Guildford Fire Station

Excavation of a Late Upper Palaeolithic campsite in the valley of the River Wey, Surrey

by Nick Barton, Alison Roberts, Sonja Tomasso, Veerle Rots,
Elizabeth Stafford, Chris Hayden and Gerry Thacker

with contributions by
Ben Attfield, Edward Biddulph, Lisa Brown, Simon Collcutt, John Cotter, John Crowther, Mike Donnelly, Richard Macphail, Nathalie Marini, Rebecca Nicholson, Mairead Rutherford, Jean-Luc Schwenninger and Tom S White

Principal illustrators
Sophie Lamb, Gary Jones and Ian R Cartwright

Oxford Archaeology Monograph No. 37
2024

The publication of this volume was generously funded by Surrey County Council and Historic England

Designed by Oxford Archaeology Graphics Office
Edited by Chris Hayden

This book is part of a series of monographs which can be bought from all good bookshops and internet bookshops
For more information visit www.oxfordarchaeology.com

© 2024 Oxford Archaeology Ltd

Figure 1 Contains OS data © Crown Copyright (2019) and Arcworld data

Front cover – *Photograph of Refit Group 13*
Back cover – *The Late Upper Palaeolithic flint scatter under excavation*

ISBN 978-0-904220-92-6

Typeset by Production Line, Oxford
Printed in Great Britain by Short Run Press, Exter, England

Contents

List of Figures vii
List of Tables xv
Acknowledgements xvii
Summary xix
Résumé xxi
Zusammenfassung xxiii

Chapter 1 – Introduction
    INTRODUCTION 1
    SITE LOCATION, TOPOGRAPHY AND GEOLOGY 1
    BACKGROUND TO THE EXCAVATION 1
    ARCHAEOLOGICAL AND HISTORICAL BACKGROUND 6
    STRUCTURE OF THE REPORT 7
    SITE ARCHIVE 7
    DIGITAL ARCHIVE 7

Chapter 2 – Methodology
    INTRODUCTION 9
    FIELDWORK METHODS 9
        Sampling 12
    POST-EXCAVATION ASSESSMENT AND ANALYSIS 12
        The Late Upper Palaeolithic flint scatters 12
        Scientific dating, geoarchaeology and palaeoenvironment 12
        Flint 13
        Flint functional analysis 13
        Sediment analysis 14
    POLLEN 14
    CHARCOAL AND CHARRED PLANT REMAINS 14

Chapter 3 – Later prehistoric, Roman and more recent features and finds
    INTRODUCTION 15
    FEATURES 15
    PREHISTORIC POTTERY 17
    ROMAN POTTERY 18
    POST-ROMAN POTTERY 18
    CLAY TOBACCO PIPE 18
    BUILDING MATERIALS 18

Chapter 4 – Stratigraphy, dating and sediment analysis
    INTRODUCTION 19
        The site and the geoarchaeological investigations 19
        Site sedimentary sequences and chronology 21

OPTICALLY STIMULATED LUMINESCENCE DATING	25
CLAST LITHOLOGY	26
Introduction	26
Methods	26
Results	26
Comparative material and discussion	32
Conclusions	32
PARTICLE SIZE ANALYSIS	33
Introduction	33
Method	33
Results	34
MICROMORPHOLOGY, GEOCHEMISTRY AND MAGNETIC SUSCEPTIBILITY	34
Introduction	34
Methods	35
Results: bulk samples	36
Results: micromorphology	37
Discussion	44

Chapter 5 – Artefact taphonomy

INTRODUCTION	47
SIZE CLASS ANALYSIS	47
FABRIC ANALYSIS	49
Data and methods	49
Dip	50
Orientation	51
Fabric analysis	51
VERTICAL DISTRIBUTION OF THE FLINT	53
Depths of refits	55
Sorting by depth	55
REFIT ORIENTATIONS	56
Methods and data	57
Results	57
HORIZONTAL DISTRIBUTION OF THE FLINT	59
The distribution of the heat-affected flint	60
Hot spot analysis	60
Centroid diagrams	64
CONCLUSIONS	69

Chapter 6 – The lithic assemblage

INTRODUCTION	77
RAW MATERIAL	77
THE DEBITAGE ASSEMBLAGE	79
Classification	79
Cores and core rejuvenation pieces	79
Flakes, blades and bladelets	83
Debris (shatter/irregular waste)	87
Small debitage	87
STONE OBJECTS	87

THE RETOUCHED TOOL ASSEMBLAGE..89
    Typological classification 89
    End-scrapers...89
    Piercers/perforators..94
    Burins...94
    Burin spalls...100
    Truncations 101
    Notches and denticulates..101
    Backed blade/lets and points 103
    Rubbed end tools 105
    Miscellaneous retouched blade/lets and flakes 105
POST-PALAEOLITHIC ARTEFACTS 111
REFITTING ANALYSIS..111
    Introduction, methods and aims 111
    Break and spall refits and individual tool lifecycles...112
    Dorso-ventral refits and refitting groups..115
    Catalogue of artefact refit groups 115
    Site activities and discard patterns 148

Chapter 7 – Functional analysis

INTRODUCTION...151
MATERIAL AND METHODS 151
    Assemblage composition and sample selection...151
    Analytical methods...151
    Experiments 152
RESULTS..153
    Preservation state of the material 153
    Residue analysis 154
    Use-wear analysis 154
    Subsistence-related activities 154
    Butchering activities 158
    Manufacturing activities 158
CONCLUSION..169

Chapter 8 – Discussion: Guildford Fire Station and the Late Upper Palaeolithic

INTRODUCTION...171
THE GEOLOGICAL CONTEXT OF THE FLINT SCATTER.....................................171
THE PLACE OF GUILDFORD FIRE STATION IN THE LATE UPPER PALAEOLITHIC 173
    The Guildford Fire Station Late Upper Palaeolithic site in its regional context.................175
    European affinities with the Guildford Fire Station site 176
SITE COMPLEXITY AND FUNCTION 179
FUTURE STUDIES 181

Bibliography...185

Index..193

List of Figures

Chapter 1
1.1 Site location...2
1.2 The topographical situation of the site..3
1.3 The geological context of the site (bedrock and drift geology).........................4
1.4 Areas of investigation..5
1.5 Excavation area with the Fire Station and training tower in the background.............6

Chapter 2
2.1 Plan of the flint scatter and surroundings showing the excavation grid and the extent of the damage caused by the detonation of the mortar smoke round........................10
2.2 Hand excavation of the flint scatter in 1m grid squares..............................11

Chapter 3
3.1 Plan of Iron Age, Roman, post-medieval and modern features........................16
3.2 Sections of Iron Age, Roman, post-medieval and modern features....................17
3.3 Roman pottery: 1020 Jar with everted rim in sandy reduced ware; 1001 Necked globular jar with cordoned shoulder and 'figure-7' rim in sandy reduced ware......................18

Chapter 4
4.1 Test pit sample section 1010..20
4.2 Test pit sample section 1011..21
4.3 Summary of OSL date ranges...22
4.4 Section 1015 with kubienas 156 and 162 through the artefact bearing sand (G2c); the nodular flints of cobble layer G2b are visible in the foreground...............................23
4.5 Section 1016 with kubiena 167 through the artefact bearing sand (G2c)................23
4.6 Photographs of monoliths from test pit sample sections 1010 and 1011................24
4.7 Photographs of monoliths from sample grid squares................................24
4.8 Particle size data..33
4.9 M113 (Context 1051b)...37
   1: Scan - relict iron-cemented locally translocated clay-enriched reddish soil-sediment, and pale loose sands where there has been iron and clay depletion (Dep) through soil leaching. Frame width is ~50mm.
   2: Photomicrograph - *in situ* flint debitage within iron cemented sands at 270mm depth within thin section sample. Plane polarised light (PPL), frame width is ~4.62mm.
   3: As 2, under oblique incident light (OIL); iron cementation provides orange to reddish colours.
   4: Photomicrograph - *in situ* flint debitage within iron cemented sands at 245mm depth within thin section
   5: As 4, under OIL.
4.10 M113 (Context 1051b)...37
   6: Photomicrograph - iron cemented sands with iron-stained clayey pan from clayey alluvium inwash. PPL, frame width is ~4.62mm.
   7: As 6, under OIL. Note orange and red iron cementation colours, which show preferential iron impregnation of clayey textural pedofeatures.
   8: Photomicrograph - detail of clay and microlaminated clay void coatings and infills (from overbank fine alluviation). PPL, frame width is ~0.90mm.
   9: As 8, under crossed polarised light (XPL); clay void coatings and infills show good orientation and associated birefringence despite obscuring secondary iron staining.

4.11   M114 (Context 1051a) 40
   10: Photomicrograph - leaching boundary between leached loose sands and iron cemented sands with original clay void coatings and infills. PPL, frame height is ~4.62mm
   11: As 10, under OIL, showing leached sands below original iron cemented soil-sediment.
4.12   M115 (Context 1051a) 40
   12: Photomicrograph - brown clayey inwash affects burrows/biochannels. PPL, frame width is ~4.62mm.
   13: As 12, under OIL; clay of likely recent overbank fine alluviation origin, is iron depleted.
   14: Detail of probable alluvial clayey inwash in 12. PPL, frame width is ~0.90mm.
   15: As 14, under XPL; clay inwash includes fine micas.
4.13   M115 (Context 1051a) 40
   16: Photomicrograph - loose sands cemented by colourless gypsum ($CaSO_4$). PPL, frame width is ~2.38mm.
   17: As 16, under XPL; gypsum with typical low birefringence colours (first order greys)
4.14   M116B (Contexts 1051a and underlying 1051b) 40
   18: Scan - showing approximate boundary between contexts 1051a and underlying 1051b. 1051b includes both relict patches of iron-cemented sands, and pale iron and clay depleted sediment (Dep). An embedded flint flake/debitage fragment is arrowed. Frame width is ~50mm
   19: Photomicrograph (Context 1051b); iron cemented sediment includes flint flake/debitage fragment (see 18). This protects the original soil sediment below it from leaching effects. PPL, frame width is ~4.62mm.
   20: Detail of 19, showing homogenised soil-sediment containing a very fine fragment of debitage below the long flake (F). PPL, frame width is ~2.38mm.
   21: Detail of 20, under XPL. Some oriented clay coatings are just about visible.
   22: As 21, under OIL. The 'sealed' soil-sediment occupation surface is strongly iron stained, with diminishing iron staining downwards.
4.15   M116A (Context 1051a) 41
   23: Photomicrograph - vertically oriented probable reworked flint debitage material in leached and burrowed sands. PPL, frame width is ~4.62mm.
   24: As 23, under OIL.
4.16   M156 (Context 1076) 41
   25: Photomicrograph - small relict area of iron-cemented soil-sediment and flint gravel. PPL frame width is ~2.38mm.
   26: Photomicrograph - leached sands containing fragment of weathering mortar/mortared-sands. PPL frame width is ~4.62mm.
   27: As 26, under XPL; weathering micritic mortar present.
   28: As 26, under OIL, with whitish grey calcitic matrix.
4.17   M162 (Context 1076) 42
   29: Scan - iron and clay depleted loose sands (Dep) and relict patches of iron-cemented soil-sediment, and associated embedded flint flake (F). Frame width is ~50mm
   30: Photomicrograph - flint flake (F) embedded in iron cemented sands (see 29 and 33). PPL, frame width is ~4.62mm.
   31: As 30, under XPL; moderately poorly sorted sands.
   32: As 30, under OIL, showing secondary iron cementation of sands and flint flake (see 33)
   33: Detail of 30; flint flake (F) and contemporary sandy soil-sediment substrate. Clay inwash (arrowed coatings) record clayey alluviation prior to iron cementation. PPL, frame width is ~0.90mm.
4.18   M167B (Context 1077b) 42
   34: Photomicrograph - relict area of iron cemented soil-sediment (Rss), which seems to embed a charcoal fragment (Ch); Later/more recent humic burrowed soil is also recorded (Hbs). PPL, frame width is ~4.62mm.
   35: As 34, under OIL; orange coloured iron-cemented relict soil sediment (Rss) seems to embed this charcoal fragment (Ch) suggesting that it is contemporary with the Upper Palaeolithic occupation of these deposits.

List of Figures

4.19 M384 (Context 1081) 43
    36: Scan - mainly loose leached sands, with relict iron cemented soil-sediments, including probable 'ped face' (arrows). 'Pea grit' is in the form of fine gravel size ironstone, chalk, brick (Br), weathered iron slag, charcoal slag (ChS) or 'cinder' and flint. Frame width is ~50mm.
    37: Photomicrograph - 'pea grit' burrow fill, with humic soil (Bu) and inclusions of charcoal slag (ChS), and weathered vesicular iron slag (WFeS) and embedded burnt rock fragment (BR). PPL, frame width is ~4.62mm.
    38: As 37, under OIL.
    39: Photomicrograph - 'pea grit' fill, with charcoal slag (ChS), and fine gravel size quartzite (Qtz) and flints (F) including likely debitage material. PPL, frame width is ~4.62mm.
    40: As 39, under XPL.
    41: Photomicrograph - flint debitage example within sands. PPL, frame width is ~2.38mm.
    42: As 41, under OIL.
4.20 Monolith 430 and marked subsamples M430A and M430B 43
    43: Photograph - note vertical and subhorizontal leaching pattern. Such 'patterned ground' can be linked to frozen ground – here a possible short-lived permafrost-associated feature – frozen ground not allowing normal drainage.
4.21 M430B (G2A; Context 1044; see Fig. 4.20) 43
    44: Scan - massive sands with vertical and sub - horizontal leaching features (L), and two likely flint debitage fragments (arrows). Frame width is ~50mm.
    45: Photomicrograph piece of flint debitage at 120mm depth (upper arrow in 44). PPL, frame width is ~4.62mm.
    46: As 45, under OIL, showing ferruginised fine fabric in original alluvial soil-sediment.
4.22 M430A (G2b; Context 1043) 44
    47: Photomicrograph - remains of a flint core(?) in loose leached and burrowed sands. PPL, frame width is ~4.62mm
    48: As 47, under OIL; note generally iron-depleted fine fabric.

Chapter 5
5.1 Size class distribution of the flint (using maximum dimensions) for the whole scatter and the north-western and south-eastern concentrations. 48
5.2 Histogram of dip angles 50
5.3 Distribution of flint dipping at between 90° (in red) and 45° (in increasingly lighter shades) 50
5.4 Equal area rose diagram summarising the orientation of the flint 51
5.5 Stereonet summarising the orientation and dip of the flint at Guildford Fire Station 51
5.6 Benn diagram for the flint artefact fabric at Guildford Fire Station. Shaded areas representing post-depositional processes from Lenoble and Bertran 2004, fig. 16. 52
5.7 The depth of the flint projected onto an east-west aligned section 52
5.8 The depth of the flint projected onto a north-south aligned section 53
5.9 The depth of the flint, showing the mean (red) and median (blue) depths 53
5.10 Refits projected onto an east-west aligned section (the y axis (depth) has been exaggerated by a factor of 5 in relation to the x axis (easting)) 54
5.11 Refits projected onto a north-south aligned section (the y axis (depth) has been exaggerated by a factor of 5 in relation to the x axis (northing)) 54
5.12 Histogram summarising the difference in depth between all refitting pieces. The red line indicates the mean difference in depth; the blue line the median difference. 55
5.13 Cumulative frequency diagram showing the depth distribution of the flint by quintiles defined using the maximum dimensions of the flint (1 represents the smallest quintile; 5 the largest) 56
5.14 Refit orientations for Refit Group 1 57
5.15 Refit orientations for Refit Group 5 58
5.16 Refit orientations for Refit Group 9 58
5.17 Heatmap of all flint 58
5.18 Heatmap of heat-affected flint 59

5.19 Contoured versions of the heatmaps in Figs 5.17 and 5.18 60
5.20 Density of flint in 0.1m wide rings, centred on the two main concentrations 61
5.21 Hot spot analysis of the maximum dimensions of the flint using a diameter of 0.3m. The size of the dots is proportional to the deviation from the overall mean. 62
5.22 Hot spot analysis of the maximum dimensions of the flint using a diameter of 0.9m. The size of the dots is proportional to the deviation from the overall mean. 62
5.23 Boxplots summarising the distribution of centroid distances for refit groups divided into concentrated groups, concentrated groups with outliers, and dispersed groups 63
5.24 Sets of refitting groups, classified by median and maximum centroid distances 64
5.25 Concentrated refitting group 9, showing the centroid diagram, a detailed plot of the group, and its location. The circles indicate the location of the two main concentrations of flint and the red points the group median centroid. (n=11) 66
5.26 Concentrated refitting group 7 (n=13) 67
5.27 Concentrated refitting group 3 (n=9) 68
5.28 Concentrated refitting group with outliers 1 (n=69) 69
5.29 Concentrated refitting group with outliers 4 (n=11) 70
5.30 Concentrated refitting group with outliers 5 (n=11) 71
5.31 Concentrated refitting group with outliers 8 (n=11) 72
5.32 Concentrated refitting group with outliers 14 (n=8) 73
5.33 Dispersed refitting group 2 (n=14) 74
5.34 Dispersed refitting group 10 (n=9) 75

Chapter 6

6.1 Overall distribution of all artefacts. Artefacts recovered from samples have been located randomly within their grid squares 78
6.2 Overall distribution of artefacts (A) over 20mm in length and (B) under 20mm in length 79
6.3 Distribution of artefacts retaining cortex on the dorsal surface 80
6.4 Overall distribution of heated/calcined material..81
6.5 Distribution of cores and core manufacturing/modifying waste 82
6.6 Single platform blade core (c.945) and blade debitage with isolated *en éperon*-like platforms (c.921/c.989/c.988; c.295), linear platform (c.147), large plain platform (c.1709), and punctiform platform (c.4201) 84
6.7 Distribution of butt types for blades 86
6.8 Photograph of natural grooved stone (c.441) 88
6.9 Distribution of all retouched tools 90
6.10 End-scrapers (c.1625, c.1583, c.485, c.1761); double end-scraper (c.2474); short end-scrapers (c.1272, c.1408) 91
6.11 Refitting blade end-scraper (c.1315) and burin (c.1564). Refit Group 56 92
6.12 End-scrapers and burins with *rasante* retouch (c.2471, c.19, c.362, c.924/c.558/c.559)............93
6.13 Distribution of scrapers, unretouched refitting parts of scrapers, perforators and truncations 94
6:14 Micropiercers (c.991, c.1152), piercers (c.99/c.143, c.5421) and perforator (c.1428)................95
6.15 Burins. Dihedral burin on blade with *rasante* retouch (c.990/c.992); refitting burin on a break and unclassified burin (c.4691/c.2488); and dihedral burin on blade with *rasante* retouch and a refitting spall (c.1204/c.9277) 96
6.16 Burins. Dihedral burins with refitting spalls (c.142/c.1407, c.1910/c.3884); dihedral burin with refitting spall and part of original flake blank (c.596/c.6); burin on break (c.1166); burin on natural surface with refitting spall and part of original blade blank (c.1441/c.5875/c.1577)..97
6.17 Dihedral burins (c.1424, c.2451, c.365, c.2319, c.266/c.267)..98
6.18 Burins. Double burin (dihedral and on a break) with three refitting spalls and part of the original blade blank (c.319/c.524/c.692/c.2802/c.7007); two refitting burins (on a truncation and on a break) and a refitting retouched blade fragment (c.699/c.2313/c.7448); burin on a notch with a refitting spall (c.1557/c.4158); double burin (on a break and on a truncation) (c.459) with a refitting part of the blade blank (c.1242)..99
6.19 Distribution of burins, spalls and burin fragments 100
6.20 Truncations. Oblique distal truncation (c.453); straight truncations (c.45, c.1274, c.1245/c.2612) ..101

List of Figures

6.21	Notches (c.1056, c.1069, c.1725) and denticulates (c.7, c.697/c.959).	102
6.22	Distribution of denticulates and notched pieces.	103
6.23	Backed blades, bladelets and points. Oblique points (c.2378, c.4200, c.694, c.5787, c.5032); curve-backed bi-point (c.308); curved backed point (c.7482, c.508); straight backed bladelet with oblique truncation (c.948); backed blade fragments (c.4322/c.4328, c.4062, c.4486); partially backed and truncated blade (c.4735); two refitting Krukowski microburins (c.1732, c.4743)	104
6.24	Photograph of curve backed bi-point (c.308)	105
6.25	Distribution of backed material.	106
6.26	Rubbed end tools (c.205, c.2555); blades with *rasante* retouch (c.1744, c.926), blade with fine lateral retouch (c.904/c.3121/c.529/c.541/c.4194/c.6492); blade with fine and denticulated retouch (c.28/c.2056/c.649)	107
6.27	Detail of rubbed end blade (c.2555)	108
6.28	Blade tools with rasante (scalar) retouch: dihedral burin (c.1204), end-scraper (c.2471), *rasante* retouched blade (c.992, the proximal part of truncation burin c.990)	108
6.29	Distribution of retouched pieces	109
6.30	Distribution of edge-damaged pieces	110
6.31	Photograph of Mesolithic axe fragment reused as a bladelet core (c.209), surface find	111
6.32	Overall distribution of all refitting artefacts	112
6.33	Distribution of all break refits	113
6.34	Distribution of all dorso-ventral refits	114
6.35	Photograph of Refit Group 01	116
6.36	Distribution of Refit Group 01	117
6.37	Photograph of Refit Group 02	117
6.38	Distribution of Refit Group 02	118
6.39	Photograph of Refit Group 03	118
6.40	Distribution of Refit Group 03	119
6.41	Photograph of Refit Group 04	119
6.42	Distribution of Refit Group 04	120
6.43	Photograph of Refit Group 05	120
6.44	Distribution of Refit Group 05	121
6.45	Photograph of Refit Group 06	122
6.46	Distribution of Refit Group 06	122
6.47	Photograph of Refit Group 07	123
6.48	Distribution of Refit Group 07	123
6.49:	Photograph of Refit Group 08	124
6.50:	Distribution of Refit Group 08	125
6.51	Photograph of Refit Group 09	126
6.52	Distribution of Refit Group 09	126
6.53	Photograph of Refit Group 10	126
6.54	Distribution of Refit Group 10	127
6.55	Photograph of Refit Group 11	127
6.56	Distribution of Refit Group 11	128
6.57	Photograph of Refit Group 12	128
6.58	Distribution of Refit Group 12	129
6.59	Photograph of Refit Group 13	129
6.60	Distribution of Refit Group 13	130
6.61	Photograph of Refit Group 14	131
6.62	Distribution of Refit Group 14	131
6.63	Photograph of Refit Group 15	132
6.64	Distribution of Refit Group 15	132
6.65	Photograph of Refit Group 16	133
6.66	Distribution of Refit Group 16	133
6.67	Photograph of Refit Group 17	134
6.68	Distribution of Refit Group 17	134
6.69	Photograph of Refit Group 18	134

6.70	Distribution of Refit Group 18	135
6.71	Photograph of Refit Group 19	136
6.72	Distribution of Refit Group 19	137
6.73	Photograph of Refit Group 20	137
6.74	Distribution of Refit Group 20	138
6.75	Photograph of Refit Group 25	139
6.76	Distribution of Refit Group 25	139
6.77	Photograph of Refit Group 28	140
6.78	Photograph of Refit Group 31	140
6.79	Photograph of Refit Group 37	141
6.80	Photograph of Refit Group 40	141
6.81	Photograph of Refit Group 41	142
6.82	Photograph of Refit Group 42	142
6.83	Photograph of Refit Group 43	143
6.84	Photograph of Refit Group 53	144
6.85	Photograph of Refit Group 55	144
6.86	Photograph of Refit Group 56	145
6.87	Photograph of Refit Group 67	146
6.88	Photograph of Refit Group 68	146
6.89	Photograph of Refit Group 75	147
6.90	Photograph of Refit Group 81	147
6.91	Photograph of Refit Group 83	148
6.92	Overall distribution of all other refit groups containing tools	149
6.93	Combined distribution of material from the remaining refit groups (not shown in other figures)	150

Chapter 7

7.1	Distribution of all objects included in the microwear analysis	152
7.2	Examples of altered pieces: a) patination; b) heat alteration; c) post-depositional gloss; d) mechanical alteration	153
7.3	Residues with taphonomic origin: a) iron oxide residues on the ventral proximal face of scraper c.924 (100×); b) plant tissue (algae) preserved on the ventral face of piece c.5105, photographed under DIC (200×)	154
7.4	Piercer c.99/143 with a) plant tissue and starch granules on the distal right edge of c.99. Photographed under neofluar light (1000×)	155
7.5	Backed blade c.4322/4328; a) detail of the distal bending fracture with a step-fissured termination on the ventral face (16×) and later removals from heat	156
7.6	Backed blade c.4062; a) macroscopic detail of the edge damage with step and fissured termination on the dorsal face (20×); b) ventral face of the left edge with the same edge damage (20×)	156
7.7	Backed blade c.4486; a) detail of the distal edge damage: distal and lateral bending fractures (20×); b) detail of the distal edge damage associated with MLITs (25×)	157
7.8	a) microscopic detail of rounding and rough polish on an experimental scraper used on dry hide (200×); b) microscopic detail of rounding and rough polish on scraper c.1583 (200×)	159
7.9	Double end-scraper c.2474 with a) detail of the proximal used edge; b) rounding, polish and striations from scraping hide (100×); c) light rounding and striations parallel to the cutting edge, ventral face (200×)	159
7.10	End-scraper on blade with *rasante* (scalar) retouch c.924 with a) macroscopic picture of the distal dorsal (10×) and b) ventral part of the tool with well-developed rounding that postdates the distal fracture (10×); c) microscopic detail of the rounded edge with polish and striations from scraping dry or moistened hide (20×); d) rounding cut by later removals from resharpening	160
7.11	End-scraper on blade with *rasante* (scalar) retouch c.2471 with a) rounding from use, distal end (200×) and b) scarring, proximal left edge (12.5×); c) microscopic detail of the lateral edge with rounding and polish (200×); d) microscopic detail of the lateral edge with striations (500×)	161

List of Figures

7.12 Short end-scraper c.1408; a) microscopic detail of the polish on the scraper-head (100x). 161

7.13 a) Blade with *rasante* (scalar) retouch c.992 with stepped retouch, left lateral edge, dorsal face (10×); b) end-scraper on blade with *rasante* (scalar) retouch c.2471 with stepped retouch (1) cut by subsequent removals from use (2), left lateral edge, dorsal face (12.5×); c) truncation burin on blade with *rasante* (scalar) retouch c.19, dorsal face, right edge, bending-initiated scar with a hinge termination (12.5×); d) experimental tool with stepped retouch and subsequent removals from cutting and sawing bone (11.2×). 162

7.14 a) Blade with *rasante* (scalar) retouch c.926 (10×); b) detail of the lateral retouch/notch cut through by a later fracture (20×); c) truncation burin on blade with *rasante* (scalar) retouch 990 (8×); d) detail of the lateral retouched edge/notch cut through by a later fracture (16×) 163

7.15 a) microscopic detail of rounding, friction and rough polish on blade with *rasante* (scalar) retouch c.992 (200×); b) detail of the same wear patterns on an experimental tool used for cutting and shaving dry hide (200×). 163

7.16 Truncation burin on blade with *rasante* (scalar) retouch c.19 with a) microscopic detail of the polish on the right lateral edge, mesial part of the tool (200×); b) rounding, right lateral edge (200×); c) rounding and striation on the lateral left edge of the tool (200×); d) striation and light developed polish on the lateral left edge of the tool (200×) 164

7.17 Dihedral burin on blade with *rasante* (scalar) retouch c.2451 with a) detail of the distal edge damage at the tip (8×) 164

7.18 Double burin on blade with *rasante* (scalar) retouch c.319 with a) detail of the distal edge damage at the tip with polish, from use on antler or bone (200×); b) macroscopic detail of the burin tip (25.0×); c) macroscopic detail of the proximal left part of the burin with scarring related to use, cut by the transversal fracture (10.0×); d) microscopic detail of the left lateral edge with a wood-like polish (200×) 166

7.19 Rubbed end blade c.2555 with a) macroscopic picture of the sturdy distal part of the blade (12.5×); b) microscopic detail of the used edge with intense rounding and 166
       striations (100×) 167

7.20 Oblique backed point c.5032 with a) rounding on the ventral surface of the tip (200×) 167

7.21 Piercer c.5421 with a) microscopic detail of the used edge with friction polish (500×) 168

Chapter 8

8.1 Topographic relief map of south-eastern England and north-eastern France showing key sites mentioned in the text 172

8.2 Late Glacial climate and archaeology. 173

8.3 Curve-backed bi-points: Guildford Fire Station (c.308; 41mm); Wey Manor Farm (#52; 67mm) 175

List of Tables

Chapter 4
4.1 Summary of geoarchaeological analyses 19
4.2 Summary of stratigraphic units 22
4.3 Summary of OSL dating results 25
4.4 Angularity/roundness categories. These are based on verbal descriptions by Schneiderhöhn (1954, in Pryor 1971) of the categories devised by Powers (1953). Simplified from Fisher and Bridgland (1986) 26
4.5 Clast lithology analysis 26
4.6 Angularity/roundness analysis and comparative data 27
4.7 Comparative data from the Ebbsfleet Valley, Lower Thames and other British Pleistocene sites 28
4.8 Particle size analysis 33
4.9 Samples analysed for micromorphology, geochemistry and magnetic susceptibility 34
4.10 Geochemical and magnetic susceptibility data 35
4.11 Phosphate fractionation data for samples related to thin sections 36
4.12 Soil micromorphology and counts 38

Chapter 5
5.1 The average, minimum and maximum dimensions of the flint in each quintile, classified according to their maximum dimensions 55
5.2 Refit orientation statistics 56
5.3 Refit groups: summary statistics for centroid distances 65

Chapter 6
6.1 Assemblage composition (artefact class by number and percentage; 323 natural and later prehistoric objects have not been included in the analysis) 81
6.2 Cores, core rejuvenators, and crested pieces (none burnt) 81
6.3 Flakes, blades, and bladelets (unretouched): qualitative attributes. Sample size (n=) indicates the number of objects for which the attribute could be recorded 85
6.4 Composition of small debitage assemblage 87
6.5 Retouched tools, including retouched tool debitage 89
6.6 Burin typology 96
6.7 Burin spalls 101
6.8 Backed tools and fragments 105

Chapter 7
7.1 The sample selected for functional analysis 151
7.2 Summary of functional interpretations for the retouched and unretouched bladelets. The confidence level (CL) of each interpretation is scored on a scale of 1 (low certainty) to 4 (certain) 155
7.3 Summary of the functional interpretations for the analysed burins. The confidence level (CL) of each interpretation is scored on a scale of 1 (low certainty) to 4 (certain) 165
7.4 Summary of the functional interpretations with the worked materials and activities .. 168

Chapter 8
8.1 Main characteristics of British Creswellian and Federmesser assemblages (from Barton *et al.* 2003; 2009; Barton and Roberts 1996) 174
8.2 Guildford Fire Station and Wey Manor Farm (data from Jones 2013 and pers. obs.) 176
8.3 Development of Magdalenian to Federmesser/Azilian (After Valentin *et al.* 2006 with additions from Naudinot *et al.* 2019; Coudret and Fagnart 2015; Fagnart pers. comm. and Mevel pers. comm.) 178

Acknowledgements

We are very grateful to Surrey County Council for funding the excavation and to Surrey County Council and Historic England for funding the post-excavation analysis and publication. We are also grateful to Jonathan Mullis of Jacobs who commissioned the work on behalf of Surrey County Council.

We are very grateful, in particular, to Nick Truckle, Tony Howe and Susan Hanford (Surrey County Council) and Helen Keeley and Jenni Butterworth (Historic England) for the considerable help they have provided in the completion of this report. We would aso like to thank Historic England's scientific advisor, Jane Corcoran, for her help, and the anonymous reviewer for their helpful comments.

We would like to thank Leigh Allen, Rebecca Nicholson, Nicola Scott, Matt Bradley, Anne Dodd and Leo Webley for managing the finds, the environmental evidence, the archive, the survey data and the post-excavation analysis. We would particularly like to thank Gary Jones for his work on the spatial analysis of the site and Mairead Rutherford for her work assessing the pollen. The project is the result of the work of a large team and we would also like to thank the following people for their work on the site, the finds, environmental samples, survey data and archive: James Archer, Ben Attfield, Thomas Booth, Ian Cook, Sharon Cook, Geraldine Crann, Mark Dodd, Mike Donnelly, Matthew Fenn, Jonathan Gill, Victoria Green, Leo Heatley, Christof Heistermann, Victoria Hughes, Michael McLean, Tony Mears, William Mills, Kev Moon, Richard Palmer, Conan Parsons, Nik Petek, Emily Plunkett, Susan Rawlings, Joanne Robinson, Alice Rose, Mairead Rutherford, Victoria Skipper, Lee Sparks, Ashley Strutt, Nicholas Taylor and Jennifer Thurstan. Thanks are due to Christof Heistermann and Charles Rousseaux for translating the summaries, and we are also very grateful to Martin Street, Jean-Pierre Fagnart and Paule Coudret for their expert help with the translations.

Summary

Excavations carried out prior to the construction of a new fire station and housing in Guildford, Surrey, revealed a well-preserved, *in situ* Late Upper Palaeolithic flint scatter. Both techno-typological analysis of the flint and Optically Stimulated Luminescence dates suggest that the scatter dates from the first half of the Late Glacial (Windermere) interstadial (*c* 14–15 KBP). The assemblage is generally comparable to that of Wey Manor Farm, Surrey, which lies 15km downstream from Guildford Fire Station. The two sites differ slightly in the typology of their backed tool forms but otherwise share many features in common including the presence of curve-backed bi-points. The finds from Guildford Fire Station raise interesting questions, examined in this volume, concerning its relationship with the Creswellian assemblages further north in Britain and Azilian/Federmesser traditions on the near continent.

Geoarchaeological analyses suggest that the site lay on cold-climate fluvial sandy gravels deposited in braided stream systems prior to the onset of the Late Glacial (Windermere) interstadial. The flint scatter itself lay within the upper part of a deposit of fine-grained sands, probably deposited by seasonal floods. Deposition of the upper sands appears to have been contemporaneous with the period of occupation of the site. During drier periods, weathering and ephemeral soil formation occurred on the surface of the sands.

Analysis of the lithic assemblage shows that it is homogeneous and that apart from initial extraction and nodule testing all stages of flint manufacture are represented. A suite of analyses examining the taphonomy of the artefacts all suggest that the flint has not suffered from significant post-depositional disturbance and was largely *in situ*. Two main concentrations of knapping are represented, 3–4m apart. The main focus of the knapping was the production of blade blanks, some of which appear to have been removed from the site. The retouched tool assemblage shows that other limited activities also took place on the site, and that this occurred outside the main knapping foci. Refitting of retouched tools reveals the lifecycle of use and discard of burins and other artefacts on the site. Additional confirmation of tool use and function comes from trace wear analyses which indicate the presence of projectiles and the processing of animal and plant materials. The site seems to represent a relatively short occupation during which flint knapping, retooling of hunting equipment, and small-scale craft activities took place. An unusual aspect of this assemblage, recognised during refitting, is the presence of products made by a novice amongst the flint debris left by more experienced flintknappers.

Résumé

Les fouilles archéologiques menées préalablement à la construction d'une nouvelle caserne de pompiers et de logements à Guildford, Surrey, ont révélé une occupation archéologique bien préservée attribuable au Paléolithique final. L'analyse typo-technologique du matériel ainsi que les datations par la méthode de l'OSL permettent de la rapporter à la première moitié du Tardiglaciaire weischélien (Windermere, 14000–15000 AP). L'industrie est globalement comparable à celle du gisement de Wey Manor Farm, Surrey, situé à 15 km en aval de Guilford. Les deux sites diffèrent légèrement par la typologie des pièces à dos, mais partagent de nombreux traits communs, notamment la présence de bipointes à dos courbe. L'identité culturelle de l'industrie de Guilford Fire Station pose la question de sa relation avec les assemblages du Creswellien britannique, dont les gisements sont situés plus au nord, et ceux de la tradition des groupes à Federmesser (Azilien) du proche continent.

Les analyses géoarchéologiques montrent à la base de la séquence des graviers fluviatiles sableux préniglaciaires, déposés dans un système de chenaux en tresses antérieur au début du Tardiglaciaire (Windermere). L'industrie lithique, quant à elle, repose à la partie supérieure d'un dépôt de sables fins (silts), probablement mis en place lors de crues saisonnières. Cette formation semble avoir été contemporaine de la période d'occupation du site. Ultérieurement, la partie supérieure des sables a été affectée par une faible pédogénèse.

L'analyse de l'assemblage lithique montre un ensemble homogène. A l'exception de l'acquisition de la matière première et du test initial des blocs, toutes les étapes de la chaîne opératoire de production lithique sont représentées. L'ensemble des analyses taphonomiques et plus particulièrement des tests de fabrique montrent que le site est bien en place et n'a pas subi de perturbations post-dépositionnelles. Les vestiges se présentent sous la forme de deux concentrations principales, distantes de 3 à 4 m. L'objectif principal du débitage est orienté vers la production de supports laminaires, dont certains ont fait l'objet d'emports hors du site. D'autres activités, situées en dehors des zones principales de débitage, sont attestées par la présence des supports transformés en outils. Les remontages effectués révèlent un cycle d'utilisation et de rejet, notamment pour les burins. L'analyse tracéologique met en évidence la présence de pointes de projectiles et d'outils dévolus au traitement des matières animales et végétales. Le gisement de Guilford représente une occupation relativement courte dans le temps, où la taille du silex est associée à des activités domestiques et cynégétiques comme le réarmement des armatures de chasse. Autre spécificité du site, les remontages montrent la présence de produits taillés par des débutants à partir d'éléments lithiques rejetés par des tailleurs plus expérimentés.

Zusammenfassung

Bei Ausgrabungen in Vorfeld des Baus einer neuen Feuerwache und eines Wohngebietes in Guildford, Surrey, wurde eine in situ gut erhaltene Feuersteinkonzentration aus dem späten Jungpaläolithikum frei gelegt. Sowohl die technologisch-typologische Analyse des Feuerstein-Inventars als auch die OSL-Datierungen deuten darauf hin, dass die Fundstelle aus der ersten Hälfte des spätglazialen (Windermere) Interstadials (ca 14–15 KBP) stammt. Das Fundinventarist im Wesentlichen mit dem der 15km flussab gelegenen Fundstelle von Wey Manor Farm, Surrey, vergleichbar. Die beiden Fundstellen unterscheiden sich geringfügig bezüglich der Typologie der rückengestumpften Geräteformen, weisen ansonsten aber zahlreiche Gemeinsamkeiten auf, einschließlich des Vorkommens von „bipointe"-Rückenspitzen. Im vorliegenden Band werden die interessanten Fragen untersucht, die von den Funden der Feuerwache Guildford bezüglich ihres Verhältnisses zu den Inventaren des weiter nördlich in Großbritannien auftretenden Creswellien und denen der Azilien / Federmesser-Traditionen auf dem nahen europäischen Festland aufgeworfen werden.

Geoarchäologische Analysen deuten darauf hin, dass die Fundstelle auf kaltzeitlichen fluviatilen sandigen Kiesen lag, die vor dem Beginn des spätglazialen (Windermere) Interstadials in einem verzweigten Flusssystem abgelagert worden waren. Die Feuersteinkonzentration selbst lag im oberen Teil einer Schicht von feinkörnigen Sanden, die wahrscheinlich von jahreszeitlich wiederkehrenden Hochwässern abgelagert worden war. Die Sedimentation der oberen Sande scheint zeitgleich mit der Aufsuchung des Ortes erfolgt zu sein. Während trockener Phasen, führte die Verwitterung der sandigen Oberfläche zu einer ephemeren Bodenbildung.

Die Analyse des lithischen Fundinventars zeigt, dass es in sich homogen ist und bis auf die ursprüngliche Bergung und Prüfung der Feuersteinknollen alle Stufen der Feuersteinbearbeitung aufweist. Eine Reihe von Analysen zur Taphonomie der Artefakte deuten alle darauf hin, dass die Feuersteinkonzentration nach ihrer Niederlegung keine wesentlichen Störungen mehr erlitten hat und sich weitgehend in situ befand. Zwei Hauptkonzentrationen innerhalb des Schlagplatzes liegen 3–4m voneinander entfernt. Schwerpunkt der Feuersteinbearbeitung war die Herstellung von Klingen, die zum Teil von der Fundstelle entfernt wurden. Das Inventar der retuschierten Steingeräte zeigt, dass in begrenztem Umfang auch noch andere Tätigkeiten am Fundort stattfanden, und dass diese abseits der Hauptzentren der Feuersteinbearbeitung erfolgten.

Das Zusammenpassen von retuschierten Werkzeugen verdeutlicht den Lebenszyklus von Sticheln und anderen Artefakten am Fundort, von der Verwendung bis zur Entsorgung. Eine zusätzliche Bestätigung für den Verwendungszweck und die Funktion von Werkzeugen lieferte die Gebrauchsspurenanalyse, die das Vorhandensein von Projektilen und die Bearbeitung von tierischen und pflanzlichen Materialien belegt. Der Fundplatz scheint einen vergleichsweisen kurzen Aufenthalt zu repräsentieren, während dessen die Bearbeitung von Feuerstein, die Instandsetzung von Jagdwaffen und in geringerem Umfang weitere handwerkliche Aktivitäten erfolgten. Eine Besonderheit, die beim Zusammenpassen der Feuersteinartefakte festgestellt wurde, ist der Nachweis von Erzeugnissen, die von einem Anfänger hergestellten worden waren, vermischt mit dem von erfahreneren Feuersteinschlägern hinterlassenen Abschlagmaterial.

Chapter 1

Introduction

INTRODUCTION

This report describes the results of excavations carried out at Guildford Fire Station in 2013 prior to the construction of a new fire station and housing. The excavations revealed a rare example of a well-preserved Late Upper Palaeolithic open air site. Since it was apparent at an early stage of the excavation that the worked flint (no non-flint lithic artefacts were recovered) was in an exceptionally fresh, unabraded condition, the excavation strategy was designed to retrieve the artefacts in pristine condition, as fully as possible, and to record their distribution in detail. Subsequent analysis has shown that the flint assemblage is homogeneous and contains all of the stages of flint manufacturing apart from the initial stages of flint extraction and testing. Two main knapping foci have been identified. The main focus of activity was blade blank manufacture and some of the blades were removed from the site. The retouched tool assemblage also indicates, however, that other limited activities took place around the foci of knapping.

SITE LOCATION, TOPOGRAPHY AND GEOLOGY

The excavations took place on land adjoining Guildford Fire Station, Ladymead, Guildford, Surrey (NGR SU 9965 5081, Figs 1.1 and 1.5) between 1 July and 4 October 2013.

The site of the Fire Station is located on the outskirts of the town of Guildford in a relatively low-lying position at c 30m OD in the valley of the River Wey (Fig. 1.2). The Chalk escarpment of the North Downs lies 2km to the south. The elongated ridge formed by the North Downs between Farnham and Guildford reaches elevations of c 150m OD and is known locally as the Hog's Back. The River Wey cuts through the escarpment in a narrow, steep-sided valley before meandering through a wider floodplain which runs through the centre and north of Guildford.

The geological context of the site (Fig. 1.3) is described in more detail in relation to the archaeology in Chapter 4. In brief, the underlying solid geology of the site is Eocene London Clay deposited c 55–44 million years ago. Clays, silts and sands of the older Lambeth Group (Upnor, Reading and Woolwich Formations) outcrop c 0.5km to the south, along with the Cretaceous Newhaven and Seaford Chalk Formations at 0.85km (Fig. 1.3; BGS 2001; Ellison *et al.* 2002).

Quaternary drift deposits in the area, overlying the bedrock, are of Pleistocene (>12,000 yrs BP) and Holocene age (<12,000 yrs BP). The River Wey probably adopted its approximate current course at some point during the Pleistocene. The valley bottom around Guildford is infilled and flanked by a sequence of river terraces consisting of coarse sands and gravels deposited under cold climate conditions. BGS mapping of the area indicates that the Fire Station is underlain by gravels of the upper floodplain, correlated with the early to middle Devensian Kempton Park Terrace of the Middle Thames (deposited >30,000 yrs BP; Bridgland 1994; Gibbard 1985). Older (undifferentiated) river terrace deposits at higher elevations are mapped along the valley sides c 1km north of the site. The Downs escarpment to the south of the site is incised by a series of dry valleys or 'coombes' infilled by a series of slope deposits or 'Head'. The Head comprises Pleistocene cold-climate solifluction deposits, although it may also include later colluvium or ploughwash of Holocene age. The current floodplain zone of the River Wey is mantled by river alluvium deposited over the last c 12,000 years.

BACKGROUND TO THE EXCAVATION

The initial heritage statement for the Fire Station site (Jacobs 2012), submitted in support of the planning application, identified the potential for prehistoric evidence to be present. This archaeological potential was identified largely on the basis of a collection of 65 struck flints, dated mainly to the Mesolithic period, which had been recovered from gardens along Ladymead. An arrowhead of late Neolithic or early Bronze Age date was also noted, although its precise find spot had not been recorded. There was deemed to be a low potential for archaeology of other eras to be present, with the exception of the medieval and post-medieval periods, which were represented by several standing buildings and structures within the vicinity of the site.

Due to the site's archaeological potential, a condition requiring preliminary archaeological evalua-

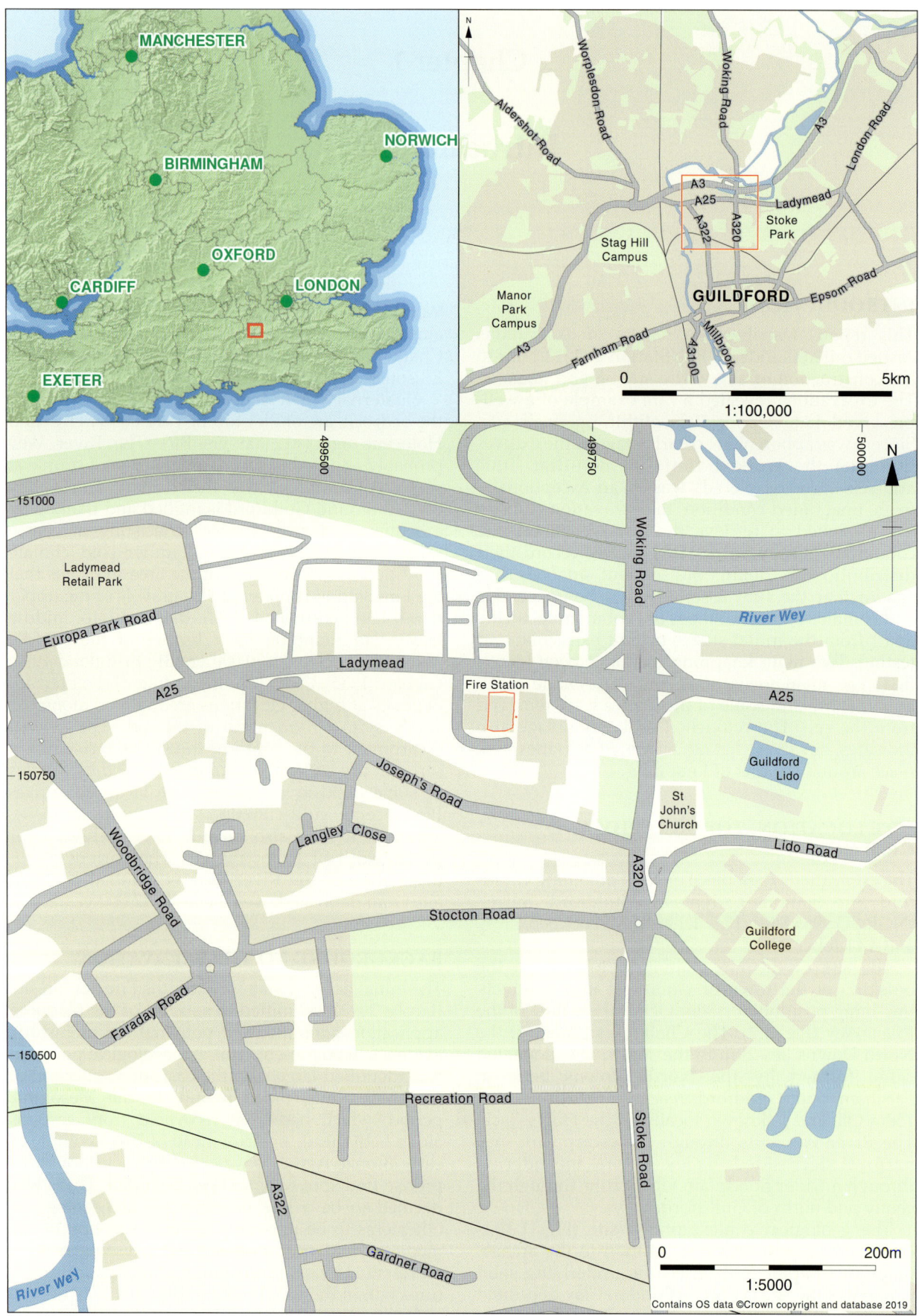

Fig. 1.1 Site location

Chapter 1

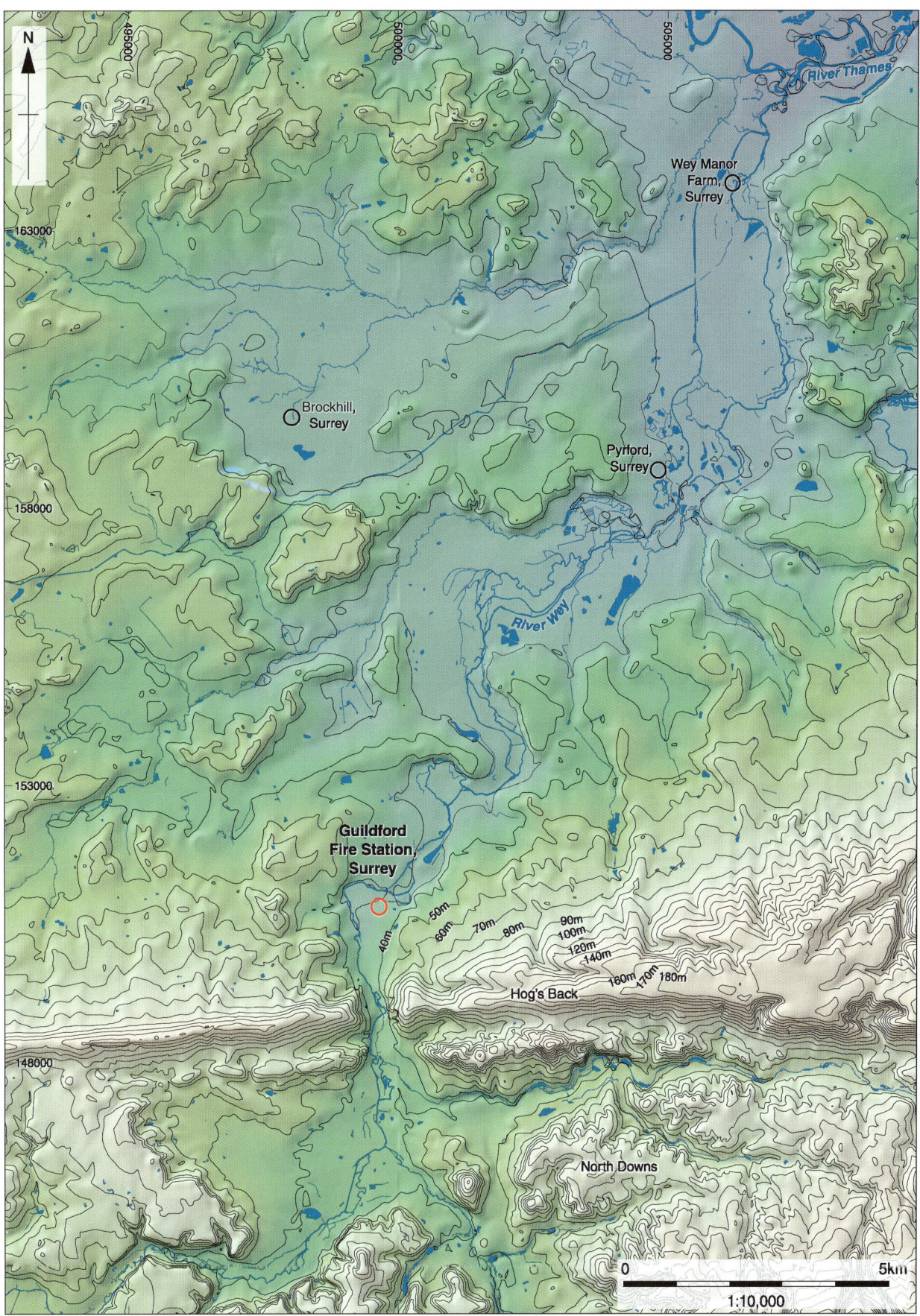

Fig. 1.2 The topographical situation of the site

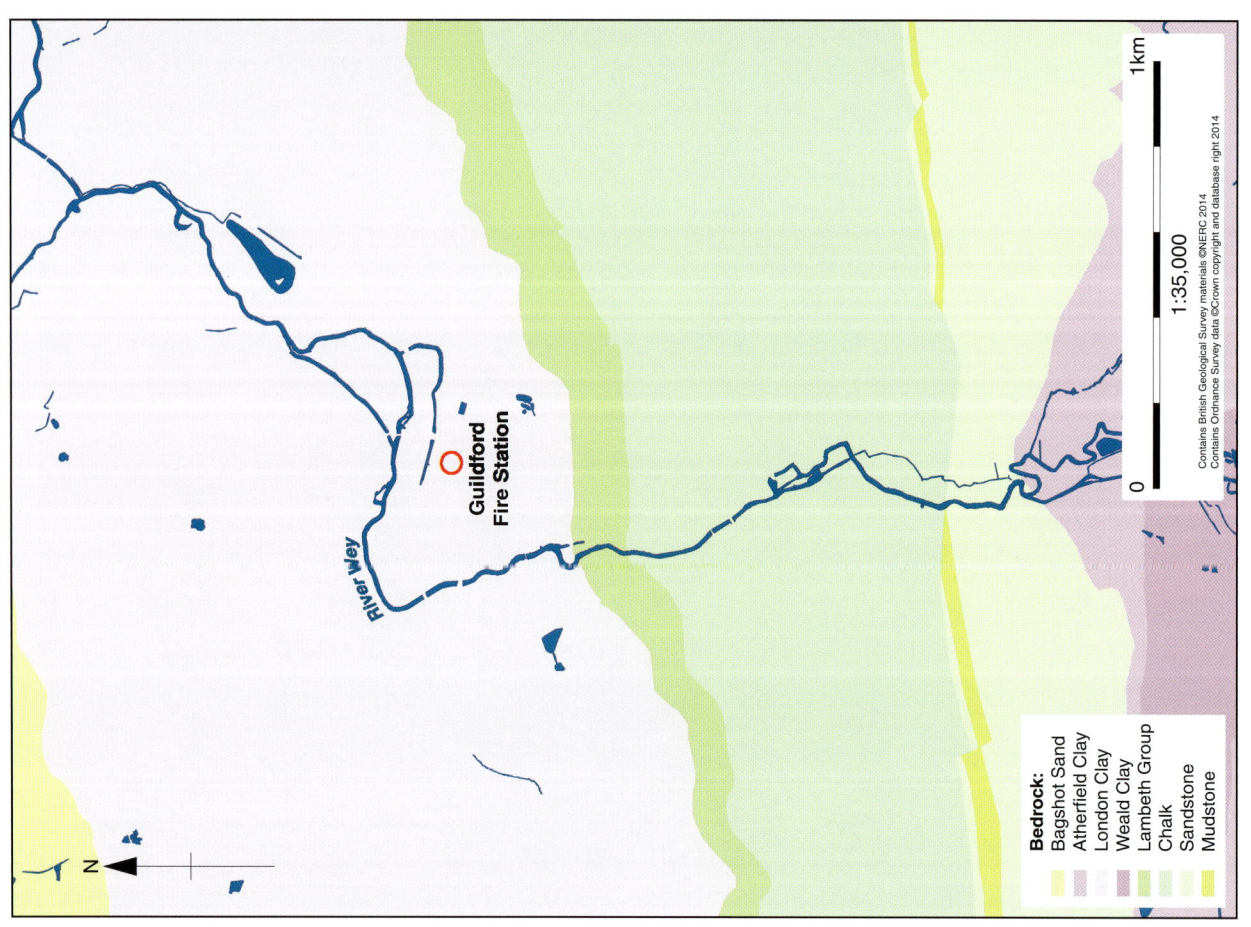

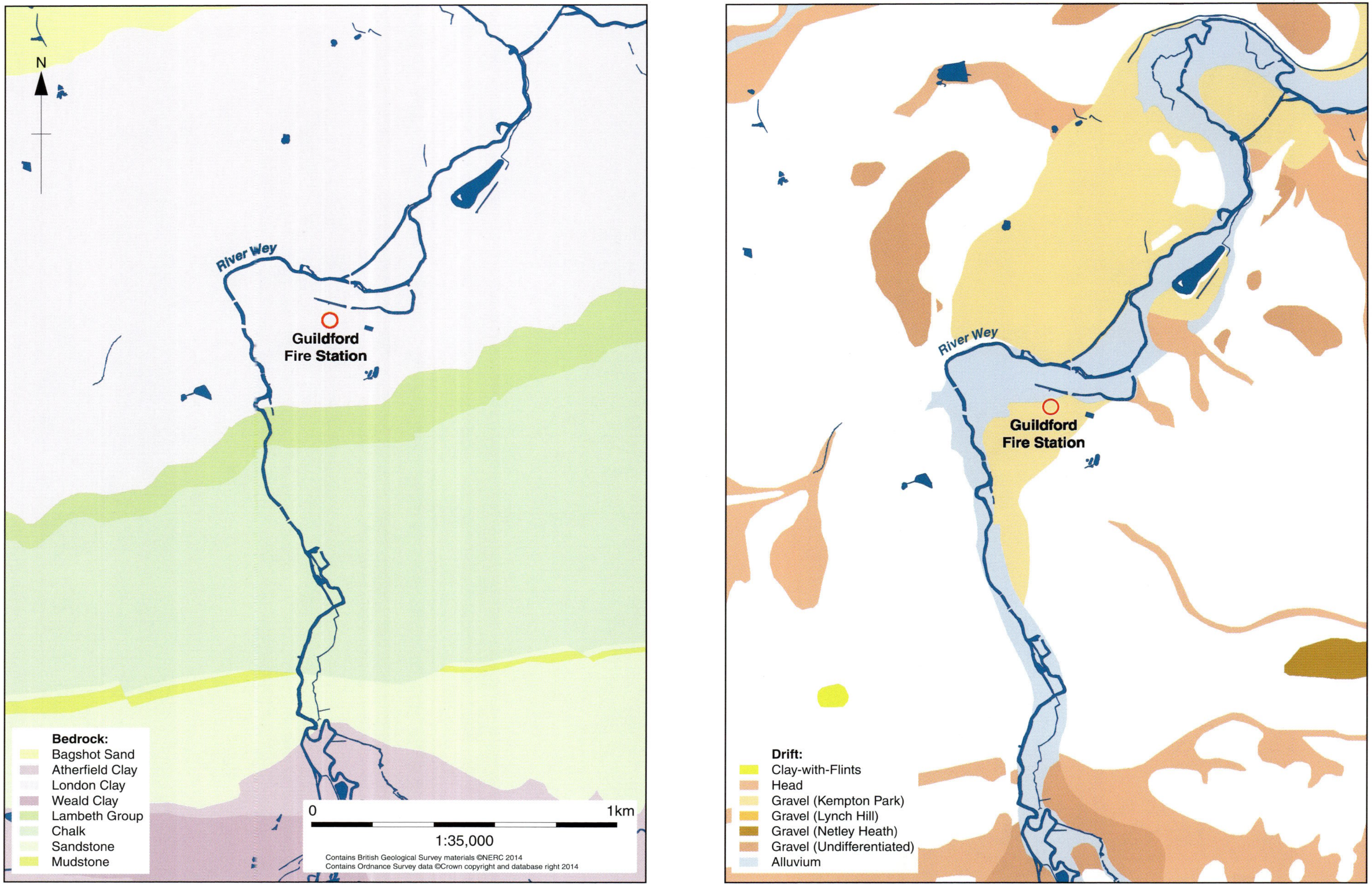

Fig. 1.3 *The geological context of the site (bedrock and drift geology)*

tion was set by Nick Truckle, Archaeological Officer for Surrey County Council (SCC). Jacobs produced a written scheme of investigation (WSI; Jacobs 2013a) for the evaluation fieldwork, and Oxford Archaeology (OA) were appointed to undertake the work, which also included a programme of historic building recording on the principal 1930s fire station building fronting onto the A25, a later 20th-century 'smoke-house' and a multistorey training tower (OA 2013b).

The intrusive evaluation comprised an array of seven trial trenches, six measuring 10m by 1.6m and one measuring 5m by 1.6m (Fig. 1.4; OA 2013a). The trenches were opened by a mechanical excavator under close archaeological supervision, and revealed a west–east orientated ditch which was potentially present in two trenches, terminating in one. Struck flints of probable Mesolithic or early Neolithic date were recovered from the ditch fills, but were thought to be residual. Tellingly, several struck flints thought to be of similar date were also recovered from the interface between the subsoil and natural geology, which manifested as a clean yellow sand. A north–south orientated ditch or former hedge line was also uncovered, but remained undated. Ceramic roof tile fragments of late medieval or post-medieval date were recovered from the subsoil which sealed the archaeological features. Other trenches revealed features of recent date including buried services and a wide shallow cut probably associated with the construction of an adjacent tarmac road.

Following the submission of the evaluation and building recording report (OA 2013a), Nick Truckle determined that further excavation was required, covering the area where the ditches had been identified in order to further understand them. OA was therefore commissioned by Jacobs UK Ltd, on behalf of SCC, to undertake an archaeological strip, map and sample (SMS) excavation in the western part of the evaluated area. The excavation area measured 34m by 23m and was focused on the area covered by evaluation trenches 1–4 in which the ditches had been found (Figs 1.4–1.5). All work was undertaken in accordance with local and national planning policies and the WSI agreed between Jacobs UK Ltd and SCC (Jacobs 2013b). The excavation revealed pits, postholes and two ditches which, on the basis of the pottery they contained, appeared to date to the Iron Age, Roman and post-medieval periods. These features and the finds from them are described in Chapter 3 of this volume.

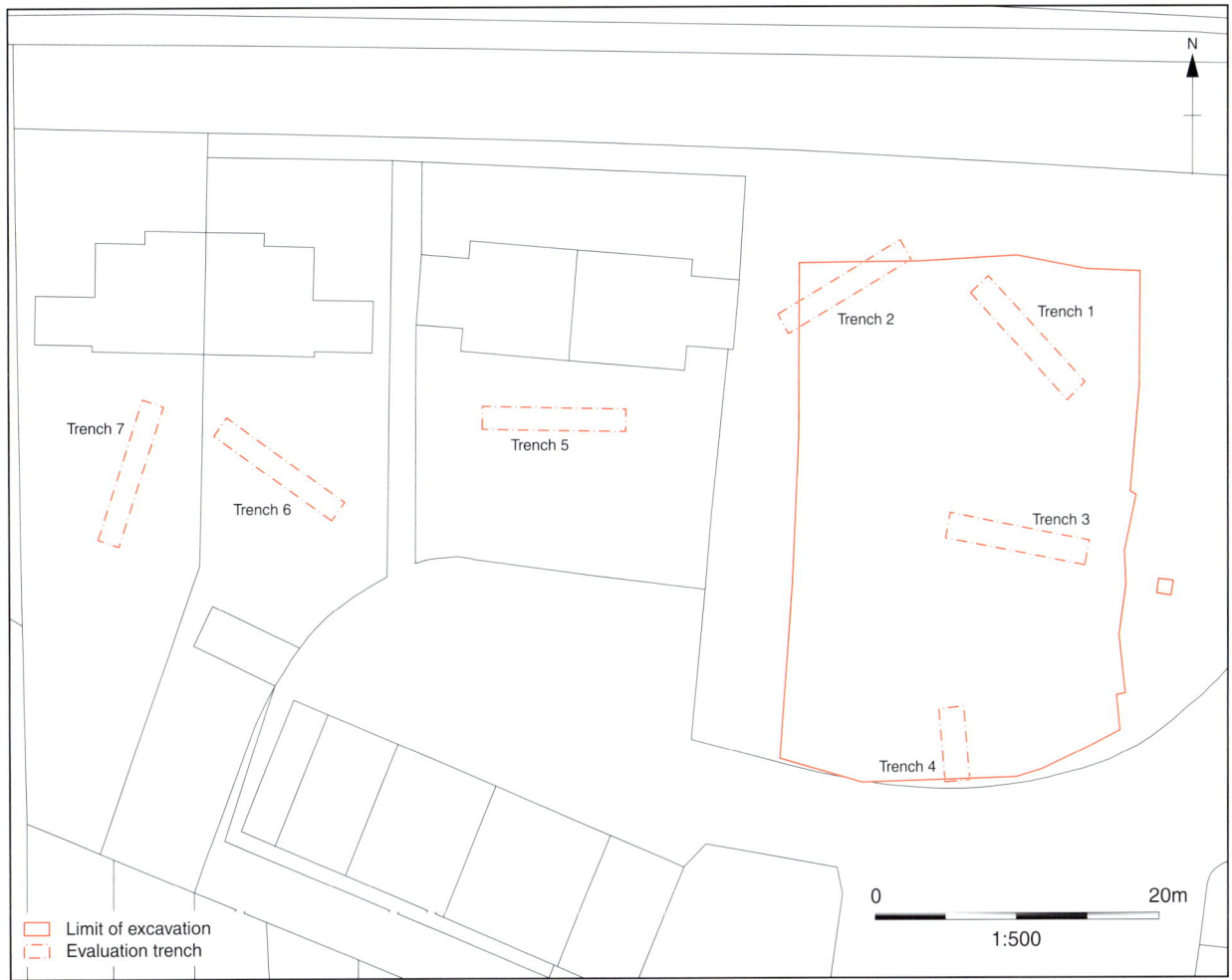

Fig. 1.4 Areas of investigation

Fig. 1.5 Excavation area with the Fire Station and training tower in the background

During the excavation an area *c* 8m by 8m near the south-eastern corner of the site was found to contain a surface scatter of around 80 struck flints (Fig. 2.1). Further investigation by two 1m by 1m test pits recovered an assemblage of around 100 further struck flints stratified within a natural sand layer. Initial assessment suggested that the assemblage almost certainly belonged to the Creswellian (Later Upper Palaeolithic) or Federmesser (Final Upper Palaeolithic) industries of the Late Glacial period, and the fresh state of the flint suggested an *in situ* assemblage. Sites of this period in the UK are extremely rare and as such the assemblage from Guildford Fire Station was considered to be potentially of national importance. In consultation with Nick Truckle (SCC) and Jon Mullis (Jacobs UK Ltd) a strategy for the full and detailed excavation of the flint scatter was formulated (OA 2013c). The analysis of this scatter and its stratigraphic context make up the main subject matter of this report and the methods used for the excavation are described in Chapter 3.

ARCHAEOLOGICAL AND HISTORICAL BACKGROUND

The Guildford Fire Station Heritage Statement (Jacobs 2012) described the known heritage assets within a 500m study area centred on the site, and was based on data gathered from both the Surrey Historic Environment Record and the Archaeology Data Service online catalogue.

The collection of 65 worked flints found in the gardens of numbers 22–26 Ladymead and during the excavations of the foundations of a pedestrian bridge over Ladymead to the north of the Fire Station has already been mentioned above. The assemblage dates mainly to the Mesolithic period and includes cores, scrapers, blades, saws and waste material.

Evidence for activity in the Neolithic period is attested by only a late Neolithic/early Bronze Age arrowhead found within material collected from the vicinity of the Fire Station, although no specific find spot was recorded.

There is no recorded evidence for any archaeology of Iron Age date, and the only archaeology of Roman date noted from within the study area was the find spot of a single bronze coin of Constantine the Great (*c* AD 317) recovered from material imported during the creation of rose beds at Guildford Lido in 1963.

Further afield at Broadstreet Common, some 2km due west of the Fire Station site, a Roman corridor-type villa with at least five rooms was discovered in the 19th century. More recent work on the site, adjacent to Barnwood School (Hayman 1994; Poulton 2005), revealed evidence for ancillary buildings, a corn dryer, fenced enclosures, postholes, pits and a boundary ditch. Occupation of the site appears to have commenced in the late 1st or early 2nd century AD, and continued into the 4th century AD. The villa building itself was probably constructed during the 3rd century AD. Hypocaust tiles recovered during the works may indicate that the villa had a detached bath house.

Within the northern part of Guildford, at Christ Church Common, around a kilometre to the north-west of the fire station, evidence for Roman rural settlement was uncovered during evaluation works (Lambert 2007). A large pit or waterhole and a probable ditch were recorded, associated with pottery dating broadly to the 2nd–3rd centuries AD. At Manor Farm, to the south-west of the fire station, evaluation by the Surrey Archaeological Society (Davies 1999; English 2000) revealed a number of ditches enclosing an area of domestic occupation. This took the form of at least one, possibly two, subrectangular buildings with flint wall footings. Pottery indicates that the site was occupied from the late Iron Age to the mid-2nd century AD. Elsewhere, at Guildford Park, Park Barn and Stoke Hill, the *Rural Settlement of Roman Britain* online resource records field systems of Roman date (Allen *et al.* 2018).

Historically, Guildford was first referred to as *Gyldeford* in AD 880, which is taken to mean the 'ford where golden flowers grew' (Ekwall 1980). The area around the fire station was known as *Stochæ* by the time of the Domesday survey (1086), and was later referred to as *Stoke next Guildford*, which was settled by 24 villagers and ten small-holders with 20 ploughs (Jacobs 2012, 15). Guildford grew considerably during the medieval period, and two heritage assets of medieval date are noted in the Heritage Statement. The Church of St John the Evangelist Stoke Juxta Guildford dates from the early 14th century, and is located immediately to the east of the site. The site of a historic bridge is first referred to in the late medieval period, and is marked on the 1806 Ordnance Survey map as 'Woodbridge'. The bridge was rebuilt in brick between 1847 and 1848 (Malden 1911).

Eleven heritage assets of post-medieval date are located within the study area. All of the assets comprise built structures which vary in date between the late 16th century and 19th century, and include timber-framed buildings, a former mill house and the Wey and Godalming Navigations canal which was constructed from 1653.

The site of the fire station is shown as being under open fields on the earliest maps consulted, including the 1806 Ordnance Survey, the 1842 Stoke next Guildford tithe map and the subsequent Ordnance Survey maps of 1881 and 1912. The fire station itself is first shown on the six-inch to the mile Ordnance Survey map of 1934.

STRUCTURE OF THE REPORT

The specialist reports describing the Upper Palaeolithic evidence are presented in Chapters 4 to 7 of this report. Chapter 4 presents the stratigraphy of the site, the Optically Stimulated Luminescence (OSL) dating, clast lithology, particle size analysis, micromorphology, geochemistry and magnetic susceptibility. Studies of artefact taphonomy, assessing the potential post-depositional processes which might have affected the site are presented in Chapter 5. The flint is described in Chapter 6 and the functional analysis of it in Chapter 7. Chapter 8 provides a synthetic and interpretative discussion of the Upper Palaeolithic site, assessing the evidence for its date and its geological context and discussing how the flint was worked and what it was used for, as well as placing the site in its regional and European context.

The preceding chapters set out the methods which were used during the fieldwork and in the post-excavation analysis (Chapter 2) and the later prehistoric, Roman and post-medieval features and finds which were recovered from the site (Chapter 3).

SITE ARCHIVE

The site archive will be deposited in the Guildford Museum under accession number GUIHS.2015.008.

DIGITAL ARCHIVE

Digital records created during the project have been deposited with the Archaeological Data Service (ADS: http://archaeologydataservice.ac.uk). The records include digital copies of paper site records (context sheets, plans, sections, photographs, and finds and sample registers), a full catalogue of the flint, shape files recording its location, and a catalogue of the results of the functional analysis of the flint.

Chapter 2

Methodology

INTRODUCTION

This chapter describes the methods which were used during the fieldwork and the post-excavation assessment and analysis. Further details of the methods used for the final post-excavation analysis of the flint and sediments are included in the relevant chapters below. During the initial post-excavation assessment (Barton *et al.* 2016) samples taken for charred plant remains and charcoal and for pollen were also assessed. Since the results of these assessments indicated that this material had very little or no potential to contribute to our understanding of the site they were not subject to full analysis. The results are, however, briefly described here.

FIELDWORK METHODS *by Gerry Thacker and Ben Attfield*

The whole site was covered with topsoil (1000), which was around 0.20m thick, and subsoil (1001), which was between 0.30m and 0.42m thick. The subsoil is interpreted as a buried plough soil of post-medieval date, and relates to the site's agricultural use before the original fire station was built. The top- and subsoil were stripped using a 13 tonne mechanical excavator fitted with a toothless ditching bucket under close archaeological supervision down to the upper surface of a sand deposit. This surface was then hand cleaned and digitally mapped, and the features which were revealed were sample excavated and recorded. During the initial stripping of the site, the mechanical excavator unearthed an unexploded ordnance round. This later proved to be a mortar smoke round (76mm; 3") of Second World War date, which was subject to a controlled explosion by the Royal Logistic Corps Bomb Disposal team, damaging an area around 7m by 5m across in the south-eastern corner of the site, and removing an unknown portion of the flint scatter (Fig. 2.1).

Late in the excavation, a number of struck flints were noted to have weathered out from the surface of the underlying sand geology in the south-eastern part of the excavation area. Following a site meeting between the representatives of Surrey County Council, Jacobs and OA it was decided that two 1m by 1m test pits would be hand excavated into the flint-bearing sediments in order to determine the stratigraphy, quantity and date of the flints. The initial test pits yielded a large quantity of struck flints of Late Upper Palaeolithic date which clearly formed part of a larger scatter, estimated to measure around 8m by 8m.

Following these findings OA produced an addendum to the Jacobs WSI (OA 2013c) detailing the approach to the further excavation of the flint scatter. The aims of the fieldwork outlined in the addendum were:

1. To define the total area of the flint scatter
2. To recover 100% of the flint artefacts and debitage from the area of the flint scatter
3. To locate each flint of above 10mm maximum linear dimension (MLD)
4. To obtain a scientific date for the flint-bearing sediment(s), either through direct dating or from recovered biological material
5. To understand the formation processes of the flint-bearing sediment(s) through scientific analysis
6. To recover sufficient environmental samples from the flint-bearing sediment(s) to test for the presence and/or absence of environmental remains
7. To publish the results of the excavation in an appropriate journal or monograph.

One of the stipulations made by Nick Truckle of SCC was that an appropriate specialist in Upper Palaeolithic archaeology should be involved in the project, and Prof. Nick Barton of the University of Oxford agreed to oversee and advise on the excavation work.

In order to undertake the excavation of the flint scatter, the excavation area was gridded into 1m squares, aligned roughly north–south, but adjusted to incorporate the previous two test pits (Fig. 2.1). The grid was extended to the north, south and west, so that the full extent of the lithic scatter could be established by systematically testing the surrounding area. A further 1x1m grid square on the same alignment as the site grid was also located to the east on the grassed area between the fire station and the area of excavation, to test whether

Guildford Fire Station

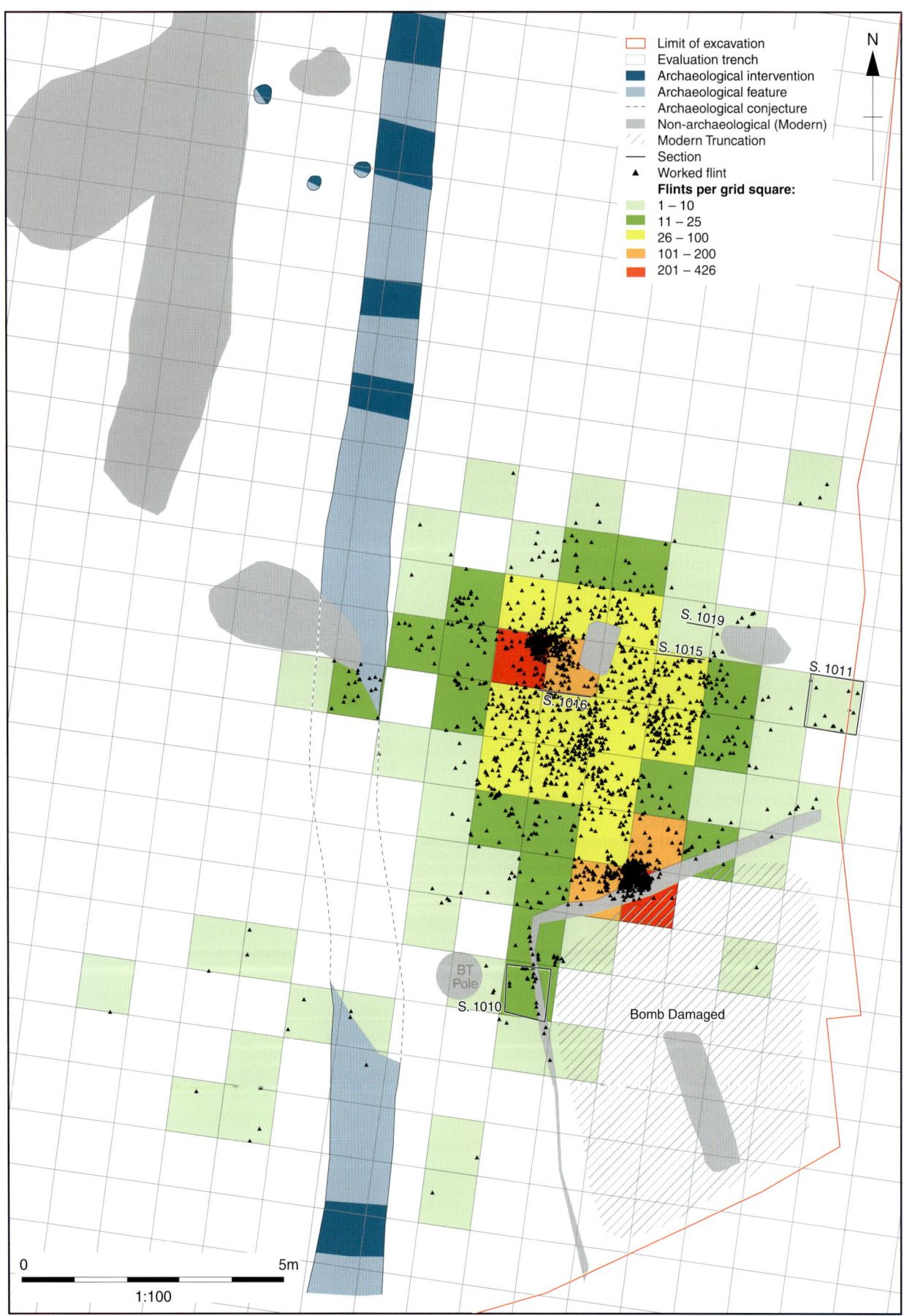

Fig. 2.1 Plan of the flint scatter and surroundings showing the excavation grid and the extent of the damage caused by the detonation of the mortar smoke round

the scatter extended in that direction (see Fig. 3.1). Although a few struck flints were recovered from the topsoil and subsoil in this extension, none was present in the sand below.

The grid squares were hand excavated by trowel in spits 0.05m thick (Fig. 2.2). Each square was assigned a block of unique context numbers. The spits were to be reduced in depth if additional horizons were observed so that finds from different contexts would not be mixed. However, no additional horizons within the lithic-bearing deposit were noted.

Flints with one dimension greater than 10mm (MLD) were left *in situ*, often on plinths of sediment if necessary, and each completed spit was photographed facing east from as high an angle as was possible before the lithics were lifted. In some cases, where the density of the flints was very high, spits had to be reduced in stages as it was not possible to expose all of the flints at one time.

The centre point of each flint measuring over 10mm MLD and of smaller recognisable tool fragments under 10mm was recorded in three dimensions using a total station theodolite. In addition, the direction of the dip along the longest axis each of the flints, and the relative angle of this dip within the sediment, was recorded. Whether the ventral or dorsal surface was visible in plan and, if not flat, the direction in which it was facing was also recorded. Although it was possible to record this information in the vast majority of cases, a few flints became dislodged during excavation and their relative angles were recorded as unknown. All of the flints recovered over 10mm MLD were issued a unique identifying small finds number and were bagged individually. Burnt flint recovered in this way, of a size potentially suitable for thermoluminescence dating, was wrapped in tin foil and bagged. Flints under 10mm MLD and not recognisably tool fragments were located by context (grid square and spit).

Spits were excavated until no more flint was present in each grid square, this level corresponding with the upper surface of the underlying gravel deposits (Unit G2b, see below). Further spits were excavated through these underlying deposits at regular intervals to test for the presence/absence of lithics but none was found.

The grid was excavated from the perceived middle of the scatter outward, initially in a chequerboard fashion, until the density of flints began to drop off and the edges of the scatter were defined. Further test squares were then dug at the extremes of the grid to check for the presence/absence of lithics, and to ensure that all worked flint was recovered.

During excavation it became apparent that the flint scatter extended below a raised, unstripped grassed area to the south-west, formerly the location of a telegraph pole. This was stripped with

Fig. 2.2 Hand excavation of the flint scatter in 1m grid squares

a mechanical excavator under constant archaeological supervision, and the grid extended into the newly stripped area. The grid was also extended further into the southern area where the density of recovered lithics was very high. This area had, however, been truncated to a significant depth by the destruction of the mortar smoke round. Many lithics were discovered along this truncated edge, and at the time, it was uncertain whether they were *in situ* or had been disturbed as the lithic-bearing sediment had become very loose. Flints recovered from this area were assigned to the relative spit (according to depth along the truncation) and their grid square. Records were made on the small finds register of whether or not the flints were thought to be *in situ*. Further test squares were dug below the base of the truncated level, but no flints were found, and the likelihood remains that significant flint-rich squares were lost as a result of this truncation.

Sampling

The sediment sampling strategy was agreed with Jane Corcoran, the English Heritage (now Historic England) Science Advisor, Elizabeth Stafford (Head of Geoarchaeology at OA) and Rebecca Nicholson (Head of Environmental Archaeology at OA) during an onsite meeting. Within the flint scatter area 100% of the sediment from each spit was retained. Of these samples, 10 litres was retained for flotation and sieving, primarily for the recovery of charred remains and charcoal (that could potentially be used for radiocarbon dating) and for microdebitage. The remainder was sieved for the recovery of the smaller flints. Initially it was intended that the remaining sediment be dry sieved onsite through a 2mm mesh. However, because of poor weather conditions this strategy was abandoned as the sediment became too damp. The sediment was stored onsite in 10 litre buckets for processing at a later date. This later processing was partially undertaken using a mechanical sieving system at OA's facility at Bourn, Cambridgeshire.

A number of sections were inspected during site meetings and key locations identified for sediment, palaeoenvironmental and scientific dating samples. Undisturbed monoliths were taken along with bulk samples to allow for a range of sediment work and pollen assessment. The acidic nature of the deposits onsite negated specific sampling for faunal remains and molluscs. The agreed sampling strategy was overseen and implemented by the onsite geoarchaeologist, Elizabeth Stafford. Sampling for OSL dating was carried out by Jean-Luc Schwenninger and David Peat of the Luminescence Dating Laboratory at Oxford University.

POST-EXCAVATION ASSESSMENT AND ANALYSIS

Following the excavation, a post-excavation assessment was carried out in order to assess the potential significance of the discoveries and to formulate a programme for their full analysis (Barton *et al.* 2016). On the basis of the assessment, and with reference to national and regional research frameworks (*Research and Conservation Framework for the British Palaeolithic* (Pettitt *et al.* 2008); *The South East Research Framework* (Pope *et al.* 2019); *Surrey Archaeological Research Framework 2006* (Bird 2006)), a series of revised research aims for the full analysis was proposed:

The Later Upper Palaeolithic flint scatters

- To determine the lateral and vertical extent, density, technological composition and spatial patterning of the flint scatters
- To place the activity more accurately within the Late Glacial period and determine whether the flint scatters primarily exhibit attributes characteristic of Creswellian and/or later Federmesser industries
- To characterise the range of activities that may have taken place. Specifically, in the absence of bone preservation at the site, by analysis of use-wear
- To address issues of site longevity (ie do the scatters represent a single episode or event, a short-lived occupation or activity over a very extended period of time)
- To determine whether the site was visited by one or more groups of hunter-gatherers
- To address issues of group mobility and seasonality
- To address the likely group size and whether technological and spatial patterning reveals anything of group composition and social organisation
- To compare and contrast the results of the analysis to other sites of similar period within the region (eg Wey Manor Farm and Brockhill) and the wider national and international context.

Scientific dating, geoarchaeology and palaeoenvironment

- To characterise the sedimentary sequence, environments of deposition, site formation processes and address taphonomic issues that may have affected preservation of the flint scatters and associated biological remains
- Specifically, to determine whether the deposit in which the flint scatters lay exhibits pedogenic features indicative of an undisturbed remnant palaeosol
- To provide an independent chronology for the sequence of sediment deposition at the site through OSL dating
- To place the site within a local and regional

landscape including aspects of geology, topography and hydrology
- In the absence of contemporary biological remains at the site, to review regional palaeoenvironmental proxy data pertaining to flora and fauna
- To consider the evidence within the wider context of Late Glacial climate studies.

Flint

During the assessment, an initial catalogue of the flint assemblage was compiled following OA's standard system of broad artefact/debitage type (Bradley 1999). Where, however, this methodology differed markedly from Barton's (1992) scheme – which has been used since the excavation of Hengistbury Head for nearly all British Later Upper Palaeolithic material – the latter system was used instead.

For the full analysis a more detailed catalogue, which included flaking pattern, terminal and bulb type, all metric characteristics (length, breadth and width, length to width ratio, platform width and depth), degree of dorsal cortex, cortex type, colour and blank profile was compiled. For cores and tools, the number and location of platforms, core histories, location and type of retouch was also recorded, again following the methods used for the site of Hengistbury Head. The flint was also marked.

An intensive refitting exercise was carried out in order to address the following issues:

- To assess the integrity of the lithic scatter, whether the site was a palimpsest or was occupied only once, and the taphonomic processes, including any post-depositional disturbance, which have affected the site
- To characterise lithic technology and methods of manufacture
- To examine individual tool lifecycles
- To identify the location of activities and discard patterns
- To provide a proxy for tool use even if the tools themselves have been removed from the site
- To identify artefacts prepared for later use (forward planning)
- To identify the unique gestures of individual flintknappers and thus potentially help identify the minimum number of people present on the site.

The refitting was carried out in a dedicated room in the Ashmolean Museum which provided the large space necessary to lay out the artefacts. The refitting began with the areas of greatest finds density and proceeded across the whole site, starting with the conjoining of ancient breaks and continuing to refitting spalls to tools and dorsal to ventral refits of blades, flakes and cores. Reversible (acetone-soluble) adhesives were used to lightly glue pieces together.

All of the flint artefacts greater than 10mm (MLD) were plotted using a GIS, which provided a means of visualising the spatial patterning within the scatter, and which was used to produce the figures in this report.

Flint functional analysis

A preliminary evaluation of the state of preservation of the worked flint was undertaken during the assessment in order to assess its potential for functional analysis. This analysis was performed using both a binocular stereoscopic microscope with magnifications up to 56x (Olympus SZX7) and a metallurgical microscope with magnifications ranging from 50 up to 500x (Olympus BX51M, bright and dark field, polarisation). Following this assessment it was recommended that a wider study was undertaken with the following aims:

- To assess the intensity of tool use at the site (were retouched tools used expediently for short-term purposes or were they curated and reused/resharpened over prolonged periods?)
- To characterise the range of activities taking place at the site and to identify possible 'activity areas', and to detail the use-histories of specific tools
- To examine the question of whether any of the tools at the site were hafted or whether they were used directly in the hand
- To test the idea that retouch on specific tools (blades with stepped and scaled retouch) was an extreme form of edge-damage resulting from use, or whether the retouch was a deliberate method of resharpening the edge during use
- To investigate the evidence for the use of armatures, especially with regard to points and backed fragments
- To place the Guildford site within a wider research context by allowing comparison with sites of similar type and age from continental Europe where similarly detailed functional studies have been undertaken.

The functional analysis was undertaken in three stages. The assemblage was first assessed macroscopically and a maximum sample of pieces – including all tools, resharpening flakes, pieces with macroscopic signs of use, and debitage products with useful edges – was defined and was assessed using a binocular microscope to evaluate the state of preservation and signs of use. The second stage involved examining all surfaces for traces of use on the basis of which the sample was divided into used, possibly used and unused pieces, which were then divided into broad functional categories. In the third stage a detailed study was made of the wear traces of a selection of pieces, covering all of the broad functional categories. Full details of the methods used for the third, detailed stage of analysis are given in Chapter 6.

Sediment analysis

During the post-excavation assessment the 17 monoliths taken for sediment analysis were photographed and logged to augment the interpretation of the stratigraphy made during the fieldwork, and to provide subsamples for pollen analysis and for archiving. On the basis of the assessment, a programme of further work intended to elucidate the depositional environment and taphonomic processes which had affected the deposits containing the flint was recommended. The further work involved micromorphological and lithological analysis of the full sediment sequence (Units G2a-d) to allow comparisons to be made and to detect the presence of remnant soils or occupation surfaces. Full details of the methods employed are described in Chapter 4.

POLLEN *by Mairead Rutherford*

Six subsamples were submitted for pollen assessment. The assessment showed that the samples were all barren of pollen. This may be due to the minerogenic nature of the sediments which are not suitable for preservation of pollen.

CHARCOAL AND CHARRED PLANT REMAINS *by Rebecca Nicholson*

A total of 42 samples, each of 10 litres, were processed by water flotation using a modified siraf-style tank. Two of these (samples 1 and 2, from posthole 1007 and ditch 1027) were taken from archaeological features which lay above the flint-scatter horizon. The remaining 40 came from a representative selection of spits and grid squares (20%, from across the site, making a total of 400 litres processed from unit G2c), and were taken in order to check whether charred remains were present within the flint scatters and, if present, whether any were suitable for radiocarbon dating. Each flot was quickly scanned to determine the types and quantities of material present.

All 42 samples produced flots containing charred material (see Appendix 4 in Barton *et al.* 2016), and all the flots include a similar range of material, albeit in slightly different quantities. In all cases, clinker and coal are common components, together with variable quantities of charcoal. The majority of the charcoal is highly comminuted but occasional roundwood or twiggy fragments are present in a number of samples as well as some fragments >2mm in diameter which are potentially identifiable to taxon. A significant proportion of the samples contain one or more charred cereal grains, including wheat, oat/brome and probably rye. Occasional very small fragments of nutshell are present in five of the samples. Most of the flots include modern uncharred seeds, insect fragments, nematode and earthworm egg capsules, and bone and snail shells are occasionally present, the latter including the burrowing mollusc *Ceciloides acicula*. Slag and/or fragments of burnt clay occur in several samples

Given the ubiquity of coal, clinker, charred cereal grains and uncharred seeds it is clear that most, or all, of the material in the flots is intrusive from the overlying soil, almost certainly as a result of worm action. The upper levels of the sediment profile (Units G2d/c) were heavily affected by very large vertical worm burrows lined with pea grit gravel but also coal and charcoal. The flots from the later archaeological features were very similar in composition to those from Unit G2c, including the ubiquitous presence of coal, which perhaps derives from steam ploughing. While some of the charcoal and nutshell could possibly be of much earlier date, its presence together with clearly residual material argues against it.

Chapter 3

Later prehistoric, Roman and more recent features and finds

by Gerry Thacker

INTRODUCTION

As well as uncovering the Late Upper Palaeolithic flint scatter, the excavations revealed a small number of later prehistoric, Roman and post-medieval features (Fig. 3.1), which, along with the finds from them, are described in this chapter. These features were all, unless otherwise stated, cut through the upper surface of the flint-bearing sands (1002) but were sealed by the top- and subsoil layers (1000 and 1001).

FEATURES

The earliest dated feature was a north–south aligned linear ditch (1381) which contained a single small sherd of pottery dated to the middle Iron Age (Fig. 3.1). The ditch, which had clearly been truncated, probably by later ploughing, was excavated in two locations, including the terminal end which was situated 9m south of the northern limit of excavation. A section across the central part of the ditch (1021, section 1007; Fig. 3.2) exhibited a concave profile which measured 0.44m wide and 0.18m deep. The terminal end of the ditch (1015, section 1004; Fig. 3.2) had a similar profile. The single ditch fill in both excavated locations was a mid- to dark grey-brown sandy silt, which, in addition to the pot sherd, contained occasional residual struck flints. An environmental sample (Sample 9) taken from the ditch fill contained occasional fragments of charcoal but no other charred plant remains. A further ditch uncovered during the evaluation (203) ran west at right angles to ditch 1381 at its northernmost plotted extent. This second ditch also contained residual struck flint, but otherwise remained undated.

A second ditch (1382) initially noted during the evaluation works (303) ran broadly parallel to and around 6m to the east of ditch 1381 This ditch (1382) was investigated through five hand-dug interventions (Fig. 3.1) which showed that only the base of the ditch survived, to a depth of between 0.05m and 0.12m (Fig. 3.2: Sections 1000, 1005, 1008 and 1009). The ditch became shallower to the north, until it disappeared altogether around 6m from the northern baulk. The ditch measured between 1.0m and 1.4m wide and the remaining profile indicated that the base of the feature was flat. The fill of the ditch was similar in all excavated locations and comprised a brownish-grey silty sand. Two sherds of pottery recovered from the southernmost intervention (1019, fill 1020) could only provide a broad Roman date. Residual struck flints were also present within the fill. An environmental sample (Sample 2) contained charcoal fragments and a charred wheat grain.

A pit (1023) was located 1.5m to the east of ditch 1381 (Fig. 3.1). It was subcircular in plan and measured 0.38m across but only 0.02m deep. The fill (1024), a dark brown sandy silt, contained two sherds of pottery, one of post-medieval date (*c* 1550–1700), and the other a residual sherd probably of medieval date (*c* 1150–1300).

A further pit (1013) was located around 4m to the south-west of pit 1023 (Fig. 3.1). The pit was ovoid in plan, with a deep, concave profile (Fig. 3.2, section 1003), and measured 0.6m at its widest and was up to 0.3m deep. The single fill, a mid- to dark grey-brown sandy silt, contained no finds.

Immediately to the west of ditch 1382, a cluster of three small postholes also remain undated (Fig. 3.1). The postholes (1007, 1009 and 1011) all had steep sides and concave bases, and measured 0.2m in diameter and between 0.14m and 0.16m deep (Sections 1000, 1001 and 1002; Fig. 3.2). The fills were mid- to dark brownish-grey sandy silts. An environmental sample (Sample 1) from the fill of posthole 1007 contained charcoal, charred grain and charred straw.

The subsoil deposit (1001) contained a number of finds including three sherds of middle Iron Age pottery, and 16 sherds in a local Roman fabric, many from a necked globular jar (Fig. 3.3, 1001). These finds are likely to have originated within the ploughed-out upper fills of the two ditches. Struck flints, seven pottery sherds dating from 1150–1300, two fragments of peg tile (13th–14th century), and a clay pipe stem (1700–50) were also recovered from this deposit.

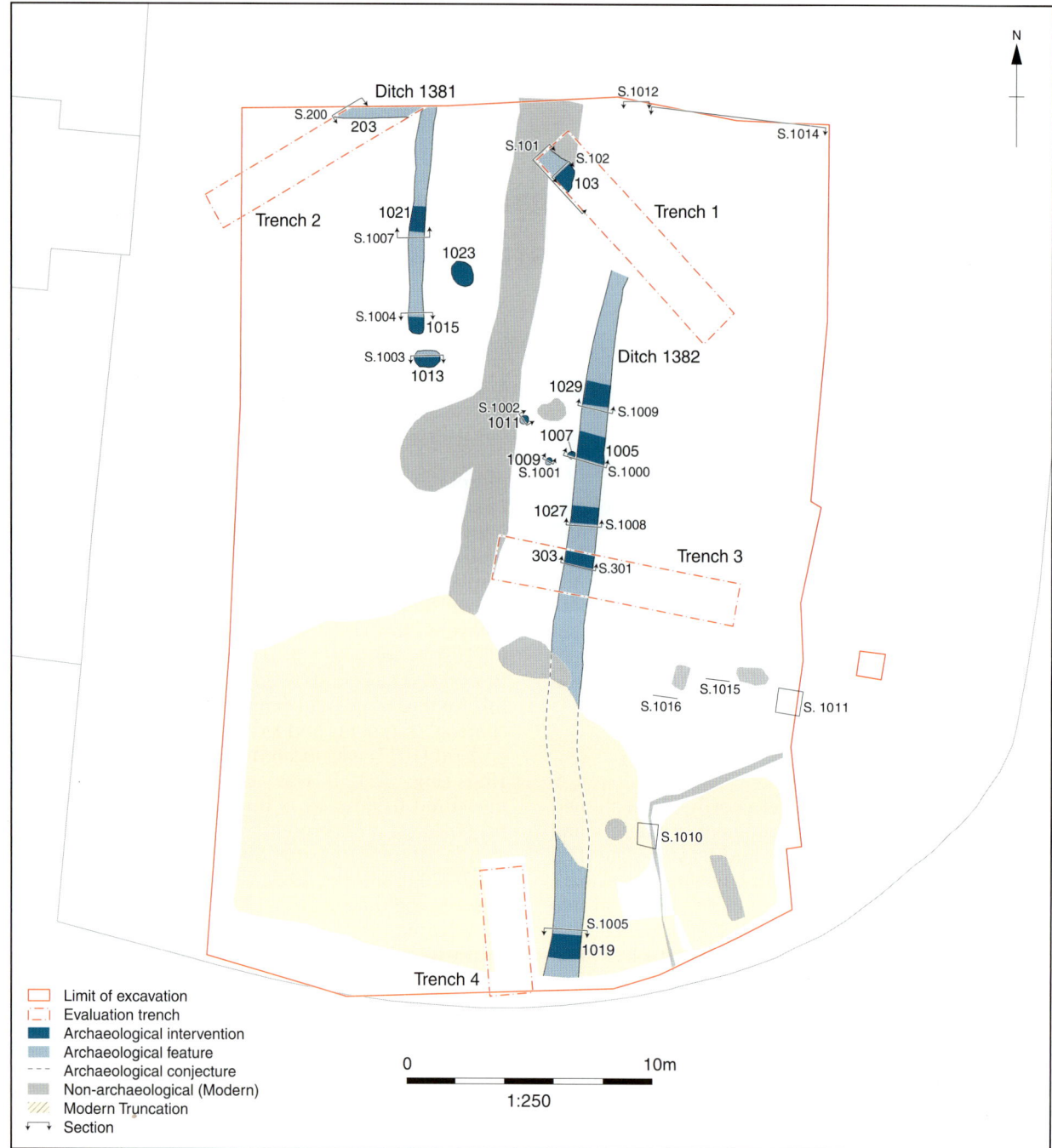

Fig. 3.1 Plan of Iron Age, Roman, post-medieval and modern features

Towards the surface of the subsoil, within the south-eastern corner of the site, a Second World War era practice mortar smoke round was uncovered. This discovery necessitated the controlled explosion of the device *in situ*, resulting in damage to the surrounding sediments (Fig. 2.1).

Other features of 20th-century date included numerous small pits and postholes, all of which contained concrete and occasional brick fragments, and a linear feature which ran north-south between ditches 1381 and 1382 (Fig. 3.1). All of these features were cut through the surface of subsoil 1001.

The ditches interpreted as being of Iron Age and Roman date are not well dated in terms of the volume of finds, and ditch 1382 had a profile perhaps more reminiscent of a plough furrow than of a ditch. However, the presence of a larger assemblage of Roman pottery in the subsoil is suggestive of a focus of activity in the area, and more pottery was recovered than would perhaps be expected in a field boundary removed from a focus of settlement. In the light of this evidence it may be postulated that a further farmstead could be located in the vicinity of the Fire Station site to add to those recorded at Manor Farm and Christ Church Common.

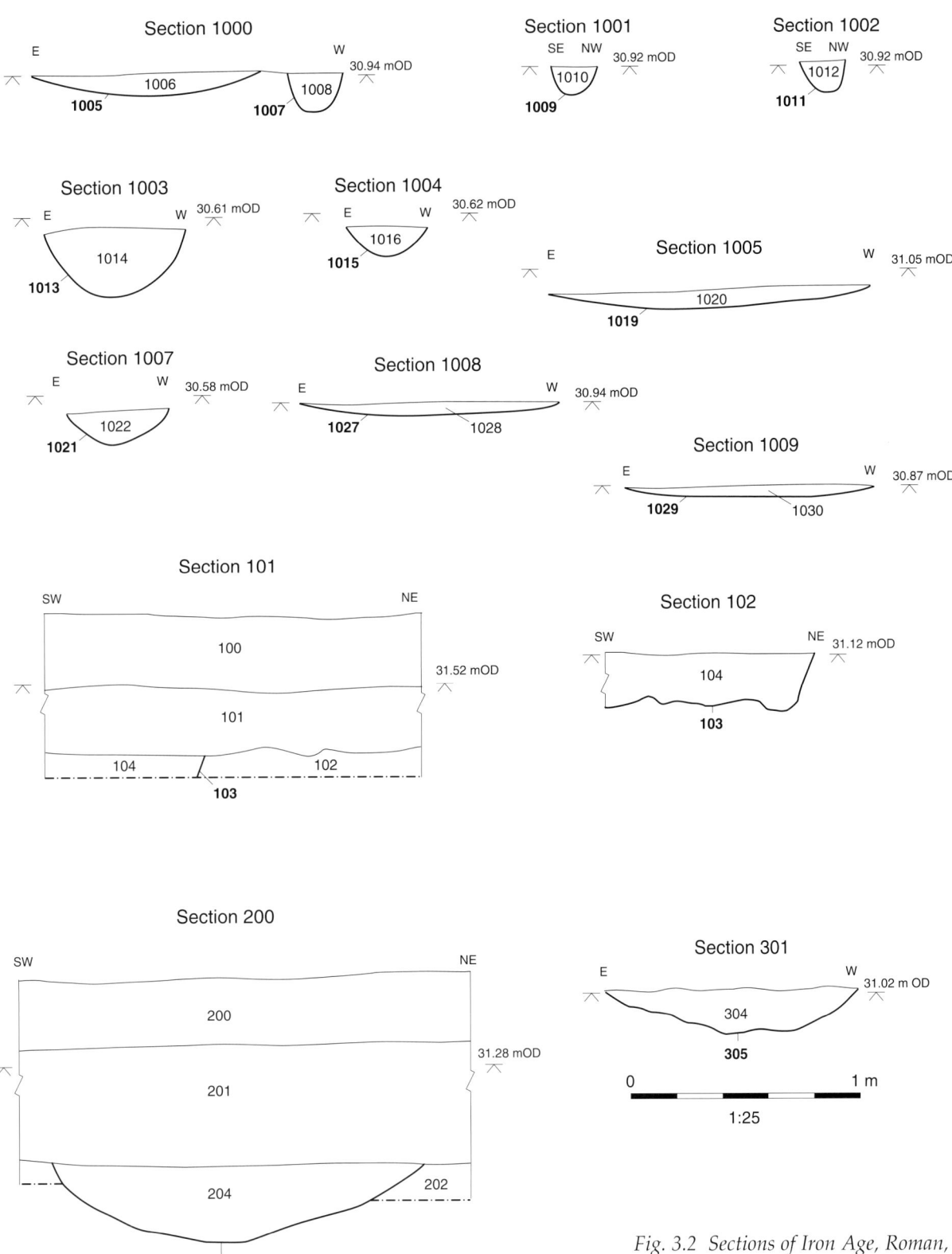

Fig. 3.2 Sections of Iron Age, Roman, post-medieval and modern features

PREHISTORIC POTTERY *by John Cotter and Lisa Brown*

A total of just four sherds of prehistoric pottery weighing 81g was recovered from three contexts: ditch 1381, the subsoil (1001) and an area of modern disturbance (1064). All of the sherds are in a hard, dark grey, very sandy, medium–coarse fabric with abundant rounded quartz up to 2mm across (including iron-stained grains) and rare flint inclusions. The vessels are from handmade jars and are probably of middle Iron Age date (*c* 400–150 BC).

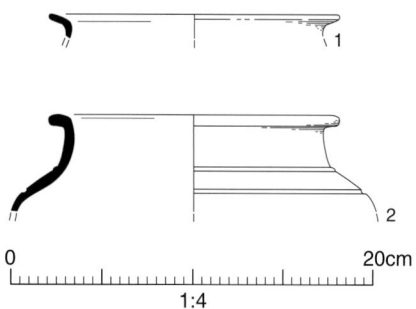

Fig. 3.3 Roman pottery: 1) Jar with everted rim in sandy reduced ware; 2) Necked globular jar with cordoned shoulder and 'figure-7' rim in sandy reduced ware

ROMAN POTTERY *by Edward Biddulph*

A small group of Roman pottery, totalling 18 sherds and 234g, was recovered from the site, largely from the subsoil layer (1001) but also from ditch 1382. The group comprised the substantial remains of a globular jar in a sandy reduced ware from the subsoil (Fig. 3.3, no. 2), a rim from a second reduced ware jar from ditch 1382 (Fig. 3.3, no. 1), and body sherds in reduced ware and oxidised ware. None of the pottery can be dated particularly closely within the Roman period, although the globular jar is likely to date to the later 1st century or first half of the 2nd century. The jar rim from ditch 1382 (context 1020) could not be identified to type, but it may be another jar with a 'figure-7' rim of similar date to the globular jar. All the fabrics were unsourced, but are presumably of local origin. The globular jar was recovered from the subsoil (1001), which also contained medieval pottery, and is therefore residual. The condition of the vessel, however, suggests that a focus of Roman occupation is located near the excavation area.

Illustrated Roman pottery (Fig. 3.3)

1   Jar with everted rim in sandy reduced ware. 1 sherd, 5g, 0.07 EVE. Context 1020, cut 1019, ditch 1382.
2   Necked globular jar with cordoned shoulder and 'figure-7' rim in sandy reduced ware. 13 sherds, 196g, 0.3 EVE. Context 1001. Subsoil. SF1012.

POST-ROMAN POTTERY *by John Cotter*

A total of 12 sherds of medieval and post-medieval pottery weighing 93g was recovered from five contexts. The assemblage is in a fragmentary condition with both worn and fresh sherds present. Ordinary domestic pottery types are represented. There are sherds from two medieval vessels, both residual. The seven small sherds in the subsoil (1001) are from a single cooking pot base in a grey sandy ware, probably Limpsfield-type ware (c 1150–1300) from east Surrey. A body sherd in the fill of pit 1023 is possibly from another Limpsfield-type product but also contains abundant chalk/limestone and some flint. Alternatively, it may be a more local late Saxon or early medieval fabric type. Other sherds in the assemblage are from local and regional post-medieval glazed earthenwares of the 17th and 18th centuries. The latest pieces comprise mass-produced Staffordshire-type whitewares including a sherd of pearlware (c 1780–1840) and a dish rim sherd in refined white earthenware which could be as late as the 20th century.

CLAY TOBACCO PIPE *by John Cotter*

A single piece of worn clay pipe stem, widening towards the bowl-end, weighing 7g was recovered from the subsoil (1001). It is of a fairly early 'chunky' type with a stem bore diameter of 2mm, suggesting a date in the first half of the 18th century.

BUILDING MATERIALS *by John Cotter*

Five pieces of building material weighing 502g were recovered from the subsoil (1001) and from the fill (1038) of an animal burrow. The pieces from the subsoil included two fragments from a crude peg tile in a hard, light orange-brown fabric with abundant medium–coarse rounded quartz, moderate very coarse lenses and platelets of red-brown ironstone or iron-rich mudstone up to 13mm across, and sparse cream clay pellets. The tile is unusually thick (18mm) and of very crude manufacture with a sub-squared edge on both pieces. Although the presence of a nail hole suggests that the fragments derive from a peg tile (probably an early example, dating to the 13th to 14th century), the thickness might indicate that this is a ridge tile as the latter can occasionally have nail holes too.

The remaining fragments, from context 1038, consisted of 19th- or 20th-century roof tile, asbestos from a tile or other covering, and a slab like object made of hard cream-coloured cement with abundant coarse quartz sand.

Chapter 4

Stratigraphic, dating and sediment analysis

by Elizabeth Stafford, John Crowther, Richard Macphail, Nathalie Marini,
Jean-Luc Schwenninger and Tom S White

INTRODUCTION *by Elizabeth Stafford*

This chapter first provides an interpretative overview of the results of the sediment analysis and dating of the site, defining its geological contexts and the processes which led to its formation and preservation. It also includes specialist reports on the Optically Stimulated Luminescence (OSL) dating, clast lithology, particle size analysis and soil micromorphology, geochemistry and magnetic susceptibility upon which these interpretations are based.

The site and the geoarchaeological investigations

The site is located in a slightly elevated position at the very edge of the Upper Floodplain Terrace of the River Wey (see Figs 1.2–1.3). The terrace has been correlated by the BGS with the Mid-Devensian Kempton Park Gravel of the Thames system. The Lower Floodplain Terrace, an equivalent of Late Glacial Shepperton Gravel, lies immediately to the north at lower elevations, buried beneath a blanket of Holocene alluvium. The modern channel of the River Wey is located *c* 200–500m north of the site. At Guildford Fire Station the basal fluvial sandy gravels are overlain by approximately 0.5–1.0m of fine-grained deposits comprising fine to medium sands, the upper parts of which contained the large and well-preserved lithic scatter, dated on typological grounds to the Late Upper Palaeolithic period (LUP). OSL dating of the sands suggests occupation of the site occurred at the beginning of the Late Glacial (Windermere) interstadial. The topographic location and character of the sediment sequences has many similarities with the sequences recorded at the LUP site of Wey Manor Farm, located 17.7km downstream from Guildford (Jones 2013).

In order to understand the sedimentary context and depositional environment associated with the

Table 4.1 Summary of geoarchaeological analyses

Section no.	Sample no.	Contexts	Sample type	Pollen	OSL dating	Thin section	Geo-chemistry	Particle size	Clast lithology
1010	52–55	1052, 1051b, 1051a	OSL Tube (x4)		X				
	110	1051a, 1051b	Monolith	X			X	X	
	113	1051b	Monolith			X	X		
	114	1051b, 1051a	Monolith			X	X		
	115	1052, 1051b, 1051a	Monolith			X	X		
	116	1051b, 1051a	Monolith			X	X		
	117	1051a, 1049	Monolith	X					
	422	1052	Bulk (30L)						X
1011	58–62	1044, 1043, 1042, 1041	OSL Tube (x5)		X				
	428	1042, 1041, 1040	Monolith	X			X	X	
	429	1044,1042	Monolith	X			X	X	
	430	1044, 1043	Monolith			X	X		
1015	156	1076	Kubiena			X	X		
	162	1076	Kubiena			X	X		
1016	167	1077	Kubiena	X		X	X		
1019	384	1081	Kubiena	X		X	X		
1014	395	1070	Bulk (30L)						X

lithic scatters at Guildford Fire Station, geoarchaeological investigations, involving the detailed recording and sampling of several exposed sections across the site, were carried out. The sections included the profiles of two test pits (Sections 1010 and 1011; Figs 4.1–4.2), excavated through the full sequence of deposits, as well as examination of standing baulks around the edges of the site, and sections through the lithic-bearing deposits within the grid squares. The locations of the sampled sections are illustrated in Figures 2.1 and 3.1.

The sediment recording was carried out onsite by a geoarchaeologist, and the sampling strategy was formulated in discussion with various specialists along with the Historic England Science Advisor (Jane Corcoran) during site visits. The sampling of the sequences included taking monoliths for micromorphology and supporting geochemical analysis, bulk samples for the study of clast lithology, and a suite of samples for OSL dating. In addition, 197 spatial bulk samples (10 litres) were collected from the grid squares containing the flint scatter for the recovery of charred plant remains, charcoal and microdebitage.

Following a preliminary assessment which included examination of the monoliths and initial OSL dating of three samples, selections of samples considered to be representative of the site sequences were submitted for detailed geoarchaeological analysis and OSL dating (Table 4.1), the

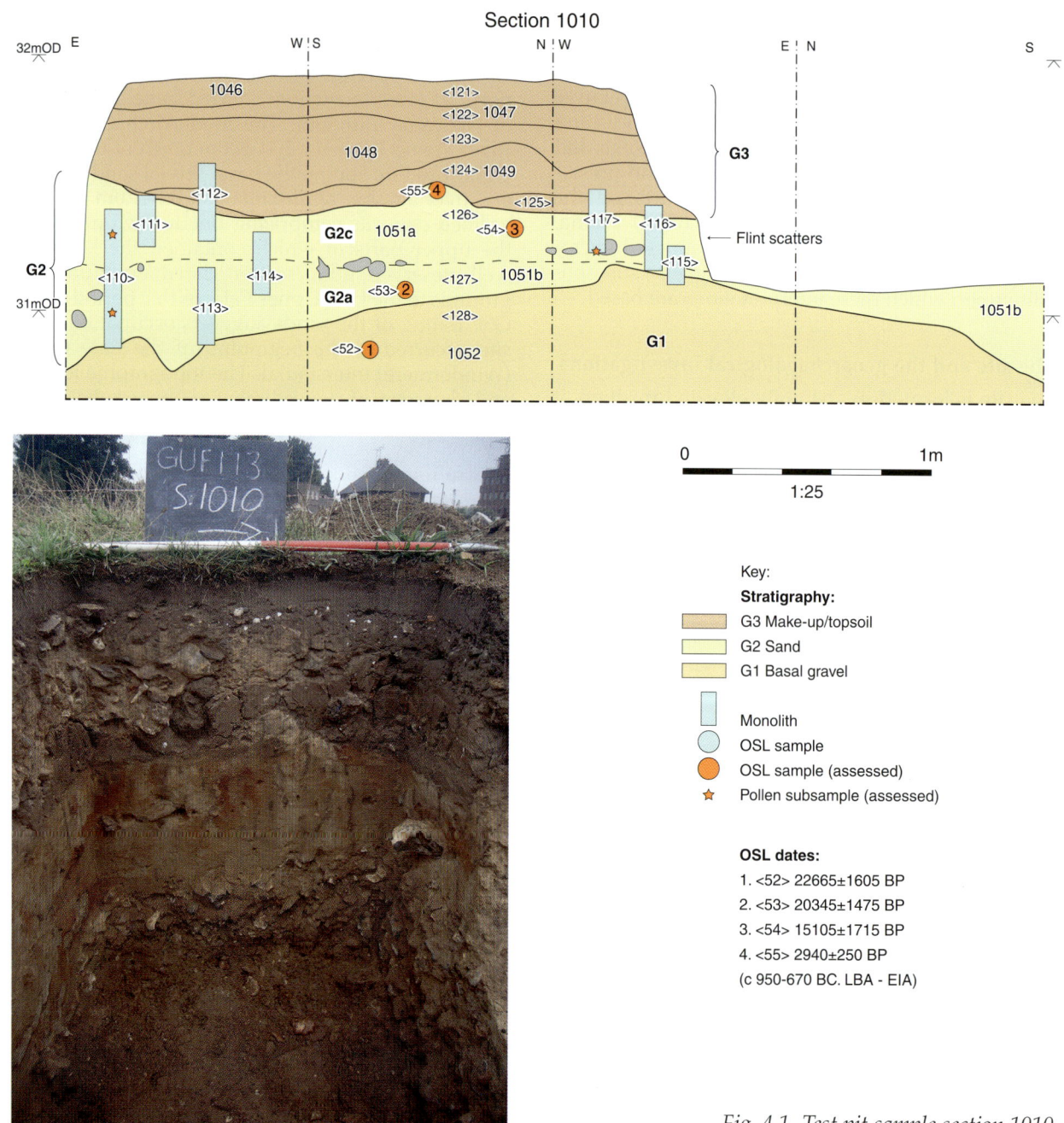

Fig. 4.1 Test pit sample section 1010

results of which are presented below. A rapid assessment of a small number (x6) of subsamples for pollen preservation provided negative results and no further work was carried out on this category of material. Equally, the results of the flotation of 42 (21%) of the bulk samples at the assessment stage for charred material were negative (see above, Chapter 2). Although charcoal was present in low quantities, it was highly comminuted and occurred alongside charred cereal grains, clinker, coal and slag, strongly suggesting it consisted of intrusive material as a result of earthworm burrowing. Consequently, processing of the remaining samples was confined to sieving for the recovery of microdebitage.

Site sedimentary sequences and chronology

Based on observations in the field, sediments were correlated into a number of broad stratigraphic units illustrated in the two key sample sections from the test pits (Figs 4.1–4.2) and summarised in Table 4.2. Detailed lithological descriptions from the monolith recording are included in the site archive.

The Basal Fluvial Gravel (G1) generally comprised poorly sorted yellowish brown sandy flint gravel, in places interbedded with medium to coarse sand, sometimes ripple bedded. This unit was observed where deeper test pits were dug across the site through the overlying sand deposits

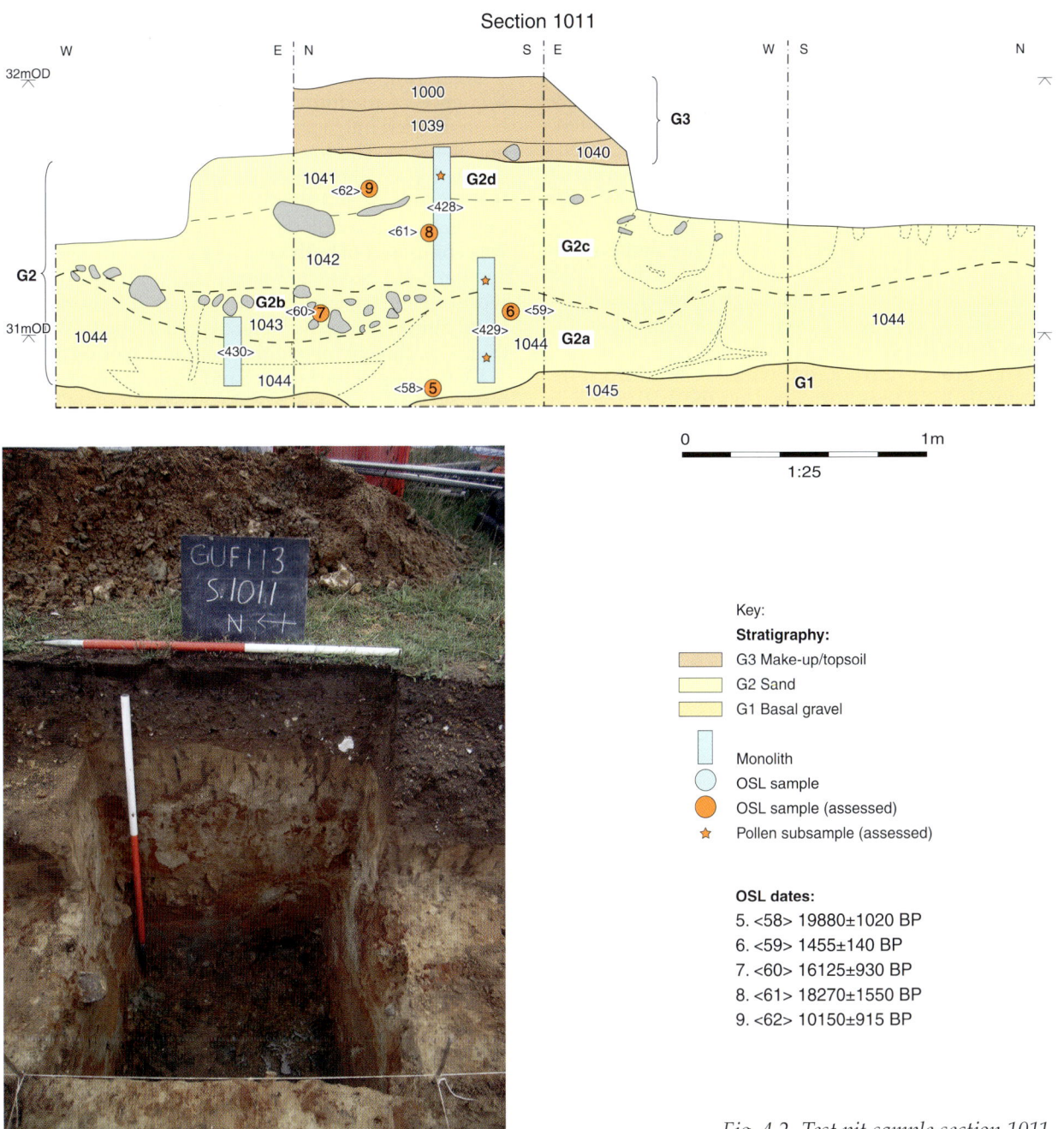

OSL dates:
5. <58> 19880±1020 BP
6. <59> 1455±140 BP
7. <60> 16125±930 BP
8. <61> 18270±1550 BP
9. <62> 10150±915 BP

Fig. 4.2 Test pit sample section 1011

Table 4.2 Summary of stratigraphic units

Unit	Description
G3	Modern topsoil and made ground
G2d	Sandy subsoil
G2c	Upper sand (containing flint scatter)
G2b	Cobble layer
G2a	Lower sand
G1	Basal fluvial gravel

and is recorded as contexts 1052 and 1045 in Sections 1010 and 1011 respectively (Figs 4.1–4.2).

Clast analysis of two samples from G1 (see White below) revealed it to be predominantly made up of nodular and weathered flint clasts, with some greensand lithologies and a significant local ironstone component. The data for G1 strongly resembles the lithological signature of 'Wealden' southern rivers that now form right-bank tributaries of the post-Anglian Thames, especially that of the Burleigh Gravel, for which an Anglian (MIS 12) age is likely. However, younger gravels in the Wey system (such as those at Guildford Fire Station) are likely to contain material derived from older terraces, including the Burleigh Gravel and its equivalents, and will therefore have similar lithological signatures.

The gravel terrace on which Guildford Fire Station is located is correlated on the 1:50,000 BGS map of the region with the Kempton Park Gravel (Upper Floodplain Terrace) of the Middle Thames (Fig. 1.3), deposited by fluvial processes in cold-climate braided stream systems during the mid-Devensian. Bridgland (1994) ascribes aggradation of the Kempton Park Gravel to MIS 4–2, and Gibbard (1985) suggested deposition had ceased by c 30,000 BP. Gravel deposits of the Lower Floodplain Terrace, known locally in the Lower Wey Valley as the Wisley Gravel or the Wey Valley Gravel (ibid., 84), are correlated with the Late Devensian Shepperton Gravel of the Thames, and largely underlies the Holocene alluvium at lower elevations adjacent to the current channel of the River Wey. The Fire Station site is located at the very interface between the Upper and Lower Floodplain Terraces as mapped by the BGS. Ground levels based on 1m DTM LiDAR data average c 31–32m OD (although the majority of the terrace to the south lies at c 33–34m OD). Ground levels on the modern floodplain adjacent to the river are lower, averaging c 27–29m OD. OSL dating of a sand bed within G1, sample 52 (Fig. 4.1), produced an age estimate of 22,665 ± 1605 BP (Fig. 4.3; see Schwenninger below), placing deposition of the upper part of this stratum within the Last Glacial Maximum (LGM).

Overlying the Basal Fluvial Gravel (G1) was a sequence of medium to fine sands (G2) that have been divided into a number of subunits (Figs 4.1–4.2 and 4.4–4.5). The lower part of the profile (G2a) is divided from the upper (G2c) by a discontinuous bed of cobble- and pebble-sized clasts recorded as unit G2b. The cobble layer was quite distinctive. It was composed of both very large flint nodules and a smaller component of greensand chert (Fig. 4.4). The worked flint artefact scatters recovered from the site were almost exclusively recovered from layer G2c (Fig. 4.5), directly above the Cobble Layer G2b.

OSL dating of the Lower Sand (G2a) in Section 1010 (sample 53) provided a date of 20,345 ± 1475 BP, whereas a date from Section 1011 (sample 58) provided a date of 19,880 ± 1020 BP, placing deposition towards the end of the LGM (Fig. 4.3). An additional sample (59) from Section 1011 produced an anomalous date of 1455 ± 140 BP and is interpreted as a result of intrusive material, possible due to burrowing. Single OSL dates from sands within the Cobble Layer G2b in Section 1011 (sample 60) produced an age estimate of 16,125 ± 930 BP, and from the Upper Sand (G2c) in Section 1010 (sample 54) of 15,105 ± 1715 BP. These dates place deposition just prior to, or at the beginning of, the warmer Late Glacial interstadial which, based on Greenland ice cores, began c 14,700 BP. A date on G2c in Section 1011 (sample 61) was a little earlier at 18,270 ± 1550 BP. As the other dates in the sequence are stratigraphically consistent, this perhaps suggests some contamination issue with sample 61 as a result of bioturbation or burrowing, as with sample 59, which was also in Section 1011. The deposits in this section did appear more disturbed than Section 1010 as a result of bioturbation (burrowing), but they also had possible cold-climate deformation structures (involutions?) and vertical fissures. The uppermost part of the sand sequence in Section 1011 – Sandy Subsoil (G2d) – provided a significantly later age estimate (than sample 62) at 10,150 ± 915 BP. In addition, in Section 1010, sample 55, from immediately beneath the made ground, produced an even later date of 2940 ± 250 BP,

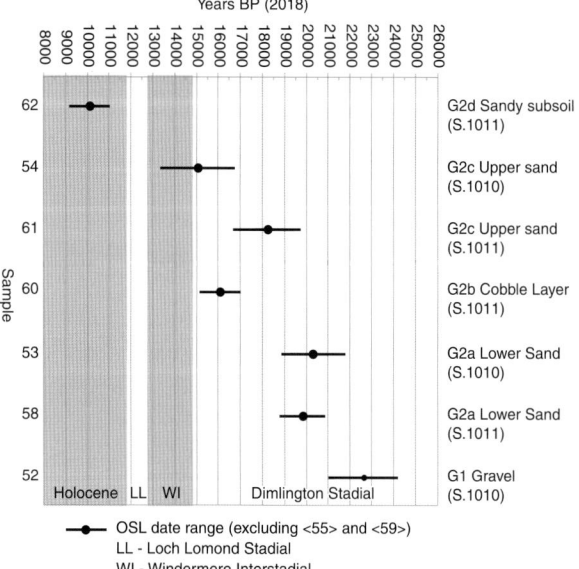

Fig. 4.3 Summary of OSL date ranges

Fig. 4.4 Section 1015 with kubienas 156 and 162 through the artefact bearing sand (G2c); the nodular flints of cobble layer G2b are visible in the foreground

Fig. 4.5 Section 1016 with kubiena 167 through the artefact bearing sand (G2c)

consistent with the level at which Iron Age activity was recorded. Overall, the OSL dates suggest that the accumulation of sand began towards the end of the LGM and continued throughout much of the earlier part of the Late Glacial period, with deposition largely ceasing, perhaps during the Late Glacial interstadial or Loch Lomond stadial (c 12,900–11,700 BP; Fig. 4.3).

Particle size analysis (0.01–2000 microns) undertaken from the two profiles from G2 in Sections 1010 and 1011 produced similar results, with very little variation throughout the profile, each sample being largely dominated by sand (66–88%) with peaks in the 100–600 micron range, with some silt (9–26%) and a little clay (1–7%; see Fig. 4.8 and Marini below). The only variation was a slightly increased clay content in G2a in Section 1011. Overall, the sands appeared to been affected significantly by localised post-depositional processes: weathering, leaching and ferruginisation, particularly at the interface of Upper Sand G2c and the Cobble Layer G2b where heavy iron mineralisation was noted. This also, however, occurred down root channels throughout the Upper Sand. Large vertical earthworm burrows filled with pea grit were clearly visible in the Upper Sand G2c. Geochemical analysis (see Crowther and Macphail below) generally recorded consistently low loss on ignition (LOI) values, only small amounts of carbonate, and a neutral to slightly alkaline pH (7.3–7.6). With reference to magnetic susceptibility, the χ values were also all consistently low, χ_{max} values were moderately high with variability assumed to be attributable to post-depositional mineralisation. The resulting χ_{conv} values were all very low and provide no evidence of susceptibility enhancement as might be associated with heating/burning or natural fermentation processes in former topsoil horizons.

Fifteen thin sections were processed from various horizons across the site (see Macphail and Crowther below). This included monoliths extracted from the two main sample profiles (Section 1010, samples 113, 114, 115, 116, Fig. 4.1, and Section 1011, sample 430, Figs 4.2 and 4.6) as well as monoliths taken from the lithic-bearing sand G2c within the grid squares (samples 156, 162, 167, 384, Figs 4.4–4.5 and 4.7). In summary, the thin section analysis suggests that the sands were largely homogeneous, having been heavily affected by post-depositional processes and bioturbation (eg worm burrows). However, some localised fine bedding structures were detected, as was occasional fine gravel. This, along with data from the particle size analysis, suggests that the sands were primarily deposited by alluvial processes adjacent to an active (braided?) channel. Periglacial rivers commonly deposit large quantities of silt and sand over extensive outwash plains through seasonal flooding, often during peak

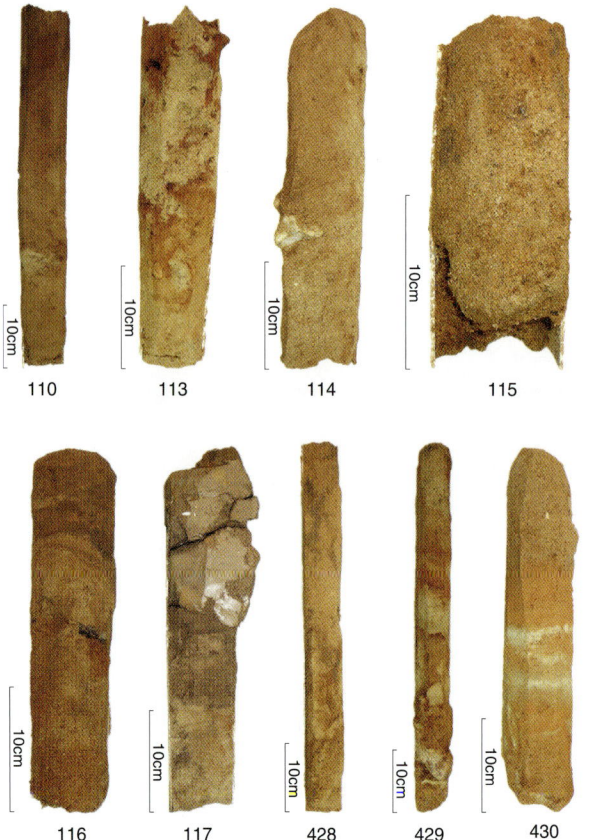

Fig. 4.6 Photographs of monoliths from test pit sample sections 1010 and 1011

Fig. 4.7 Photographs of monoliths from sample grid squares

discharge in spring and early summer. However, localised wind erosion and deflation processes can also occur in late summer and winter over bare or sparsely vegetated braid bars and sand flats (Ballantyne and Harris 1994, 155). This may perhaps go some way to explaining the concentration of clasts represented by Cobble Layer G2b. Analysis indicates that the worked flint assemblage does not derive from this material (see Chapter 6), and the very large size of the intact flint nodules within a fine-grained sand body is not consistent with fluvial and/or alluvial deposition. If not intentionally collected and brought to site by the flintknappers, one must assume a natural depositional process, perhaps related to cold-climate periglacial conditions. The site is located c 800m north of surface outcrops of Cretaceous Newhaven and Seaford Chalk Formations, as mapped by the BGS (Fig. 1.3). Between the Chalk and the Tertiary London Clay – the latter underlying Guildford Fire Station – lies an outcrop Tertiary deposits of the Lambeth Group (formerly the Woolwich-and-Reading Beds). The north-facing slopes of the Hog's Back ridge and Netley Heath (itself capped by high-level Tertiary sands and gravels) are dissected by several sinuous dry valleys that extend as far as the low-lying river terrace in the vicinity of Guildford Fire Station. These valleys are filled with Head deposits – the product of weathering and erosion of bedrock material – which, during the Pleistocene, largely occurred in cold climate conditions through processes such as solifluction. It is possible that the clasts are remnants of soliflucted material that had been subject to deflation under cold, dry conditions, the winnowing out of finer material resulting in a concentrated gravel lag deposit. Examination of a sample of the clasts provided little evidence of the frost shattering that might be expected from cold-climate mass movement deposits (see White below), although this might not have been as prevalent if conditions had been relatively arid. Certainly, vertical and horizontal fissuring/leaching identified during thin section analysis of the underlying Lower Sand G2a in Section 1011 (sample 430) is interpreted as potential evidence of cold climate conditions and periglacial 'patterned ground'.

The thin section analysis indicates that incipient soil formation associated with the lithic-bearing sand G2c probably occurred seasonally under conditions of reduced channel flow. Seasonal reactivation of the channel system probably occurred during periods of higher discharge with renewed alluviation of fine sediment and inwash of clay into voids. Fluctuating groundwater during and after deposition led to iron deposition and leaching. This could conceivably also be related to waterlogging and frozen ground during the Loch Lomond stadial (c 12,900–11,700 BP).

OPTICALLY STIMULATED LUMINESCENCE DATING *by Jean-Luc Schwenninger*

A total of nine samples from the sedimentary sequences were processed for OSL dating at the Luminescence Dating Laboratory at Oxford University. The initial sampling was carried out from two open section faces during a specialist visit to the excavation in September 2013. An initial assessment of three samples in 2014 indicated good signal characteristics including high sensitivity, low thermal transfer, low variability between multiple measurements as well as good recycling and negligible infrared signals indicative of feldspar contamination. There was some uncertainty in the assessment of the mean water content of the sediment during the burial period, but it was not considered reason to question the veracity of the calculated age estimates and their corresponding error margins. Subsequently the full suite of samples from the two sections was processed in 2017.

Table 4.3 presents a summary of the OSL dating results. The results are based on luminescence measurements of sand-sized quartz (180–255μm) extracted from the samples using standard preparation techniques including wet sieving, HCl (10%) treatment to remove carbonates, HF treatment (48%) to dissolve feldspathic minerals and heavy mineral separation with sodium polytungstate. Results for

Table 4.3 Summary of OSL dating results

No.	Section no.	Sample no.	Lab code	Burial depth (m)	Water content (%)	Palaeodose (Gy)	Dose rate (Gy/ka)	Age estimate BP (2018)	Stratigraphic unit
1	1010	52	X6362	1.2	4	18.64 ± 0.96	0.82 ± 0.04	22665 ± 1605	Basal gravel (G1)
2	1010	53	(X6363)	0.8	6.7	21.95 ± 1.25	1.08 ± 0.05	20345 ± 1475	Lower sand (G2a)
3	1010	54	(X6364)	0.61	4.9	14.31 ± 1.45	0.95 ± 0.05	15105 ± 1715	Upper sand (G2c)
4	1010	55	X6365	0.45	3.5	3.12 ± 0.20	1.06 ± 0.06	2940 ± 250	Upper sand (G2c)
5	1011	58	X6366	1.2	11.1	24.54 ± 0.63	1.23 ± 0.05	19880 ± 1020	Lower sand (G2a)
6	1011	59	X6367	0.95	11.9	2.16 ± 1.19	1.48 ± 0.05	1455 ± 140	Lower sand (G2a, intrusive, burrow?)
7	1011	60	X6368	0.93	11.4	17.69 ± 0.49	1.10 ± 0.06	16125 ± 930	Cobble layer (G2b)
8	1011	61	(X6369)	0.64	8.4	15.78 ± 1.09	0.86 ± 0.04	18270 ± 1550	Upper sand (G2c)
9	1011	62	X6370	0.46	5.2	9.27 ± 0.70	0.91 ± 0.05	10150 ± 915	Sandy subsoil (G2d)

samples with laboratory codes inserted in brackets were reported in 2014 but the age estimates presented here have been recalculated using updated dose rate conversion factors by Guerin et al. (2011) rather than the older values of Adamiec and Aitken (1998). The dose rate calculations now also take account of the effects of the radioisotope concentrations of rubidium. The three previously reported samples were measured in a Lexsyg Research luminescence reader (Richter et al. 2013) fitted with a novel type of ring source to enable uniform irradiation (Richter et al. 2012). Blue light stimulated UV emissions (375nm) were detected through a Hoya U340 and Delta BP 365/50 filter pack with a Hamamatsu H7360-02 photomultiplier tube. The new set of measurements on the remaining samples were measured in a Lexsyg Smart device manufactured by Freiberg Instruments (Richter et al. 2015) using identical filter and detector configurations to those used in the previous measurements. ASAR post-IR blue OSL measurement protocol (Murray and Wintle 2000; Banerjee et al. 2001; Wintle and Murray 2006) was used for all the measurements.

CLAST LITHOLOGY by Tom S White

Introduction

This report provides details of the analysis of three gravel samples from the site. Two samples from the Basal Fluvial Gravel G1 were studied as standard clast lithology samples, and the third, derived from the Cobble Layer G2b, was examined in order to provide additional supporting information regarding the depositional environment. Comparative clast lithological data from nearby localities in Wealden south-bank Thames tributaries and from the main Thames are included and discussed.

Methods

The samples were separated by wet sieving into 16–32mm and 11.2–16mm fractions for clast analysis (as recommended in the appropriate QRA Technical Guide: Bridgland 1986). Clast-lithological analysis was applied to both size fractions and, as a separate procedure, the angularity/roundness characteristics of the flint component of the coarser fraction was also assessed. The latter analysis used a modified version of the Powers (1953) method, adapted for gravel-sized clasts (Fisher and Bridgland 1986) and using the categories defined in Table 4.4. This has been standard practice among most researchers undertaking clast lithological analysis for several decades, although some older published data must be integrated with caution (eg Gibbard 1982) due to the use of atypical size fractions.

Results

Data from the analysis of the samples are presented separately in Table 4.5 (clast lithological analysis), Table 4.6 (angularity/roundness analysis) and Table

Table 4.4 Angularity/roundness categories. These are based on verbal descriptions by Schneiderhöhn (1954, in Pryor 1971) of the categories devised by Powers (1953). Simplified from Fisher and Bridgland (1986)

Category	Abbreviation	Characteristic features
Well rounded	WR	No flat faces, corners or re-entrants discernible; a uniform convex clast outline
Rounded	R	Few remnants of flat faces, with corners all gently rounded
Subrounded	SR	Poorly to moderately developed flat faces with corners well rounded
Subangular	SA	Strongly developed flat faces with incipient rounding of corners
Angular	A	Strongly developed faces with sharp corners
Very angular	VA	As angular, but corners and edges very sharp, with no discernible blunting

Table 4.5 Clast lithology analysis

| Sample | Context | Size fraction | Flint | | | | Southern | | Exotic | | Total |
			Tertiary	Nodular	Weathered	Broken	Greensand chert	Greenstone sandstone	Local ironstone	Vein quartz	
395	1070	16–32 mm	8	122	110		160	7	21		428
		%	1.9	28.5	25.7		37.4	1.6	4.9		
		11.2–16 mm	21	81	156	2	94	15	48	1	418
		%	5.0	19.4	37.3	0.5	22.5	3.6	11.5	0.2	
422	1052	16–32 mm	13	107	112		191	15	72		510
		%	2.5	21.0	22.0		37.5	2.9	14.1		
		11.2–16 mm	9	52	98	1	144	66	25		395
		%	2.3	13.2	24.8	0.3	36.5	16.7	6.3		

Table 4.6 Angularity/roundness analysis and comparative data

Locality	WR	R	SR	SA	A	VA	Total
Guildford Fire Station							
<395> (1070)				21.8	72.4	5.8	225
<422> (1052)			0.5	11.2	78.1	9.3	215
Comparative material							
Thames southern (right-bank) tributary gravels							
Southfleet Ringmain <1> (74960)			0.8	23.8	70.5	4.9	122
Eastern Quarry, Swanscombe <3> (68990)			1.9	23.1	73.1	1.4	216
Eastern Quarry, Swanscombe <50> (7403)				4.0	79.8	16.1	124
Eastern Quarry, Swanscombe <51> (7403)				9.8	73.2	17.1	82
Eastern Quarry, Swanscombe <60> (8205)			0.5	4.9	85.4	9.3	205
Eastern Quarry, Swanscombe <96> (12706)			3.5	30.0	61.1	5.7	283
Eastern Quarry, Swanscombe <101> (12708)			2.0	43.3	48.4	6.3	252
Crossways Business Park <18> (1104)			2.0	56.9	29.4	11.7	197
Crossways Business Park <19> (1003)				7.5	72.6	19.9	146
Northfleet Cement <5> (602)			1.1	55.2	37.9	5.8	377
Northfleet Cement <9> (1003)			0.6	61.0	32.8	5.5	344
Northfleet West Sub-station <104>			1.4	12.8	52.0	32.4	148
Northfleet West Sub-station <106>			0.8	61.4	34.8	3.0	132
Northfleet West Sub-station <203>			3.1	21.9	62.5	12.5	32
Eastern Quarry <2> (61040)		0.6	1.7	36.3	42.9	18.4	347
Southfleet Road <4> (61040)			2.7	26.4	52.1	18.8	261
Southfleet Road <8> (61040)				6.9	48.3	44.8	58
Southfleet Road <10> (61040)				5.3	67.5	27.2	206
Southfleet Road EBS <40361> (40164)				7.3	79.2	13.5	82
Southfleet Road <40420> (40167)				6.7	75.5	17.8	279
Southfleet Road <40001>			1.1	9.7	66.7	22.6	93
Southfleet Road <40002>				9.0	67.0	24.0	100
Southfleet Road <40003>				8.5	59.8	31.6	117
Southfleet Road <40004>				7.1	65.7	23.9	67
Springhead 1121/1				5.6	59.0	35.4	178
Springhead 1121/3				7.8	72.0	20.3	232
Dartford Paper Mill <4> (83550)			2.2	52.7	41.0	4.1	160
Pleistocene beaches							
Boxgrove 1	1.9	5.8	23.0	29.9	21.0	18.0	618
Boxgrove 2	1.4	7.4	38.5	28.8	19.1	4.8	351
Bembridge 1	9.6	21.0	30.5	24.6	11.4	2.9	509
Bembridge 2	4.6	11.7	30.0	35.9	13.6	4.3	582
Southwold 1	37.7	27.1	16.9	10.7	3.2	4.4	591
Pleistocene fluvial gravels							
Barvills Farm 1	24.8	7.2	3.1	24.1	21.2	19.6	638
Barvills Farm 1			1.0	36.8	32.3	29.9	418
Shakespeare Pit 2A	24.1	6.9	1.3	18.5	22.3	26.8	622
Shakespeare Pit 2A			0.7	27.1	32.8	39.4	424
Aylesford 1			0.8	31.1	17.6	50.4	119
Aylesford 2		0.7	0.7	26.8	28.9	43.0	142
Little Hayes 1			0.6	26.7	34.8	37.9	546
Little Hayes 2			0.6	30.5	41.0	28.6	466
Rampart Field 4				18.3	54.5	27.2	226
Knettishall 2			1.5	14.1	52.0	32.3	474
Solifluction gravels							
Great Fanton Hall 1			0.6	35.2	34.4	29.8	540
St Mary's Marshes 1			0.6	15.7	32.9	50.9	540
Skinners Wick 1				0.6	18.9	74.8	222
Lodge Hill 1			0.7	14.6	27.2	57.6	151

Table 4.7 *Comparative data from the Ebbsfleet Valley, Lower Thames and other British Pleistocene sites*

Deposit/Terrace	Site	Sample	Tertiary	Flint Nodular	Total
Southern tributaries	LUP Guildford (Mole-Wey)	<395> (1070)	1.9	28.5	56.1
		11.2–16	5.0	19.4	62.2
		<422> (1052)	2.5	21.0	45.5
		11.2–16	2.3	13.2	40.5
Data from Gibbard (1982)			*Rounded*	*Angular*	
Note – categories slightly	Easthampstead Gravel	Chobham Ridges	12.72	83.04	95.76
different and some	Chobham Common Gravel	Chobham Common	24.93	47.11	72.04
lithologies excluded		Kings Hill	23.94	48.39	72.33
from published dataset	Burleigh Gravel	Burleigh	8.61	52.78	61.29
		Sunninghill	18.2	48.86	67.04
South–bank Thames tributary	Southfleet Road ARC342W02	<4001>	78.9	3.3	93.9
		11.2–16	89.0	0.9	97.1
		<4002>	90.0	2.4	97.6
		11.2–16	94.5	1.6	99.1
		<4003>	94.4	4.0	99.2
		11.2–16	93.2	0.5	98.2
		<4004>	87.2	4.5	96.2
		11.2–16	91.5	1.1	97.9
South–bank Thames tributary	Springhead	<1121/1>	92.6	1.1	96.8
		11.2–16	92.6	0.7	96.6
		<1121/3>	89.5	3.1	96.8
		11.2–16	95.3	0.8	99.2
South–bank Thames tributary Main Thames	Eastern Quarry Swanscombe	<50> (7403)	71.5	18.5	94.2
		11.2–16	76.5	15.0	97.0
		<51> (7403)	70.7	16.2	94.2
		11.2–16	78.6	9.3	97.4
		<60> (8205)	90.6	5.6	98.8
		11.2–16	91.7	3.0	98.0
		<96> (12706)	80.0	4.1	94.3
		11.2–16	81.4	2.0	95.5
		<101> (12708)	60.1	7.5	93.4
		11.2–16	67.0	3.6	93.6
Main Thames	Swanscombe Southfleet Road School	Lower Middle Gravel	63.9	7.4	94.3
		11.2–16	52.3	4.7	89.2
		Trench D	66.4	7.3	95.7
		11.2–16	51.5	6.3	90.5
		Trench E	46.0	13.2	93.1
		11.2–16	42.0	7.1	91.6
		Trench K	71.6	8.1	95.0
		11.2–16	60.6	3.7	91.4
		Trench P	51.9	13.9	93.5
		11.2–16	42.1	6.5	89.8
Main Thames	Crossways Park	<19> 1003	65.1	17.4	96.9
		11.2–16	66.3	18.1	98.4
		<18> (1104)	48.5	9.3	91.9
		11.2–16	50.8	4.2	91.9
Main Thames	Southfleet Ringmain	<1> (74960)	56.8	5.7	94.3
		11.2–16	52.4	3.0	90.3

Chapter 4

Chalk Chalk	Southern/Local Greensand Chert	Ironstone	Total	Quartz	Quartzite	Exotics Carboniferous Chert	Rhaxella Chert	Igneous	Total	Total count
	37.4	4.9	43.9	0.0					0.0	428
	22.5	11.5	37.6	0.2					0.2	418
	37.5	14.1	54.5	0.0					0.0	510
	36.5	6.3	59.5	0.0					0.0	395
	3.99			0.25					0.25	401
	28.0			0.00					0.00	329
	27.5			0.20					0.20	482
	38.3			0.27					0.27	728
	33.0			0.00					0.00	276
	6.1		6.1							213
	2.0		2.4							456
	2.0		2.0							250
	0.7		0.7							438
	0.8		0.8							248
	1.4		1.4							621
	3.2		3.2							156
	2.1		2.1							281
	1.1		1.1							380
	0.8		0.8							1101
	1.1		1.1							551
	0.6		0.6							1331
	5.8		5.8							260
	2.5		3.0							200
	5.2		5.8							154
	2.6		2.6							150
	0.4		0.4	0.1	0.1				0.2	461
	0.6		1.4							1042
	4.8		4.8	0.2	0.4				0.7	459
	3.1		3.7	0.1	0.3	0.3		0.1	0.8	1027
	3.4		3.4	2.0	1.0	0.2			3.2	411
	3.9		4.1	1.5	0.5	0.1	0.2		2.4	1234
	1.5		1.5	0.6	2.7	0.6	0.2	0.2	4.2	474
	2.6		3.0	2.1	3.9	0.6	0.1	0.4	7.5	1085
	1.8		1.8	0.3	1.0	0.6	0.3	0.2	2.5	672
	2.8		3.0	1.4	3.6	0.8		0.1	6.5	1055
	3.6		3.6	1.1	0.8	0.5	0.3		3.3	889
	3.3		3.4	0.9	2.8	0.8	0.5	0.1	5.0	1089
	2.0		2.5	0.2	1.5	0.3		0.2	2.3	641
	1.8		1.9	1.8	3.1	0.6	0.3	0.1	6.5	791
	1.7		1.7	0.2	3.2	0.2	0.3	0.2	4.8	584
	3.7		3.8	1.7	3.4	0.4	0.3	0.2	6.4	999
	3.1		3.1	1.6	0.3	0.9			3.1	287
	2.4		2.7	0.8	0.1	0.1	0.4		1.6	1069
	5.7		5.7	0.6	0.3	0.3	0.3		1.8	332
	4.8		4.8	1.5	0.6	0.4	0.1	0.2	3.0	826
	2.6		2.6	1.7	0.4	0.4	0.4		2.9	229
	2.6		2.6	3.2	2.0	0.6	0.6	0.2	6.6	538

Table 4.7 continued

Deposit/Terrace	Site	Sample	Tertiary	Flint Nodular	Total
Main Thames	Northfleet Cement Works	<5> (602)	61.2	7.0	94.3
		11.2–16	62.4	3.1	94.8
		<9> (1003)	68.1	4.9	95.3
		11.2–16	72.2	2.0	96.3
Boyn Hill Gravel	Barnfield Pit	1D	58.2	9.8	93.9
	Lower Middle Gravel	11.2–16	50.9	5.3	89.9
		2D	48.5	12.7	92.7
		11.2–16	41.6	5.5	89.7
Boyn Hill Gravel	Barnfield Pit	3D	55.5	8.3	94.3
	Lower Gravel	11.2–16	36.5	5.9	89.0
		4D	30.5	11.8	94.1
		11.2–16	28.1	8.8	90.6
East Tilbury Marshes Gravel	East Tilbury Marshes	1	58.9	9.9	96.2
		11.2–16	49.5	6.6	92.2
Mucking Gravel	Lion Pit upper gravel	1	67.1	5.9	95.3
		11.2–16	59.4	3.2	94.2
	lower gravel ('floor')	1	47.8	35.9	97.5
		11.2–16	50.2	19.6	95.7
	Mucking	1A	64.0	9.3	97.0
		11.2–16	57.70	4.90	92.10
		1B	37.4	13.3	92.5
Corbets Tey Gravel	Stifford	1A	51.6	8.4	94.0
		1B	52.5	#	92.9
		11.2–16	39.2	8.3	88.3
	Purfleet, Esso Pit	1A	44.8	16.9	91.8
		11.2–16	36.3	7.6	86.6
		1B	47.7	18.1	95.0
	Globe Pit	1	57.9	11.2	93.1
		2	50.2	10.5	93.2
		11.2–16	40.7	5.4	90.5
		3	64.6	8.9	94.4
	Barvills Farm Pit	1	67.9	11.8	92.9
		11.2–16	55.6	5.6	91.8
Orsett Heath Gravel	Hornchurch Railway Cutting	1	41.8	0.7	92.6
		2	28.9	11.7	90.2
	Hornchurch Dell	1	54.0	7.7	91.7
	Globe Pit North	1A D	41.4	9.0	90.4
	Linford	1D	64.6	11.6	96.0
		2D	84.2	4.0	95.7
		11.2–16	28.0	3.6	91.3

4.7 (comparative data). Brief descriptions of the samples are as follows:

Basal Fluvial Gravel G1, sample 395, context 1070

The 16–32mm size-fraction of this sample (428 countable clasts) consisted predominantly of flint (56.1%) and greensand lithologies (39.0%), with a significant local ironstone component (4.9%). Flints of clear nodular origin (ie with identifiable nodular cortex) formed 28.5% of the sample, with weathered flint clasts (probably nodular in origin) forming 25.7%. Broken and intact pebbles reworked from 'Lower London Tertiary' strata accounted for a minor component (1.9%) of the gravel. The non-flint material consisted entirely of 'southern' greensand

Chalk	Southern/Local					Exotics				
Chalk	Greensand Chert	Ironstone	Total	Quartz	Quartzite	Carboniferous Chert	Rhaxella Chert	Igneous	Total	Total count
	4.0		4.0	0.7	0.4	0.3			1.6	670
	3.0		3.0	0.9	0.1	0.1	0.1		1.3	1293
	3.2		3.2	0.7	0.1				1.1	758
	2.0		2.0	0.8	0.1	0.2		0.1	1.3	1203
	0.9		1.2	2.4	1.8	0.5			4.8	1081
	2.1		2.3	4.4	2.0	0.8		0.1	7.7	17.3
	1.9		2.0	1.9	1.8	0.5	0.1	0.2	5.0	992
	3.0		3.1	3.5	1.5	0.5	0.2	0.2	6.8	1785
	1.0		1.0	2.3	1.3	0.5	0.2	0.1	4.5	931
(0.1)	2.5		2.7	4.0	2.9	0.5	0.1	0.1	8.3	1391
(0.4)	2.7		2.8	1.1	0.8	0.4	0.1		2.7	857
(0.3)	3.5		3.8	2.7	1.5	0.9	0.2		5.6	1494
	0.9		1.1	0.9	0.7	0.5	0.3	0.3	2.7	745.0
	1.5		1.6	3.2	1.4	0.6	0.2	0.1	6.1	979
	0.8		0.8		3.5				3.9	255.
	1.1		1.1	1.9	1.5	0.4	0.4		4.7	465
(1.1)	0.7		0.7	0.7	1.1				1.8	276
(0.3)	0.6		0.6	1.8	0.9	0.6		0.3	3.7	327
	1.1		1.1	0.9	0.6		0.1		1.8	708
	1.90		1.90	3.10	1.20	1.10	0.20	0.10	6.00	901
	4.9		4.9	1.2	0.6	0.6	0.3		2.6	345
	0.4		0.4	2.9	1.2	0.6	0.1	0.4	5.5	730
	0.9		1.0	3.5	1.4	0.5	0.1		5.9	918
	1.1		1.4	6.0	2.6	1.1	0.2	0.1	10.3	1277
	0.5		0.5	2.5	3.0	1.6			7.4	366
	1.0		1.1	3.9	3.7	3.1	0.5	0.2	11.7	618
(37.3)	1.5		1.5	0.8	1.5	0.8	0.4		3.5	260
	3.2		3.5	0.8	1.1	1.1	0.2		3.4	653
	3.1		3.1	1.3	0.7	0.7	0.8		3.7	617
	4.4		4.7	2.1	0.8	1.2	0.2	0.1	4.5	1456
	2.4		2.4	1.5	1.0	0.4			3.2	463
	3.3		3.3	1.7	1.1	0.4	0.1		3.6	722
	2.7		2.9	2.2	1.1	1.1	0.3	0.3	5.3	1138
	2.3		2.3	2	1.4	0.6	0.6		5.1	352
	1.6		1.9	1.9	2.3	1.6	0.9	0.9	7.9	429
	1.5		1.5	2.1	2.8	1.2	0.4		6.7	676
	4.1		4.4	0.6	1.4	1.6	0.3		5.2	365
	2.2		2.4	0.7		0.2		0.2	1.7	424
	1.4		1.6		0.5		0.2	1.2	2.7	625
	1.1		1.2	3.9	2.3	0.5	0.2	0.5	7.4	665

lithologies; these included greensand chert (37.4%), greensand sandstone (1.6%) and local ironstones (4.9%). Similar proportions were observed in the 11.2–16mm size-fraction (418 countable clasts), which had a slightly higher proportion of weathered flints (37.3%) in comparison to clasts of demonstrable nodular origin (19.4%) and some broken flint clasts of uncertain provenance (0.5%). Tertiary pebbles were also marginally more common in the smaller size fraction (5.0%). The only other lithology identified was a single clast of vein quartz.

Basal Fluvial Gravel G1, sample 422, context 1052
This 16–32mm size-fraction of this sample was similarly dominated by flint clasts (45.5%) but had

rather higher proportions of greensand material (up to 40.4%) and local ironstone lithologies (14.1%). The proportions of nodular and broken flint clasts were correspondingly slightly lower, but the general composition of the gravel was generally similar to that of sample 395.

Cobble layer G2b

A sample of large (>32mm) pebbles were examined for basic identification. The sample consisted mainly of nodular flint with a few clasts of greensand chert. This is not surprising, given that these are the most durable lithologies to be found in the local bedrock strata. Some of the flint clasts had been recently broken, presumably during excavation or transport. There was little evidence of frost shattering, suggesting that the clasts had not been subjected to repeated reworking or solifluction.

Observations

Angularity/roundness analysis shows that both samples are characteristic of fluvial gravels, with proportions of angular and sub-angular clasts similar to data from other south-bank Thames tributaries. Comparative angularity/roundness data from earlier publications by Gibbard (1979; 1982) differs from the accepted 'standard' that emerged with the publication of Bridgland (1986) in that it is presented simply as 'rounded' and 'angular', but examination of Table 4.6 shows strong correspondence with samples from fluvial deposits.

Apart from a single clast of vein quartz in the smaller size-fraction of sample 395, none of the 'exotic' Midlands lithologies associated with the main channel of the post-Anglian Thames were encountered. Quartz is also present in the high level 'Pebble Gravels' that were also reworked into rivers draining the London Basin (Moffat 1986), which is the likely source of this clast.

Comparative material and discussion

The gravel samples analysed here are undoubtedly fluvial in origin and clearly represent a river system draining the northern Weald, part of the Mole-Wey system that has existed since at least the early Middle Pleistocene (Gibbard 1979). Older studies of the Wey catchment (eg Linton 1930) did not include formal clast lithological analyses, so most of the comparative data (Table 4.7) has been taken from summaries of the clast types characteristic of Wealden rivers provided by, for example, Gibbard (1982) and Bridgland (1999). Rivers draining northwards in the Guildford area, most notably the Mole-Wey (but also the nearby Blackwater-Loddon tributary systems, part of which was captured by the Wey) entrain most of their durable pebbles from only a few sources, due to the majority of local bedrock strata being soft clays and sands. Amongst the most extensive gravel deposits in the Guildford area are the high-level 'plateau gravels' that form the watershed between the Blackwater system and the tributaries of the Wey (Thomas 1961), which are probably the source of the Tertiary flint pebbles and the quartz clast in sample 395. Apart from flint, which is plentiful throughout south-east England and therefore not diagnostic of regional drainage patterns, the most characteristic lithology indicative of a 'southern' provenance is greensand chert, which occurs in the Hythe Beds throughout the northern Weald (Bridgland 1999). Rocks from the Hastings Beds are also important indicators of Wealden provenance, and include sandstones, ironstones and siltstones that can form up to 80% of the rudaceous components of local gravels (see Bridgland 1999 and Table 4.5 for clast lithological data). Gravel samples from Thames tributaries to the east, notably those of the catchments in the Swanscombe area, contain markedly more Tertiary pebbles derived from the Pebble Gravels and clearly differ from the Guildford samples that are dominated by greensand chert.

Conclusions

The available data indicate that the Guildford samples strongly resemble the lithological signature of 'Wealden' southern rivers that now form right-bank tributaries of the post-Anglian Thames. The composition of southern Thames tributary gravels varies mainly in terms of the proportion of local lithologies; there was no injection of northern rocks to provide chronological markers within the gravel signatures, as is the case in the main Thames where the Anglian Glaciation (MIS 12) supplied various distinctive lithologies, most notably Rhaxella chert, into the Thames system. However, it has been suggested that the relative proportions of flint:greensand chert could be used as a means of identifying terrace aggradations within the catchments of the south-bank Thames tributaries (Gibbard 1982). Comparison of the Guildford samples with the gravels of the river systems in north Surrey (Table 4.7) indicates that they match most closely with those of the much older MIS 12 Burleigh Gravel, which consists of Wealden-derived material with 61–67% flint and 34–39% greensand chert, with a trace of quartz (cf Gibbard 1982). The Burleigh Gravel was interpreted by Gibbard as a correlative of the St George's Hill Gravel of the Mole-Wey system (Gibbard 1979; 1982) which downstream is correlated with the Dollis Hill Gravel north of the modern Thames valley. The pre-Anglian Mole-Wey was blocked by the Anglian ice advance, which diverted the Thames into its current valley, so that the northern part of the pre-Anglian Mole-Wey became the post-Anglian Lower Lea valley, its drainage reversed to the newly diverted Thames (Bridgland 1994). However, given the much more recent age for the Guildford samples indicated by OSL dating (see above), the similarity to much older deposits in the area probably reflects derivation of clasts from older terrace deposits, including the Burleigh Gravel and its equivalents, giving younger gravels in the Wey system a similar lithological signature.

PARTICLE SIZE ANALYSIS *by Nathalie Marini*

Introduction

This report summarises the particle size analysis undertaken by Quaternary Scientific (QUEST), University of Reading. Fifteen bulk samples from monoliths 110, 428 and 429 (Sections 1010 and 1011) were submitted for particle size analysis with the aim of broadly characterising the deposits.

Methods

Fifteen samples were selected for particle size analysis. Prior to particle size distribution analysis by laser granulometry (range 0.01–2000 microns), a representative sample was gathered from the main bulk sample. The sample was then mixed with a spatula to form a homogeneous 'paste'. A sub-sample was placed on a plastic watchglass and a weak dispersant solution (c 0.5ml 3.3% Calgon) was added in order to aid dispersion of the material (Blott *et al.* 2004). Physical disaggregation on a clean watchglass with a rubber pestle was carried out. Any particles observed to be greater than 2mm were removed. The sample was then washed with distilled water into the analyser. Particle size distribution measurements for particles falling within the size range 0.01 to 2000 microns was measured by laser granulometry using a Malven Mastersizer 3000. The results are shown in Table 4.8 and Figure 4.8.

Table 4.8 Particle size analysis

Monolith	Context	Relative depth (mm)	Clay (0.01–2 μ)	Silt (2–63 μ)	Sand (63–2000 μ)
110	1051a	10–20	2.66	18.73	78.61
	1051a	110–120	2.15	16.59	81.25
	1051a	210–202	1.31	9.71	88.99
	1051b	310–320	2.35	12.75	84.9
	1051b	410–420	3.25	18.99	77.76
	1051b	510–520	2.6	15.06	82.34
428	1041	50–60	1.8	13.47	84.73
	1041	150–160	1.82	12.27	85.92
	1042	250–260	2.57	15.33	82.1
	1042	350–360	3.16	19.31	77.53
	1042	450–460	2.58	15.33	82.1
429	1044	180–190	7.55	26.45	66
	1044	280–290	4.28	19.28	76.44
	1044	380–390	5.34	25.47	69.19
	1044	480–490	5.35	22.03	72.62

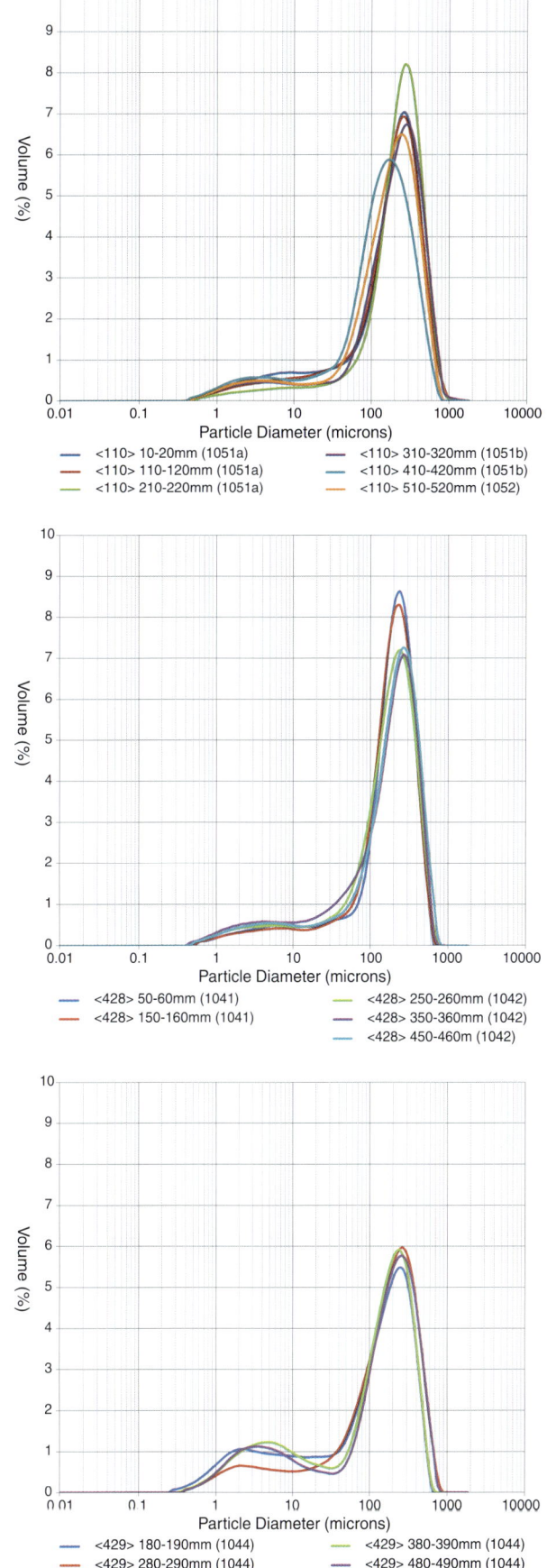

Fig. 4.8 Particle size data

Results

The results indicate that the composition of the three groups of samples from monoliths 110, 428 and 429 is fairly similar, each largely dominated by sand (66–88%), with silt (9–26%) and clay (1–7%), although samples from profile 429 present a greater input of clay (average of 5%) and silt (average of 23%), and therefore a reduced amount of sand (average of 71%), compared to samples from profiles 110 and 428, which show a similar average of clay (2%), silt (15%) and sand (82%) for both profiles. Detailed results as presented in Figure 4.8 confirm that samples from 110 and 428 show a similar profile, with a single peak of volume percentage of particles around 100–600 microns. However, samples from sequence 429 present a slightly different profile, with two peaks of volume percentage of particles, around 1–10 microns and 100–600 microns, which is much lower than the peaks observed in locations 110 and 428.

MICROMOPHOLOGY, GEOCHEMISTRY AND MAGNETIC SUSCEPTIBILITY
by Richard I Macphail and John Crowther

Introduction

In the present study, 12 thin sections (with three duplicates) and 34 bulk samples were analysed for their soil micromorphological characteristics, pH, magnetic susceptibility and LOI (organic matter estimates), carbonate and fractionated phosphate content. The samples were analysed in order to characterise various key contexts as detailed in Table 4.9.

Table 4.9 Samples analysed for micromorphology, geochemistry and magnetic susceptibility

Section	Context	Monolith	Relative depth (mm)	Thin section	Bulk sample
1010	1051b	113	200–280	M113	x1051b leached
1010	1051b	113	200–280	M113	x1051b ferruginised
1010	1051a	114	20–90	M114	x1051a
1010	1051a, 1051b, 1052	114	20–90	M114	x1051b
1010	1051a, 1051b,	115	40–120	M115	x1051a
1010	1051a, 1051b	115	40–120	M115	x1051b
1010	1050, 1051a, 1051b	116	85–165	M116A	x1051a
1010	1051a	116	165–180	M116B	x1051a
1010	1051b	116	180–240	M116B	x1051b
1011	1043	430	0–80	M430A	x1043
1011	1044	430	80–160	M430B (1 and 2)	x1044 (blue grey+brown)
1011	1044	430	80–160	M430B (1 and 2)	x1044 (orange brown)
1015	1076	156	0–75	M156	-
1015	1076	162	15–90	M162	x1076
1016	1077	167	25–100	M167A	x1077a
1016	1077	167	10–175	M167B	x1077b
1019	1081	384	65–145	M384	x1081
1010	1051a	110	0–10	-	110/0–1
1010	1051a	110	50–60	-	110/5–6
1010	1051a	110	100–110	-	110/10–11
1010	1051a	110	150–160	-	110/15–16
1010	1051a	110	200–210	-	110/20–21
1010	1051a	110	250–260	-	110/25–26
1010	1051b	110	300–310	-	110/30–31
1010	1051b	110	360–360	-	110/36–36
1010	1051b	110	400–410	-	110/40–41
1010	1051b	110	450–460	-	110/45–46
1010	1052	110	500–510	-	110/50–51
1011	1041	428	100–110	-	428/10–11
1011	1042	428	200–210	-	428/20–21
1011	1042	428	300–310	-	428/30–31
1011	1042	428	400–410	-	428/40–41
1011	1042	429	130–140	-	429/13–14
1011	1042	429	230–240	-	429/23–24
1011	1042	429	330–340	-	429/33–34
1011	1044	429	430–440	-	429/43–44

Methods

Bulk samples

Analysis was undertaken on the fine earth (ie < 2mm) fraction of the samples. LOI (loss-on-ignition) was determined by ignition at 375°C for 16 hours (Ball 1964; previous experimental studies having shown that there is normally no significant breakdown of carbonate at this temperature); carbonate content (expressed here as $CaCO_3$ equivalent) by subsequent ignition at 950°C for 2 hours (Heiri *et al.* 2001); and pH (1:2.5, water) using a combination electrode.

In addition to χ (low frequency mass-specific magnetic susceptibility), measurements were made of χ_{max} (maximum potential magnetic susceptibility) and χ_{hf} (high frequency susceptibility), thus enabling χ_{conv} (fractional conversion) and χ_{fd} (frequency-dependent susceptibility) to be calculated. χ_{max} was determined by subjecting a sample to optimum conditions for susceptibility enhancement in the laboratory. A Bartington MS2 meter was used for magnetic susceptibility measurements. χ_{conv} (fractional conversion), which is expressed as a percentage, is a measure of the extent to which the potential susceptibility has been achieved in the original sample, viz: $(\chi/\chi_{max}) \times 100.0$ (Tite 1972; Scollar *et al.* 1990). In many respects this is a better indicator of magnetic susceptibility enhancement

Table 4.10 Geochemical and magnetic susceptibility data

Sample	LOI (%)	CO_3 (%)	pH	Phosphate-P ($mg\ g^{-1}$)	$\chi (10^{-8}\ m^3\ kg^{-1})$	χ_{max} ($10^{-8}\ m^3\ kg^{-1}$)	χ_{conv}(%)	χ_{hf} ($10^{-8}\ m^3\ kg^{-1}$)	χ_{fd}(%)
Samples related to thin sections analysed									
x1051b leached	0.584	1.15	7.4	0.657	3.7	1460	0.25	3.2	**13.5***
x1051b ferruginised	**1.62***	1.36	7.3	**3.71****	8.6	**3330***	0.26	8.1	5.81
x1051a	0.960	1.07	7.4	0.660	5.8	**3560***	**1.63***	5.6	3.45
x1051b	0.815	0.842	7.3	0.702	5.0	2870	0.17	4.4	**12.0***
x1051a	0.915	1.18	7.3	0.747	6.2	**3390***	0.18	5.9	4.84
x1051b	0.768	0.817	7.3	**0.991***	5.2	2310	0.23	4.8	7.69
x1051a	0.725	0.854	7.3	**0.849***	4.5	2170	0.21	4.1	8.89
x1051b	0.783	0.801	7.3	0.609	**15.3***	1510	**1.01***	14.5	5.23
x1076	0.763	0.861	7.4	0.486	6.8	2820	0.24	6.4	5.88
x1077a	0.746	0.861	7.3	0.500	**14.9***	2570	0.58	14.3	4.03
x1077b	0.782	0.927	7.3	0.453	**20.2***	2680	0.75	17.8	**11.9***
x1081	0.882	1.28	7.3	0.708	6.7	**3050***	0.22	5.8	**13.4***
x1043	0.778	1.28	7.4	0.432	5.6	**3020***	0.19	5.4	3.57
x1044 blue grey	0.736	**2.40***	7.6	0.327	5.2	1620	0.32	4.7	9.62
x1044 orange brown	0.901	**1.51***	7.6	0.535	7.0	3420	0.20	6.5	7.14
Samples from Section 1011									
428/10–11	0.558	0.785			7.9	1570	0.50	7.3	7.59
428/20–21	0.553	0.802			5.9	1770	0.33	5.8	1.69
428/30–31	0.953	1.17			6.5	**3420***	0.19	6.4	1.54
428/40–41	0.909	1.25			6.9	**3380***	0.20	6.6	4.35
429/13–14	**1.06***	**1.61***			8.3	**3760***	0.22	7.9	4.82
429/23–24	0.770	1.48			6.8	2400	0.28	6.6	2.94
429/33–34	**1.01***	**1.86***			9.1	2610	0.35	8.3	8.79
429/43–44	0.975	**2.27***			7.6	2760	0.28	7.5	1.32
Samples from Section 1012									
110/0–1	0.849	0.998			9.2	2630	0.35	8.7	5.43
110/5–6	0.915	1.05			**10.3***	2860	0.36	10.1	1.94
110/10–11	0.892	1.04			**10.7***	2810	0.38	9.5	**11.2***
110/15–16	0.796	0.963			8.0	2600	0.31	7.8	2.50
110/20–21	0.740	0.874			6.7	2890	0.23	6.5	2.99
110/25–26	0.813	0.976			5.8	**3490***	0.17	5.3	8.62
110/30–31	0.797	1.03			5.5	3330	0.17	4.9	**10.9***
110/36–36	0.805	1.41			6.6	2070	0.32	6.3	4.55
110/40–41	0.674	1.33			6.7	2360	0.28	6.1	8.96
110/45–46	0.671	1.22			5.1	2620	0.19	4.9	3.92
110/50–51	0.611	1.24			4.6	2130	0.22	4.5	2.17

* Figures in bold have somewhat higher values: LOI ≥ 1.00%; Carbonate ≥ 1.50%; Phosphate-P * = slightly enriched (0.750–0.999 $mg\ g^{-1}$),
** = strongly enriched (≥ 2.50 $mg\ g^{-1}$); χ ≥ $10.0 \times 10^{-8}\ m^3\ kg^{-1}$; χ_{max} ≥ $3000 \times 10^{-8}\ m^3\ kg^{-1}$; χ_{conv} ≥ 1.00%; χ_{fd} ≥ 10.0%

than raw χ data, particularly in cases where soils have widely differing χ_{max} values (Crowther and Barker 1995; Crowther 2003). χ_{max} was achieved by heating samples at 650°C in reducing, followed by oxidising, conditions. The method used broadly follows that of Tite and Mullins (1971), except that household flour was mixed with the soils and lids placed on the crucibles to create the reducing environment (after Graham and Scollar 1976; Crowther and Barker 1995). Very small ferrimagnetic minerals, known as superparamagnetic particles (SPs), are often present in topsoils and increase as a result of burning (Dearing *et al.* 1996). These contribute to magnetic susceptibility at low frequencies, but not at high frequencies. χ_{fd} (frequency-dependent susceptibility), which is an expression of the percentage difference between these two measures, therefore reflects the proportion of SP minerals in the sample.

Phosphate-P_i (inorganic phosphate) and phosphate-P_o (organic phosphate) were determined using a two-stage adaptation of the procedure developed by Dick and Tabatabai (1977) in which the phosphate concentration of a sample is measured first without oxidation of organic matter (P_i) using 1N HCl as the extractant (after a slight excess of HCl has been added to remove any carbonate present); and then on the residue following alkaline oxidation with sodium hypobromite (P_o), using 1N H_2SO_4 as the extractant. Phosphate-P (total phosphate) has been derived as the sum of phosphate-P_i and phosphate-P_i, and the percentages of inorganic and organic phosphate calculated (ie phosphate-P_i:P and phosphate-P_o:P, respectively).

Soil micromorphology

The undisturbed monolith subsamples (Table 4.9) were impregnated with a clear polyester resin-acetone mixture; samples were then topped up with resin, ahead of curing and slabbing for 75x50mm-size thin section manufacture by Spectrum Petrographics, Vancouver, Washington, USA (Goldberg and Macphail 2006; Murphy 1986).

Duplicates of M162, M430A and M430B were also received. Thin sections were further polished with 1000 grit papers and analysed using a petrological microscope under plane polarised light (PPL), crossed polarised light (XPL), oblique incident light (OIL) and using fluorescent microscopy (blue light: BL), at magnifications ranging from x1 to x200/400. Thin sections were described, ascribed soil microfabric types (SMTs) and microfacies types (MFTs) and counted according to established methods (Bullock *et al.* 1985; Courty 2001; Courty *et al.* 1989; Macphail and Cruise 2001; Stoops 2003; Stoops *et al.* 2018).

Results: bulk samples

The key analytical data are presented in Table 4.10, with features relating to individual samples highlighted, and the phosphate fractionation data in Table 4.11.

In summary, geochemical analysis revealed that the samples are all highly minerogenic, with LOI ranging from 0.553–1.62%. Only one sample (x1051b ferruginised), which is from Unit G2a, stands out as having a notably higher LOI (1.62%) than the other samples. Equally, only small amounts of carbonate were recorded in the samples (range: 0.785–2.40%), with only five having concentrations ≥ 1.50%. All sediments were neutral to slightly alkaline in reaction, with values ranging from pH 7.3 to 7.6. As would be anticipated, because of past leaching, the concentrations of phosphate-P (total phosphate) in the sediments are mostly quite low, with only one of the 15 samples analysed being ≥ 1.00 mg g^{-1} and 12 having concentrations ≤ 0.747 mg g^{-1}; and the majority of the phosphate present is in inorganic forms, with phosphate-P_i:P ranging from 69.1% to 93.4%. Interestingly, the highest phos-

Table 4.11 Phosphate fractionation data for samples related to thin sections

Sample	Phosphate-Pi (mg g⁻¹)	Phosphate-Po (mg g⁻¹)	Phosphate-P (mg g⁻¹)	Phosphate-Pi:P (%)	Phosphate-Po:P (%)
x1051b leached	0.556	0.101	0.657	84.6	15.4
x1051b ferruginised	3.47	0.244	3.71	93.4	6.6
x1051a	0.484	0.176	0.660	73.3	26.7
x1051b	0.551	0.151	0.702	78.5	21.5
x1051a	0.579	0.168	0.747	77.5	22.5
x1051b	0.831	0.160	0.991	83.9	16.1
x1051a	0.703	0.146	0.849	82.8	17.2
x1051b	0.494	0.115	0.609	81.1	18.9
x1076	0.338	0.148	0.486	69.5	30.5
x1077a	0.349	0.151	0.500	69.8	30.2
x1077b	0.327	0.126	0.453	72.2	27.8
x1081	0.547	0.161	0.708	77.3	22.7
x1043	0.317	0.115	0.432	73.4	26.6
x1044 blue grey	0.226	0.101	0.327	69.1	30.9
x1044 orange brown	0.405	0.130	0.535	75.7	24.3

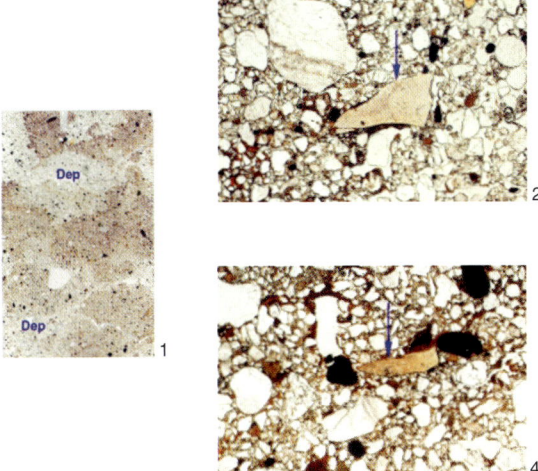

Fig. 4.9 M113 (Context 1051b)
1: Scan - relict iron-cemented locally translocated clay-enriched reddish soil-sediment, and pale loose sands where there has been iron and clay depletion (Dep) through soil leaching. Frame width is ~50mm.
2: Photomicrograph - in situ flint debitage within iron cemented sands at 270mm depth within thin section sample. Plane polarised light (PPL), frame width is ~4.62mm.
3: As 2, under oblique incident light (OIL); iron cementation provides orange to reddish colours.
4: Photomicrograph - in situ flint debitage within iron cemented sands at 245mm depth within thin section
5: As 4, under OIL.

phate-P concentration (3.71 mg g^{-1}), with the highest phosphate-P$_i$:P ratio, was recorded in the sample (x1051b ferruginised) which also has the notably higher LOI.

The χ values recorded are all consistently low, with values ranging from 3.7×10^{-8} m^3 kg^{-1} to 20.2×10^{-8} m^3 kg^{-1}, and only five samples $\geq 10.0 \times 10^{-8}$ m^3 kg^{-1}. The χ_{max} values are moderately high (range: 1460–3760 $\times$ 10^{-8} m^3 kg^{-1}), with the variability observed presumably being attributable in part to variations in the degrees of post-depositional mineralisation that has occurred (Crowther 2003; Crowther and Barker 1995). The resulting χ_{conv} values are all very low, with only two being $\geq 1.00\%$ (maximum: 1.63% in sample x1051a), and provide no evidence of susceptibility enhancement as might be associated with heating/burning or natural fermentation processes in former topsoil horizons (Dearing et al. 1996). Determinations were also made of χ_{hf} in order to establish χ_{fd} (frequency dependent susceptibility), increases in which can also indicate enhancement through heating/burning or in topsoils. χ_{fd} ranges from 1.32% to 13.5% with six samples having values $\geq 10.0\%$.

Results: micromorphology

Results are presented in Table 4.12 (and in more detail in the archive) and are illustrated in Figs 4.9–4.22. A total of 21 characteristics were identified and counted from 18 subunits/units in the 12 thin sections analysed.

Context 1051b (M113): This unit is heterogeneous with reddish orange massive cemented moderately

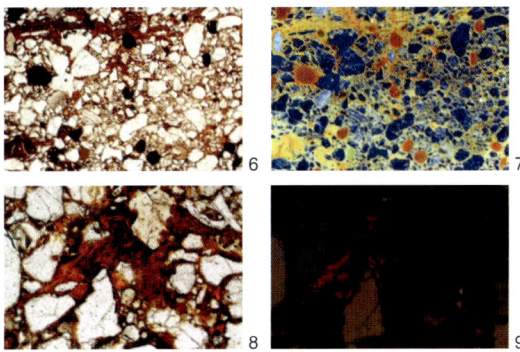

Fig. 4.10 M113 (Context 1051b)
6: Photomicrograph - iron cemented sands with iron-stained clayey pan from clayey alluvium inwash. PPL, frame width is ~4.62mm.
7: As 6, under OIL. Note orange and red iron cementation colours, which show preferential iron impregnation of clayey textural pedofeatures.
8: Photomicrograph - detail of clay and microlaminated clay void coatings and infills (from overbank fine alluviation). PPL, frame width is ~0.90mm.
9: As 8, under crossed polarised light (XPL); clay void coatings and infills show good orientation and associated birefringence despite obscuring secondary iron staining.

poorly sorted sands (with possible diffuse coarse silt-sand laminae) and patches, channels and sub-horizontal zones of dusty grey to pale yellow sands (Fig. 4.9, 1). Very little gravel (max 7mm), examples of possible flint debitage at 245mm (sub-horizontally oriented, 1.2mm size) and at 270mm (possibly sub-horizontally oriented, 1.5mm size), occur (Fig.

Table 4.12 Soil micromorphology and counts

Context	Soil thin section	Depth (mm)	MFT	SMT	Voids	Stones
1051b	M113	200–280	A2	1b	30–35%	*
1051b	M113	200–280	A1	1a	20%	*
1051a	M114	20–90	A1/A2	1a/1b	10–20%/45%	f
1051a, 1051b, 1052	M114	20–90				
1051a, 1051b	M115	40–120	A1/A3	1a/1b(2a)	10%/35%	*
1051a, 1051b	M115	40–120				
1050, 1051a, 1051b	M116A	85–165	A3	1b,2a(1a)	40–45%	*
1051a	M116B	165–180	A2	1b	35%	*
1051b	M116B	180–240	A1, A2	1a,1b	20%/35%	*
1043	M430A	0–80	A2	1b(1a)	45%	f
1044	M430B(1and 2)	80–160		1a,1b	~30%	*
1076	M156	0–75	A4	1a,2a(1b)	20% & 35%	*
1076	M162	15–90	A1,A3	1a,1b,2a	30–40%	*
1077	M167A	25–100	A3	1b,2a(1a)	35%	*
1077	M167B	10–175	A3	1b,2a(1a)	35%	
1081	M384	65–145	A4	1a,1b,2a	10 & 35%	*(ff)

* - very few 0–5%, f - few 5–15%, ff - frequent 15–30%, a - rare <2% (a*1%; a-1, single occurrence), aa - occasional 2–5%, aaa - many 5–10%, aaaa - abundant 10–20%

4.9). Occasional poorly oriented very thin (~25mm) dusty grey clay void and grain coatings are present in depleted sediment areas, whereas often secondary iron-obscured very abundant very thin (~25mm) to thick (0.5mm), sometimes micro-laminated grain and void coatings and infills of often well-oriented clay (rare microlaminated clay pans also present ~250mm thick) were recorded in ferruginised sediment (Fig. 4.10). Very abundant moderate to total iron and clay depletion of fine fabric, very abundant orange to opaque iron cementation of sands, especially areas of clayey textural pedofeatures; trace amounts of yellowish possible iron phosphate void infills, and many thin and broad burrows in iron-depleted sediments, were found.

The moderately poorly sorted coarse silts and fine to coarse sands, with very little gravel, and original character, were best preserved in ferruginised (iron cemented) areas. Here, minor sub-horizontal compacted zones and possibly horizontally oriented flint debitage fragments suggest ephemeral exposure of now very diffusely laminated sandy River Wey alluvium (of braided stream origin?). Subsequent alluviation, and seasonal flooding led to clay inwashing into sediment packing-voids (Brammer 1971) as recorded elsewhere (eg Harding et al. 2014; Macphail 2010). More recent leaching along burrows and likely root channels produced thin dusty clay coatings and local contamination produced very minor amounts of possible secondary iron-phosphate deposition.

Context 1051a (M114): This layer consists of heterogeneous and horizontally zoned reddish orange poorly

Flint deb.	Charc. slag	Brick	Iron slag	Chalk	Thin burrows	Broad burrows	V. thin O-M excr.	Thin O-M excr.
					aaa	aaa		
a-2								
					aaaa	aaaa		
					aaa	aaaa	a	
(core)								
					aaaa	aaaa	aaa	
a-1 (flakes)	a-1				aaaa			
					aaa	aa		
aa					aaaa	aaaa		
a-1?					aaa	a		
a-2?								
a-1	aa	a*			aaaa	aaaa		a
a-1					aaa	aa	a	
					aaaa	aaaa	aa	
a-1?	a-1				aaa	aaa	a*	
a*(aa)	aa	a-1	a-1	aa				

sorted sands and patches and sub-horizontal zones of dusty grey to pale yellow sands, with little small gravel (quartzite – max 4mm, and ironstone – max 3mm; Fig. 4.11). There is a trace of fine charcoal (max 300mm) in structureless sands. Textural and depletion pedofeatures are the same as in M113 with only trace amounts of clayey panning. In addition there are anomalous rare mm-size concentrations of gypsum embedding sands (see M115), very abundant orange to opaque iron cementation of sands, especially areas of clayey textural pedofeatures, and abundant thin and broad burrows in iron-depleted sediments. The braided River Wey stream fluvial origins of 1051a are probably the same as described from M113. A trace amount of fine charcoal may occur through post-Upper Palaeolithic/recent burrowing. The patch of gypsum is probably modern contamination through use of gypsum cement (Portland Cement) on the site.

Context 1051a/1051b (M115): Here, ferruginised sediment is mainly present between 40–70mm, with leached sands below (70–120mm), and few dusty brown clay soils in burrows, possibly inwash. Very little rounded gravel (max >2mm; ironstone) occurs, but bulk subsampling of the monolith sample found a small flint core at 90mm. Rare patches of poorly oriented very thin dusty grey clay void and grain coatings occur in depleted sediment areas, where occasional channel/burrow partial infills of pale brown clay are also present (Fig. 4.12). In terruginised sediment and often secondary iron-obscured, are occasional grain and void clay coatings and infills. Very abundant moderate to total iron and clay deple-

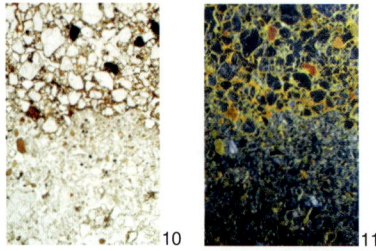

Fig. 4.11 M114 (Context 1051a)
10: Photomicrograph - leaching boundary between leached loose sands and iron cemented sands with original clay void coatings and infills. PPL, frame height is ~4.62mm
11: As 10, under OIL, showing leached sands below original iron cemented soil-sediment.

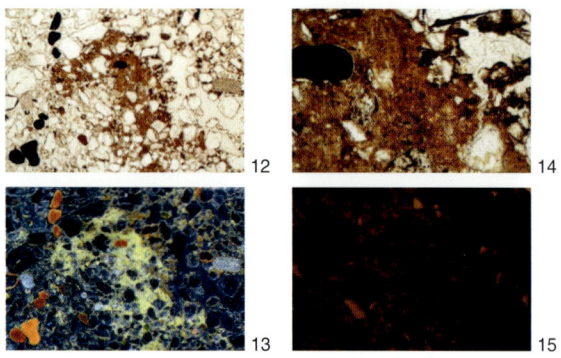

Fig. 4.12 M115 (Context 1051a)
12: Photomicrograph - brown clayey inwash affects burrows/biochannels. PPL, frame width is ~4.62mm.
13: As 12, under OIL; clay of likely recent overbank fine alluviation origin, is iron depleted.
14: Detail of probable alluvial clayey inwash in 12. PPL, frame width is ~0.90mm.
15: As 14, under XPL; clay inwash includes fine micas.

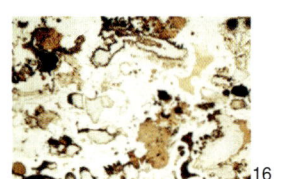 

Fig. 4.13 M115 (Context 1051a)
16: Photomicrograph - loose sands cemented by colourless gypsum ($CaSO_4$). PPL, frame width is ~2.38mm.
17: As 16, under XPL; gypsum with typical low birefringence colours (first order greys).

tion of fine fabric, anomalous occasional 30mm-wide concentration of gypsum embedding sands at 50–60mm (Fig. 4.13), many orange to opaque iron cementation of sands, especially areas of clayey textural pedofeatures, many thin and probably abundant broad burrows in iron-depleted sediments, and rare trace of very thin organo-mineral excrements along channels with brown clay infills.

Context 1051a and its junction with 1051b show strong leaching and loss of iron and clay and its

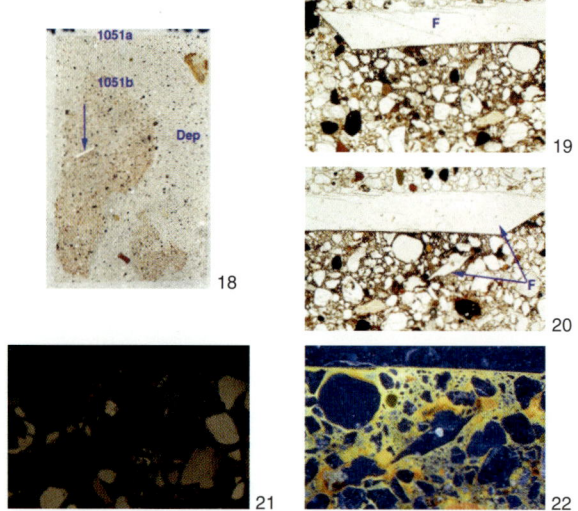

Fig. 4.14 of M116B (Contexts 1051a and underlying 1051b)
18: Scan - showing approximate boundary between Contexts 1051a and underlying 1051b. 1051b includes both relict patches of iron-cemented sands, and pale iron and clay depleted sediment (Dep). An embedded flint flake/debitage fragment is arrowed. Frame width is ~50mm
19: Photomicrograph (Context 1051b); iron cemented sediment includes flint flake/debitage fragment (see 18). This protects the original soil sediment below it from leaching effects. PPL, frame width is ~4.62mm.
20: Detail of 19, showing homogenised soil-sediment containing a very fine fragment of debitage below the long flake (F). PPL, frame width is ~2.38mm.
21: Detail of 20, under XPL. Some oriented clay coatings are just about visible.
22: As 21, under OIL. The 'sealed' soil-sediment occupation surface is strongly iron stained, with diminishing iron staining downwards.

original massive structural integrity. A small flint core was found just above this unit boundary, but no microstructural features were noted. The site may have been affected by more recent overbank fine alluviation which deposited clay in channels utilised by a few invertebrate mesofauna. The uppermost part of this sample was also probably affected by gypsum Portland Cement contamination, possibly from foundation works.

Context 1051b (M116B): Here, the layer is heterogeneous with common patches of cemented reddish orange moderately poorly sorted sands and coarse silts within grey to pale yellow sands (Fig. 4.14, 18). There is very little fine gravel (max 3mm, iron-stained rounded flint) and occasional angular flint debitage (max 8mm) protecting relict silt-rich 'soil' surface and a 1mm-size flint fragment/debitage (Fig. 4.14). Many generally thin clay grain and void coatings, often partially obscured by ferruginisation, rare dusty clay grain coatings in loose sands, very abundant moderate to total iron and clay depletion of fine fabric, with a depletion-protected zone under the example of flint debitage/flake, very abundant orange to opaque iron cementation of sands, especially areas of clayey textural pedofeatures and preserved below the flint flake, and abundant thin and probably occasional broad burrows in iron-depleted sediments.

The sample found a small preserved area of deposit where there is a history of silt and sand sediment homogenisation and possible compaction. This appears to be a putative 'surface' containing flint debitage, which as elsewhere was followed by alluvial clay deposition (Brammer 1971; Duchaufour 1982). Later/penecontemporaneous iron cementation was followed by subaerial possibly vertical leaching. This left some relict iron cemented nodules as discussed here, which included a totally *in situ* flint flake-protected soil-sediment surface example.

Context 1051a (M116B): This is composed of loose structureless grey to pale yellow sands, with very little gravel (max 9mm, partially iron-stained rounded flint; Fig. 4.14, 18).

Context 1051a (M116A): Upwards, this unit is composed of heterogeneous grey silts and sands, with trace amounts of orange cemented sands, with frequent broad burrow fills of yellow brown sands. Very little fine gravel (max >2mm, eg quartzite) was encountered, and in the broad burrows are examples of vertically oriented possible flint debitage (max 3mm at 9.5mm depth; Fig. 4.15) and wood char (charcoal slag, 1.7mm); flint flakes were found at 110mm during bulk subsampling. There are many dusty clay grain coatings in loose sands, with a trace of thin clay grain obscured by ferruginisation, very abundant moderate to total iron and clay depletion of fine fabric, a trace of iron cementation of sands, abundant thin and broad burrows in iron-depleted sediments, and many very fine (pellety) organo-mineral excrements in broad burrowed areas. These are totally leached soils, with one worked flake present, although other flakes were found during subsampling. Recent burrowing has also introduced wood char (charcoal slag).

Context 1076 (M156): Context 1076 is heterogeneous with common loose dusty grey sands, very few iron-cemented orange sands (Fig. 4.16, 25) and brown burrowed soil and dominant weathered cemented/mortared-sands. There is very little fine gravel (ironstone and rounded flint, max ~7mm) present. An example of a fragmented 2mm-size flint flake, vertically oriented in a burrow at 15mm depth, very abundant mainly decalcified cemented sands, with rare intact mortar material/mortared sands (Fig. 4.16, 26–28), a trace of brick (4mm), iron nodules and occasional charcoal and wood char (max 4mm), with a possible example of an earthworm granule present, were recorded. The following were found: a trace of clay and dusty clay void and grain coatings, very abundant iron and clay depletion of sands and

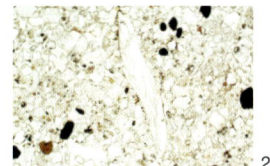
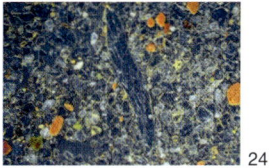

Fig. 4.15 M116A (Context 1051a)
23: Photomicrograph - vertically oriented probable reworked flint debitage material in leached and burrowed sands. PPL, frame width is ~4.62mm.
24: As 23, under OIL.

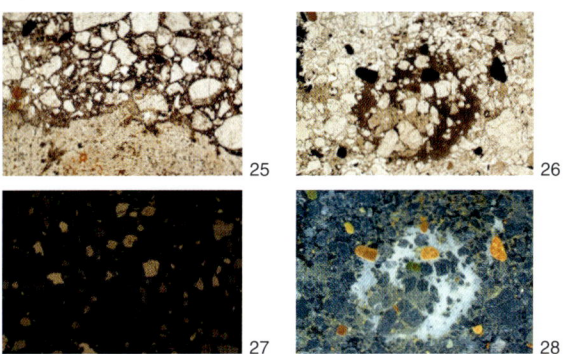

Fig. 4.16 M156 (Context 1076)
25: Photomicrograph - small relict area of iron-cemented soil-sediment and flint gravel. PPL frame width is ~2.38mm.
26: Photomicrograph - leached sands containing fragment of weathering mortar/mortared-sands. PPL frame width is ~4.62mm.
27: As 26, under XPL; weathering micritic mortar present.
28: As 26, under OIL, with whitish grey calcitic matrix.

very abundant decalcification of once-cemented/mortared sands, occasional void and grain coatings as micritic and rarely microsparitic calcite, including possible root pseudomorphs, rare iron cementation of sands and gravel, many thin and abundant broad burrows, and occasional thin organo-mineral excrements associated with broad burrows.

Only very few patches of the original iron cemented sandy soil-sediments remain, after leaching of 1) the original Pleistocene sands and 2) the more recent cemented/mortared-foundations took place. One flint 'flake' was found at around 15mm depth in a burrow. Broad, probable earthworm burrowing (possible earthworm granule present) has mixed-in brick, mortar and charcoal/charcoal slag. One product of the weathering of cemented sands (foundations?) are secondary calcium carbonate features, including probable root pseudomorphs.

Context 1076 (M162): Unit 1076 is made up of heterogeneous grey silts and sands, with common orange cemented sands, with few broad burrow fills of yellow brown sands; very little fine gravel

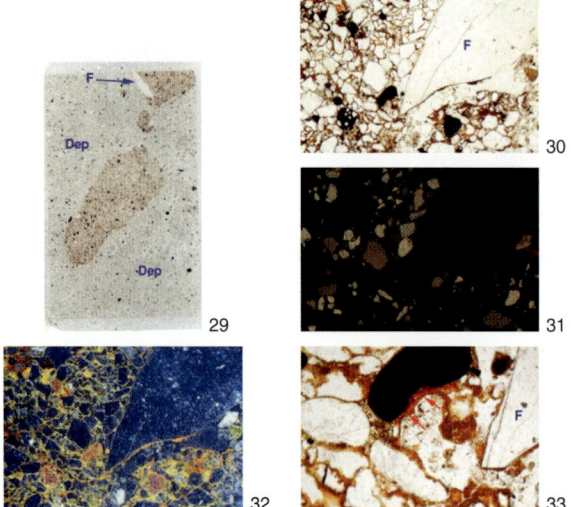

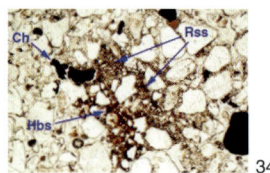 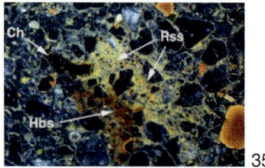

Fig. 4.18 M167B (Context 1077b)
34: Photomicrograph - relict area of iron cemented soil-sediment (Rss), which seems to embed a charcoal fragment (Ch); Later/more recent humic burrowed soil is also recorded (Hbs). PPL, frame width is ~4.62mm.
35: As 34, under OIL; orange coloured iron-cemented relict soil sediment (Rss) seems to embed this charcoal fragment (Ch) suggesting that it is contemporary with the Upper Palaeolithic occupation of these deposits.

Fig. 4.17 M162 (Context 1076)
29: Scan - iron and clay depleted loose sands (Dep) and relict patches of iron-cemented soil-sediment, and associated embedded flint flake (F). Frame width is ~50mm
30: Photomicrograph - flint flake (F) embedded in iron cemented sands (see 29 and 33). PPL, frame width is ~4.62mm.
31: As 30, under XPL; moderately poorly sorted sands.
32: As 30, under OIL, showing secondary iron cementation of sands and flint flake (see 33)
33: Detail of 30; flint flake (F) and contemporary sandy soil-sediment substrate. Clay inwash (arrowed coatings) record clayey alluviation prior to iron cementation. PPL, frame width is ~0.90mm.

(max >2mm) occurs (Fig. 4.17, 29). An example of >10mm-size sloping flint debitage/flake embedded on edge in iron cemented sands at 25mm was recorded (Fig. 4.17). Occasional dusty clay grain coatings in loose sands, with many thin (~50mm) clay grain and void coatings often obscured by ferruginisation (Fig. 4.17, 30–33), very abundant moderate to total iron and clay depletion of fine fabric, abundant iron cementation of sands, especially affecting clayey coatings, many thin and occasional broad burrows in iron-depleted sediments, and rare very fine (pellety) organo-mineral excrements in broad burrows. These are partially iron and clay depleted alluvial silts and sands, with relict iron cemented sands recording the presence of flint flake debitage in probably ephemeral soil-sediment surfaces followed by alluvial clay inwash and iron cementation.

Context 1077b (M167B): This unit is heterogeneous with very dominant dusty grey and pale yellow stoneless sands, with frequent broad burrow fills of dusty brown and finely humic soil, and trace of iron cemented orange sands. A possible sand-size example of flint debitage and sand-size charcoal slag, with an example of 0.5mm-size charcoal possibly partially embedded in iron cemented sands (Fig. 4.18), were noted. There are rare dusty clay grain coatings in loose sands, very abundant moderate to total iron and clay depletion of fine fabric, traces of iron cementation of sands, many thin and broad burrows, and a trace of very fine (pellety) organo-mineral excrements in broad burrows. This is an almost totally leached and bioworked sandy alluvium, with possible trace amounts of original Pleistocene soil-sediment that could embed a fine charcoal fragment.

Context 1077a (M167A): Upwards, context 1077a is heterogeneous with dominant dusty grey and pale yellow sands, with common broad burrow fills of dusty brown and finely humic soil, and very few of iron cemented orange sands, and very little fine gravel (ironstone, flint; max 3mm). A flint was found during subsampling at 75mm. There are occasional dusty clay grain coatings in loose sands, and trace amounts of iron-stained clay void coatings in patches of orange sands, very abundant moderate to total iron and clay depletion of fine fabric, rare iron cementation of sands, abundant thin and broad burrows, and occasional very fine (pellety) organo-mineral excrements in broad burrows. These are leached and burrowed Pleistocene sands, with one flint flake found during subsampling.

Context 1081 (M384): A heterogeneous context with common iron cemented orange sands, with frequent broad burrow fills of dusty brown and finely humic soil and dusty grey and pale yellow sands (Fig. 4.19, 36). These are now poorly sorted silts and sands, because the original very limited fine gravel (max 5mm-size flint) component is now augmented by concentrations of gravel-sized ironstone, chalk and recent anthropogenic inclusions (sometimes confusingly mixed with what may be flint debitage). An example of possible flint debitage at 107mm depth, and concentrations of occasional flint debitage (max 6mm) in a broad burrow (earthworm aestivating burrow?) with occasional vesicular charcoal slag (max 5mm), and examples of mortar (max 4mm), weathered vesic-

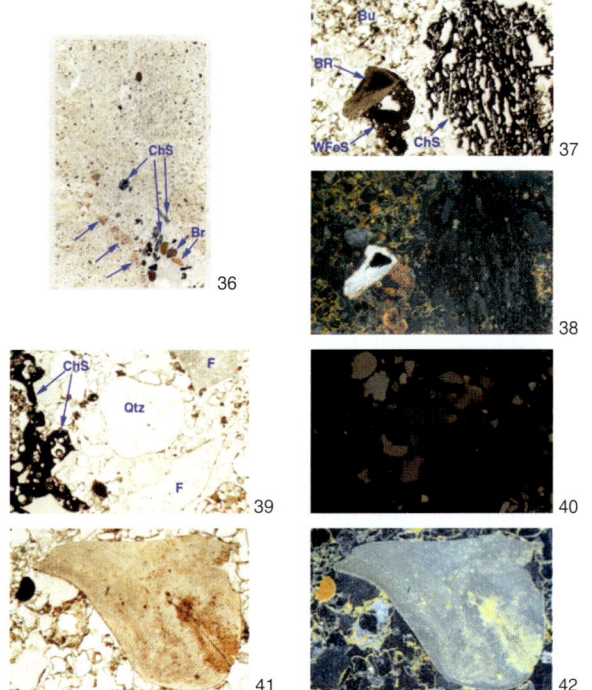

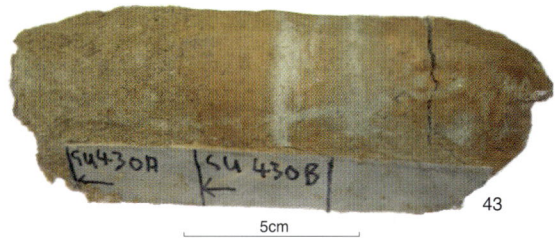

Fig. 4.20 Monolith 430 and marked subsamples M430A and M430B
43: Photograph - note vertical and subhorizontal leaching pattern. Such 'patterned ground' can be linked to frozen ground – here a possible short-lived permafrost-associated feature – frozen ground not allowing normal drainage.

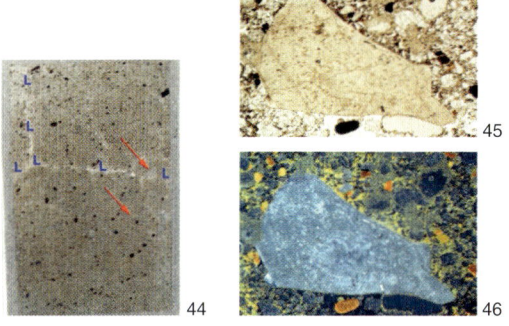

Fig. 4.19 M384 (Context 1081)
36: Scan - mainly loose leached sands, with relict iron cemented soil-sediments, including probable 'ped face' (arrows). 'Pea grit' is in the form of fine gravel size ironstone, chalk, brick (Br), weathered iron slag, charcoal slag (ChS) or 'cinder' and flint. Frame width is ~50mm.
37: Photomicrograph - 'pea grit' burrow fill, with humic soil (Bu) and inclusions of charcoal slag (ChS), and weathered vesicular iron slag (WFeS) and embedded burnt rock fragment (BR). PPL, frame width is ~4.62mm.
38: As 37, under OIL.
39: Photomicrograph - 'pea grit' fill, with charcoal slag (ChS), and fine gravel size quartzite (Qtz) and flints (F) including likely debitage material. PPL, frame width is ~4.62mm.
40: As 39, under XPL.
41: Photomicrograph - flint debitage example within sands. PPL, frame width is ~2.38mm.
42: As 41, under OIL.

Fig. 4.21 M430B (G2A; Context 1044; see Fig. 4.20)
44: Scan – massive sands with vertical and sub-horizontal leaching features (L), and two likely flint debitage fragments (arrows). Frame width is ~50mm.
45: Photomicrograph piece of flint debitage at 120mm depth (upper arrow in 44). PPL, frame width is ~4.62mm.
46: As 45, under OIL, showing ferruginised fine fabric in original alluvial soil-sediment.

ular iron slag, and brick, were found (Fig. 4.19). The following pedofeatures were also recorded: occasional dusty clay grain coatings in loose sands and iron-stained clay void coatings and infills in cemented sands, very abundant moderate to total iron and clay depletion of fine fabric, abundant iron cementation of sands, with ironpan formation (including 3mm wide channel hypocoating), many thin and broad burrows, and occasional very fine (pellety) organo-mineral excrements in broad burrows. Both loose weathered sands and original Pleistocene soil-sediment (containing flint debitage) are present, with evidence of clay inwash in sandy alluvium, its cementation by iron in the groundwater, iron and clay depletion through soil leaching subsequently, and lastly probable earthworm aestivating activity concentrated not only recent artefact material (mortar, charcoal slag and iron slag) and gravel size ironstone and chalk but also probable flint debitage material. This is an example of the 'pea grit' reported from the site.

G2A; Context 1044 (M430B^1 and M430B^2): This layer is heterogeneous with common iron-cemented orange sands and loose dusty grey sands in vertical and horizontal bands (~110–120mm depth), containing very little fine gravel (max >4mm, iron-stained chert, ironstone and flint; Figs 4.20–21, 43–44). Probable fine flint debitage was found at 110mm (1.5mm-size) and 120mm (4mm; Fig. 4.21). Many generally very thin clay grain and void coatings, often partially obscured by ferruginisation, and rare traces of dusty clay grain coatings in loose sands, many vertical and sub-horizontal zones of moderate to total iron and clay depletion of fine fabric, very abundant orange to opaque iron cementation of sands, especially areas of clayey textural pedofeatures, and because of manufacturing artefacts there are probably many thin and

Fig. 4.22 M430A (G2b; Context 1043)
47: Photomicrograph - remains of a flint core(?) in loose leached and burrowed sands. PPL, frame width is ~4.62mm
48: As 47, under OIL; note generally iron-depleted fine fabric.

rare broad burrows in iron-depleted sediments. These are alluvial sands with very little fine gravel containing possible examples of flint debitage, in soil-sediments affected by alluvial inwash clays and later ferruginisation. It is conceivable that mixed vertical and horizontal fissuring/leaching is a component of 'patterned ground' formed by last Late Glacial cold conditions (Avery 1990; Catt 1986; 1990; Jarvis *et al.* 1984). A period of frozen ground would have aided the development of poor drainage and this pattern of leaching.

G2b; Context 1043 (M430A^1 and M430A^2): This upper layer is characterised by mainly homogeneous loose grey and pale brown dusty sands, with very few patches and relict concentrations of iron-cemented orange sands, with little fine gravel to small stones (weathered flint or possible artefact (18mm-size); Figs 4.20, 43 and 4.22, 47–48). This could be a possible outer flint core residue at 35–45mm depth. There is a trace amount of very thin clay grain and void coatings, often partially obscured by ferruginisation, and rare dusty clay grain coatings in loose sands, very abundant areas of mainly total iron and clay depletion of fine fabric, a trace of orange to opaque iron cementation of sands, and because of manufacturing artefacts there are probably abundant thin and broad burrows in iron-depleted sediments. These overlying sediments have lost their original interstadial soil-sediment character through leaching and bioworking, and if the relict flint core remains are an artefact, they are unlikely to be exactly *in situ*.

Discussion

Although the site is mapped as urban space by the Soil Survey of England and Wales, locally, soils along the Wey River valley are Gleyic argillic brown earths or Typical argillic gley soils formed in loamy to sandy River Terrace Drift (eg Shabbington and Waterstock soil series; Jarvis *et al.* 1983). The artefacts are concentrated in some 15cm of sandy subsoil, ~0.40–0.50m below the modern ground surface. In addition, a large number of other post-depositional processes and factors have to be considered before attempting to interpret the soil and sedimentary environment contemporary with the Upper Palaeolithic archaeology. As noted by the excavators, the most obvious post-depositional features are burrowing, including earthworm burrowing, and the concentration of pea grit. Soil micromorphology showed that the latter is composed of fine gravel-size ironstone, quartzite and chalk, as well as more obviously anthropogenic materials: brick, mortar, iron slag and vesicular charcoal slag ('cinders'). It can be noted that pea grit also includes fine gravel-size flint, some of which is probably debitage. The deposits have also been affected by recent constructional activity, and some sands appear to have been mortared, others show secondary gypsum ($CaSO_4$) deposition, presumably from the use of gypsum cements (Portland Cement), and some secondary calcium carbonate ($CaCO_3$) formation is also probably the result of cement and mortar weathering. These thin section study findings are thus generally consistent with the current neutral to weakly alkaline pH and the small amounts of carbonate measured in the soils (see above). In addition, there is an example of possible, but minor, weakly enhanced organic matter content and secondary phosphate deposition recorded in the seemingly intact Late Glacial soil sediments which include *in situ* flint debitage (x1051b ferruginised).

The deposits show that in the past, much weathering and leaching had taken place, producing many areas of generally loose, structureless sands (Courty *et al.* 1989; Duchaufour 1982). Leaching and concomitant ferruginisation of these sands (Vepraskas *et al.* 2018) is also reflected in the magnetic susceptibility (see above). Flint debitage within them may show the effects of reworking, and, for example, be anomalously vertically oriented in burrowed soil. This is probably one reason why some flint may not be completely 'fresh' or show some kind of abrasion. Leaching and burrowing, and other earlier site formation processes (see below), create geomorphological 'noise' typical of Pleistocene sites (Macphail and Goldberg 2018, 32–4).

Despite these weathering factors, some parts of the deposits show seemingly intact Late Glacial deposits, contemporary with the Upper Palaeolithic occupation, that appear to have been preserved by ferruginisation; specific samples may also have associated geochemical and possible slight magnetic susceptibility signatures. In the field, in the monoliths and in the thin sections, this was observed as iron mottling. Site formation processes penecontemporaneous with the Upper Palaeolithic archaeology are now presented.

The deposits are generally moderately poorly sorted coarse silts, fine and medium sands, which sometimes contain very little or little fine gravel. In some instances, poorly bedded coarse silts and sands occur, which is consistent with River Wey braided stream deposition (see particle size analysis). Where preserved, the following site formation processes can be recognised, from locations where artefacts are embedded in ferruginised sediments (as in the instance of an area of artefact-protected sediment in 1051b; M116B):

- Braided stream alluviation of silts, sands, sometimes with little gravel, and occasionally as finely bedded sediments
- Possible seasonal, presumed biological homogenisation of these into soil-sediments (Fedoroff *et al.* 2010; Fedoroff and Goldberg 1982; Macphail and Goldberg 2018, 136–65, 174–8) forming an Upper Palaeolithic occupation/knapping surface (deposition of tools, debitage and possibly charcoal),
- Seasonal (?) reactivation of the stream and renewed alluvial sedimentation, which also led to the deposition of fine overbank alluvium, and inwash of clay into underlying more coarse sediments (silts and sands), and leading to the formation of clay void and grain coatings (Brammer 1971; Kühn *et al.* 2018; cf 'lamellae' in Bullock and Mackney 1970), and finally,
- Penecontemporaneous(?) and later fluctuating ground-water deposition of iron, which preferentially impregnated these clayey textural pedofeatures, and formed iron-cemented sediments overall (Vepraskas *et al.* 2018); fluctuating water tables within river sediments also led to patchy leaching producing iron- and clay-depleted deposits. Conceivably, Late Glacial (Loch Lomond Stadial?) frozen ground may have caused waterlogging and the formation of patterned ground in some underlying soil-sediments (see Monolith 430; Avery 1990; Catt 1986; Catt 1990; Jarvis *et al.* 1984). The discovery of artefacts in similar sediments also occurred at Upper Palaeolithic Farndon Fields, Nottinghamshire (Harding *et al.* 2014). Here and elsewhere (eg Upper Palaeolithic Colne River, Kingsmead Quarry, Horton, Berkshire; Barclay *et al.* 2017; Macphail and Crowther 2017), no subaerial soil formations such as frost lensing features occurred (cf Barton *et al.* 2009; Macphail and Crowther 2008). This is presumably because ephemeral surfaces were perhaps unaffected by post-interstadial cold conditions, because they too were buried by continuing alluvial sedimentation.

Chapter 5

Artefact taphonomy

by Chris Hayden

INTRODUCTION

The geoarchaeological investigations discussed in Chapter 4 provide an indication of some of the kinds of depositional and post-depositional processes which might have affected the flint scatter. The particle size analysis and the presence of localised fine bedding structures suggest that the sands from which the flint was recovered lay adjacent to an active river channel and were deposited by alluvial processes. Thin section analysis of the main lithic-bearing sand deposit (G2c) indicates incipient soil formation which probably occurred seasonally when channel flow was reduced. It is possible, then, that the distribution of the flint after it was deposited was affected by fluvial processes. The geoarchaeological analyses also provide clear indications of other processes that are likely to have affected the distribution of the flint after it was deposited. Large earthworm burrows and root channels indicate that it was affected by bioturbation. Leaching and iron deposition indicate that the deposit was impacted by fluctuations in groundwater which may have affected the distribution of the flint through shrink-swell processes. The deposits may also have been subject to freeze-thaw processes. In addition to these natural processes, the distribution of the flint may well have been affected by anthropogenic processes such as trampling. Although the flint was generally in an exceptionally fresh, unabraded condition, the use-wear analysis revealed wear resulting from abrasion and friction of differing intensities on much of the flint.

The aim of this chapter is to evaluate how, and to what extent, the distribution of the flint was affected by depositional and post-depositional processes, and thus to test the hypothesis that the site is a rare example of an *in situ* flint scatter in primary context. Such an assessment forms an important prerequisite for the behavioural interpretation of the scatter presented in Chapter 8. To do so, it will analyse the size-class distribution of the artefacts, the artefact fabric of the scatter, the vertical distribution of the flint, refit orientations, and, using hot spot analysis and an analysis of centroid diagrams, the horizontal distribution of the flint (cf. Pope 2002).

The size class distribution, hot spot and fabric analyses provide little indication of significant fluvial disturbance, although there are signs that bioturbation and frost heave may have moved the flint vertically. The site itself probably derives from a number of episodes of activity during a single, short-term period of occupation. Two main concentrations, located around 4m apart (1 to the northwest and 2 to the south-east; Fig. 5.17), represent episodes of knapping activity, but the functional analysis and the distribution of retouched tools suggest that other activities were also carried out in the area around these main foci of knapping. The distribution of burnt flint is also distinct from that of the unburnt flint, and this may reflect both the location of a hearth between the two knapping scatters and the fact that not all of the flint derives directly from the main foci of knapping. The flint includes, nonetheless, a high proportion of small debitage (<10mm) and chips (<5mm) which is characteristic of *in situ* knapping areas. Whilst it is likely that activity on the site contemporary with the deposition of the flint caused some horizontal movement, and the flint may have suffered from some further subsequent dilation, much of the structure expected of *in situ* knapping scatters has been retained. The extent of post-depositional disturbance thus appears to have been limited.

SIZE CLASS ANALYSIS

The geoarchaeological analyses suggest that fluvial processes could have had a major effect on the distribution of the flint. The first way in which the possible effects of such processes have been assessed involves analysis of the size-class distribution of the flint. Schick (1986, 21–32) and Bertran *et al.* (2012, 3150) have shown that although differing raw materials and knapping strategies do produce slight differences (ibid., 3151–4), the artefact size-class distributions produced by knapping, even given differences in raw materials and knapping

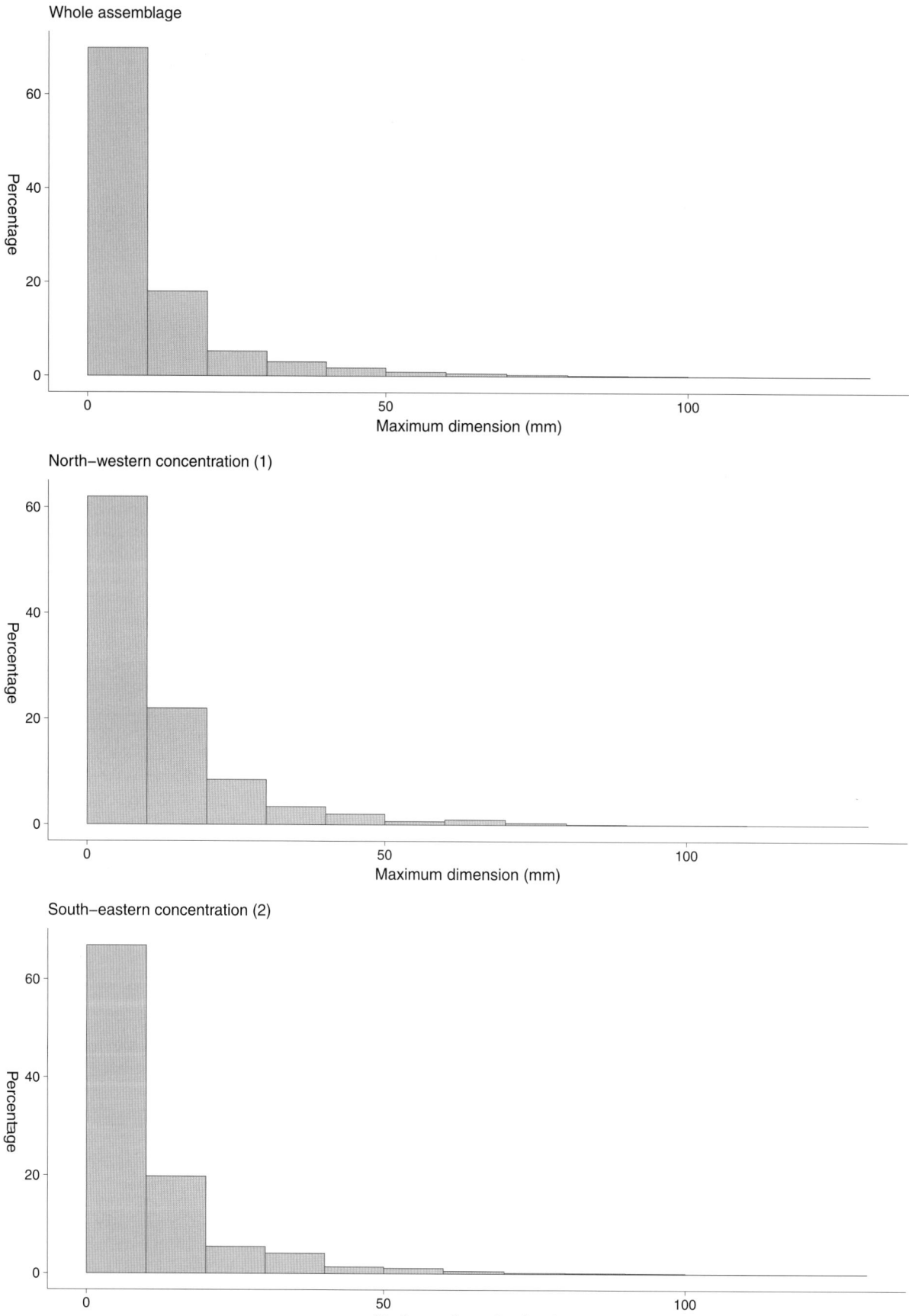

Fig. 5.1 Size class distribution of the flint (using maximum dimensions) for the whole scatter and the north-western and south-eastern concentrations

strategies, are remarkably consistent. The distributions are strongly skewed towards the smallest debitage as a result of what Schick (1986, 28; see also Bertran *et al.* 2012, 3150) calls the 'mechanics of stone fracture': each blow, however it is made and no matter what the raw material, will produce not only the intended end-product but also a range of smaller fragments. Given the consistency of experimentally produced size-class distributions, comparison of the size-class distribution of the flint from the scatter at Guildford with those derived from experimental knapping can provide an indication of whether any debitage has been removed from the site. In the case of the Guildford scatter, the primary interest is in whether fluvial processes have removed the smaller pieces of flint.

The length, width and thickness of all of the flint greater in size than 20mm was measured. Most of the pieces below this size were divided into three size categories based on their length: <5mm (chips), 5–10mm (small debitage) and 10–20mm (classified by type). A sample of these smaller pieces was also measured, including refits, tools, and most of the pieces recorded in three dimensions.

To analyse the size class distribution of the flint, it was classified into decimetre size classes using its maximum dimensions. In the case of the Guildford flint the maximum dimension is almost always the length, but there are 356 pieces – largely flakes but also including some core tablets, rejuvenation flakes and other types – which were wider than they were long. At the bottom end of the scale, as Schick (1986, 22) notes, flint fragments grade into the size ranges of sedimentary particles, and there is, as a result, no clearly defined lower limit to the size classes. In practice, however, a lower limit is defined by the smallest mesh size which was used to recover the flint. At Guildford, sediment from the flint-bearing layer was sieved with a 2mm mesh, making that the lower limit of the size classes. The lack of microdebitage (<1mm) found at the site may be due to this sieving strategy. Microdebitage was, however, identified in the samples subject to soil micromorphological analysis (see Chapter 4).

The analysis was carried out for the assemblage as a whole, and for each of the two concentrations (represented by the flint from the four surrounding 1m grid squares).

The resulting distributions (Fig. 5.1) are consistent with all of the flint having remained on the site, and do not provide any indication of selective removal of smaller pieces by fluvial processes. The distributions are heavily skewed towards the smallest size class which account for nearly 70% of the flint from the assemblage as a whole (and 62% for the north-western concentration and 67% for the south-eastern concentration). The remaining larger size classes have progressively fewer pieces: just 18–22% for the next smallest size class (10mm to 20mm), then 5–9%, 3–4%, 1–2%, and so on. Bertran (*et al.* 2012, 3148) used widths rather than maximum dimensions in their analyses, and a different set of size classes designed to mimic the effect of sieving, making it difficult to directly compare their results with those for Guildford. It is nonetheless striking that the overall distribution of the flint from Guildford is very similar to their experimentally produced data: their smallest category contained between 70% and 80% of the flint, the next category between 10% and 20%, and so on.

The refitting (see Chapter 6) indicates that some blades were removed from the site (or were, at least, not present within the excavated area). These pieces, however, would have fallen into one of the larger size categories, and whilst their removal will have lowered the proportion of pieces in these categories, its effect appears to have been slight in the context of the assemblage as a whole, and it did not produce a measurable effect on the overall distribution of the flint.

FABRIC ANALYSIS

The extent to which the deposition of the flint was affected by fluvial site formation processes and subsequently by bioturbation, shrink-swell processes and frost heave can also be examined using fabric analysis (Bertran and Texier 1995; Bertran and Lenoble 2002; Lenoble and Bertran 2004). Artefact fabric analysis is the analysis of the orientation and dip of artefacts. Although originally developed to characterise geological deposits (eg Watson 1965; 1966; Woodcock 1977; Benn 1994), it has been applied to Palaeolithic sites in a range of contexts (Lenoble and Bertran 2004, 457–8), and has been developed recently in particular by Bertran, Lenoble and Texier (eg Bertran and Texier 1995; Bertran and Lenoble 2002; Lenoble and Bertran 2004; see also McPherron 2005). Comparisons with the results they have collated provide the basis for interpreting the results at Guildford Fire Station.

Data and methods

Dip and orientation were recorded for all artefacts with a maximum linear dimension over 10mm where such measurements could be made. Dip was recorded along each piece's longest axis to the nearest 5°, between 0° (representing horizontal pieces) and 90° (representing vertical pieces). Orientation was recorded only in terms of minor compass points – N, NNE, NE, ENE, E etc – to the nearest 22.5°. In practice, however, it is clear from the data that there was a strong tendency to favour the simpler directions – N, NE, E etc – and hence that the recording tends to be to the nearest 45°. This limitation in the recording of the flints' orientations is very evident when the data is plotted out (Fig. 5.5), and in future, it would be better if the data were recorded following the method described by McPherron (2005, 1004), in which a total station is used to take two measurements at each end of an artefact. For horizontal pieces, the orientation was recorded only as axial data (ie a piece lying N–S is equivalent to a piece lying S–N). Where the pieces dipped, the orientation was recorded as the direction down to which the piece dipped (as polar data). Most of the analyses use only axial data.

Dip

Before examining the dip and orientation data together, it is helpful to look at each attribute separately. Figure 5.2 summarises the dip data. It shows that most of the flint lay flat or nearly flat and that the quantities of flint generally fall as the angle increases. Very little of the flint lay at angles over 45%. Overall, then, the distribution is quite strongly planar, and provides little indication of disturbance.

There are, however, a small number of pieces (52 out of 1416: 3.7%) which were vertical, although there were very few pieces with dips of between 50° and 85°. Figure 5.3 shows the distribution of the vertical pieces of flint (in red) and of the pieces between 45° and 85° (in increasingly lighter shades as the angle approaches 45°). The vertical and near-vertical pieces are distributed across more or less the whole area of the flint scatter. The data thus suggests that the dip of the flint was affected by a general process which affected the whole site (rather than a localised form of disturbance) which tended to leave pieces vertical rather than steeply sloped.

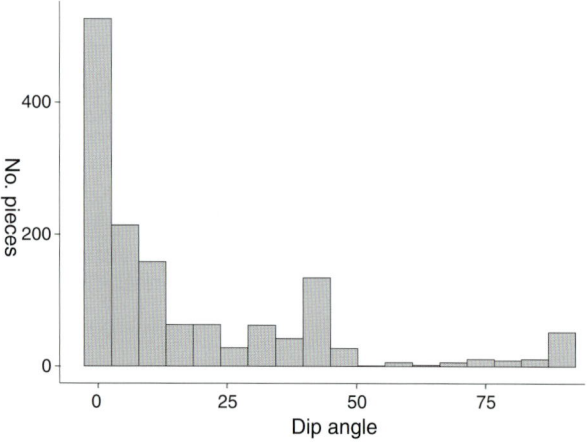

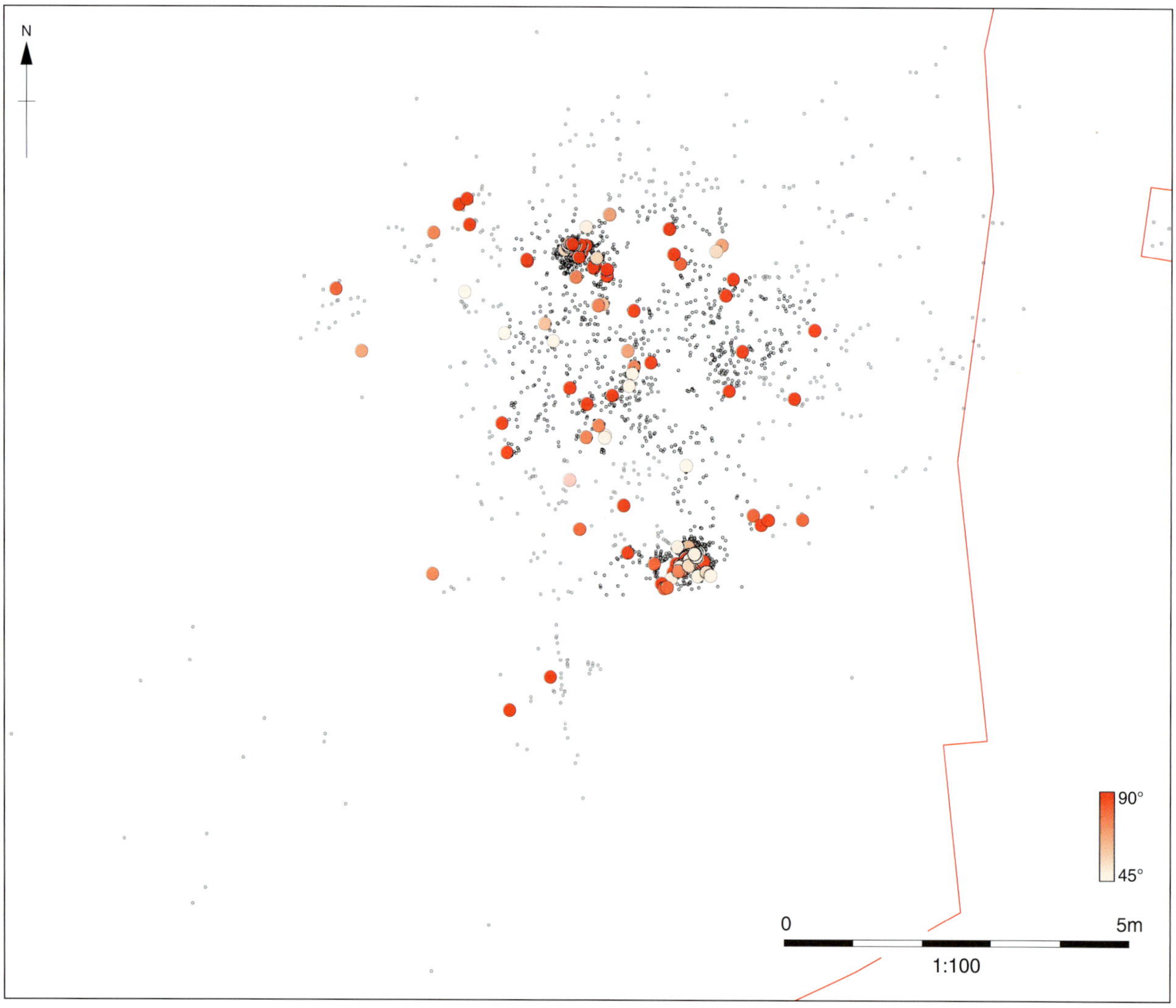

Fig. 5.2 Histogram of dip angles

Fig. 5.3 Distribution of flint dipping at between 90° (in red) and 45° (in increasingly lighter shades)

It has already been noted in the soil micromorphology report (see Chapter 4) that earthworm burrowing may be responsible for some of the vertical pieces of flint, and such a process could explain the propensity for pieces to have been found in vertical positions rather than between 45° and 85°. It is also possible that frost heave has pushed some of the flint into vertical positions (Wood and Johnson 1978, 340; Johnson *et al.* 1977; Johnson and Hansen 1974), although it seems likely that heave would have produced a more even distribution of orientations and would also have resulted in some size sorting (Wood and Johnson 1978, 343) which is not evident in the flint from Guildford (see below).

Orientation

The orientation data is summarised in Figure 5.4. This figure shows only axial data (ie orientation and not direction) and is, therefore, symmetrical through 180°. Overall, the orientations are quite evenly distributed. There is a curious absence of pieces oriented WNW–ESE, but that absence is matched by slightly larger numbers of pieces oriented E–W and NW–SE, and may well reflect the biases in the recording of the orientation data noted above rather than a real pattern.

The distribution of the orientation data can be analysed more precisely using Curray's vector magnitude L (Curray 1956; Lenoble and Bertran 2004, 458–9) which provides a measure of the extent to which the flint was oriented randomly or following a particular direction. L varies from 0% to 100%, 0% indicating a random distribution and 100% indicating that all of the pieces were oriented in the same way. The flint at Guildford Fire Station produces a value of 3.9%, indicating that its orientation is close to random. (The probability of obtaining a greater value of L from a random selection of orientations is 0.14; that is, there is a 14% chance that a random selection of orientations would have produced a higher L value.)

Lenoble and Bertran (2004, 463) have found a strong correlation between vector magnitudes and the extent to which sites slope, and the low figure for Guildford Fire Station is consistent with the site being essentially level. The result thus suggests that the site has not suffered from the post-depositional processes associated with slopes (such as the creep of stones). It also suggests that other processes, such as flooding, that might have affected the orientation of the flint have not had a significant effect.

Fabric analysis

The fabric of the artefacts, defined by both their orientation and dip, has been characterised using Benn's (1964) eigenvalue method (following Lenoble and Bertran 2004, 459). Benn defined two indices – an isotropy index and an elongation index – which can be used to characterise the degree to which fabrics are isotropic, planar or linear. These indexes have been used in archaeological contexts by Lenoble and Bertran (eg 2004; Bertran *et al.* 2005) and comparison with their results provides a means of interpreting the results for Guildford Fire Station. The eigenvalues were calculated using Orient (v.3.12.0: Vollmer 1995; 2015) which was also used to plot the rose diagram (Fig. 5.4) and stereonet (Fig. 5.5).

The data for Guildford are summarised in a stereonet in Figure 5.5. In this diagram, the angle of dip is represented by proximity to the edge of the circle – vertical pieces at 90° plotting at the centre and horizontal pieces at 0° at the edge. The shading indicates the proportions of pieces with each orientation and dip – red indicating a high proportion

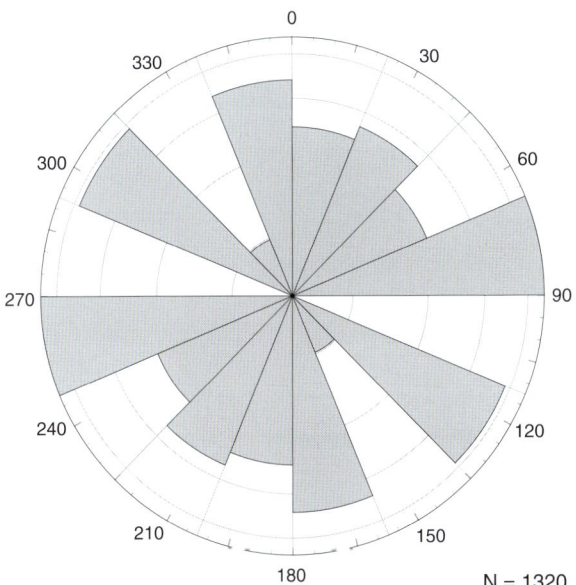

Fig. 5.4 Equal area rose diagram summarising the orientation of the flint

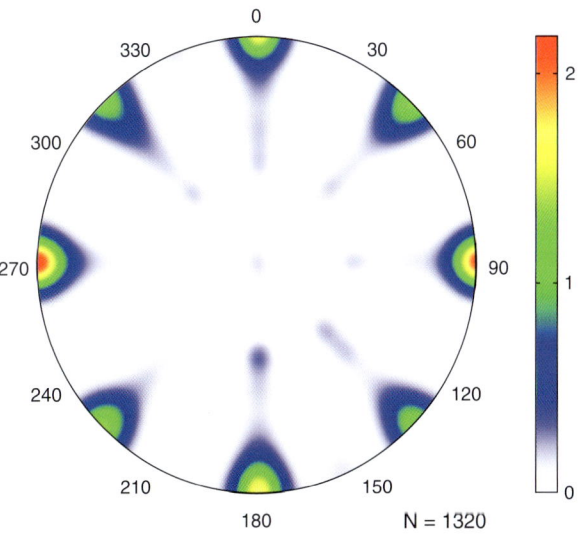

Fig. 5.5 Stereonet summarising the orientation and dip of the flint at Guildford Fire Station

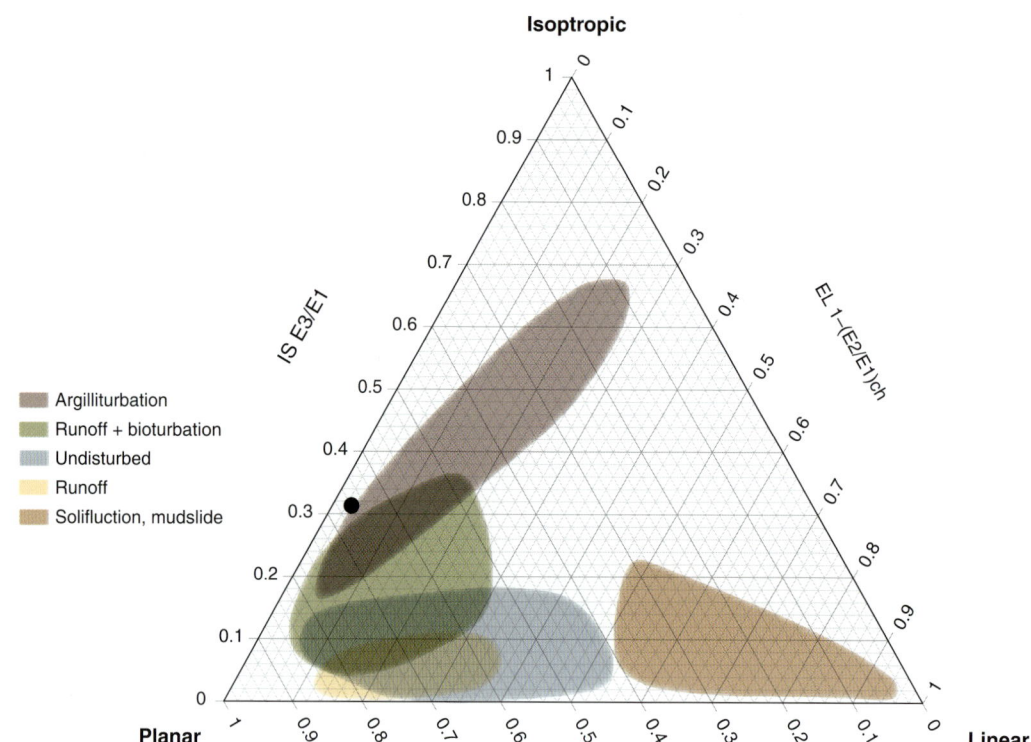

Fig. 5.6 Benn diagram for the flint artefact fabric at Guildford Fire Station. Shaded areas representing post-depositional processes from Lenoble and Bertran 2004, fig. 16

and blue to white a low proportion. As has been noted above, the majority of the pieces were horizontal and thus cluster around the edge of the plot, and only a small number of pieces were vertical (and are indicated by the faint blue dot at the centre of the diagram). The orientation of the pieces is shown by their position around the circle. The tendency to record orientations to the nearest 45° is very evident. The shading is clearly clustered round the points corresponding to the cardinal points at 45°.

The Benn diagram for the Guildford data is shown in Figure 5.6. Not surprisingly, given the results for the dip and orientation discussed above, it indicates a quite planar fabric, which tends towards being isotropic rather than linear.

The most important conclusion that arises from this result is that the site has probably not suffered from severe disturbance. Sites analysed by Lenoble and Bertran (2004, figs 15 and 16) which have been affected by solifluction and mudslides, for example, tend to plot near the linear fabric pole, and sites affected by severe argilliturbation near the isotropic fabric pole. They also note (ibid., 465) that undisturbed sites on gentle slopes tend to plot near the planar fabric pole, a characterisation that fits the results for Guildford Fire Station well. Most significantly, any effects of flooding appear to have been limited since they would be expected to lead to a more linear fabric (equivalent to Lenoble and Bertran's (2004, fig. 16) results for runoff).

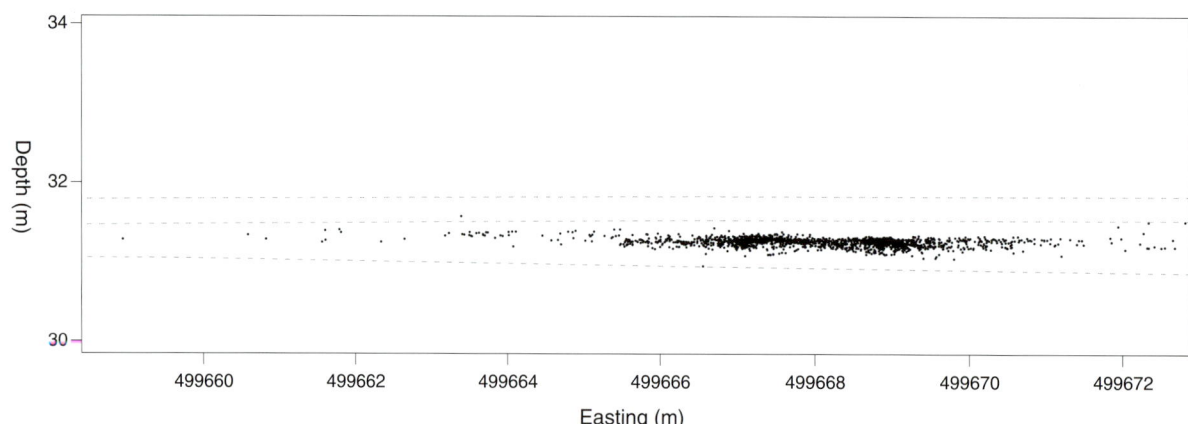

Fig. 5.7 The depth of the flint projected onto an east-west aligned section

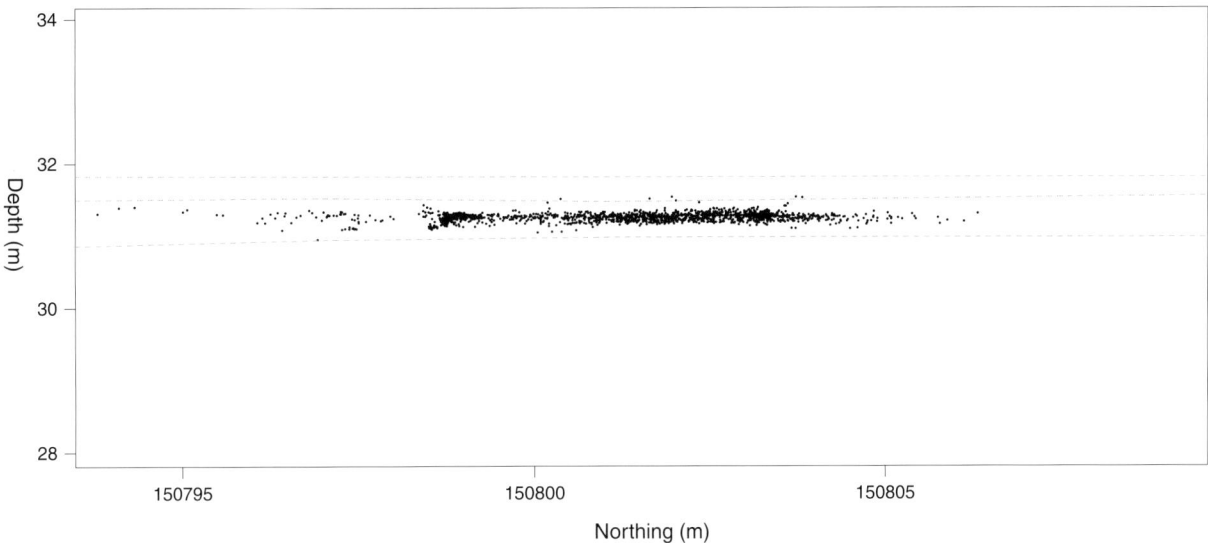

Fig. 5.8 *The depth of the flint projected onto a north-south aligned section*

The results do not, however, suggest that there has been no disturbance. Lenoble and Bertran suggest that isotropy may be increased by trampling, bioturbation, shrink/swell, frost heave and cryoturbation processes, and that whilst such processes may not have much effect on horizontal spatial patterning, they may affect the vertical position of the artefacts. Some of these processes may have affected the Guildford Fire Station site (as the presence of the vertical pieces of flint indicates) and could explain the slightly elevated isotropic index. The geoarchaeological analyses suggest that bio- and floralturbation, from earthworms and roots, is likely to have affected the site. The deposit containing the flint is predominantly sandy and contains only a small proportion of clay, so argilliturbation is unlikely to have been significant. Frost heave may, however, have had some effect (perhaps during the Loch Lomond Stadial), and might have contributed to the tendency towards isotropy. Such processes can be investigated further by looking at the vertical distribution of the flint, which they are likely to have also affected.

VERTICAL DISTRIBUTION OF THE FLINT

The depth of the flint projected onto east–west and north–south aligned sections is shown in Figures 5.7 and 5.8 (with the levels of layer G2 and the top of the topsoil interpolated from levels which were taken roughly through the centre of the flint scatter). The depth of the flint varies over a range of 0.62m. This figure is comparable to other sites on sandy substrates, such as Hengistbury Head (Barton 1992, table 3.3). The range, however, obscures the fact that most of the flint was concentrated within a quite narrow layer: 95% lay within a band with a depth of 0.19m, and 50% was concentrated within a band just 0.05m deep.

A histogram summarising the depth of the flint (Fig. 5.9) has a bell-shaped distribution. Similar distributions have been recorded at Meer, Belgium (Van Noten *et al.* 1980, 51) and the Cave Spring site, Tennessee (Hofman 1986, fig. 2). They contrast with those at Three Ways Wharf, Uxbridge (Lewis and Rackham 2011, fig. 172) and Hengistbury Head (Barton and Bergman 1982, fig. 2) which have

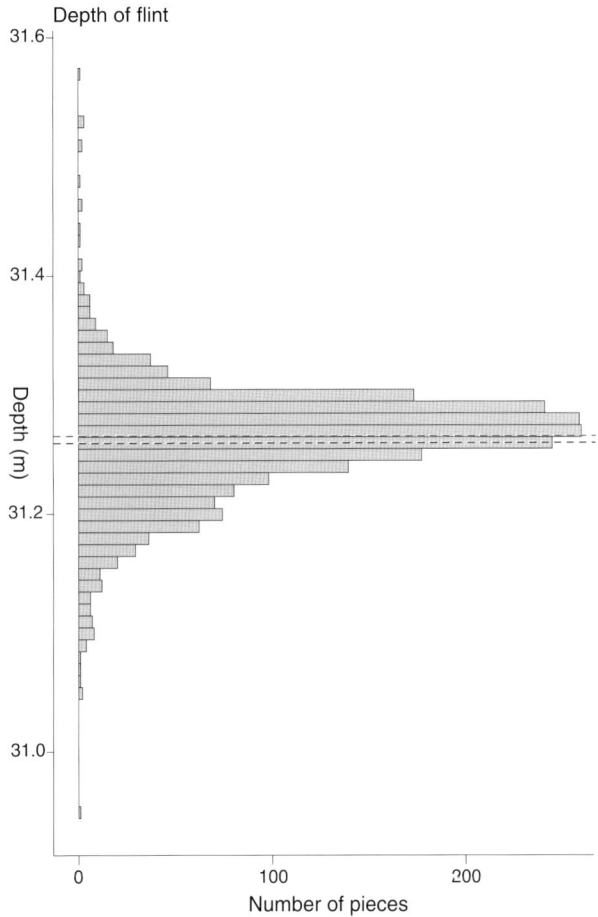

Fig. 5.9 *The depth of the flint, showing the mean (red) and median (blue) depths*

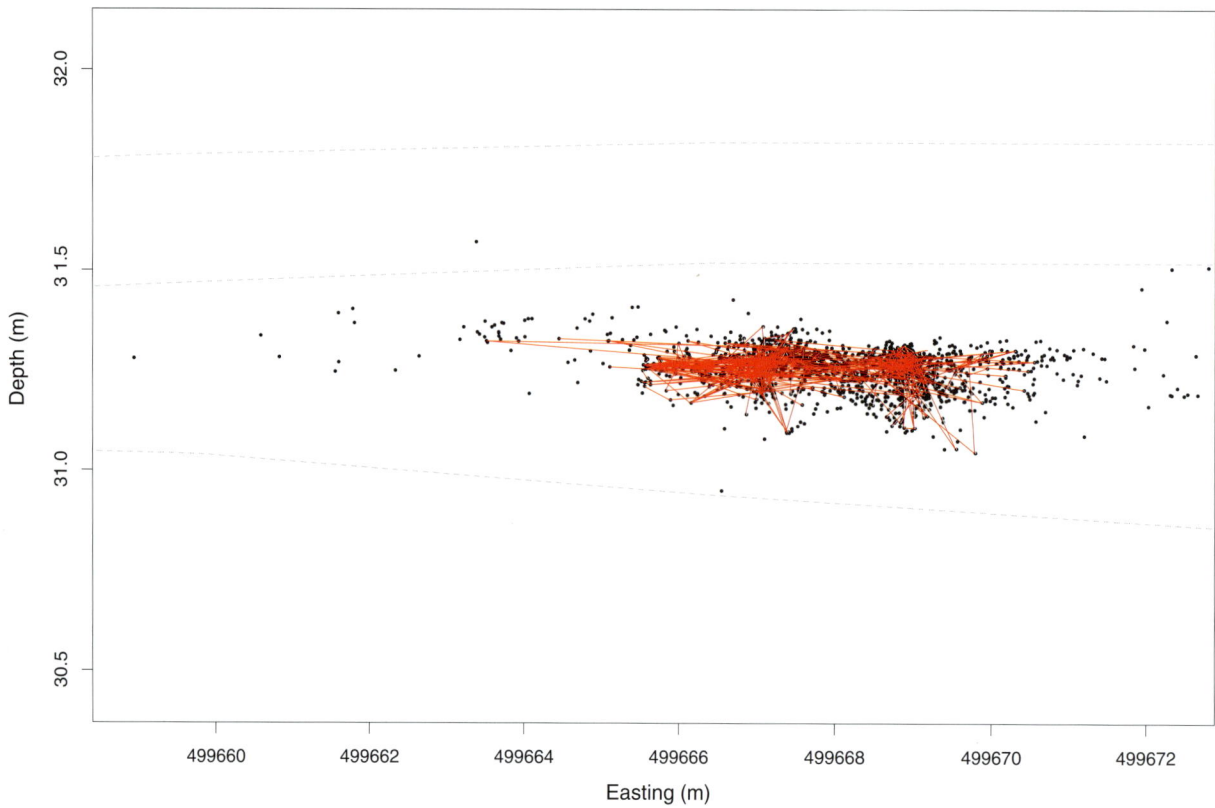

Fig. 5.10 Refits projected onto an east-west aligned section (the y axis (depth) has been exaggerated by a factor of 5 in relation to the x axis (easting))

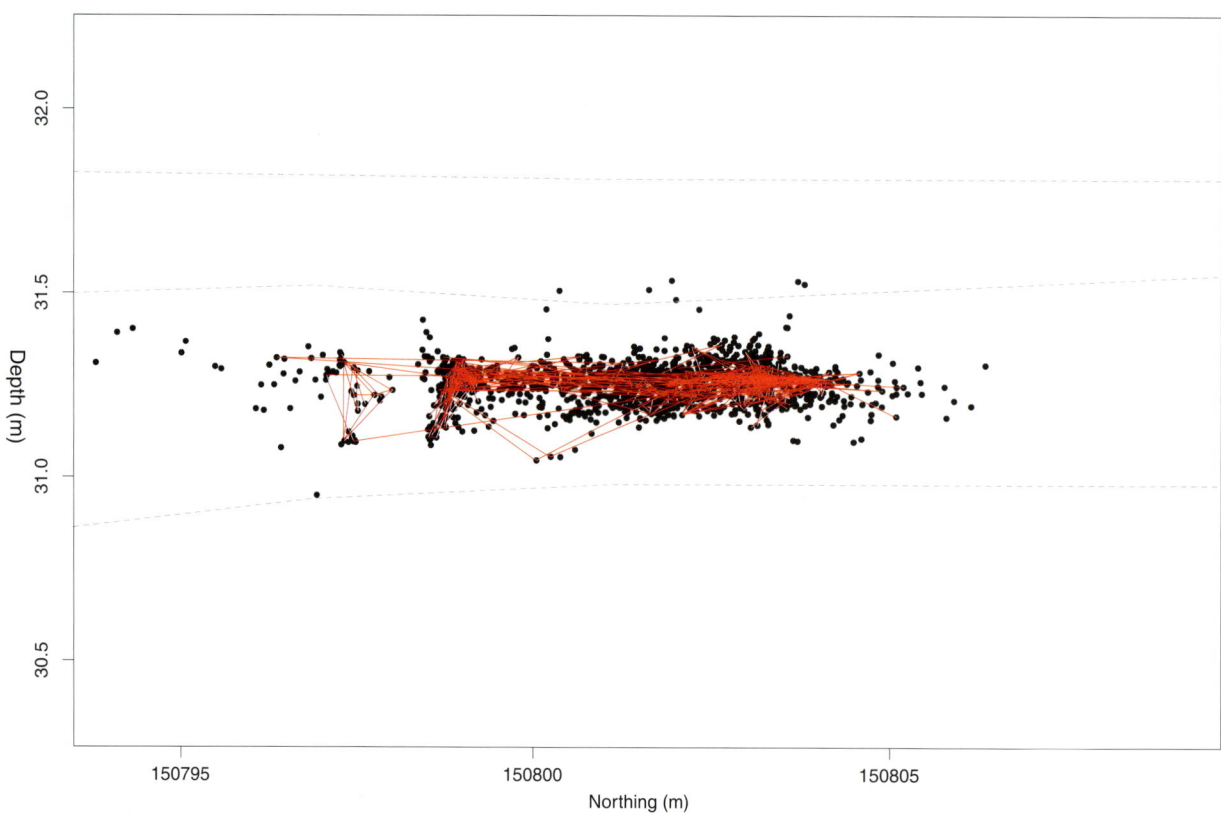

Fig. 5.11 Refits projected onto a north-south aligned section (the y axis (depth) has been exaggerated by a factor of 5 in relation to the x axis (northing))

skewed distributions in which the highest proportion of flint lies towards the top of the distribution.

Bell-shaped distributions can be produced by trampling (Gifford-Gonzalez *et al.* 1985, fig. 8), and whilst trampling would be sufficient to explain most of the difference in depth of the flint at Guildford Fire Station, especially on a sandy substrate, it would imply significant activity after the artefacts had been deposited. The effects of trampling can be seen, however, as a specific example of a more general process, involving the more or less random application of vertical force onto the sediment containing the artefacts, which might be generated in other ways (such as by shrink/swell processes). A bell-shaped distribution would be consistent with the accumulated effects of such randomly occurring small disturbances, moving pieces vertically, over a long period, from what was originally a flat surface. It is quite possible that such long-term processes, even though their short-term impact might have been small, have had more of an effect on the distribution of the flint than short-term processes such as trampling with more obvious effects.

Depths of refits

The suggestion that the vertical dispersion of the flint is the product of post-depositional processes, and does not reflect the presence of flint of different ages, can be tested by examining the differences in the depths of refitting pieces. The vertical distribution of all of the refits is shown projected onto east–west and north–south aligned sections in Figures 5.10 and 5.11 (in which the vertical axis has been exaggerated by a factor of 5 with respect to the horizontal axis) and the differences in depth are summarised in a histogram in Figure 5.12. The depths have all been calculated from the higher piece to the lower piece, and thus are all negative. It is important to stress, however, that the post-depositional movements involved could have been both up and down.

The histogram again shows clearly that whilst most of the refitting pieces were found at approximately the same depths (with a mean difference in depth of just 0.04m and a median difference of 0.02m), the differences between a small proportion

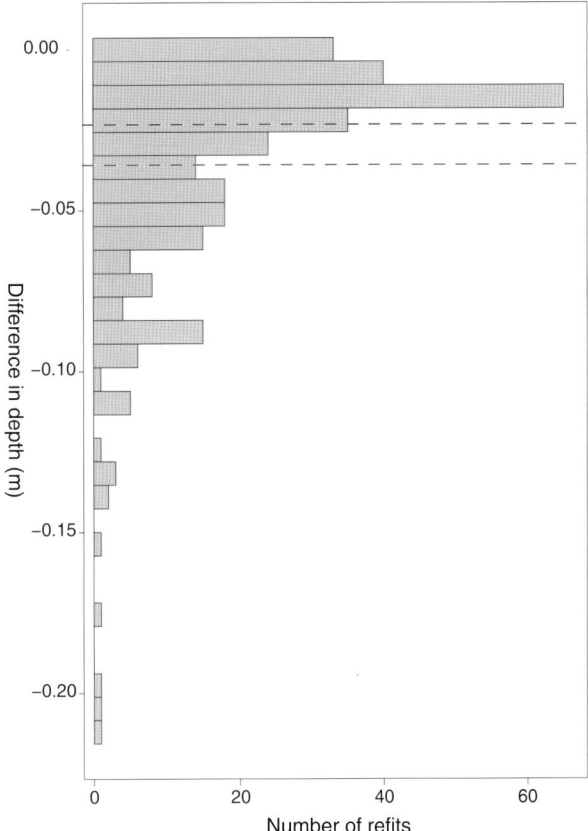

Fig. 5.12 Histogram summarising the difference in depth between all refitting pieces. The red line indicates the mean difference in depth; the blue line the median difference

of the pieces were larger, up to a maximum difference of 0.23m. Plotting out the refits against the overall distribution of flint shows that the refits cover almost the whole depth over which the flint was distributed (Figs 5.10–5.11), although again it is clear that most are focused within the most dense band of flint. The differences in the depths of refitting pieces show that flint very probably knapped at the same time occurs at quite different depths and supports the suggestion that the flint was all deposited in a single layer from which it has subsequently moved vertically.

Sorting by depth

Analysis of the vertical distribution of the flint by size could indicate whether any of the possible post-depositional processes had sorted the flint by size. Such sorting by depth can be produced, for example, by frost heave (Johnson and Hansen 1974, 88). To examine this possibility, the flints were divided into quintiles using their maximum dimensions (ie they were divided into five groups, the first containing the smallest 20% of the flint, the second, the next smallest 20% and so on). The range of sizes in each quintile are shown in Table 5.1. The cumulative proportion of flint within each quintile

Table 5.1 The average, minimum and maximum dimensions of the flint in each quintile, classified according to their maximum dimensions

Quintile	Mean (mm)	Median (mm)	Min (mm)	Max (mm)
1st (smallest)	12.1	15	2.5	15.0
2nd	17.5	15.4	15.0	24.3
3rd	32.2	35.0	24.3	35.0
4th	35.2	35.0	35.0	37.7
5th (largest)	67.4	56.3	37.7	121.7

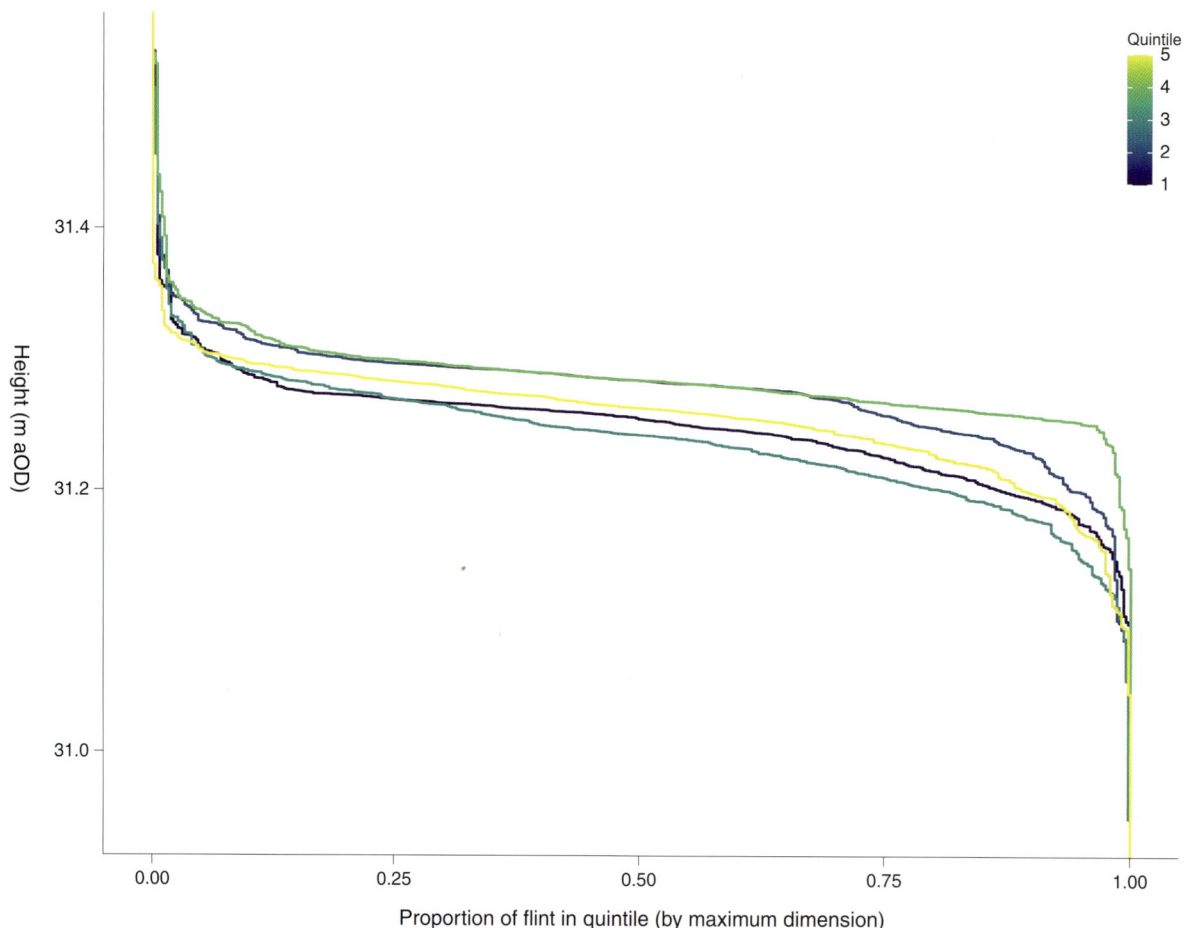

Fig. 5.13 Cumulative frequency diagram showing the depth distribution of the flint by quintiles defined using the maximum dimensions of the flint (1 represents the smallest quintile; 5 the largest)

occurring at each depth was then plotted (Fig. 5.13).

The results do not indicate any significant sorting by size. There is little difference between the depth distributions for any of the quintiles, the flint in all of them being concentrated in the same quite narrow band, between c 31.2m and 31.3m aOD. Perhaps most strikingly, the curves for the first and fifth quintiles, representing the smallest and largest pieces of flint, are very similar, and the remaining quintiles are distributed both above and below them, indicating that there is no overall pattern to the depth distribution of the difference size classes. There is, then, no indication of any sorting by size.

REFIT ORIENTATIONS

Analysis of the orientations of refits provides another means of examining whether post-depositional processes have affected the distribution of the flint. The results may, however, be less clearly

Table 5.2 Refit orientation statistics

Refitting Group	No. refits	Mean direction (degrees from north)	Median direction (degrees from north)	Rayleigh test		Kuiper's test		
				Test statistic	P-value	Test statistic	Level 0.05 critical value	P-value
RG 1	140	295	309	0.1009	0.2407	1.439	1.747	>0.15
RG 5	28	185	190	0.2031	0.3178	1.6258	1.747	> 0.05 < 0.10
RG 7	26	143	142	0.3245	0.0634	1.8373	1.747	**>0.025 < 0.05**
RG 2	22	124	123	0.4722	**0.0062**	2.0576	1.747	**< 0.01**
RG 8	21	159	168	0.4506	**0.0124**	1.973	1.747	**> 0.01 < 0.025**
RG 9	19	273	270	0.736	**0.0000**	2.5136	1.747	**< 0.01**
RG 3	18	289	323	0.1778	0.5724	1.4971	1.747	> 0.15

Figures in bold indicate significant results (p < 0.05)

indicative of such effects than the overall fabric of the artefacts. De la Torre *et al.* (2019, 4581–3) suggest that strongly oriented patterns can be produced by knapping and do not, therefore, necessarily provide an indication of post-depositional disturbance. Overall, however, the results for Guildford Fire Station suggest that the refit orientations rarely depart significantly from uniformity, and, like the fabric analysis, they do not provide any evidence of significant disturbance.

Methods and data

The analysis has been carried out following the methodology outlined by de la Torre *et al.* (2019), although no weighting has been used. They use a number of statistics to characterise the distribution of the refit orientations. Of these, the Rayleigh test for unimodal departures from uniformity is perhaps the most useful since it might be expected that either knapping itself or post-depositional disturbance would tend to create patterns which cluster in one direction. The test returns a value between 0 (when the orientations are distributed evenly) and 1 (when they are all concentrated at a single point; Pewsey *et al.* 2013, 3.4.1 and 5.1.1). A significance test can be used to assess the probability that the points derive from a uniform distribution (a probability of 0.05 or less would lead to the null hypothesis of a uniform distribution being rejected). De la Torre *et al.* also give the results of a suite of 'omnibus tests' which test for a variety of other kinds of departure from uniformity (Pewsey *et al.* 2013, 5.1.1) and which also provide similar tests of significance. The rose diagrams were plotted, and the statistics calculated, using the circular and CircStats packages in R (Agostinelli and Lund 2023; Lund and Agostinelli 2001).

Refit Group 1 (which has 72 refits) is, unfortunately, the only group at Guildford which is large enough to give interesting results. Results for the largest of the other refit groups (which have between 28 and 18 refits), are also shown in Table 5.2, but with samples this small the results of the statistical tests become erratic.

Results

The results are very varied, but rather strikingly, none of the tests suggest that the two largest refit groups – RG 1 and RG 5, with 140 and 28 refits respectively (Figs 5.14–5.15) – deviate significantly from a uniform distribution, whilst the smaller ones, with fewer than 26 refits often do, although in some cases the tests provide contrary results. Refit Group 9 most clearly tends towards a particular orientation (Fig. 5.16). Overall, however, there is little consistency in the average directions of the refitting groups, so that even when the distributions do depart from uniformity, there is little indication of any significant overall trend which might indicate the effects of, for example, flooding. Overall, then, the results are consistent with the fabric analysis and suggest that there are no trends in the orientation of the flint or the refits which might indicate the effects of post-depositional processes such as flooding.

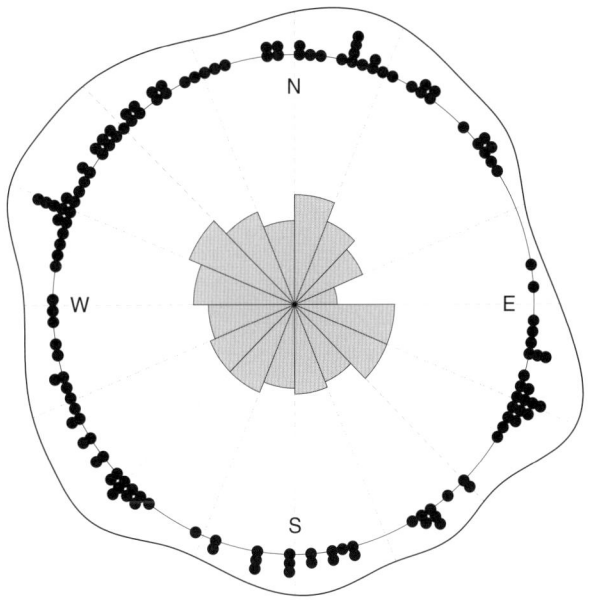

Fig. 5.14 Refit orientations for Refit Group 1

	Rao's spacing test			Watson's test		
Test statistic	Level 0.05 critical value	P-value		Test statistic	Level 0.05 critical value	P-value
141.7143	143.83	>0.05 <0.10		0.1196	0.187	>0.10
149.2857	157.65	>0.10		0.1195	0.187	>0.10
166.0769	158.52	**>0.01 <0.05**		0.2165	0.187	**>0.025 <0.05**
175.4545	160.56	**>0.001 <0.01**		0.2775	0.187	**<0.01**
158.4286	161.16	>0.05 <0.10		0.2514	0.187	**>0.01 <0.025**
187.2105	162.47	**<0.01**		0.5849	0.187	**<0.01**
181.0000	163.20	**>0.001 <0.01**		0.1109	0.187	>0.10

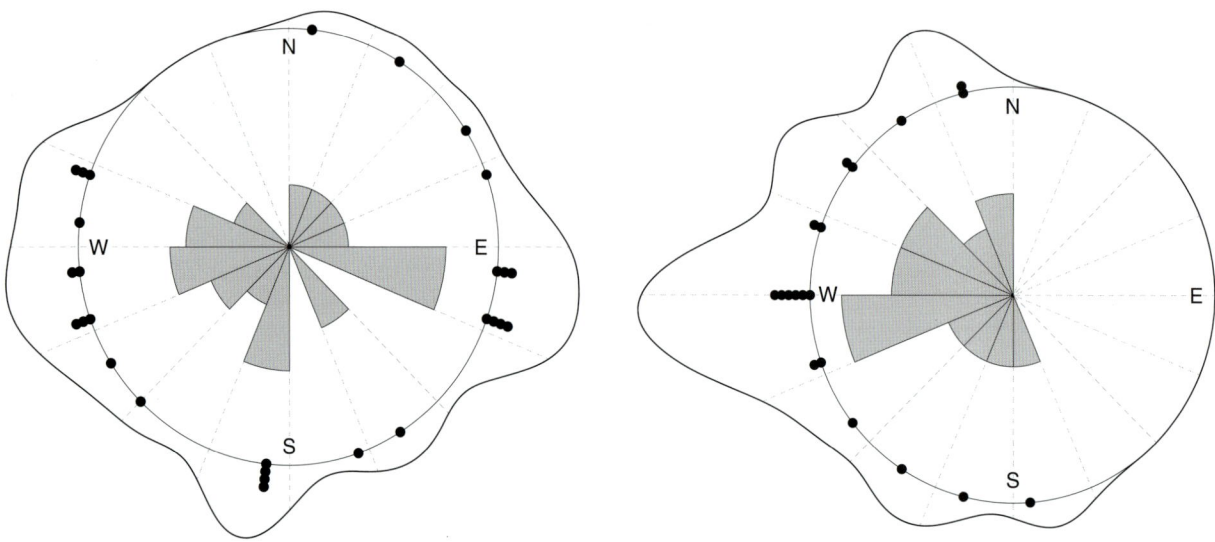

Fig. 5.15 Refit orientations for Refit Group 5

Fig. 5.16 Refit orientations for Refit Group 9

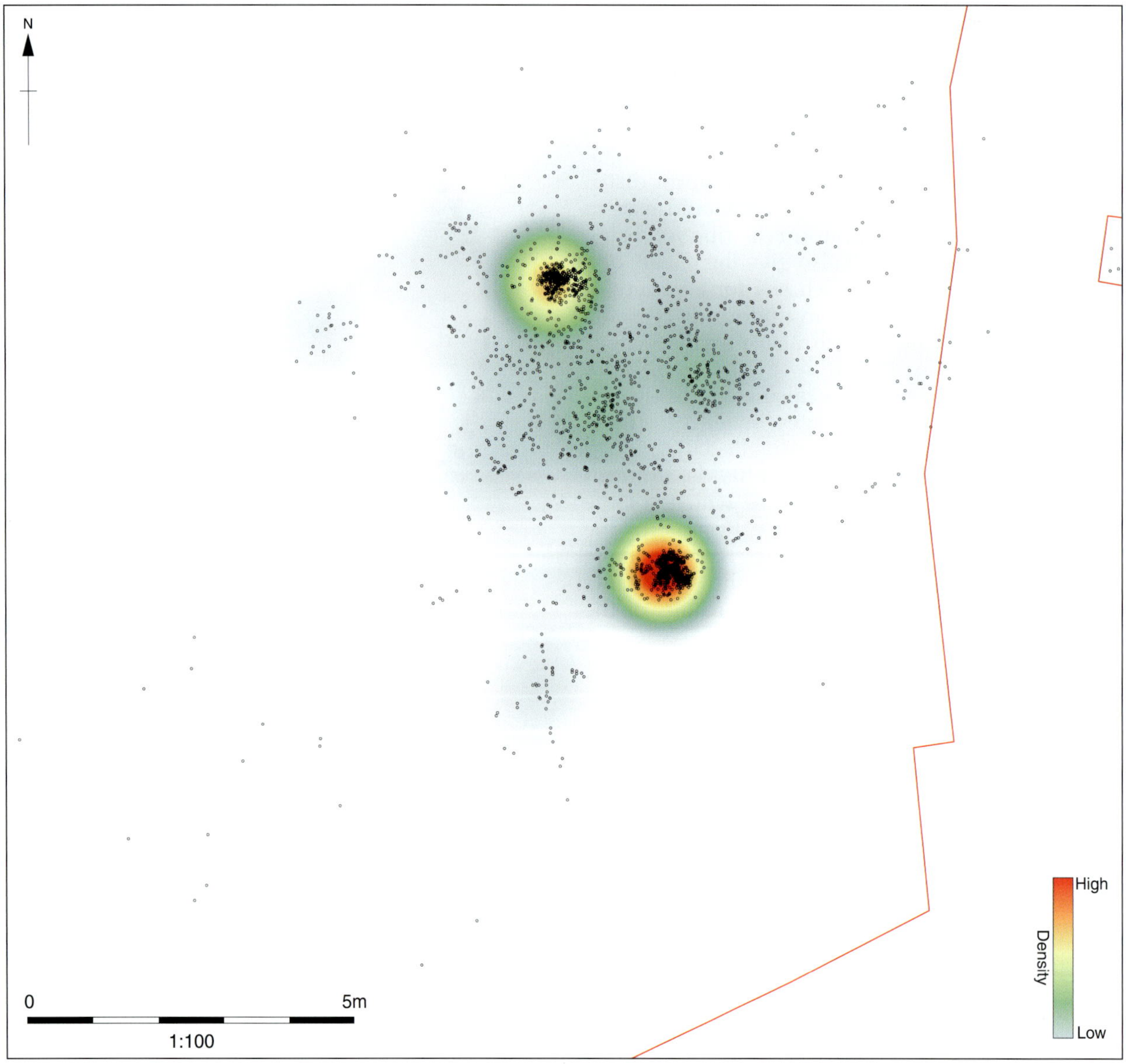

Fig. 5.17 Heatmap of all flint

HORIZONTAL DISTRIBUTION OF THE FLINT

Although there is, then, evidence that the vertical distribution of the flint has been affected by processes such as bioturbation, the lack of evidence that fluvial processes significantly affected the distribution of the flint suggests that the horizontal distribution of the flint has been relatively unaffected. This section will, therefore, examine the horizontal distribution of the flint to assess whether there are any indications that it retained any of its original structure.

Figures 5.17 and 5.18 show kernel density estimates (heatmaps) for all of the flint and the heat-affected flint. Figure 5.19 shows contoured versions of the same estimates so that the two distributions can be compared. The heat maps were generated in QGIS using a quartic kernel with a radius of 1m. The contours were also fitted in QGIS but, because there is so little burnt flint (compared to the assemblage overall), the contours for the burnt flint are fitted at much closer intervals than those for the whole assemblage, and the two sets of contours do not, therefore, show equivalent levels of density.

The heatmaps clearly show that the overall distribution includes two dense concentrations (Concentration 1 to the north-west and Concentration 2 to the south-east) which are separated by a 4m wide area in which a more general spread of artefacts was found. As is discussed further below (see Chapters 6 and 8), the two concentrations are knapping scatters and the general spread between them includes both artefacts related to the knapping scatters and which derive from other activities.

Figure 5.20 summarises the density of the flint which occurs in concentric rings at intervals of 0.1m from the centroids of the two concentrations. It shows how highly concentrated the flint was in the two knapping concentrations. The densities peak at 4000 pieces/m^2 at the centre of Concentration 2 and at 2936 pieces/m^2 in Concentration 1, and then fall off quickly over just 0.3–0.4m to very low levels. The majority of the flint is thus concentrated at the centre of these concentrations in areas with diameters of just 0.6m to 0.8m. This concentration alone suggests that the knapping concentrations have not been significantly dilated.

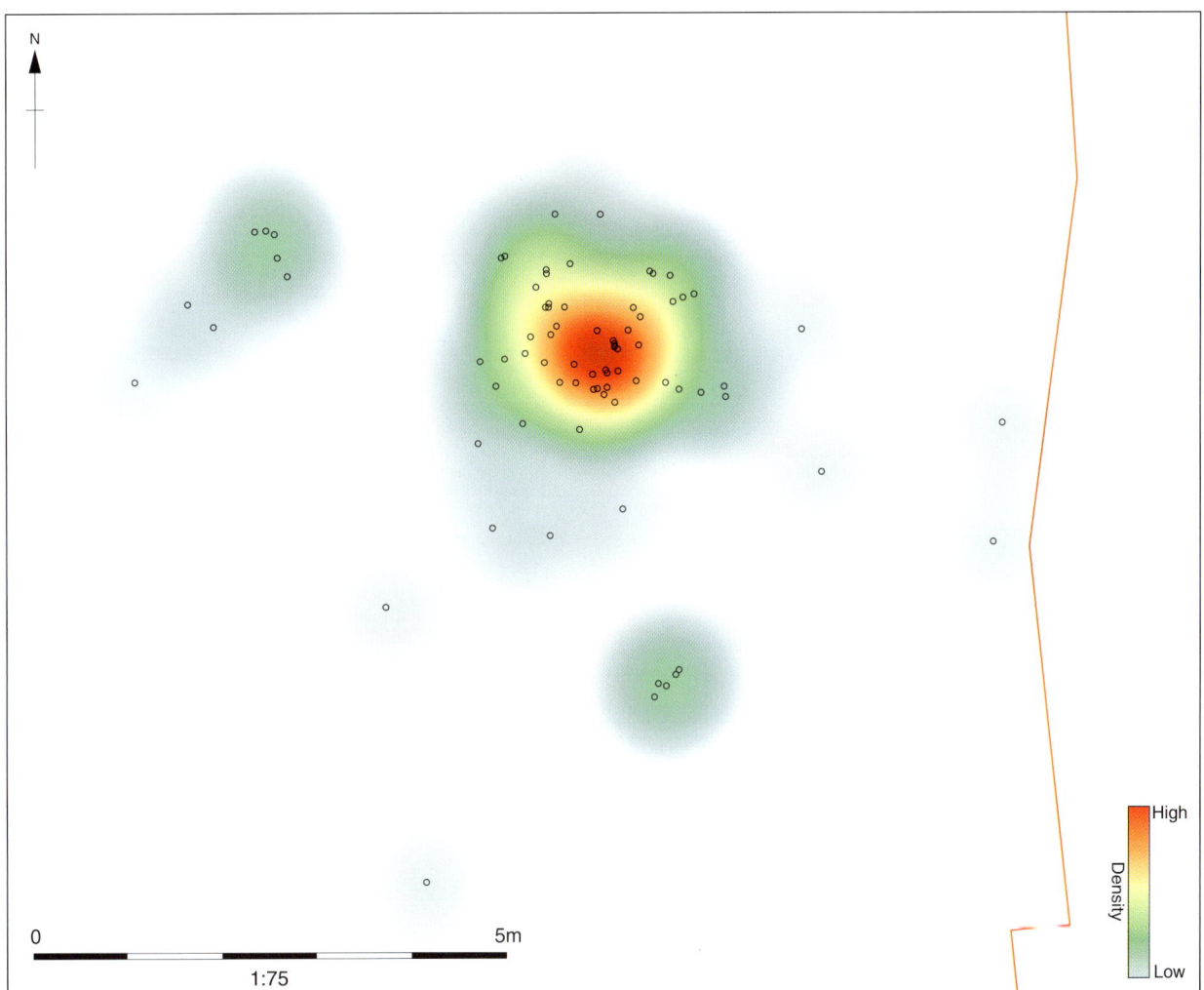

Fig. 5.18 Heatmap of heat-affected flint

The distribution of the heat-affected flint

As the contoured versions of the heatmaps show (Fig. 5.19), the distribution of the heat-affected flint does not match that of the other flint. Whilst there are no very dense concentrations of burnt artefacts, they are mostly concentrated just to the south-east of Concentration 1 (with a very small second concentration to the north-west) and this concentration could mark the former location of a hearth. The mixing of burnt and unburnt flint in this area could reflect the dispersal of burnt and heated flint after the hearth was in use (perhaps as ash was removed from the hearth; cf. Yellen 1977, 143) or the subsequent addition of unburnt flint to the area where a hearth had previously existed. Although the results are not presented here, relative risk analysis (Kelsall and Diggle 1995; Bevan 2012, 500; Baddeley *et al.* 2015, 581–3) shows that the ratio of the density of heat-affected flint relative to the density of unburnt flint is much higher in the area of the potential hearth than it is anywhere else on the site.

Hot spot analysis

To assess whether there was any horizontal sorting of the flint by size, hot spot analysis (Ord and Getis 1995; Getis and Ord 2010) has been carried out, using the maximum dimensions of the artefacts recorded in three-dimensions. Hot spot analysis provides a means of identifying clusters of large and small pieces of flint, compared to the size of the flint overall. For each piece of flint, it compares the sizes of the pieces of flint within a specified distance to the overall mean size for the site, and expresses the differences in standard deviations from the mean (as a standard or Z score). Large differences are highlighted by high scores. The statistics calculated here are Getis and Ord's local G_i^* which includes the measurements of the pieces for which the statistics are calculated within the calculation. The analysis was carried out in R using the spdep package (Bivand *et al.* 2013).

The results are dependent upon the distance around each artefact that defines which other artefacts are included in the calculations. To select this distance, Moran's I was calculated at a range of distances. Significant correlations occurred at a number of distances, and the results for one of the smallest significant distance – 0.3m – which revealed the spatial structure of the scatter with

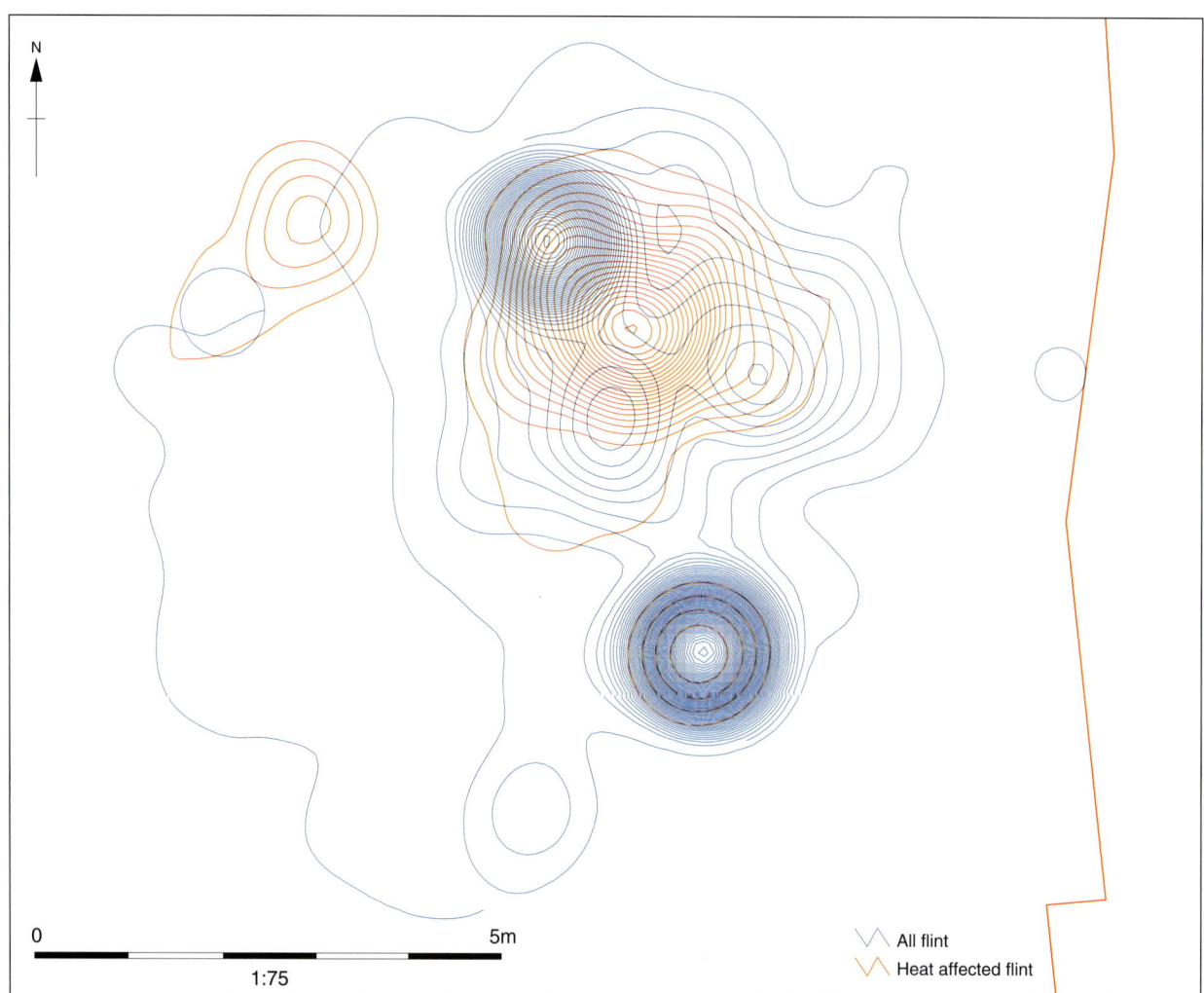

Fig. 5.19 Contoured versions of the heatmaps in Figs 5.17 and 5.18

Chapter 5

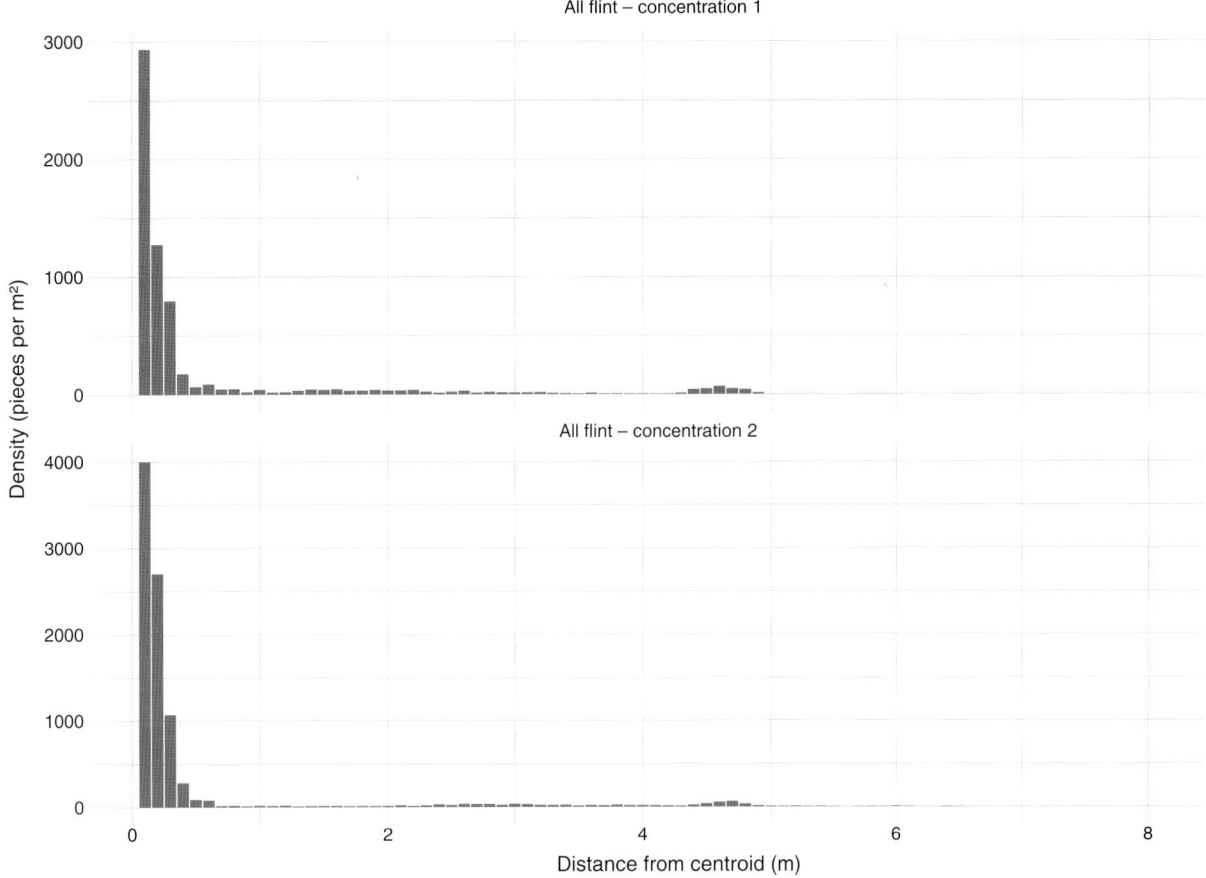

Fig. 5.20 Density of flint in 0.1m wide rings, centred on the two main concentrations

some precision, and a wider scale – 0.8m – which reveals the wider general pattern, were selected. It should be stressed that whilst it does reveal a more detailed picture of the distribution of the artefacts, the smaller distance especially is too small to encompass all of the outlying pieces. Where pieces lie more than 0.3m apart, the results will derive only from the size of the single pieces themselves, and do not provide a reliable indication of the presence of hot spots. Similarly, the results at this scale are unreliable for areas where only a small number of pieces lie within 0.3m of each other. This problem affects the larger distance – 0.8m – less significantly, but even this distance leaves some of the outlying artefacts isolated.

The results suggest that there is significant spatial structure in the scatter. In Figures 5.21–5.22, pieces falling in clusters characterised by larger-than-average-sized pieces are marked in yellow, and those in clusters with smaller-than-average pieces in blue. The size of the dots is proportional to the absolute size of the Gi* statistic: the larger the dot, the greater the deviation from the overall average.

Rather than reflecting the effects of fluvial processes, the pattern revealed by the analysis appears more likely to reflect the patterns produced by knapping, suggesting that much of the flint has suffered from very little dilation. Both of the main concentrations are marked by clusters of smaller-than-average pieces. There are also clusters of smaller-than-average pieces between the two concentrations, near the centre of the flint scatter, although the clusters here are closer to the average than those associated with the two main concentrations. The clusters of larger-than-average pieces lie beside and around both the two concentrations and the area between the concentrations. Not surprisingly, the distribution of the clusters of the larger-than-average pieces to some extent matches that of the cores and crested pieces (see Fig. 6.4), which are amongst the largest pieces. The distribution of the smaller pieces, in contrast, must be influenced by the distribution of the smallest pieces: chips and small debitage. The same broad pattern is revealed at both scales of analysis. Analysis at the smaller scale does, however, suggest a greater mixing of clusters of small and large pieces than the analysis at a larger scale.

It is important to stress that these clusters are defined using the average size of the pieces within 0.3m and 0.8m of the pieces for which the measurements were made. They do not imply that only small or large pieces occurred within the areas marked in blue and yellow in Figures 5.21–5.22, but rather that the areas contained either a high proportion of smaller or larger pieces or included exceptionally large or small pieces.

The pattern is consistent with the idea that most of the small pieces, including the chips and small

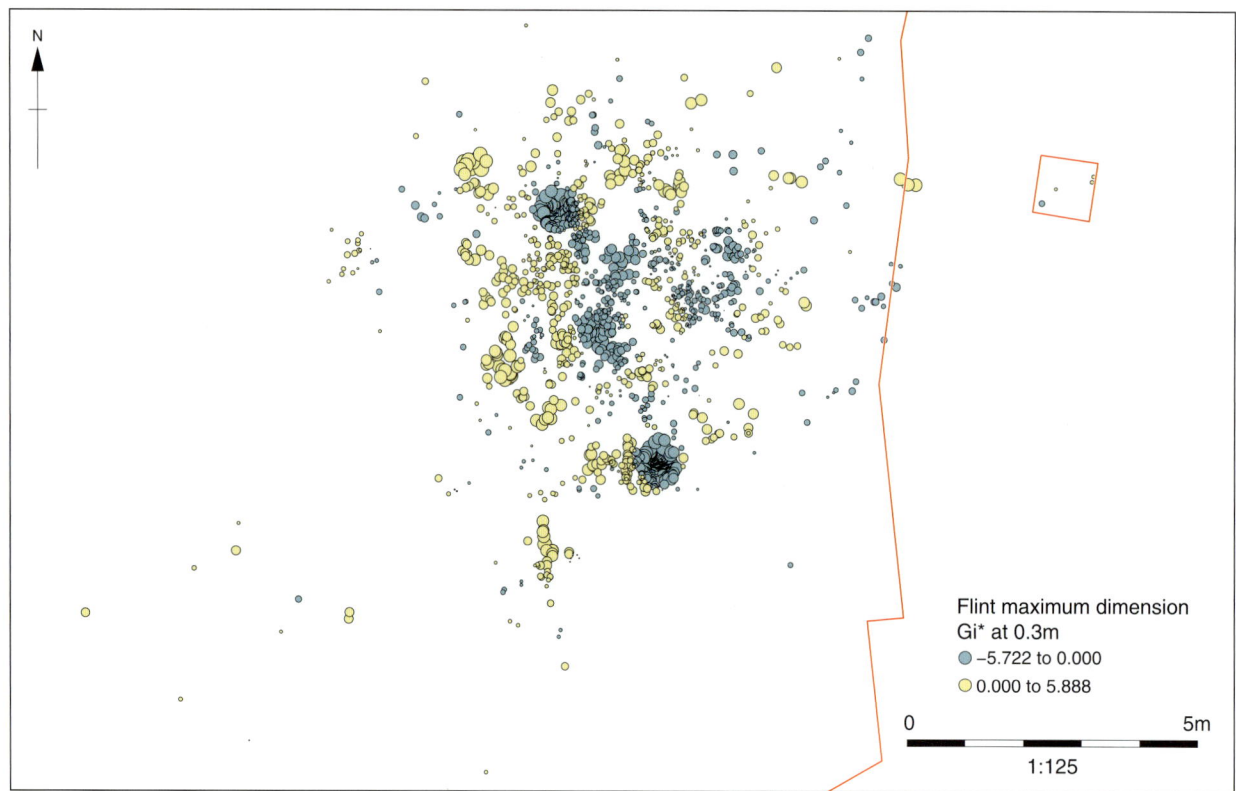

Fig. 5.21 Hot spot analysis of the maximum dimensions of the flint using a diameter of 0.3m. The size of the dots is proportional to the deviation from the overall mean.

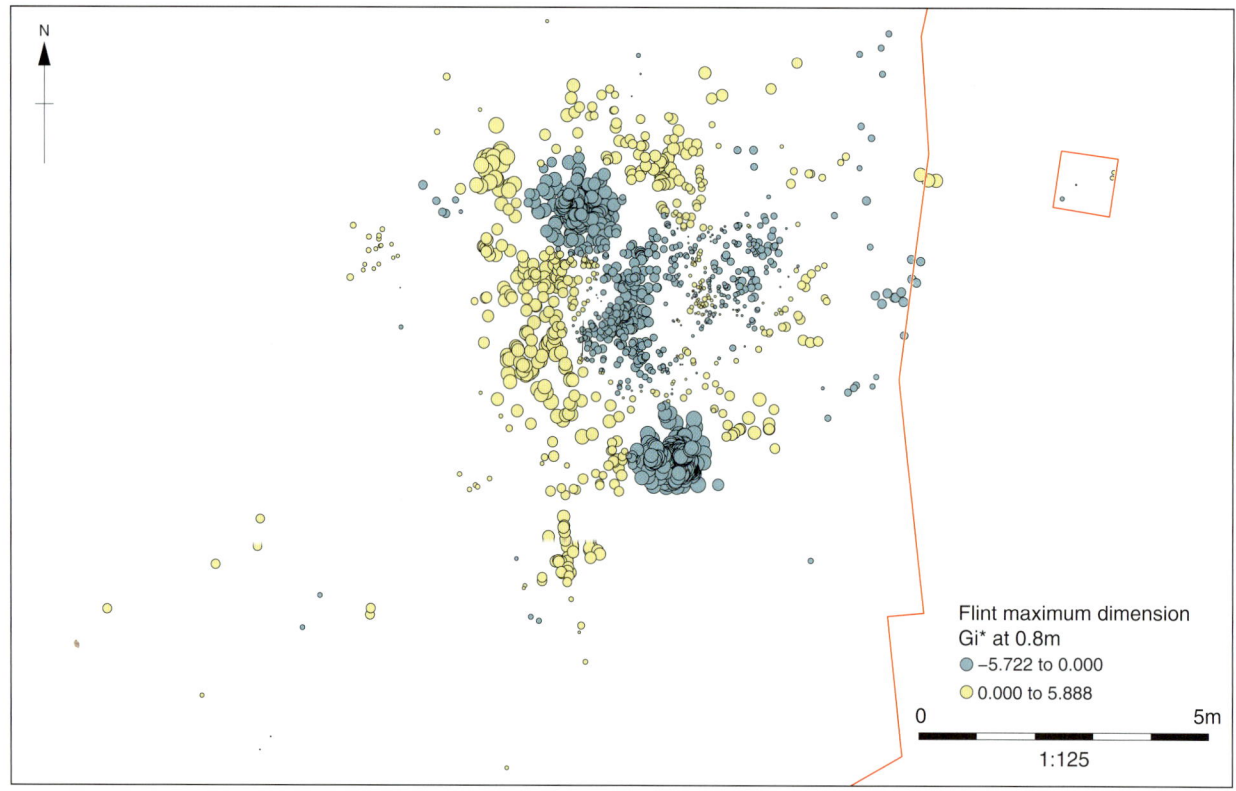

Fig. 5.22 Hot spot analysis of the maximum dimensions of the flint using a diameter of 0.9m. The size of the dots is proportional to the deviation from the overall mean.

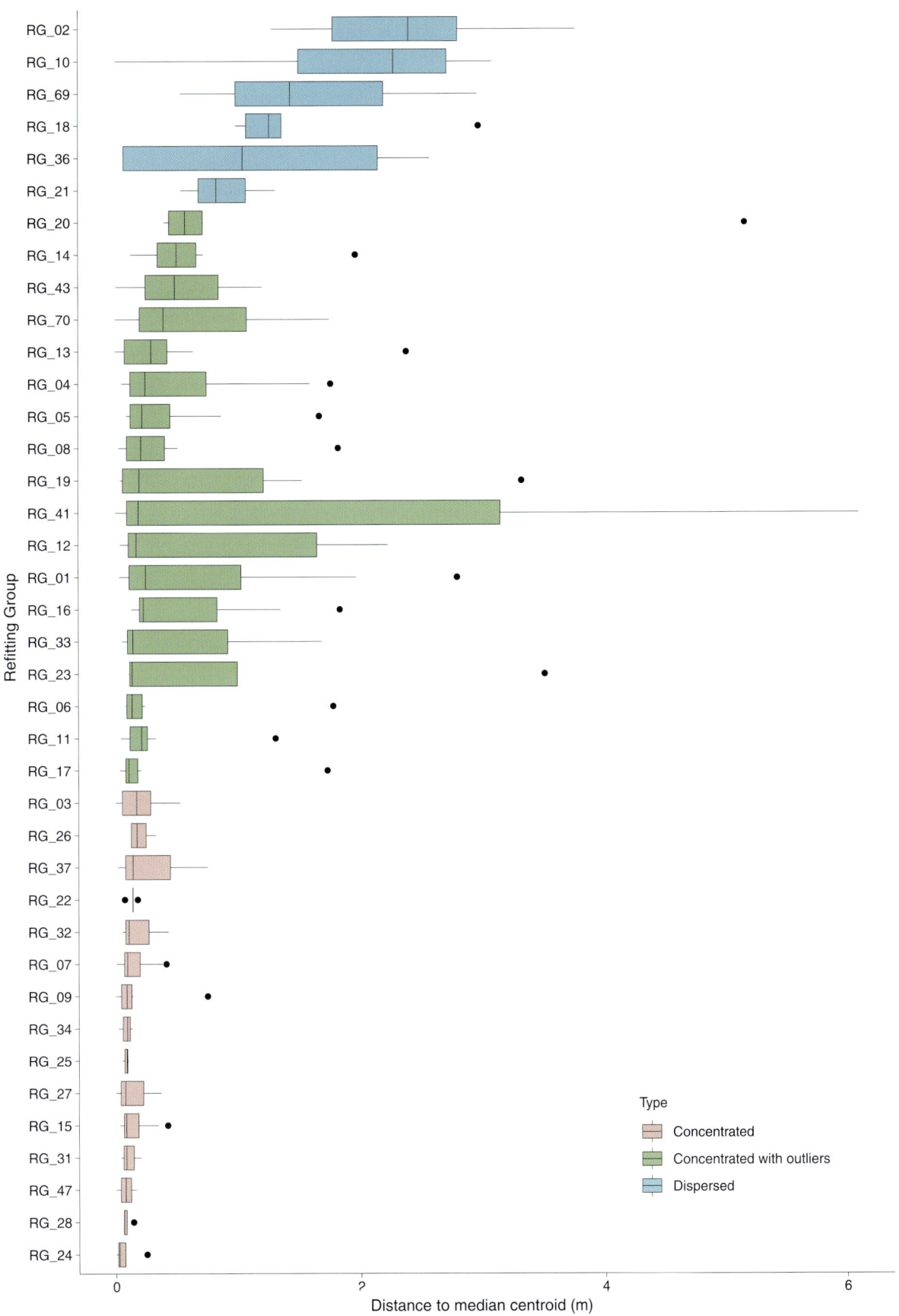

Fig. 5.23 Boxplots summarising the distribution of centroid distances for refit groups divided into concentrated groups, concentrated groups with outliers, and dispersed groups

debitage, fell close to the points where the knapping occurred (marked by the two concentrations), whilst larger pieces, including cores and crested pieces, were often deposited beside or at the edges of the concentrations. The presence of clusters of smaller-than-average pieces between the two main concentrations might even reflect the way in which the knappers sat: roughly facing each other with the smaller debitage falling in front of them whilst their bodies shielded the area behind them (although the area 'behind' or to the south of the southern concentration was disturbed by the explosion of the mortar and the absence of flints in this area may not have been real). It is also possible, however, that the clusters of smaller than average pieces between the two main concentrations might represent further locations in which more limited episodes of knapping took place.

Whatever the case, the overall pattern is not consistent with the flint having been sorted by fluvial processes. Such a process would be expected to produce a more gradual cline across the site, or at least a simpler pattern rather than the slightly mixed, roughly concentric pattern which characterises the site.

Centroid diagrams

Detailed observations of refitting show that in the northern area of the scatter a high proportion of dorso-ventral refits to break refits was found in every square examined (see Figs 6.33–6.34). This is quite unusual and again suggests both that *in situ* knapping took place in this part of the site, and that at least here the assemblage has not been greatly disturbed by processes such as contemporary trampling which could cause a higher breakage rate in the discarded debitage.

The extent to which the horizontal distribution of the flint might have been affected by dilation can also be examined in more detail using centroid

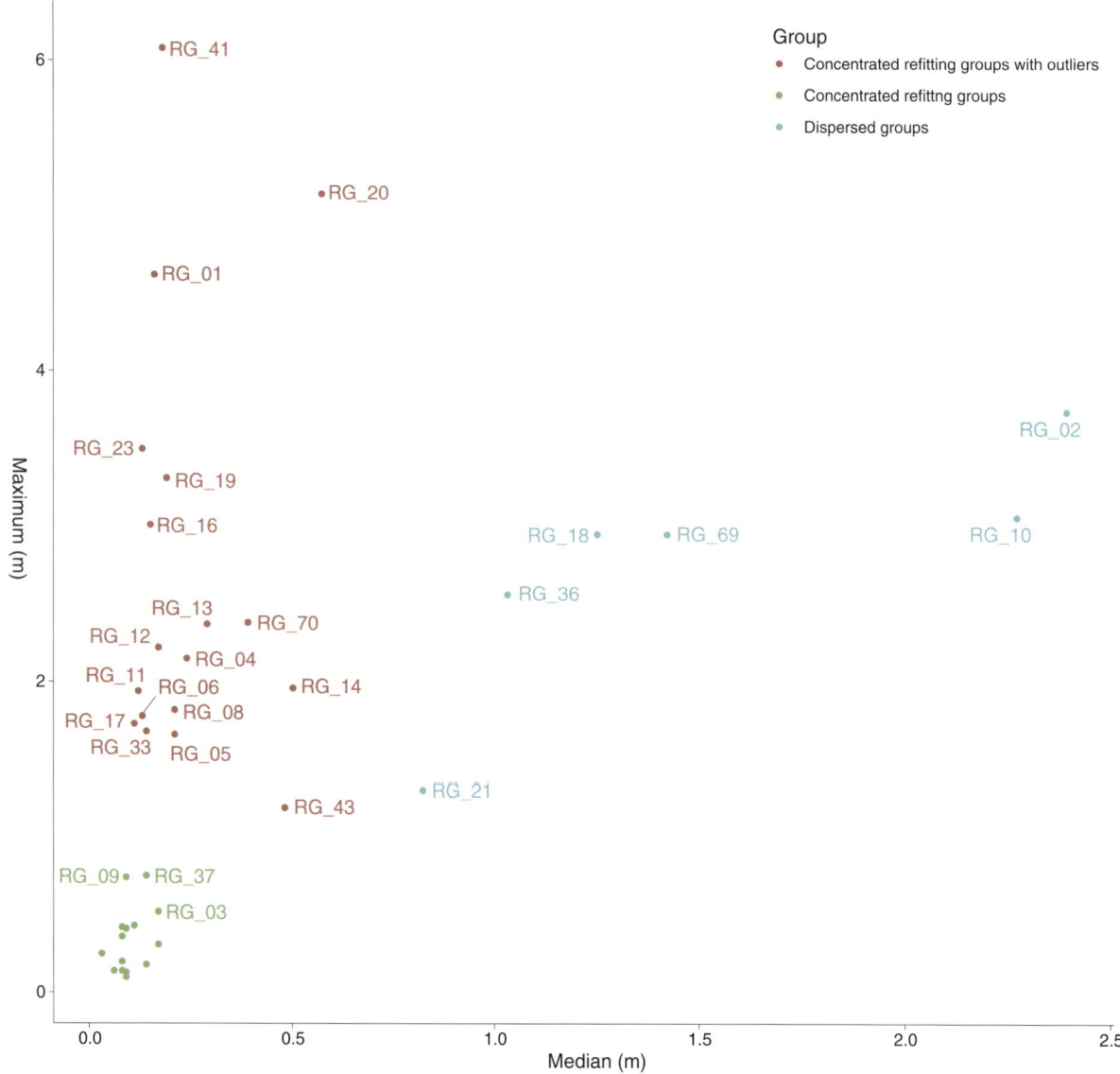

Fig. 5.24 Sets of refitting groups, classified by median and maximum centroid distances

Table 5.3 Refit groups: summary statistics for centroid distances

Group	Min.	1st Quartile	Median	Mean	3rd Quartile	Max.	No. refits	Centred on
Concentrated refitting groups								
RG 26	0.12	0.12	0.17	0.19	0.23	0.31	4	Concentration 1
RG 47	0.00	0.04	0.08	0.07	0.11	0.14	3	Concentration 1
RG 07	0.01	0.07	0.09	0.15	0.19	0.41	13	Concentration 2
RG 09	0.00	0.04	0.09	0.14	0.13	0.74	11	Concentration 2
RG 15	0.03	0.06	0.08	0.15	0.18	0.42	8	Concentration 2
RG 22	0.07	0.14	0.14	0.13	0.14	0.18	5	Concentration 2
RG 24	0.00	0.02	0.03	0.07	0.07	0.25	5	Concentration 2
RG 27	0.00	0.04	0.08	0.15	0.22	0.36	3	Concentration 2
RG 28	0.06	0.06	0.06	0.08	0.08	0.14	4	Concentration 2
RG 32	0.05	0.08	0.11	0.19	0.27	0.43	3	Concentration 2
RG 34	0.02	0.06	0.09	0.08	0.11	0.13	3	Concentration 2
RG 37	0.02	0.08	0.14	0.30	0.44	0.75	3	Concentration 2
RG 03	0.00	0.05	0.17	0.18	0.28	0.52	9	Other concentrations
RG 25	0.05	0.07	0.09	0.08	0.09	0.10	5	Other concentrations
RG 31	0.04	0.06	0.08	0.11	0.14	0.20	3	Other concentrations
Concentrated refitting groups with outliers								
RG 01	0.01	0.09	0.16	0.66	1.25	4.62	69	Concentration 1
RG 04	0.00	0.08	0.24	0.61	0.70	2.15	11	Concentration 1
RG 11	0.02	0.04	0.12	0.35	0.25	1.94	8	Concentration 1
RG 16	0.05	0.14	0.15	0.76	0.92	3.01	7	Concentration 1
RG 70	0.00	0.19	0.39	0.92	1.38	2.38	3	Concentration 1
RG 05	0.09	0.12	0.21	0.41	0.44	1.66	11	Concentration 2
RG 08	0.03	0.09	0.21	0.36	0.40	1.82	11	Concentration 2
RG 12	0.04	0.11	0.17	0.74	1.64	2.22	10	Concentration 2
RG 13	0.00	0.07	0.29	0.48	0.42	2.37	9	Concentration 2
RG 17	0.03	0.08	0.11	0.34	0.18	1.73	7	Concentration 2
RG 19	0.04	0.06	0.19	0.88	1.20	3.31	6	Concentration 2
RG 20	0.40	0.44	0.57	1.30	0.71	5.14	6	Concentration 2
RG 23	0.11	0.11	0.13	0.97	0.99	3.50	4	Concentration 2
RG 06	0.08	0.09	0.13	0.41	0.21	1.78	6	Other concentrations
RG 14	0.13	0.34	0.50	0.63	0.66	1.96	8	Other concentrations
RG 33	0.05	0.10	0.14	0.62	0.91	1.68	3	Other concentrations
RG 41	0.00	0.09	0.18	2.09	3.13	6.08	3	Other concentrations
RG 43	0.00	0.24	0.48	0.56	0.84	1.19	3	Other concentrations
Dispersed groups								
RG 02	1.27	1.77	2.39	2.46	2.78	3.74	14	Dispersed groups
RG 10	0.00	1.49	2.27	1.99	2.70	3.06	9	Dispersed groups
RG 18	0.98	1.06	1.25	1.52	1.35	2.95	5	Dispersed groups
RG 21	0.53	0.68	0.82	0.88	1.06	1.30	3	Dispersed groups
RG 36	0.07	0.07	1.03	1.17	2.14	2.56	4	Dispersed groups
RG 69	0.53	0.98	1.42	1.63	2.18	2.95	3	Dispersed groups

diagrams, which have, therefore, been constructed for all of the refitting groups which contain three or more pieces of flint. The results can be compared with the distributions produced by knapping experiments and with scatters on other sites, to assess the degree to which the refit groups have been dilated.

The centroid diagrams have been constructed using the method set out in Barton (1992, fig. 3.10), with the exception that the centroids have been calculated using median rather than mean values. Many of the refitting groups consist of quite tight clusters of flints with just one or two outlying pieces which occasionally lie considerable distances from the main clusters. These outlying pieces strongly affect the mean centroid, often pulling it away from the main cluster. They have much less effect, however, on the median centroid, and use of the median centroid thus makes it more likely that the centroid will be placed within the main cluster of pieces than does the mean. As a result, the diagrams based on a median centroid give a more intuitive representation of the refit distances relative to the location of the main concentration of flint than do those based on a mean centroid.

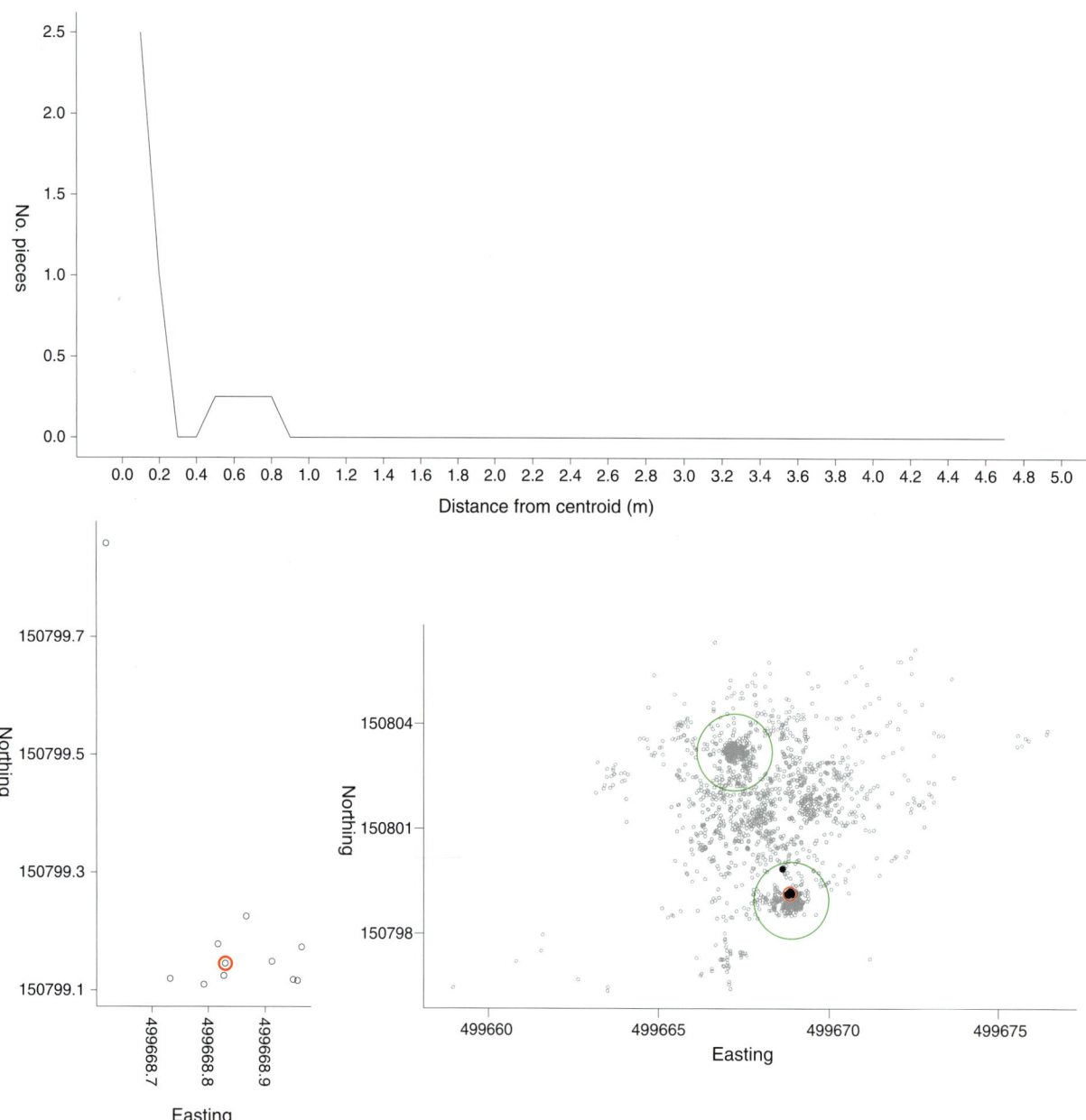

Fig. 5.25 Concentrated refitting group 9, showing the centroid diagram, a detailed plot of the group, and its location. The circles indicate the location of the two main concentrations of flint and the red points the group median centroid. (n=11)

The centroid diagrams show a running mean across four decimetres of the number of pieces of flint at specific distances from the centroid (which is represented by the origin). Plots for selected groups, alongside detailed plans of the relevant refit group and plans which show the relationship of the refit groups to the wider distribution of the flint and the two concentrations, are shown in Figures 5.25–5.34. Summary statistics for each group are shown in Table 5.3 and are represented as boxplots in Figure 5.23.

It is useful to divide the refitting groups into three categories, according to the distribution of their centroid distances (Figs 5.23–5.24). The first category consists of concentrated refitting groups, in which all of the refitting pieces are concentrated within small areas (eg Figs 5.25–5.27). These groups have small median distances, between 0.03m and 0.17m, and third quartile and maximum distances which are not much greater (between 0.07m and 0.44m for the third quartile, within which 75% of the pieces lie, and between 0.10m and 0.75m for the maximum distances). The numbers of pieces in these groups are, however, often quite small, many containing no more than three pieces. It is possible, then, that the small range of the centroid distances is partly a product of the small number of refitting pieces which it has been possible to identify.

The second category consists of concentrated refitting groups which have small numbers of

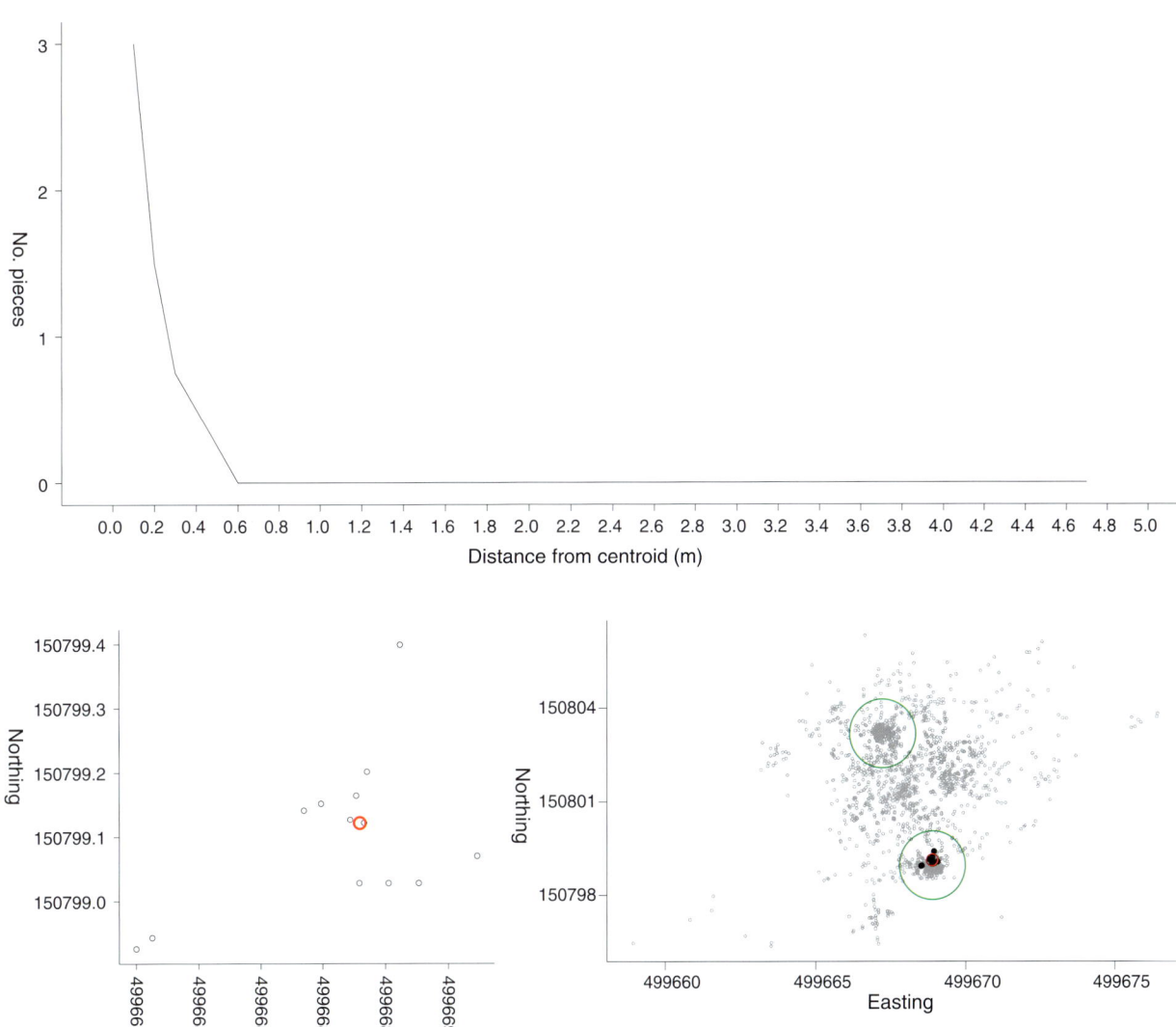

Fig. 5.26 Concentrated refitting group 7 (n=13)

outliers, often just one or two (Figs 5.28–5.32). These groups have much larger maximum centroid distances (between 1.19m and 6.08m), but the median and third quartile distances are often not much greater than those for the concentrated groups (the median ranging from 0.11m to 0.57m, and the third quartile from 0.18m to 3.31m). The large differences between the maximum distances and the median and third quartile reflect the fact that whilst most of the flint in these groups was concentrated within a small area, they also include a few pieces, sometimes tools, which were significantly further away. The groups in this set are generally larger than those which lack outliers (and include the largest group: Refit Group 1) and thus probably give a better impression of the extent to which the flint has been dilated.

The third set consists of dispersed groups, which lack any clear concentration (Figs 5.33–5.34). These groups have larger median and third quartile distances than the concentrated groups (the median ranging from 0.82m to 2.39m and the third quartile from 1.06m to 2.78m, but maximum distances (1.30m–3.74m) which are not generally larger than those of the concentrations with outliers.

The most significant observation which arises from this analysis is that much of the refitting flint remains concentrated within small areas. Whilst it is possible that fluvial processes could have concentrated flint in a particular location, the concentrated refit groups are spread across the site. Although, not surprisingly, most of the refit groups are centred in the two main concentrations, there are also other small groups elsewhere: Refit Group 3 to the south-west of Concentration 2 (Fig. 5.27), Refit Groups 14 (Fig. 5.32), 25 and 33 between the two concentrations, and others closer to the main concentrations. The preservation of such concentrations in different parts of the site suggests that any dilation is due to localised processes, such as trampling and scuffing across the site, rather than general processes such as flooding.

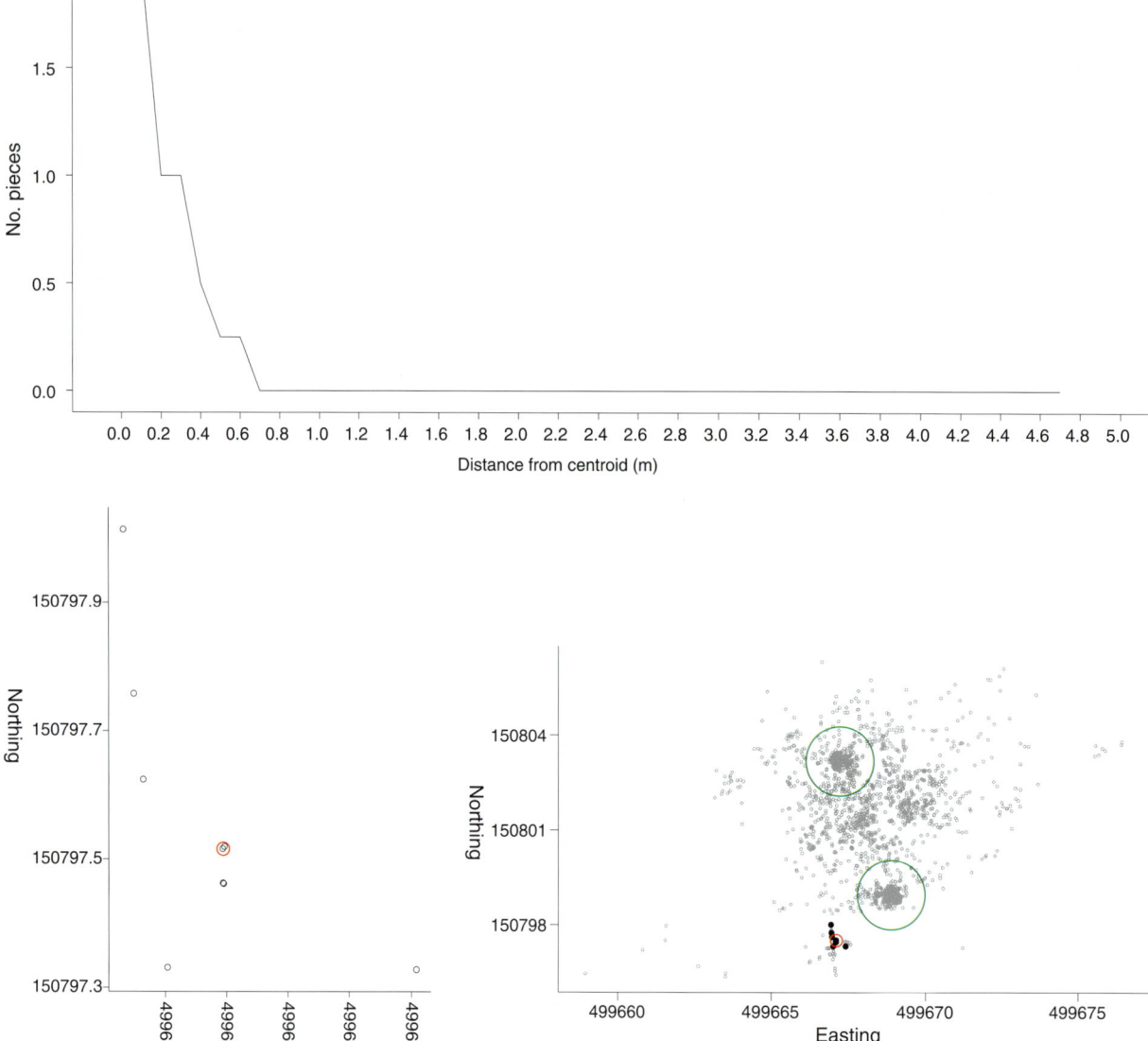

Fig. 5.27 Concentrated refitting group 3 (n=9)

The contrast between the main concentrations and the associated outlying pieces which characterises many of the larger refitting groups could correspond to the distinction made by Schick (1986, 34) between the extent of dense scatter and the wider maximum scatter which can be seen in a number of experimentally produced knapping scatters (eg Newcomer and Sieveking 1980; Kvamme 1997). This contrast can be seen particularly clearly in the largest refitting groups (RG 1 and RG 5: Figs 5.28 and 5.30). The small dimensions of the main concentrations in the groups with and without outliers are consistent with those produced by experimental knapping (Barton 1992, table 3.1), and even the slightly larger dimensions of the largest group (RG 1) are within the bounds for knapping from a raised seat or standing. Even if Refit Group 1 was produced by knapping seated on the ground, the extent of dilation would have been limited.

There are a number of ways in which the more distant outlying pieces could have been moved from the main concentrations. Some may just be small pieces which flew exceptionally far during knapping (eg Spurrell 1884, 112; Lewis Johnson 1978, 339), some could be pieces which have been moved because they were used, and others may have been scuffed across the site. The fact that only small numbers of outliers are associated with most of the refit groups again suggests that the scatters have been affected to only a limited extent by localised processes. The small number of dispersed groups (six out of a total of 39), most of which consist of only small numbers of pieces, is again

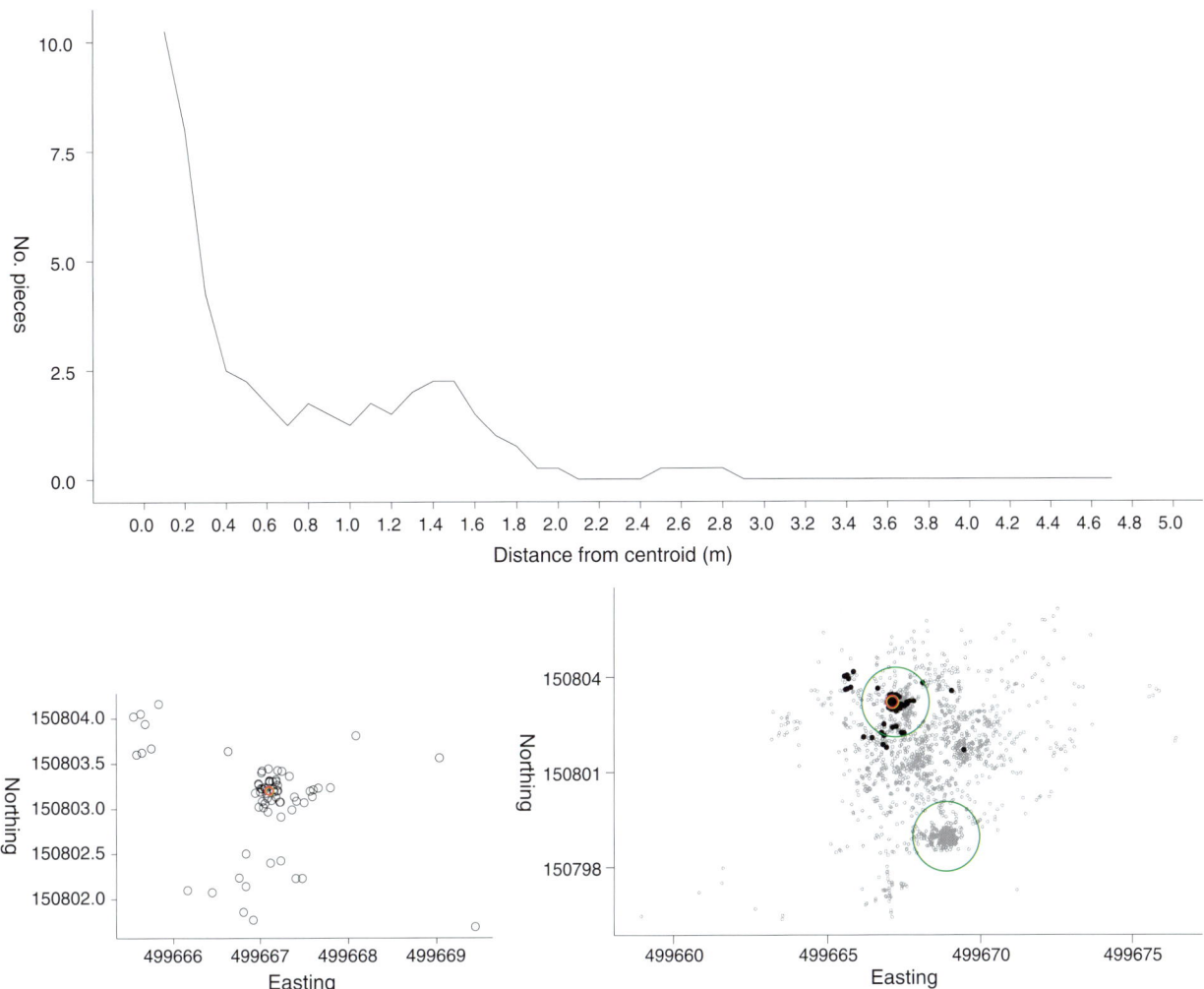

Fig. 5.28 Concentrated refitting group with outliers 1 (n=69)

consistent with only limited, localised disturbance.

Overall, then, analysis of the centroid distances suggests that flint has suffered from only limited, localised disturbance, such as might have been caused by scuffing of pieces across the site. Concentrations of refitting flint have been preserved across the site. The dimensions of these concentrations are consistent with those produced by experimental knapping and suggest only a limited degree of dilation.

CONCLUSIONS

The geoarchaeological investigations indicate that the sand deposit (G2c) from which the majority of flint was recovered lay adjacent to a river channel and was deposited by alluvial processes. Although they suggest that the distribution of the flint could have been affected by fluvial processes, the analyses presented here provide no evidence that such processes had a significant effect. They thus support the idea that the flint is still essentially *in situ*, in its primary context, and, despite evidence for vertical post-depositional movement and some localised horizontal disturbance, retains much of its original spatial structure.

The size-class distribution of the flint is consistent with experimentally produced data and suggests that all of the size classes produced by flint knapping are represented in the expected proportions and that no significant proportion of the flint, including the smaller components of the assemblage, has been removed. The refitting discussed in Chapter 6 shows that some of the end products of the flint knapping – blades – were removed from the site, but the proportion of material removed is too small to have had an appreciable effect on the size-class distribution. Artefact fabric analysis also indicates a quite planar fabric with a tendency towards being isotropic rather linear, and again provides no indication that the orientation of the flint has been affected by fluvial processes. Analysis of the orientation of refits is a less useful indicator of the effect of fluvial processes since knapping itself may produce departures from uniformity, and the numbers of refits in all but one of the refit groups are too small to produce reliable results. Again, however, the results do not provide any evidence for significant disturbance. Rather than reflecting the effects of fluvial processes, both the hot spot analysis and the centroid diagrams suggest that the

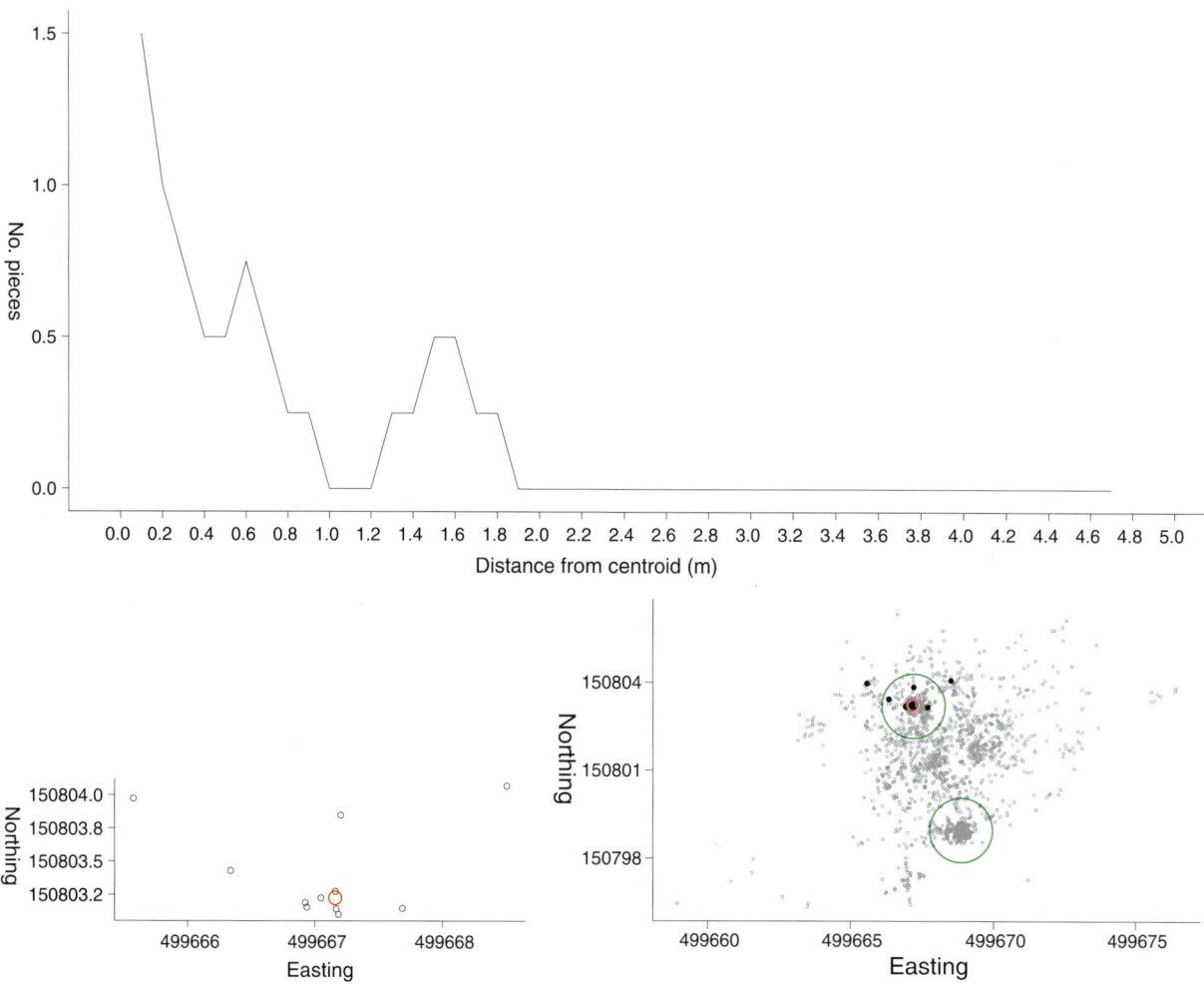

Fig. 5.29 Concentrated refitting group with outliers 4 (n=11)

horizontal distribution of the flint largely retains the patterns produced by knapping.

The geoarchaeological investigations also, however, indicate that bioturbation is likely to have affected the depth distribution of the flint and suggest that fluctuations in groundwater could also have had an effect. The effects of such post-depositional processes are clearly reflected by both the vertical distribution of the flint and the presence of a small proportion of vertically oriented flints. Although it indicates a quite planar fabric, the results of the artefact fabric analysis also suggest a degree of isotropy which may be related to bioturbation, shrink/swell processes and trampling. Although most of the flint was concentrated in a quite thin layer, overall it was distributed in a bell-shaped distribution over some depth. Analysis of the depths over which refits occur shows that differences in the depth of the flint do not reflect differences in their age but are likely to have been produced by post-depositional processes. Similar bell-shaped distributions can be produced by trampling, and whilst it is quite possible that trampling did affect the distribution of the flint, both vertically and horizontally, it has been suggested that such a distribution could have been produced by the accumulation of randomly occurring small disturbances such as might be produced by burrowing and shrink/swell processes as well as by trampling. There is, however, no indication of sorting by depth such as might be produced by freeze/thaw processes.

Despite the fact that post-depositional processes have clearly affected the vertical distribution of the flint, the analyses suggest that the horizontal distribution of the flint retains the characteristics which would be expected of *in situ* knapping scatters. The flint is concentrated in two small areas set approximately 4m apart, which appear to have been related to the two main locations in which flint was knapped. The density of flint within these concentrations was very high over areas with diameters of just 0.6m and 0.8m but falls very rapidly with distance. The hot spot analysis has also revealed spatial patterning which is consistent with the idea that much of the flint derives from knapping and has suffered relatively little dilation. The smallest pieces of flint, including relatively high proportions of chips and small debitage, were densest in the two main concentrations. Smaller than average pieces

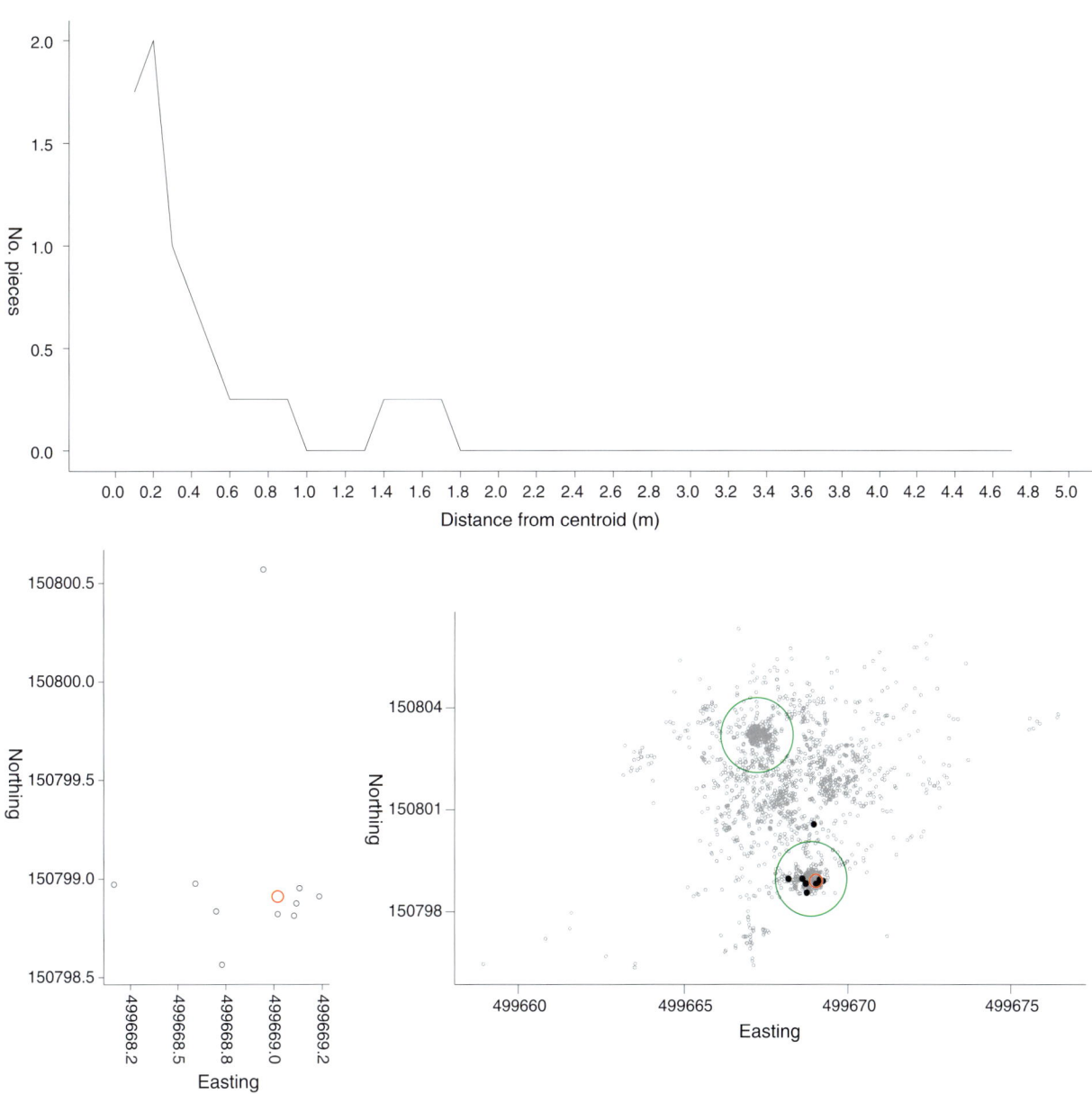

Fig. 5.30 Concentrated refitting group with outliers 5 (n=11)

were also spread between the two concentrations, but the larger pieces, including a high proportion of the cores and crested pieces, were distributed around and beside the two concentrations, in a pattern which could reflect the way in which the knappers sat, the small debitage having fallen in front of them whilst some of the larger pieces were placed beside them (cf Binford 1986, 553; Binford and O'Connell 1984, 409, fig. 3). Analysis of the refitting groups also, however, suggests that knapping was not just focused on the two concentrations but also occurred on a more limited scale in nearby locations. One striking example is provided by the evidence, discussed in Chapter 6, for the possible presence of an apprentice knapper adjacent to the north-western concentration.

Analysis of the distances between refitting pieces using centroid diagrams also shows that whilst many of the refitting pieces were concentrated within short distances of each other, a small proportion had been dispersed over distances up to 6m (although usually much less). In part, this pattern may simply be a product of knapping which typically produces a dense scatter adjacent to the knapper and a wider, less dense area of 'maximum scatter'. It is possible that some small pieces of flint may have flown quite large distances during knapping. There is, however, also evidence which suggests that a number of other processes may have contributed to the dispersal of the artefacts.

Evidence discussed in the following chapters suggests that other stages of tool production were represented at the site, including hafting and tool resharpening/replacement. These activities could also have affected the distribution of the artefacts. For example, the distribution of backed blades and

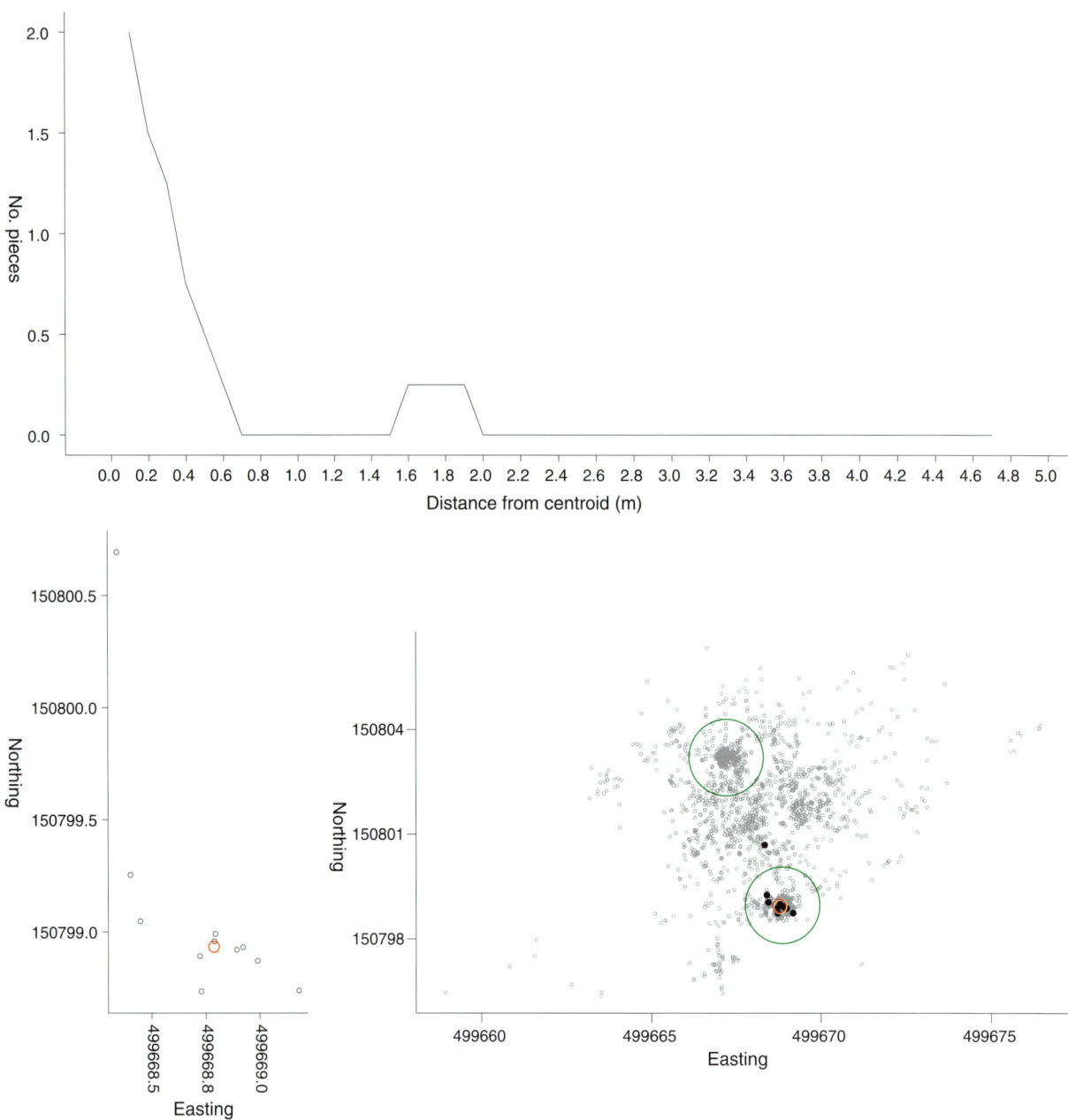

Fig. 5.31 Concentrated refitting group with outliers 8 (n=11)

points (mainly tool fragments) is concentrated in the area of the north-western concentration, adjacent to the possible hearth. These tools show a high proportion of heating compared to other tool types. This suggests that broken projectile tips may have been removed and replaced close to the hearth, perhaps so that the heat from the hearth could be used to soften an adhesive used in hafting. This type of activity would be consistent with observations made by Binford in the 1980s of an Australian Aboriginal camp where men sat beside a fire whilst warming resin to haft stone knives (1983, 150; 1986, 548–51).

It is also clear that the flint does not all derive directly from knapping and tool production, but also from the use and eventual discard of tools. The functional analysis reported below shows that the flint had been used for a variety of tasks including hide working and working plant and hard animal materials. The deposition of the flint thus involved at least two operational routes: one related to the production of tools, and the other to their discard after use. Since the production of flint blanks for tools produces large quantities of debitage, the majority of the flint almost certainly derives from the first route, and the overall spatial distribution of the flint is thus largely a product of this route. The deposition of flint via the second route – through use and discard after use – is likely, however, to account for some of the dispersal of the flint. The lithic analysis and refitting discussed in the next chapter shows that the reworking of tools was also

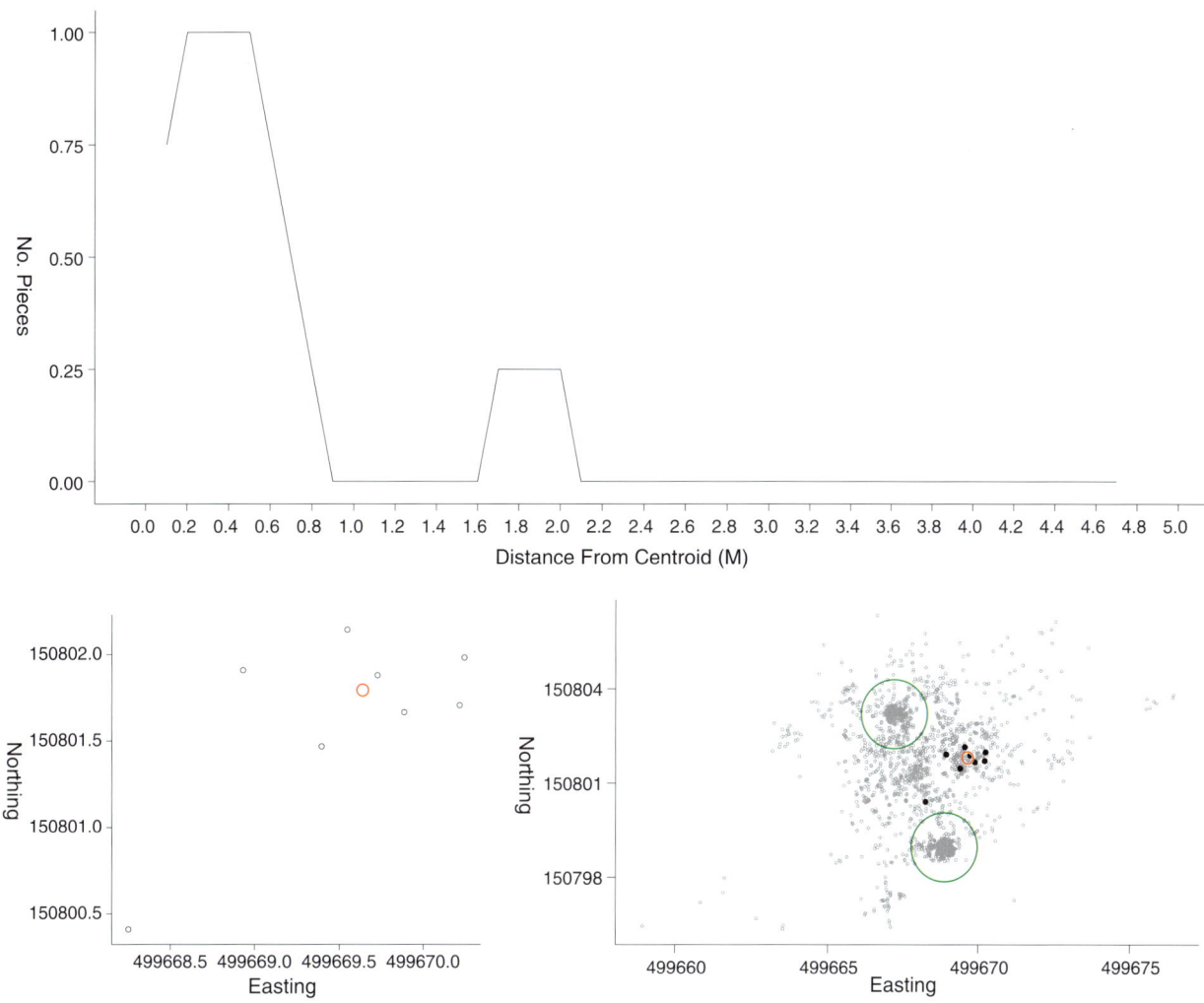

Fig. 5.32 Concentrated refitting group with outliers 14 (n=8)

represented. As has been noted above, it is likely that some of the flint was also dispersed by trampling and scuffing. The analysis presented above suggests, however, that the effects of any such processes were localised and of limited extent.

Overall, the analyses presented in this chapter provide no evidence that fluvial processes have affected the distribution of the flint artefacts. Whilst they do indicate that bioturbation and shrink/swell processes probably have affected the vertical distribution and dip of the flint, the horizontal distribution retains much of the structure which would be expected of *in situ* knapping scatters. Although the spatial distribution of the flint artefacts is likely to be largely a product of flint knapping carried out on the site, it also provides evidence for other activities including the presence of a hearth and the manufacture, use, reworking and discard of tools.

Guildford Fire Station

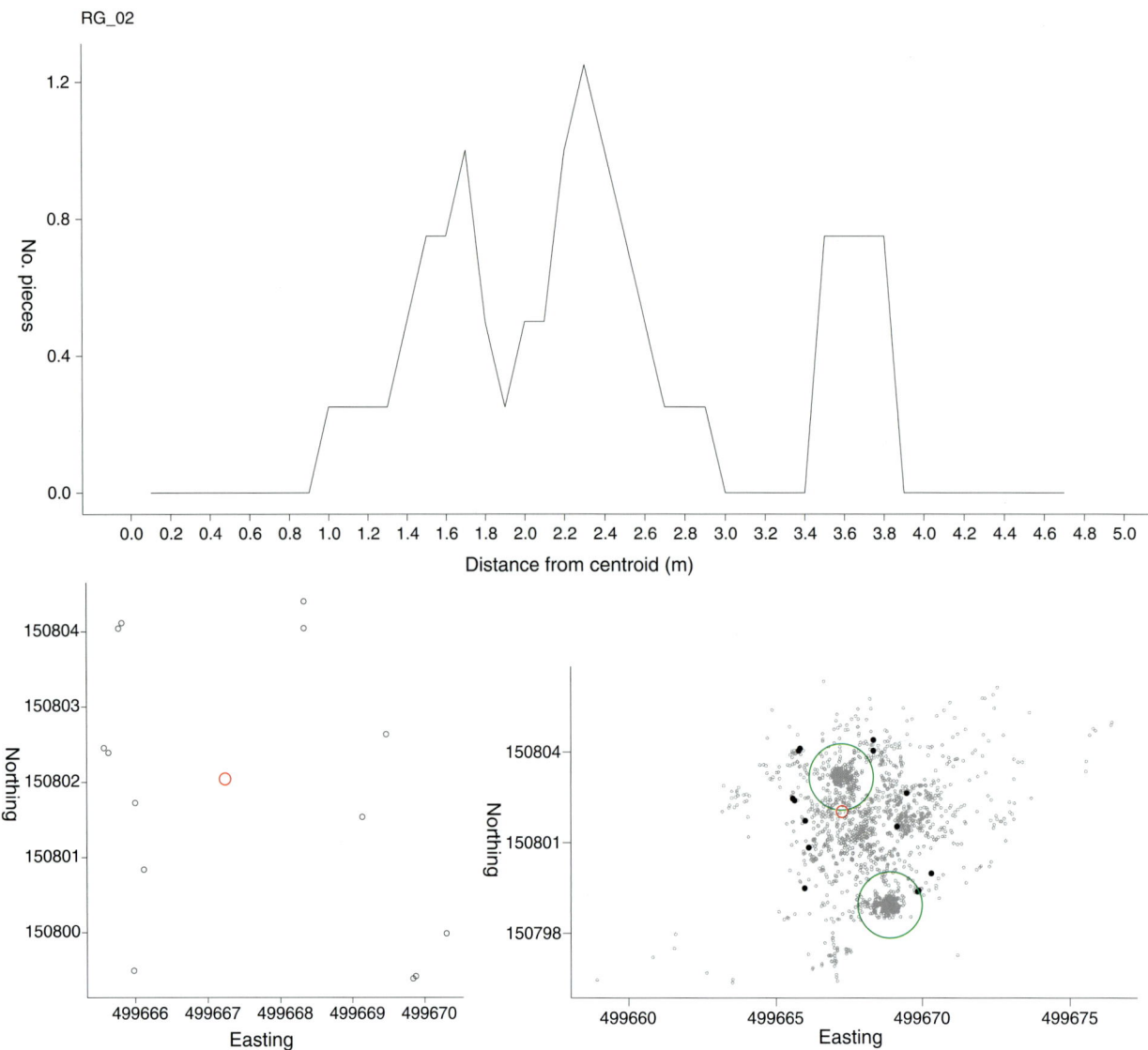

Fig. 5.33 Dispersed refitting group 2 (n=14)

Chapter 5

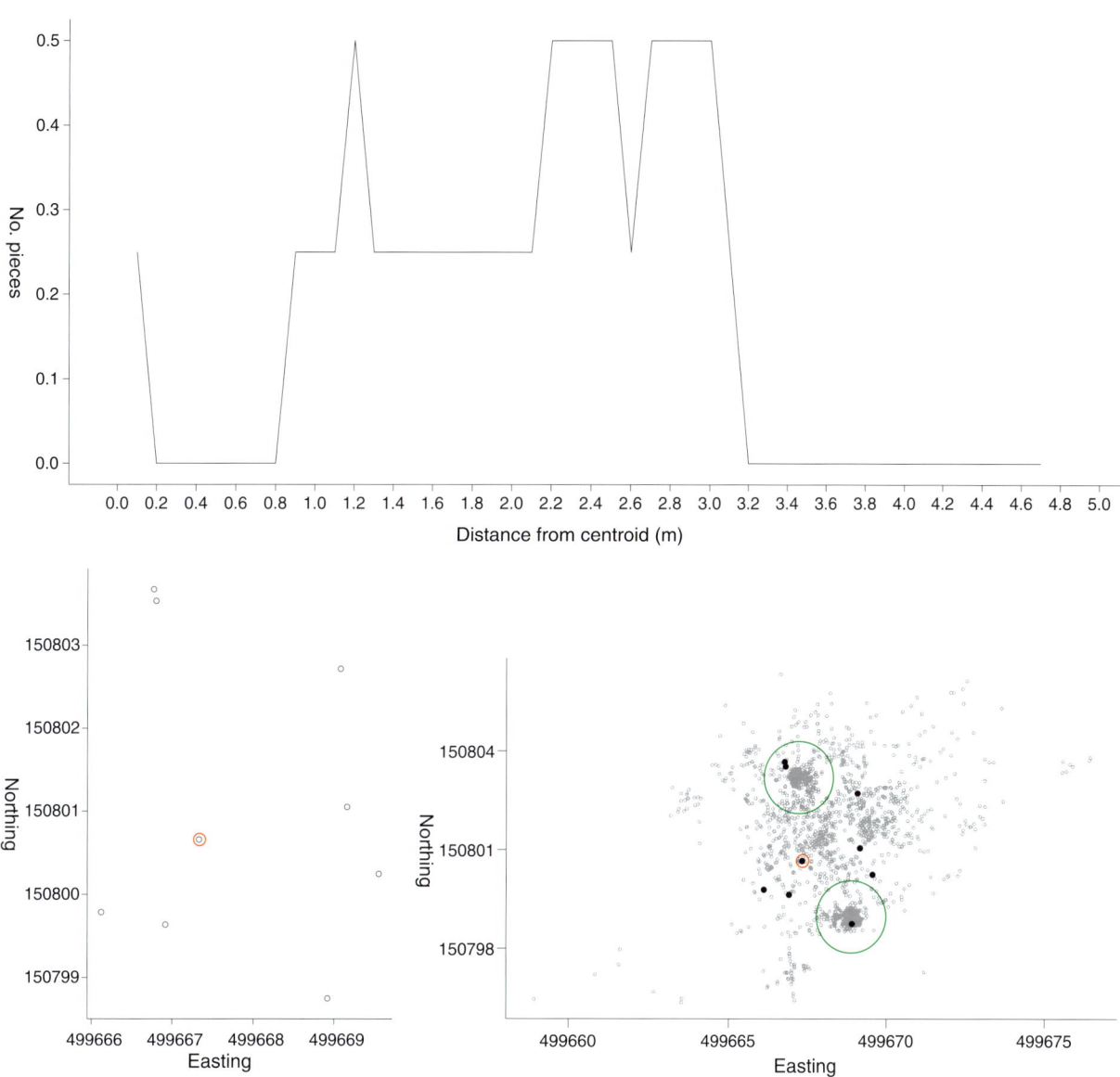

Fig. 5.34 Dispersed refitting group 10 (n=9)

Chapter 6

The lithic assemblage

by Alison Roberts and Nick Barton with Mike Donnelly and Simon Collcutt

INTRODUCTION

It became apparent early in the excavation that the artefacts were in exceptionally fresh, unabraded condition, with only light surface patination. As a result, every effort was made to retrieve the finds in pristine condition with artefacts often bagged with sediment still adhering, and the excavation strategy was specifically designed to maximise information that could be recovered. Initial assessment of the flint assemblage took place in early March 2014, and recommended that a detailed synthetic analysis of the lithic assemblage (refitting, spatial and microwear studies) should be a priority for the post-excavation analysis. The microwear analysis took place at the University of Liège in 2016, and the full results are presented in Chapter 7. While this work was in progress, Mike Donnelly assessed the artefacts recovered from the sieved samples. The complete flint assemblage was then submitted for cataloguing, refitting and spatial studies at the Ashmolean Museum by Alison Roberts and Nick Barton. This work took place in 2018. Simon Collcutt assisted with the refitting and assessed the stone objects recovered from the site. An additional phase of refitting by Alison Roberts took place in late 2019 as part of an agreed sabbatical work programme from the Ashmolean. A final phase of checking took place in 2023.

The Late Upper Palaeolithic assemblage can be shown to be typologically and technologically homogeneous and to contain all the different stages of flint manufacture apart from initial extraction and nodule testing. The assemblage also includes a high proportion of small debitage (<10mm) and chips (<5mm) that are characteristic of *in situ* knapping activity. Within the overall spread of artefacts two knapping concentrations located about 3–4m apart can be identified (Figs 6.1–6.2). One cluster can be seen to the north (northern concentration/concentration 1) and the other in the south (southern concentration/concentration 2). The presence of the two concentrations is highlighted by the related distributions of cores and related material (Fig. 6.5) and by the presence of artefacts with high proportions of cortex on their dorsal surfaces (Fig. 6.3).

Indeed, pieces with more than 60% cortex are clearly focused in these two clusters, particularly in the southern cluster. This gives a high probability that the early stages of core preparation took place there. Refitting analysis also confirms that flint core preparation, reduction and rejuvenation were focused in each of the concentrations. Of the primary knapping outputs it is clear that blade production was the main focus of activity at the site, and that some blades made there were exported elsewhere. The retouched tool assemblage demonstrates that various activities also took place at the site, and that this occurred mainly in the area around the knapping foci. The site assemblage also contains a minor component of material of later age, most of which was recovered from the surface in the initial stages of site assessment and from areas outside the main Late Upper Palaeolithic lithic scatters.

RAW MATERIAL

The predominant flint raw material in the Late Upper Palaeolithic lithic assemblage is a high-quality translucent to semi-translucent black/grey flint. Small white speckles are commonly visible in this flint, and some small fossil inclusions also occur (for example, close to cortical surfaces). Where cortex survives it usually has the characteristics of slightly weathered flint nodules derived from the Chalk. Some of the best-quality flint found at the site is a black-grey flint with internal reddish tinges, and about 14% of the formal tools are made of this material although it makes up under 1% of the assemblage as a whole.

The site is located in a relatively low-lying position close to the present-day River Wey, 2km downstream from a 'gap' where the river cuts through the North Downs chalk escarpment in a narrow steep-sided valley (Fig. 1.2). It is presumed that most of the flint used at the site originated from nodules eroded from the local chalk by river action. As the river flows north from the 'gap' to the location of the Guildford Late Upper Palaeolithic site it cuts though deposits of the Lower, Middle and Upper Chalk formations (Fig. 1.3; BGS 2001).

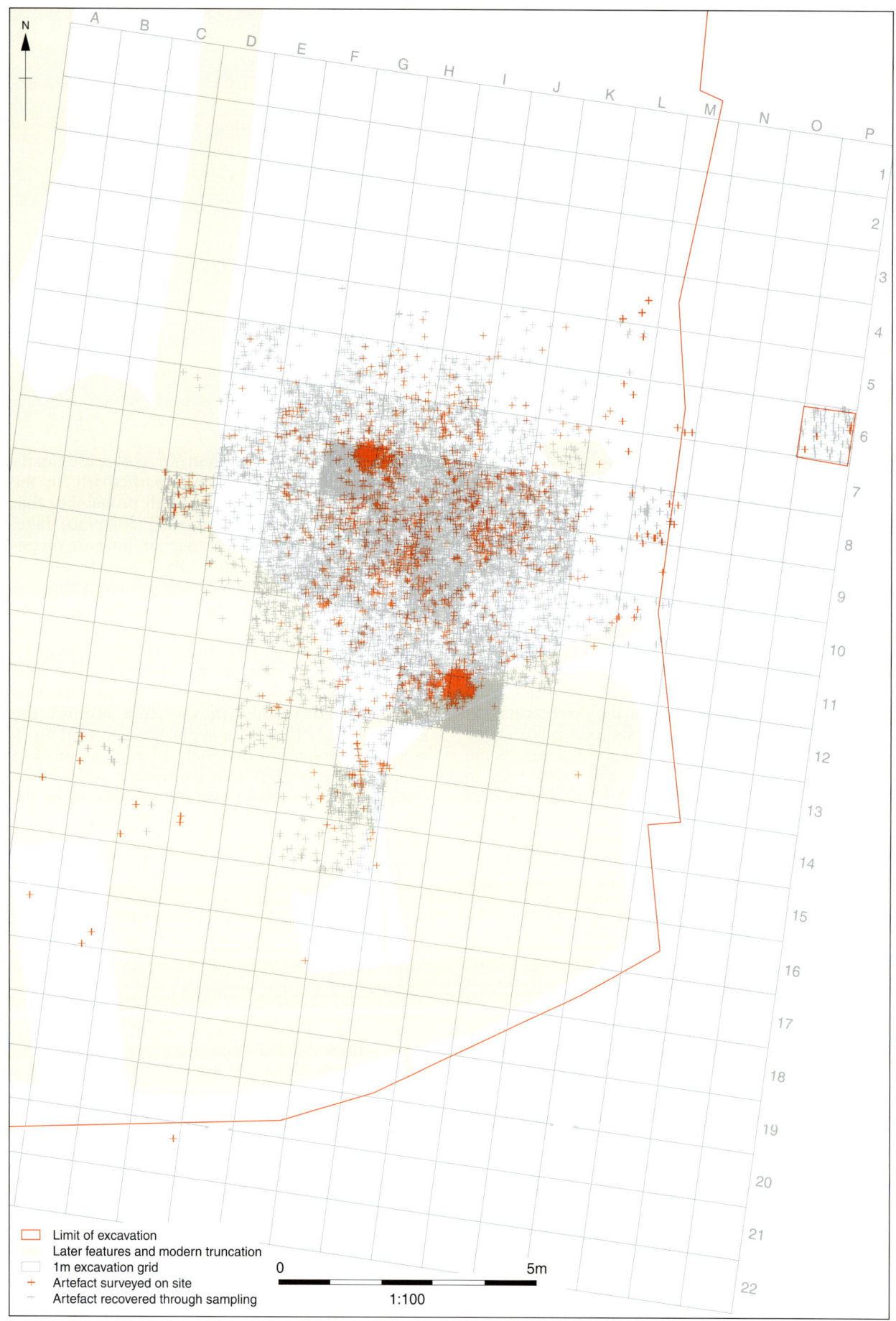

Fig. 6.1 Overall distribution of all artefacts. Artefacts recovered from samples have been located randomly within their grid squares

Chapter 6

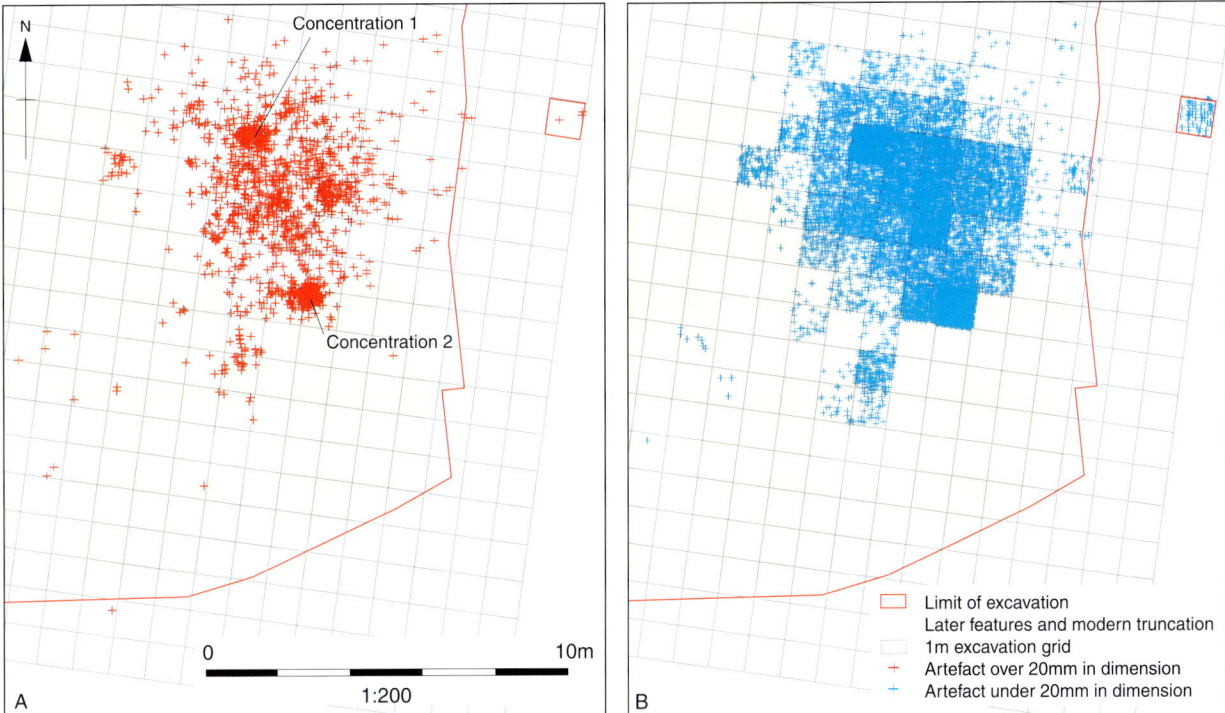

Fig. 6.2 Overall distribution of artefacts (A) over 20mm in length and (B) under 20mm in length

Of these, the Seaford Chalk Member of the Upper Chalk formation is probably the most likely original source for the nodules of flint used at the site. Flint nodules for knapping could have been collected directly from the area where they were exposed by river action, or from closer to the site if they had been washed downstream. Other possible sources of flint nodules in the area would include Clay-with-flints deposits about 4km from the site and other exposures of the Chalk. However, use of these sources seems unlikely given the proximity of the easily accessible river exposures of flint nodules near the Guildford site — indeed the availability of flint could perhaps provide one rationale for the choice of the Late Upper Palaeolithic site location.

Flint that is heavily weathered and of inferior knapping quality is known from the solifluced gravels immediately underlying the occupation layer, but it appears that this was rarely, if ever, exploited. One core and a few artefacts appear to have been made on a flint river cobble. This material could have been collected directly from the River Wey gravels. There is also a small group of material made of a grey-white flint that is often patinated and/or weathered. These artefacts appear to be mainly post-Palaeolithic in age, and the source of this raw material is unknown.

THE DEBITAGE ASSEMBLAGE

Classification

The lithic artefacts from the assemblage were catalogued according to the standard methodology for defining Upper Palaeolithic and Mesolithic assemblages in England (as described in Barton 1992). The unmodified waste, also known as debitage, was divided into two basic groups for cataloguing: cores and core preparation/rejuvenation pieces, and other debitage products. The latter consists of flakes, blades and bladelets; debris (irregular waste or shatter); and smaller debitage, including chips (henceforth 'small debitage'). The retouched tools and modified pieces are discussed in a following section. Table 6.1 shows the basic composition of the entire lithic assemblage in terms of actual numbers, actual percentages, and percentages not including the small debitage. The latter percentage figure is provided for ease of comparison with assemblages that lack the information about small debitage. Only 1.9% of the assemblage is burnt (297); most of this was recovered from the northern part of the site (Fig. 6.4).

Cores and core rejuvenation pieces

Blade cores

Most of the cores recovered at the site are Late Upper Palaeolithic blade cores (7) or fragments of such pieces (5; Table 6.2). There are four single-platform blade cores, all with faceted or partially faceted platforms and evidence of cresting at the back of the core (c.504, c.945, c.1094 and c.1940). Three have faceted or partially faceted platforms, while c.504 has plain platforms. All have the remains of some bidirectional removals suggesting that they may at some point have had an opposed platform, probably to control the flaking face.

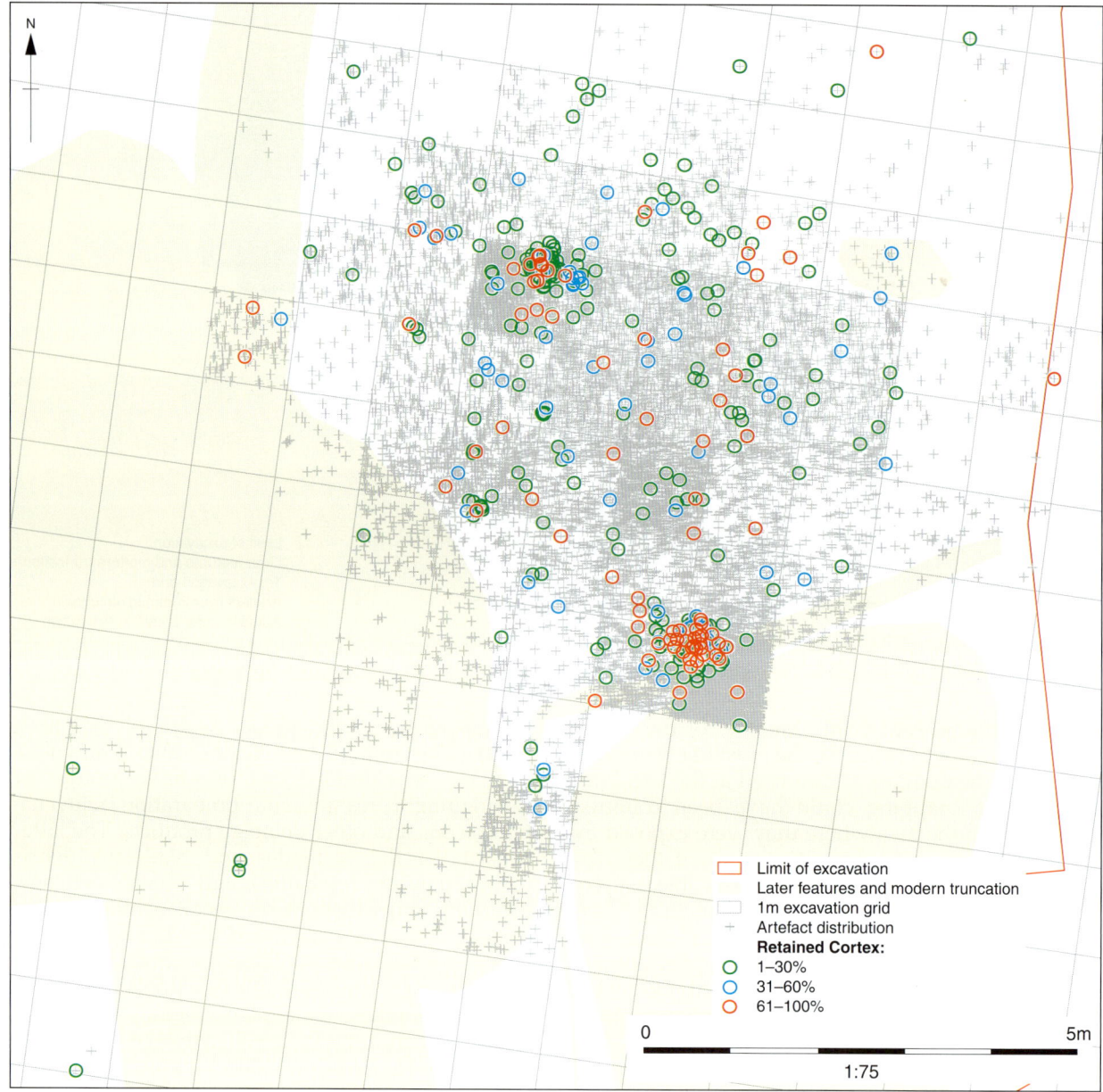

Fig. 6.3 Distribution of artefacts retaining cortex on the dorsal surface

Three of these cores have significant refitting elements: c.504 is part of refit group (RG) 01, c.1094 of RG 13, and c.1940 of RG 05. The distribution of the individual refit groups is discussed later in this chapter. Core c.945 has a single refitting flake fragment on the back of the core and is from the northern concentration (Fig. 6.6; RG 68).

Of the seven blade cores identifiable to type, three have opposed platforms, all faceted (c.1195, c.1399 and c.2353). In each case one platform appears to be related to controlling removals on the flaking face. Two of these cores are from the southern concentration, and one is unlocated (c.1399). All three have refitting elements: core c.1195 is part of RG 20; c.1399 of RG 4; and c.2353 of RG 17.

There are also five substantial fragments of cores. Three of these fragments are clearly from blade cores and are part of refit groups located near to the southern concentration. Core fragment c.675 is part of RG 10, c.1171 of RG 5, and c.2542 of RG 03. The two other fragments, c.305 and c.2435, only refit each other and a piece of irregular waste and were found some distance from each other (RG 35). These two fragments seem to be related to the initial phase of preparation of some form of a core. (Further information about the refit groups is provided below.)

From a production point of view the blade cores seem to be exhausted and at the end of their usable life for blade production. They have mainly prismatic forms and are of similar sizes, with median dimensions of about 65mm length, 50mm breadth and 45mm thickness. None of the core platform edges preserves evidence of abrasion, although the use of this technique can be seen earlier in the knapping sequence, especially in relation to blade manufacture. The scars from the

Table 6.1 Overall assemblage composition (artefact class by number and percentage). Not including natural (319), organic (11) and post-Upper Palaeolithic (16) objects

	Number	%	% less small debitage
Cores (8) and core fragments (5)	13	0.1	0.3
Core rejuvenation (128) and crested pieces (57) *	185	1.2	4.2
Blades and blade fragments, unretouched	593	3.9	13.6
Bladelets and bladelet fragments, unretouched	555	3.6	12.7
Flakes and flake fragments, unretouched	2236	14.6	51.4
Knapping debris (irregular waste)	474	3.1	10.9
Small debitage and chips	11,004	71.6	
Unclassified	14	0.1	0.3
Retouched tools and tool fragments (235) and tool debitage (54) *	289	1.9	6.6
Total	15,357		4353

* Six tools were made on core rejuvenation (2) or crested (4) pieces and also have been counted in the tools category

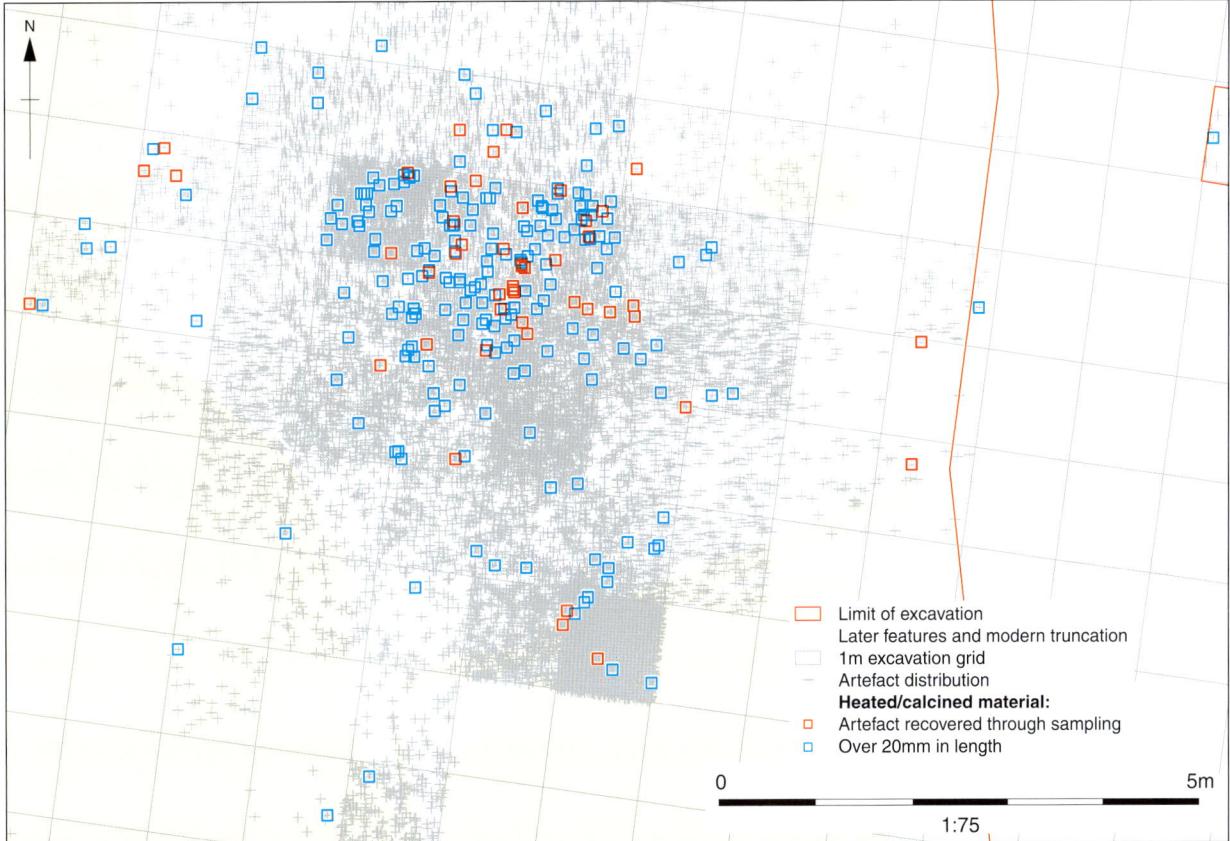

Fig. 6.4 Overall distribution of heated/calcined material

Table 6.2 Cores, core rejuvenators, and crested pieces

	Number
Blade core, one platform	4
Blade core, two platforms, opposed	3
Flake core, one platform	1
Core fragments	5
Core rejuvenation pieces: platform (100), other (23)	123
Crested pieces	56

final removals from the cores have widths of both blade (12mm and over) and flake proportions. Refit Group 13, with a refitting sequence of core modification and preparation removals, demonstrates the extensive use of one of the blade cores (c.1094) before it was abandoned (Figs 6.59–6.60). There are no specific bladelet cores in the Late Upper Palaeolithic assemblage, and bladelets found at the site appear to be by-products rather than the objective of blade manufacture. The assemblage contains no tested nodules or cores abandoned in the initial stages of use. In total five of the blade cores and core fragments derive from the northern concentra-

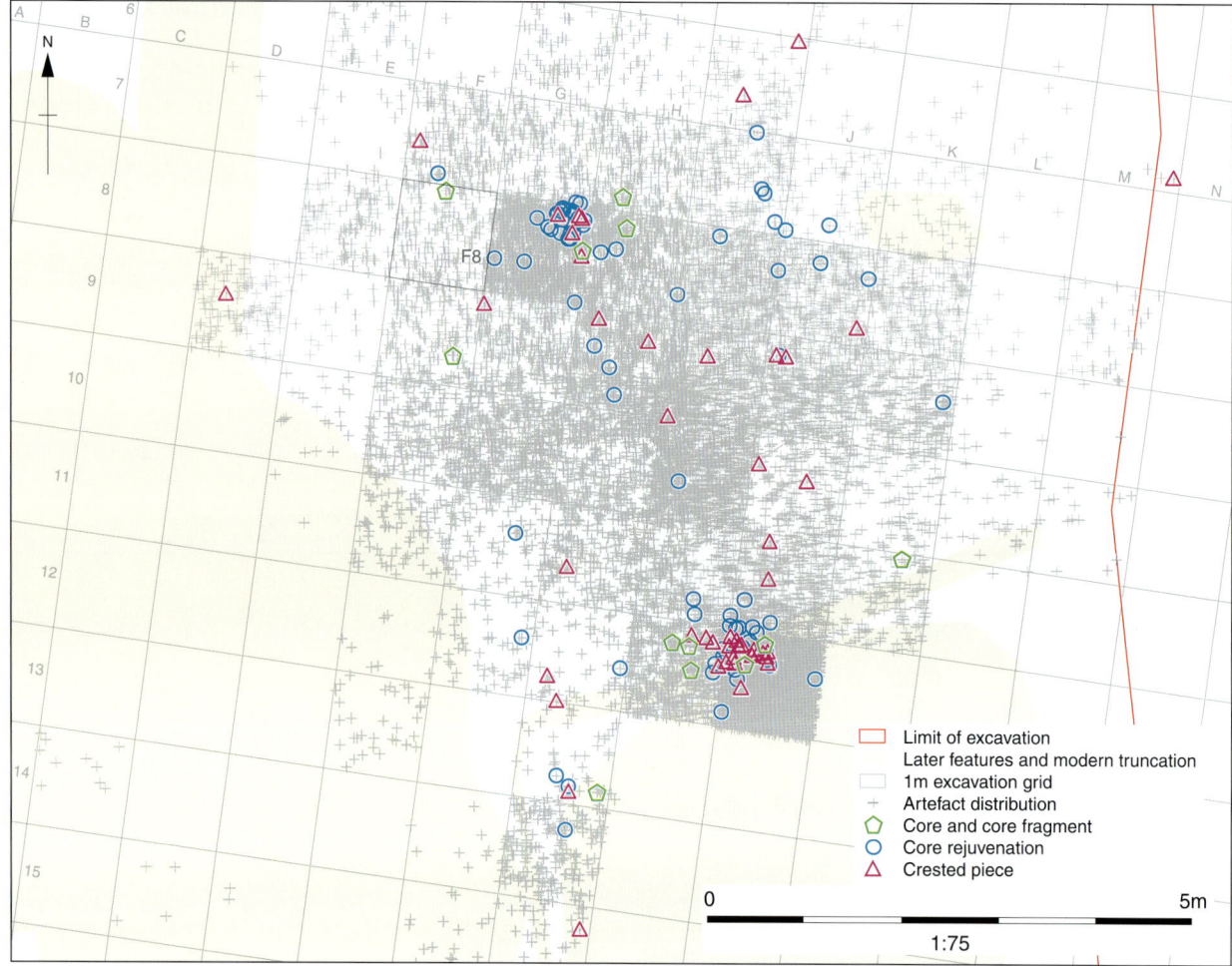

Fig. 6.5 Distribution of cores and core manufacturing/modifying waste

tion and five from the southern concentration. Two are unlocated. None of the artefacts in this category show traces of burning.

The distribution of the blade cores and core fragments shows that with one exception they were all located in or were closely linked with the two concentrations (Fig. 6.5). The one exception is core fragment c.2435, which was found with a refitting piece of irregular waste on the surface just southwest of the southern concentration (RG 35). The only other refitting element of this small refit group is another core fragment located in the northern concentration. There are no cores or core fragments in the activity area between the two concentrations.

Flake core

A single flake core, c.1905, was found close to the northern concentration (square F8). It has a single platform, a cortical back and an unprepared plain platform. It forms part of a refit group of seven artefacts (RG 06; Figs 6.45–6.46) and appears to have been abandoned at an early stage of knapping. It differs from the other cores both in that it was made from a river cobble and because the knapper apparently had a lower level of flint working skill than is displayed elsewhere in the assemblage. The core and the elements of its refit group are well integrated with the northern knapping concentration, and it is considered most likely to be the work of a novice flintknapper, perhaps a child (Roberts and Barton 2021).

Crested pieces

There are 57 crested pieces in the assemblage, over half being parts mainly of crested blades (35). Two thirds of the crested pieces with coordinates can be related to the southern concentration, and the others to the northern concentration or northern part of the site. Only one small distal fragment of a crested flake is burnt (c.1698). The crested material includes four pieces that were used as tools: a truncation burin on a crested blade (c.2207), two edge-damaged crested blades (c.1093, part of RG 67; and c.1757) and a crested blade with retouch at the tip (c1473, part of RG 53). Three of the tools were found in the southern concentration, and the burin was found in the northern part of the site. Nineteen of the crested pieces form parts of refitted groups: RGs 01, 03, 05, 12, 13, 15, 17, 24, 32, 53, 55, 67 and 81.

Cresting is a technique used in blade production to shape and maintain the core face, and 68% of the crested pieces in the Late Upper Palaeolithic assemblage have blade dimensions. Most of the crested pieces have unidirectional crests, most often to the right, with only occasional examples of bidirectional crests (eg c.1085–6, c.1668 and c.1870). Direct evidence of cresting can be observed on the backs of the blade cores. Refitting evidence shows that the technique was also used at the front of cores to prepare the core for blade manufacture, and to repair the flaking face. For example, crested flake c.103 appears to be a core correction from the opposed (non-preferential) end of a blade core. The technique was also used occasionally at the side of cores (eg core c.945; Fig. 6.6), perhaps also as a means of maintaining the flaking face. The debitage also contains examples of blades and flakes that are secondary crests or 'sous crêtes' that underlie the primary crest and preserve traces of cresting on their dorsal surface (for example see RG 53 and RG 81: Figs 6.84 and 6.90). These were not systematically counted but are unlikely to have been confused with unidirectionally crested examples where dorsal removal scars are well preserved.

The distribution of the crested pieces shows that they occur both within the two knapping concentrations and in the activity area between them (Fig. 6.5). Of the four tools on crested blades, the truncation burin, c.2207, was found close to the surface several metres away from the main Upper Palaeolithic site and the other three were found in or close to the southern concentration.

Core rejuvenation flakes

There are 128 core rejuvenation flakes in the assemblage, of which 106 (83%) are platform rejuvenation flakes. The others are off the core edge or flaking face. Some of the platform rejuvenators are large, with lengths of up to 94.1mm (c.1193) and have been used to remove the entire top of a core to completely refresh the platform (cf core tablet). Others are very small with lengths under 10mm. The majority of the platform rejuvenation flakes were used to make minor modifications to a platform during blade production. This technique is also reflected in the high proportion of faceted and dihedral butts seen in the blade(let) and flake categories (Table 6.3). About 20% of the core platform rejuvenators appear broken, but this may be an overestimate as refitting shows that some apparent breaks are instead step terminations. Only two are burnt, both from the northern part of the site. The median dimensions for platform rejuvenators are 31mm by 30mm by 8mm.

Tools have been made on three core rejuvenation flakes: a piercer (c.1428), a notched piece (c.1725) and one with significant edge damage (c.4685). Fifty-two of the core rejuvenation flakes form part of refit groups (belonging to 21 different RGs). Most of the refit groups contain 1–4 core rejuvenation flakes, but RG 8 contains 9 and RG 13 contains 6. Not unexpectedly, the distribution of core rejuvenation flakes shows that the greatest concentrations were in the two main knapping scatters near to the cores (Fig. 6.5). There was no difference in the distribution of platform and other rejuvenation flakes.

The distribution of the core rejuvenation flakes shows that they occur both within the two knapping concentrations and in the activity area between them (Fig. 6.5). The three tools were located either in the northern scatter (c.1725) or outside it (c.1428 and c.4685).

Flakes, blades and bladelets

Cataloguing of the Late Upper Palaeolithic assemblage included recording a series of basic attributes for all artefacts, and more detailed information for tools and debitage other than small debitage and chips. Flakes, blades and bladelets are distinguished by different length/width ratios: flakes have a length/width ratio of approximately 1:1, whilst blades have a length/width ratio of at least 2:1 (de Sonneville-Bordes 1960; Whittaker 1994). Bladelets are small blades with a width of less than 12mm (Barton 1992; Tixier 1963). These artefact categories are the primary debitage products at the site and provide essential information about the knapping reduction methodology and other related behavioural aspects (collectively referred to as the *chaîne opératoire*). The basic attributes recorded for debitage included: artefact type, completeness, thermal damage (burning), condition, patination, cortex presence and type, and flint raw material. More detailed attributes recorded for selected examples included: basic dimensions and weight, butt type, platform abrasion, distal termination, blank profile and direction of dorsal scars. In addition, where possible, an assessment was made regarding flaking mode (hard stone, soft stone, or soft organic hammer type; Ohnuma and Bergman 1982; Pelegrin 2000). Table 6.3 summarises the attributes recorded for all flakes, blades and bladelets.

Blades

The assemblage contains 755 blades and blade fragments, 162 of which have been retouched or modified (22%). Thirty-six pieces are burnt (5%), and of these 14 are tools or tool fragments made on blades. There are 244 complete, unmodified blades, some of which have been reconstructed from refitting fragments (break refits). Based on this sample the mean dimensions and standard deviations for blades are: length 60.2 ± 17.4mm, width 21.2 ± 7.2mm, and thickness 5.6 ± 3.2mm.

Butt types (striking platform features) for the blade assemblage as a whole are dominated by plain and linear examples (57%), with a higher proportion of faceted and dihedral types (25.5%)

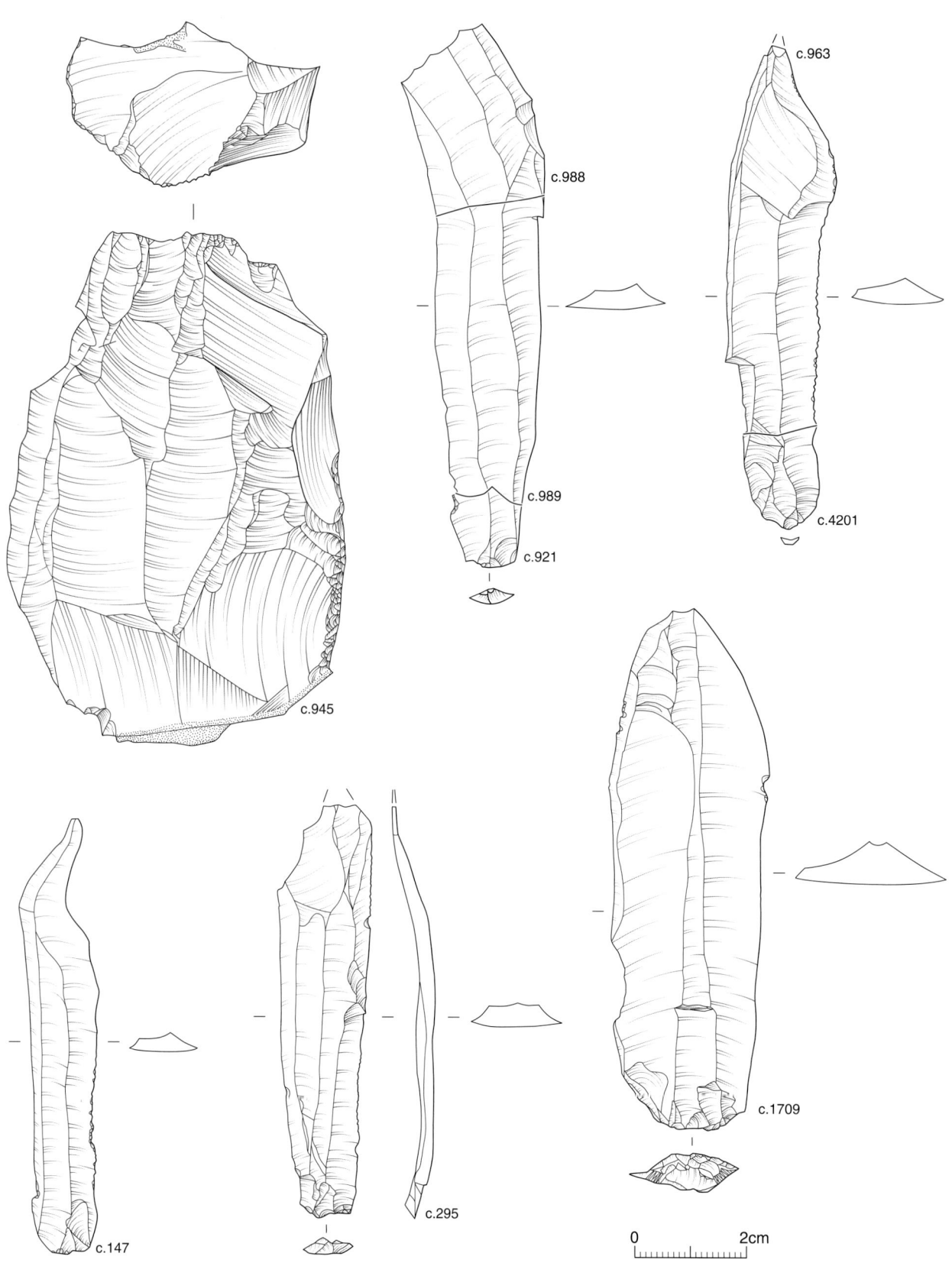

Fig. 6.6 Single platform blade core (c.945) and blade debitage with isolated en éperon*-like platforms (c.921/c.989/c.988; c.295), linear platform (c.147), large plain platform (c.1709), and punctiform platform (c.4201).*

Table 6.3 Flakes, blades and bladelets, not including core rejuvenation pieces: qualitative attributes

Attribute	Blades	Bladelets	Flakes
Complete (or refitted)	22%	13%	61%
Retouched/modified (excluding tool waste)	22%	1.5%	7%
Formal tools	11%	0.5%	3%
Burning/thermal damage	5%	2%	2%
Butt type (classifiable)			
Faceted (including isolated)	19.5%	6%	10%
Dihedral	6%	0%	5.5%
Plain and linear	57%	65%	67%
Punctiform	3%	18.5%	5.5%
Cortical	1%	3%	4%
Indeterminate (damaged or modified)	13%	8%	8%
Platform abrasion (presence)	59%	43%	24%
Flaking mode (classifiable)			
Hard hammer	5%	0%	4%
Soft stone hammer	84%	68%	67%
Soft hammer	11%	32%	29%
Distal termination (classifiable)			
Feathered	61%	77%	67%
Hinge fracture	18%	13%	24%
Step fracture	21%	10%	16%
Profile (classifiable)			
Straight	59%	79%	54%
Curved	38%	19%	35%
Twisted/irregular	3%	2%	11%
Dorsal scars (classifiable)			
Single	74%	91%	60%
Crossed	9%	5%	19%
Opposed	13%	1%	3%
Multi-directional	<1%	0%	6%
Indeterminate and irregular	3%	3%	12%
Cortex type (presence)			
Chalk (slight weathering)	98%	82%	93%
Pebble/cobble	2%	18%	7%
Cortex proportion			
0%	72%	89%	57%
1–30%	22%	9%	26%
31–60%	5%	<1%	7%
61–100%	<1%	2%	10%
Total number	755	566	2289

than for flakes (15.5%) and bladelets (6%). Within the faceted category are 19 examples in which the platform has been isolated in a manner similar, but not exactly identical, to the *en éperon* technique (Fig. 6.6; see Chapter 8). Eight of the blades with this butt feature were made into tools (89%), three with *rasante* (scalar) retouch. Blades with small plain punctiform butts also make up a significant proportion of all blade tools where this could be determined (14%). Figure 6.7 shows the distribution of butt types for blades. Plain cortical butts were unsurprisingly located mainly in the two knapping concentrations and are consistent with core preparation and maintenance activities. Both blades with plain (non-cortical) and dihedral/faceted butts were distributed across the site, in both knapping scatters and in the areas in between. Interestingly, the blades displaying small, isolated butts were distributed almost exclusively in the area between the two concentrations, and especially close to the northern concentration, while three were found in the centre of the southern concentration. This perhaps indicates that the technique was employed by the knapper in the southern concentration, but the resulting blades were often used or moved into the northern part of the site.

Platform abrasion is found on just over half of the blades (59%), indicating careful preparation of platforms during blade manufacture. The number of blades detached with a hard hammer (5%) is lower than those detached with a soft stone (84%) or soft organic hammer (11%). The dominance of the soft stone knapping mode indicates that this was the preferred method of knapping at the site. Distal terminations of blades are mainly feathered (61%), with fewer hinge (18%) or step fractures/breaks (21%). The similarity of these proportions for both blades and flakes suggests that a similar method of knapping was used for both types of removals. There seems to be no association between distal termination type and location on the site. There are higher numbers of blades with straight profiles (59%) than with curved (38%) or twisted/irregular (3%) profiles. Similar proportions of straight to curved profiles also occur for the retouched blades and do not seem to be related to the amount of cortex present on the dorsal surface.

Dorsal scars on blades are dominated by unidirectional scar patterns (74%). Opposed dorsal scars are seen on far fewer blades (13%) and seem mainly to be from non-preferred platforms and related to controlling the core flaking face. Crossed dorsal scars are seen on 9% of blades and are likely to relate to cresting and core rejuvenation activity. Refitting confirms the interpretation of both opposed and crossed dorsal scar patterns. The majority of blades have no trace of cortex on their surface (72%). Of the ones that do preserve such traces, most (98%) can be attributed to lightly weathered nodules of chalk flint.

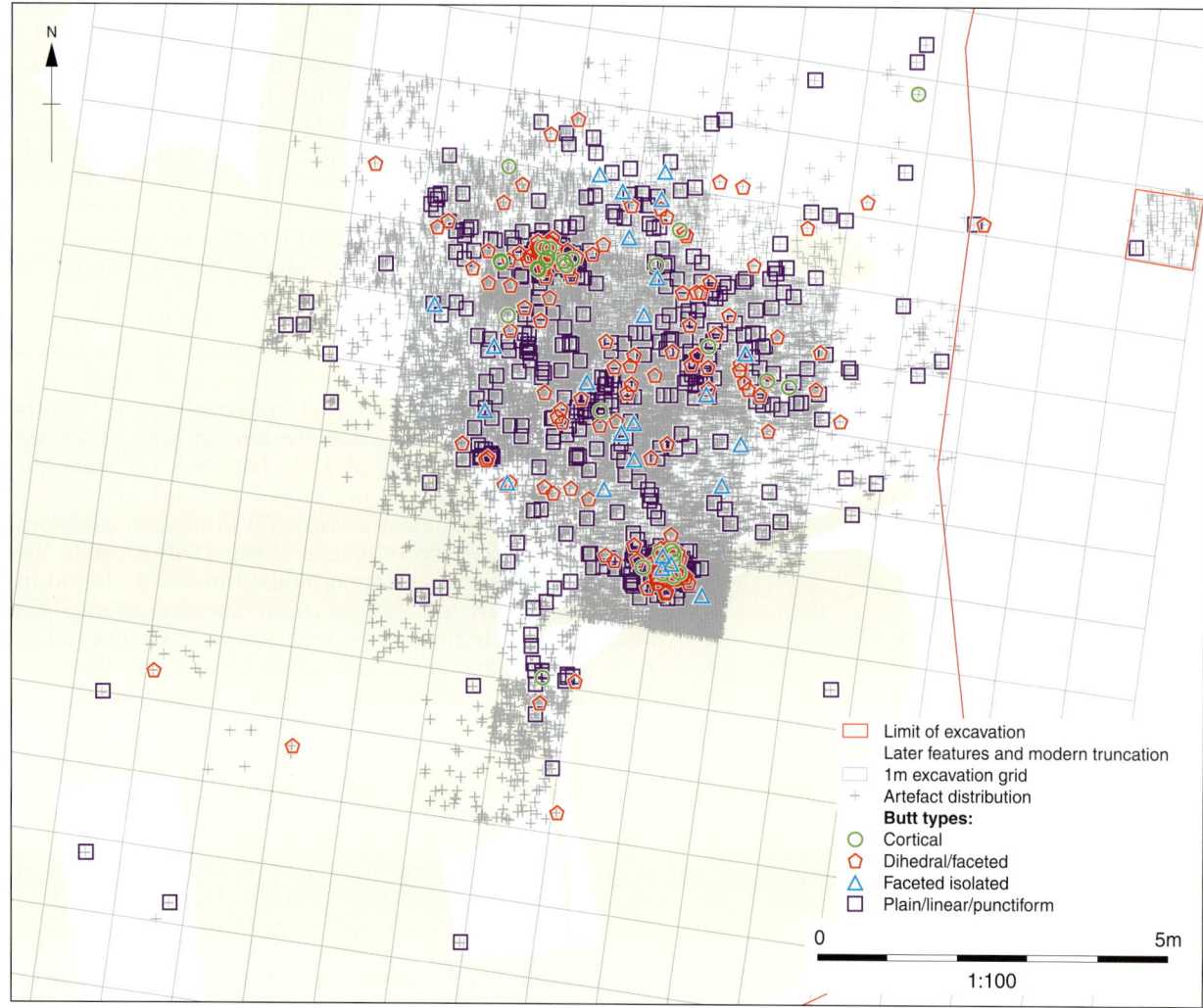

Fig. 6.7 *Distribution of butt types for blades*

Bladelets

The assemblage contains 566 bladelets and bladelet fragments (13% of the assemblage). Of these four have been modified as formal tools (c.948, c.2589, c.5032 and c.5114), and seven have miscellaneous retouch or edge damage. Fourteen pieces are burnt (2%), and none of these are tools. There are 72 complete, unmodified bladelets, some of which have been reconstructed from refitting fragments. Based on this sample the mean dimensions and standard deviations for bladelets are: length 20.6 ± 11mm, width 7.3 ± 3mm, and thickness 1.7 ± 0.8mm.

The butts of bladelets are usually plain or linear (65%), with 18.5% being punctiform. In contrast to the blades there are few with dihedral or faceted butt types (6%), and none of these show the distinctive technique of isolating the bulb. Four unmodified bladelets with plain butts have the bulb located at the edge of the platform. Platform abrasion is found on less than half of the bladelets (43%). There were no examples of bladelets detached by a hard hammer. They were produced by either soft stone (68%) or soft organic (32%) hammers. Distal terminations are mainly feathered (67%), with some hinge (13%) or step (10%) fractures. A majority of the bladelets have a straight profile (79%), more than four times the number of those with a curved profile (19%). This perhaps indicates that many bladelet removals did not travel the full distance of a core. The dorsal scars are almost exclusively unidirectional (91%). Only a single distal bladelet fragment (c.853) has opposed dorsal scars, but it should be noted that this has a width of 11.9mm and therefore is at the edge of the range between blades and bladelets. Most bladelets have no trace of cortex on their surface (89%). Of the ones that do preserve such traces (22), most can be attributed to cortex from lightly weathered nodules of chalk flint and only four have features of pebble/cobble flint.

The lack of bladelet cores in the assemblage, combined with the under representation of platform abrasion or other evidence of careful platform preparation, seems to indicate that bladelet production at Guildford Fire Station was probably a by-product of core maintenance activities rather than a deliberate goal of manufacture. It is also interesting that very few bladelets were transformed into tools and that the overall distribution of bladelets also closely parallels that of the cores and core rejuvenation pieces, suggesting that they were not moved far from the place of knapping.

Flakes

The assemblage contains 2289 flakes and flake fragments. Of these 21 have been modified as formal tools, and 25 have miscellaneous retouch or edge damage. Fifty-six pieces are burnt (2%), and of these one is a tool retouch flake. There are 1390 complete, unmodified flakes, some of which have been reconstructed from refitting fragments. Based on this sample the mean dimensions and standard deviations for flakes are: length 29.3 ± 20mm, width 22.6 ± 14.6mm, and thickness 4.8 ± 4.4mm. The wide standard deviations are indicative of a range of flake sizes, resulting from different stages of blade core preparation, reduction and maintenance.

The butts of these pieces are mainly plain or linear (67%), with only 15.5% being dihedral or faceted. There are four examples of the use of faceting to isolate a bulb, none of which are tools. The feature of a bulb and point of percussion occurring at one end of a platform either to the right or the left of centre is also occasionally observed. Twenty-six unmodified flakes and a tool retouch flake have this feature, 25 of them with plain butts. This feature is also occasionally seen on blade(let)s. Platform abrasion is only found on 24% of flakes, and this feature is most common on flakes with little or no cortex. Only 4% (24) of flakes were detached with a hard hammer, a similar proportion to that for blades. Twenty-one of these hard hammer struck flakes form parts of refit groups and they often represent the initial stages of core preparation. The majority of flakes were made with a soft stone (67%) or a soft organic (29%) hammer. The use of soft organic and soft stone hammers appears to be more prevalent on flakes with little or no cortex. Distal terminations are mainly feathered (67%) or hinged (24%). Some of the 16% of flakes with step fractures seem to be related to core maintenance activities. There is a predominance of flakes with a straight profile (53%), with over half of the flakes showing a curved profile also having at least 50% cortex preserved on their dorsal surface. The dorsal scars are overwhelmingly dominated by a unidirectional scar pattern.

Debris (irregular waste/shatter)

The term debris is used here to refer to knapping debitage 'when the means by which it was fractured cannot be identified' (Inizan *et al.* 1999, 34). This is commonly known as 'irregular waste' or 'shatter'. The assemblage contains 474 pieces of knapping debris that are distributed across the site although there are concentrations of debris corresponding to the two main knapping scatters. Thirty-one pieces of debris are burnt and 22 of these were associated with the northern concentration or were found elsewhere in the northern part of the site. Nineteen pieces of debris form parts of refit groups (RGs, see below). RGs 03, 07, 10, 11, 15, 35, 45, 51, 67 and 74 contain only one piece of debris. RG 08 contains three refitting pieces of debris. RGs 35 and RG 54 only contain refitting pieces of debris, three and two pieces respectively, and appear to be related to the initial stages of core preparation.

Small debitage

A total of 11,004 artefacts were classified only as small debitage or chips (Table 6.4). Following standard accepted definitions, chips are defined as complete lithic artefacts less than 5mm in length (Newcomer and Karlin 1987). Although the term 'small debitage' has been in the literature for several decades (eg Patterson and Sollberger 1978; Clarke 1986), it has not been precisely defined. For the purposes of this report the term is used for otherwise unclassified lithic flaking residue between 5–10mm in maximum dimension. This includes both artefact fragments and complete pieces. The composition of the small debitage assemblage is summarised in Table 6.4. The large numbers of small debitage and chips recovered at Guildford Fire Station is consistent with *in situ* knapping having taken place there. Not surprisingly, the highest concentrations of small debitage were recovered from the areas of the two lithic concentrations.

Microdebitage is defined as lithic flaking residue less than 1mm in maximum dimension (Fladmark 1982). There are no catalogued pieces of microdebitage recorded from the site, and this is presumed to be due to the difficulty of recovering such small pieces from sediments sieved to 2mm. However, sediments found adhering to artefacts from the densest parts of the two scatters have been examined under magnification and only a few examples of microdebitage have been found. It is possible that an alternative explanation might be that these smallest elements of lithic debitage were lost from the sediments, perhaps due to a winnowing effects of the wind and/or overbank flooding (see Chapter 4).

Table 6.4 Smaller debitage composition

	Number	%	Burnt
Small debitage (5mm – <10mm)	8253	75%	4%
Chips (1mm – <5mm)	2751	25%	0.3%

STONE OBJECTS

Several stone objects were recovered during the excavation that were initially thought to have been brought to the site and used. One stone object with an apparent groove running down the middle, found beyond the northern concentration (c.441; Fig. 6.8), was originally thought to be a possible

Fig. 6.8 Photograph of natural grooved stone (c.441)

polissoir (polishing stone) or shaft-smoother. Another roughly spherical stone object from the area of the southern concentration (c.821) was tentatively designated as a hammerstone. Other stone objects were collected based on the find location or shape, or because they displayed apparent red staining. Twenty-five of the stone objects recovered from the site were examined non-intrusively by Dr Simon Collcutt in 2021 who judged that they were all natural examples of weathered metamorphosed sandstone, quartzite or indeterminate silicate-rock, with no unequivocal signs of human modification. He has summarised his report (available in full in the archive) below.

Stone object c.441 is a granular pseudo-bedded rock weighing 296g which is most likely a sandstone that has undergone relatively low-grade metamorphism (Fig. 6.8). It has a superficial dark-coloured iron-manganese veneer, which is a pedogenic effect. The rock has a high density (specific gravity) of $c\ 3.7\mathrm{g/cm}^3$ (estimated by water displacement), significantly higher than an 'ordinary' silica sandstone. The most likely cause would be the inclusion of large amounts of iron bound in the cement; note, however, that glauconite is not apparent on the available surfaces. The rock may be rounded due to having been in a fluvial/marine environment or due to long-term weathering. It could have originated from a variety of deposits in the Guildford region, although there is no evidence that it reached its final position other than by geomorphic means. The pseudo-bedding visible on this object seems a function of coherence, either inter-grain or of the cement, and is the principal characteristic governing the present 'scalloped' form of the rock. There seem to be no veins of secondary mineralisation or crystal intergrowths. However, there are some, rather irregular (curved or wavy) features that pass through the rock roughly at right angles to the pseudo-bedding. Depending upon the reaction of the particular pseudo-bed it is crossing, a perpendicular feature may be expressed as a healed suture or as a weaker linear band at the surface, in the latter case now often resembling a 'groove' (due to recent erosion). Such perpendicular features are typical of low-grade metamorphism. The grooves in c.441 are not convincing as artefactual, especially since the surface grains in the base of the grooves show absolutely no sign of wear-faceting or polish.

Sandstone specimen c.2535 is similar to c.441 but at a higher grade of metamorphism. The 'rippling' on one surface of this stone seems to be the result of the interaction of original bedding and the lithification processes. This is probably 'warping' rather than original cross-bedding. There are no signs of human modification. Other similar stones are c.656, c.1480, c.1525, and an unnumbered stone from context 1033 that is a strongly contorted and metamorphosed rock, almost a true quartzite.

Stone object c.821, originally thought to be a possible hammerstone, is a strongly weathered pseudo-bedded quartzite with no sign of human modification or percussive use. None of the other quartzites collected from the site (see below) show any signs of percussive use.

Four stones were observed in the field to have a red staining on some surfaces. Three of these (c.934, c.960 and c.1080), all weathered quartzites, apparently show 'red ochre' (haematitic iron ore) applied on some of their surfaces. This effect could have happened naturally if this rock lay against another iron-rich one (there being various 'ironstone' types in the local gravels) and both were weathering. Stone c.241 is a relatively sharp quartzite pebble fragment and has natural manganese and some red iron staining on the fracture face.

Nine other specimens of quartzite were collected. Two have cemented surface deposits of reddish iron-rich sand with some rounded grains and tiny pebbles and are probably from a stream or secondary fluvial deposit (c.398 and c.939). Three are strongly weathered quartzites, two of which were probably originally stream pebbles (c.936, c.937 and c.938). There are also three pieces of weathered tabular quartzite (c.973, c.1072 and c.1165) and a further small piece of quartzite (c.1178). Stone c.1072 might have been heated.

Five other stones are best labelled as indeterminate silicates: c.318 is a stream pebble of reasonably homogenous dark silicate, more likely to be a chert than a quartzite; c.1179 is a hydrated silicate common in the region's gravel bodies; c.2058 is a weathered granular silicate; c.2077 is a deeply weathered small silicate pebble; and weathered silicate c.1175 might possibly have been heated.

THE RETOUCHED TOOL ASSEMBLAGE

Typological classification

The retouched tools have been broadly grouped according to the de Sonneville-Bordes and Perrot type-list for describing Upper Palaeolithic tools (1953; 1954; 1955; 1956a and b) with some additional categories (cf Barton 1992). Under this simplified scheme, tools are classified according to their principal morphological characteristics (Table 6.5), with any variation being described under each of the main groupings.

The retouched tool assemblage contains 288 artefacts. The total collection consists of some 108 formal retouched tools and fragments. These comprise 10 end-scrapers, 7 piercers or perforators, 36 burins, 7 truncations and 20 backed blades, bladelets and points. There are also significant numbers of notches (22), denticulates (4) and rubbed end pieces (2). The majority of formal tools are made on blades (76%). The remainder of the tool assemblage can be described as consisting of miscellaneous retouched blade/lets and flakes (79) and pieces with edge damage (47). Apart from there being overlap between the latter two categories, 'edge damage' can be particularly difficult to determine and may have arisen under a number of different circumstances ranging from post-depositional effects (eg damage due to trampling or natural bioturbation) or to deliberate utilisation. The identification of these types is necessarily more subjective than for the other categories. The retouched tool category also includes identifiable by-products of tool manufacture, such as burin spalls (45) and small flakes from retouching tool edges such as end-scrapers (9). The distribution of all tools is shown in Fig. 6.9. The following sections present data on each of the main individual tool categories.

End-scrapers

There are 10 end-scrapers (Figs 6.10–6.13) consisting of six complete or nearly complete tools and four fragments. In terms of scraper typology, the majority are simple end-scrapers (7), two can be classified as short end-scrapers (*grattoirs courts*) and there is one double end-scraper (c.2474). The two short end-scrapers were made on flakes, and all of the others were made on blade blanks. One of the blade end-scrapers is on a blank with secondary

Table 6.5 Retouched tools, including retouched tool debitage

Retouched tool categories	Number
End-scrapers	10
Piercers/perforators	7
Burins	36
Truncations	7
Backed blade/lets and points	20
Notches and denticulates	26
Rubbed end tools	2
Miscellaneous retouched blade/lets and flakes	
Blades with *rasante* retouch	10
Retouched blade/lets and flakes	46
Blade/lets with fine retouch	23
Edge-damaged blades and flakes	47
Total (excluding tool debitage)	234
Retouched tool debitage	
Burin spalls	45
Tool retouch flakes	9
Total (including retouched tool debitage)	288
Post-Palaeolithic artefacts	13

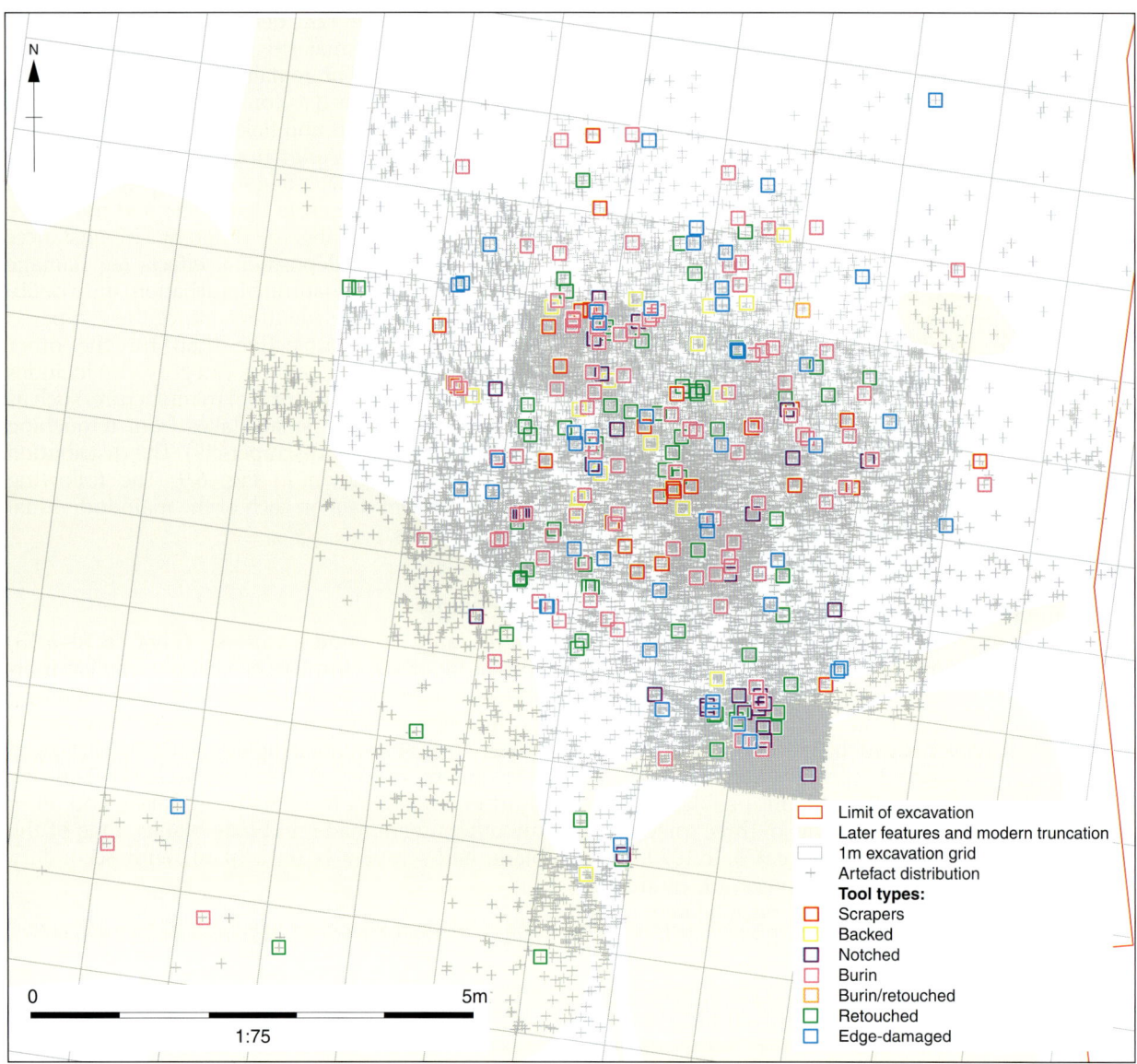

Fig. 6.9 Distribution of all retouched tools

cresting (c.1625), while another displays heavy abrasive rubbing on the dorsal ridge near the scraper end (c.1315), and one shows visible rounding on the scraper edge itself (c.485). Two of the end-scrapers (c.558/c.559/c.924, made up of three broken fragments, and c.2471; Fig. 6.12) are on retouched blades displaying an invasive stepped and scaled *rasante* retouch (Bodu and Mevel 2008, fig. 10). The same retouch type is also present on eight unmodified blades in the assemblage as well as on ten other formal tools (see below). None of the scrapers shows any evidence of burning.

The measurements of the complete blade end-scrapers vary in length from 111.3mm to 78.2mm. The longest examples with parallel sides are relatively narrow (<26.3mm), while the double end-scraper and scraper with secondary cresting have widths of >34mm. One of the blade-end scrapers (c.1315) can be joined to the dorsal surface of a dihedral burin on a blade (c.1564) (Fig. 6.11; Refit Group 56, Fig. 6.86). No further artefacts can be refitted to this sequence although other tools and debitage in the same type of high-quality black flint with red tinges are present elsewhere on the site. No other scrapers form parts of refitted groups. The morphological characteristics of the scraper edges appear to be fairly uniform. The retouched edge is almost always semicircular in plan and located at the distal end of the blank, although on two tools the retouch is located proximally (c.485 and c.2474; Fig. 6.10). The scraper edge is usually formed by semi-abrupt retouch (Tixier *et al.* 1980), which is always direct. The edge angles may vary slightly but the majority are between 40° and 70°. Occasionally the scraper edge is more abrupt, probably as a result of resharpening (c.1625; Fig. 6.10).

In profile, the scraper blanks are slightly curved (Fig. 6.10), with a concave ventral surface. On some tools (c.1583 and c.2474) this feature seems to have been deliberately favoured since the tool's

Chapter 6

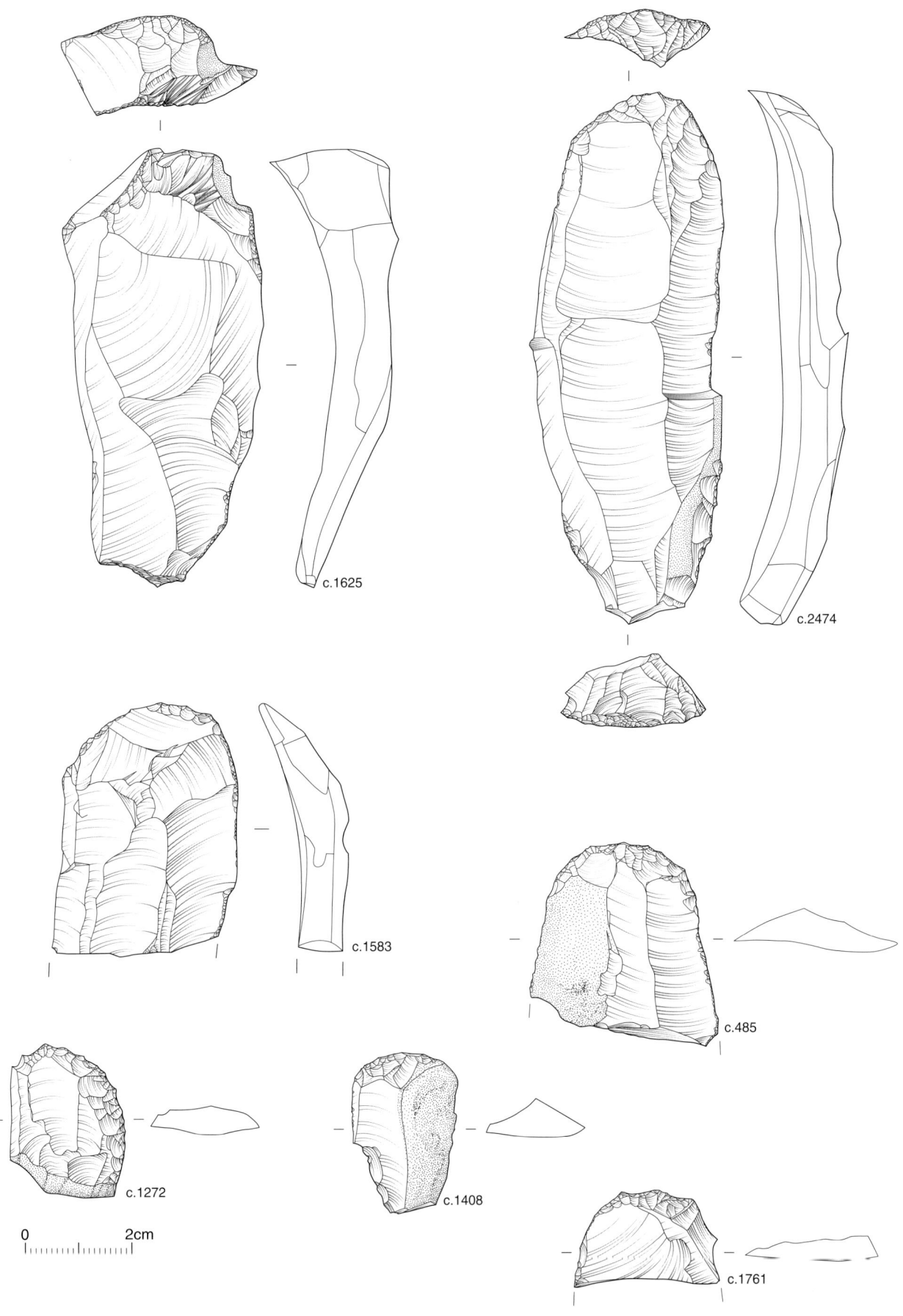

Fig. 6.10 End-scrapers (c.1625, c.1583, c.485, c.1761); double end-scraper (c.2474); short end-scrapers (c.1272, c.1408)

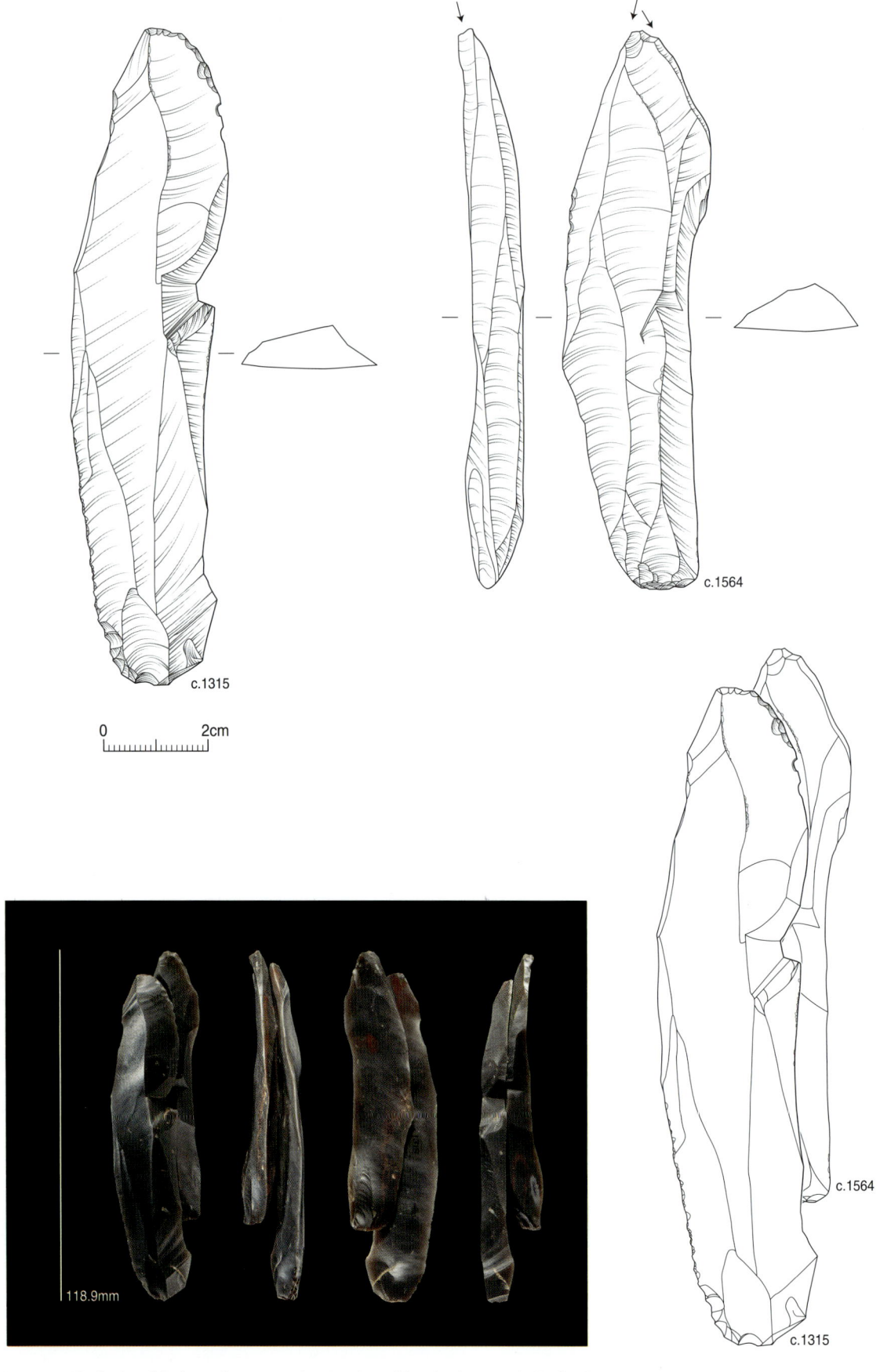

Fig. 6.11 Refitting blade end-scraper (c.1315) and burin (c.1564). Refit Group 56

edge was located near the maximum point of curvature, giving the scraper a hooked appearance in profile.

Despite a careful search through the small debitage, relatively few tool retouch chips have been found (9) of which some may have been from sharpening end-scrapers. It is possible that others were overlooked because of their similarity to small rejuvenation flakes relating to core reduction.

Functional use wear traces have been described on a number of the scrapers (see Chapter 7).

The distribution of end-scrapers indicates an interesting spatial pattern with most of them located between the northern and southern scatters (Fig. 6.13). Only one such artefact (c.485), a broken portion of an end-scraper, was situated in the northern concentration. Wear trace analysis indicated that it had been hafted and used in hide-working (see Chapter 7).

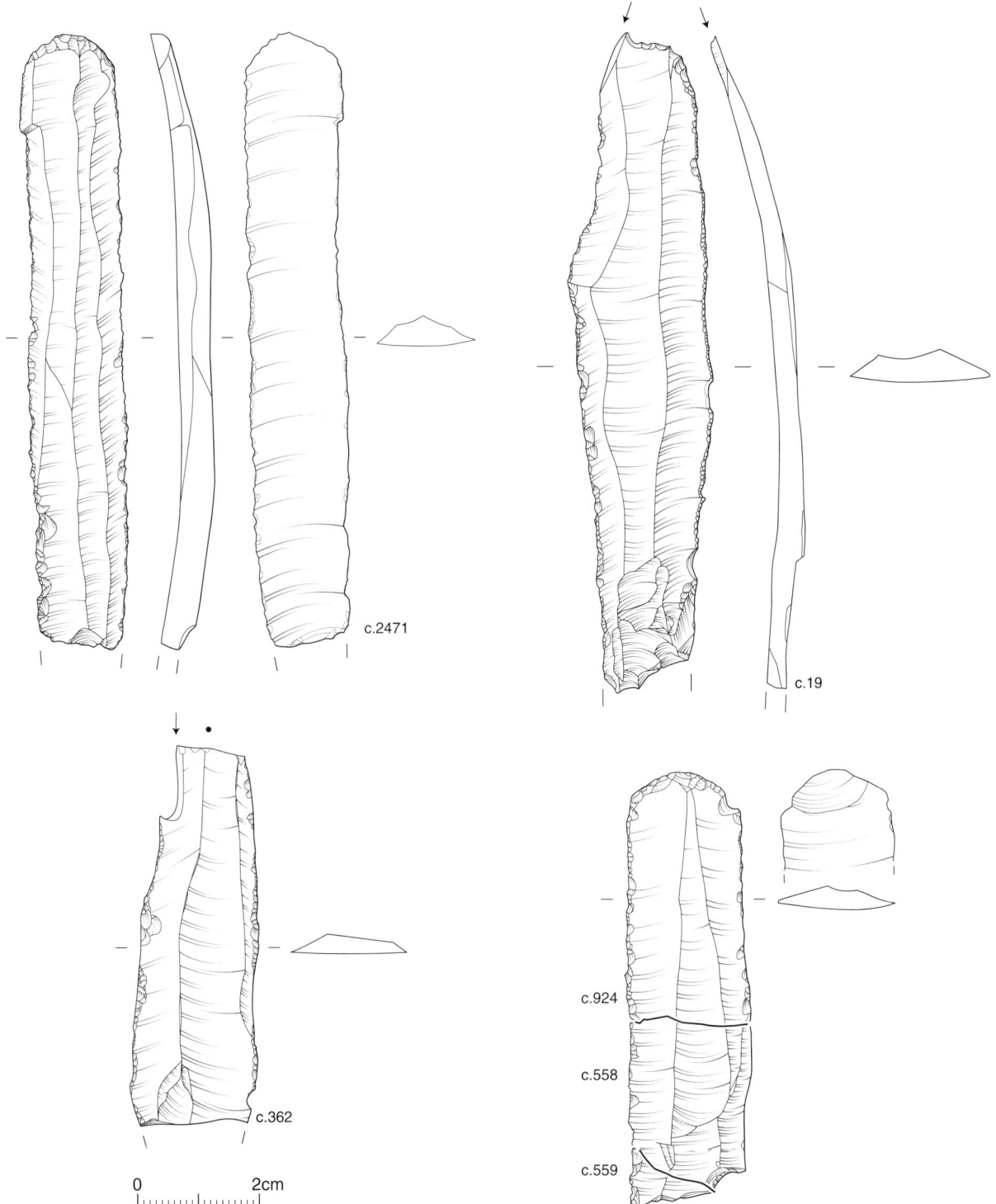

Fig. 6.12 End-scrapers and burins with rasante *retouch (c.2471, c.19, c.362, c.924/c.558/c.559)*

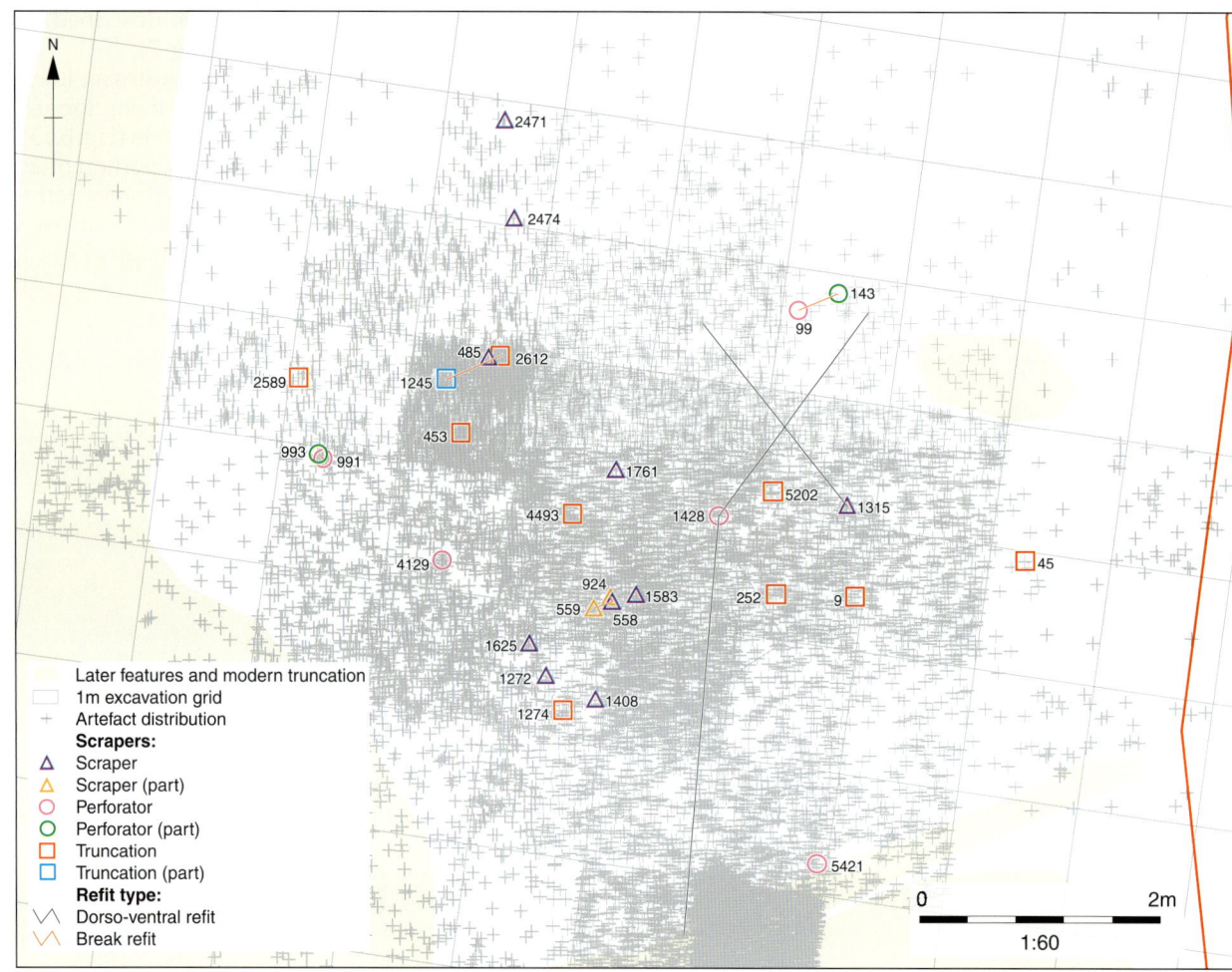

Fig. 6.13 Distribution of scrapers, unretouched refitting parts of scrapers, perforators and truncations

Piercers/perforators

Six of the seven tools in this category are piercers; only one (c.1428) has a robust tip and is described as a perforator (Fig. 6.14). Five of the tools are made on blades (one on a break refit) and two on flakes (one a mended break). The retouched tip in all but one case is situated at the distal end, the exception being a proximal example, c.1152. The orientation of the tips generally follows the central axis of the blank but the size of the projection differs from tool to tool. The smallest examples (3) have tiny retouched projections <3mm long (Fig. 6.14). None of the piercers/perforators shows any evidence of burning. One of the illustrated pieces is particularly interesting. It is made on a blade from the main stages of reduction (*plein debitage*; c.99/c.143) that measures 91mm long (Fig. 6.14). The proximal end of the blade displays an isolated butt similar to an *en éperon* type. Its tip at the distal end is slightly offset to the main axis of the blank, and formed by abrupt direct retouch converging from both lateral edges. The tip itself displays a very small burin-like facet on the left-hand side that might be evidence of use. The left edge also displays a combination of abrupt fine retouch running most of the length of the blade with some *rasante* (scalar) retouch. Interestingly, microwear traces were identified on this piece but on its right lateral edge which also displays some signs of fine retouch or edge damage (see Chapter 7). Perforator c.1428 is the only tool in this category that forms part of a refitted group (RG 18).

The distribution of artefacts in this tool class shows that the majority lie between the two main knapping concentrations. One tool (c.1428) has a refit connection with the edge of the southern concentration (Fig. 6.13).

Burins

Out of a total of 36 burins, 12 are dihedral, 9 are on a truncation, there are 2 transverse burins, 2 double burins, 6 burins on a break, 1 on a natural surface and 2 on a notch, with the remaining 2 too fragmentary to classify (Figs 6.15–6.19; Table 6.6). In three examples, burins made on the same blade can be refitted to other burins showing successive stages of manufacture and use (c.699 and c.2313, Fig. 6.18; c.2488 and c.4691, Fig. 6.15; c.1204 and c.9277, Fig. 6.15). Burins also included additional proximal (3), mesial (2) and distal (2) parts that could be refitted

Chapter 6

but would not have been recognised as burins in themselves. All but one of the typed burins is made on a blade. The burin edges are generally simple in form with only four examples of three or more facets forming the burin edge (three dihedral and one transverse burin); the burin edges are most commonly located at the distal end of the blank (31 out of 36). The majority of tools (30) have no cortex or only minimal dorsal coverage indicating that they were made on blanks from the main stages of reduction (*plein débitage*). Except in a few cases, most of the burins are on shorter blades and flakes. It is interesting to note that the ones made on longer supports (5 or 6) are on straight blades and often carry signs of additional retouch down one or both edges, indicating extended usage. For example, truncation burins c.19 (Fig. 6.12) and c.990/c.992 (Fig. 6.15) illustrate examples with lateral *rasante* retouch. Only one burin (c.3120, a transverse type) shows evidence of burning.

Dihedral burins constitute the most numerous subtype. Five of them have burin facets along the central axis of the blade (symmetrical forms: c.142, c.596, c.887, c.1564 and c.2451); seven are slightly offset (asymmetrical forms: c.266, c.319, c.365, c.1424, c.1910, c.2319 and c.1204). All of the dihedral

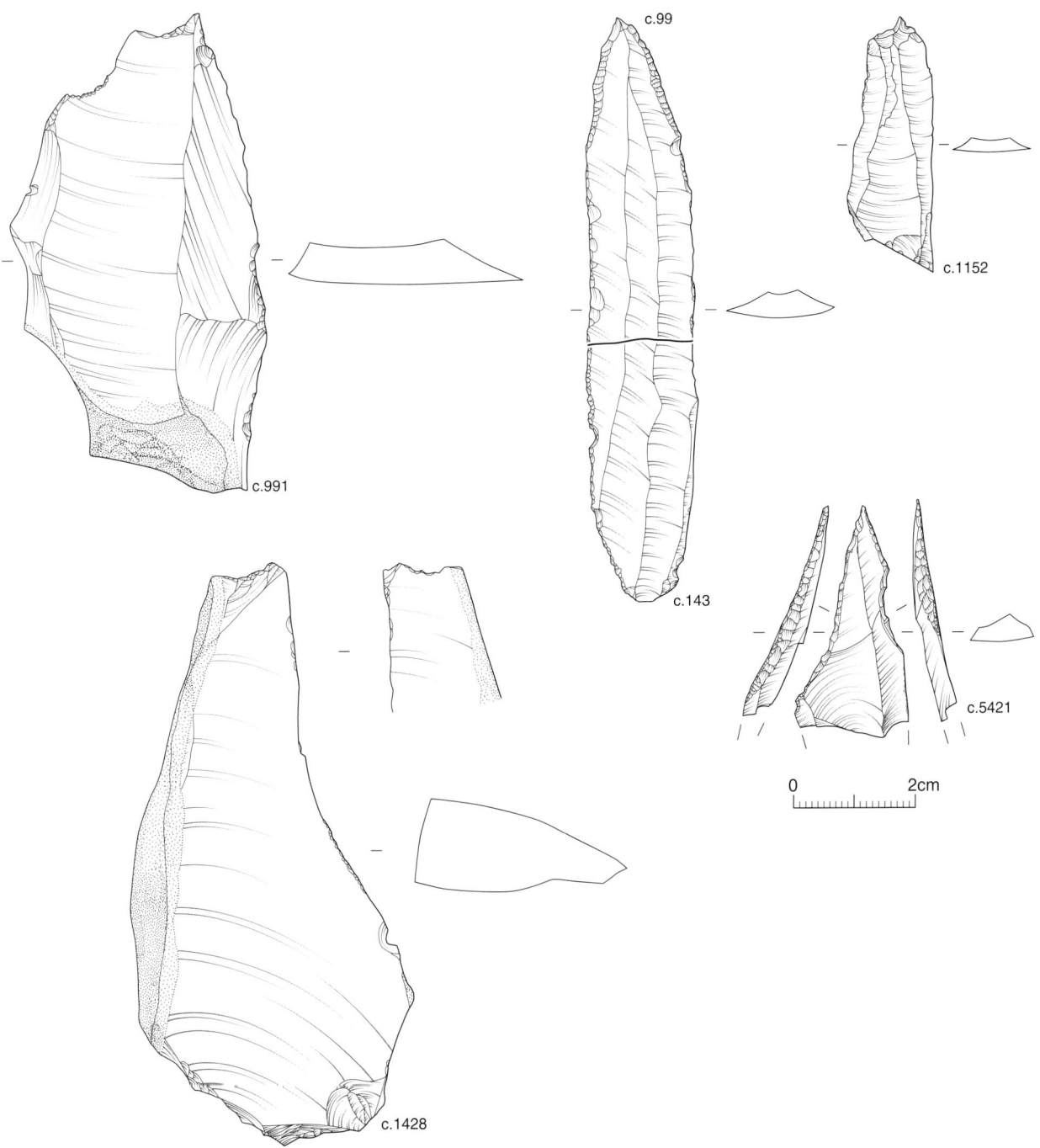

Fig. 6:14 Micropiercers (c.991, c.1152), piercers (c.99/c.143, c.5421) and perforator (c.1428)

burins are burinated at the distal end. It is noteworthy that on three of the burins small irregular retouch scars occur directly adjacent to the burin facets on the lateral edge (c.142, c.365 and c.1564). This may have been due to modification of the edge prior to the removal of the burin spall. In four of the dihedral examples (c.142, c.319, c.1204 and c.2451) the blades feature evidence of *rasante* retouch (ventrally in the case of c.2451). The retouch seems to have been executed prior to burination in two of the burins (c.142 and c.2451) and following burination in the remaining two. This suggests that the modifications may have been linked to related activities. Of the nine dihedral burins examined for microwear traces, evidence of use was demonstrated in five cases, with possible use on two others (see Chapter 7). *Rasante* retouch is present on

Table 6.6 Burin typology

Typological category	Number
Dihedral asymmetrical burin	7
Dihedral symmetrical burin	5
Burin on an oblique truncation	5
Burin on a concave/other truncation	4
Double burin	2
Transverse burin	2
Burin on a break	6
Burin on a natural surface	1
Burin on a notch	2
Unidentified/broken	2
Total	36

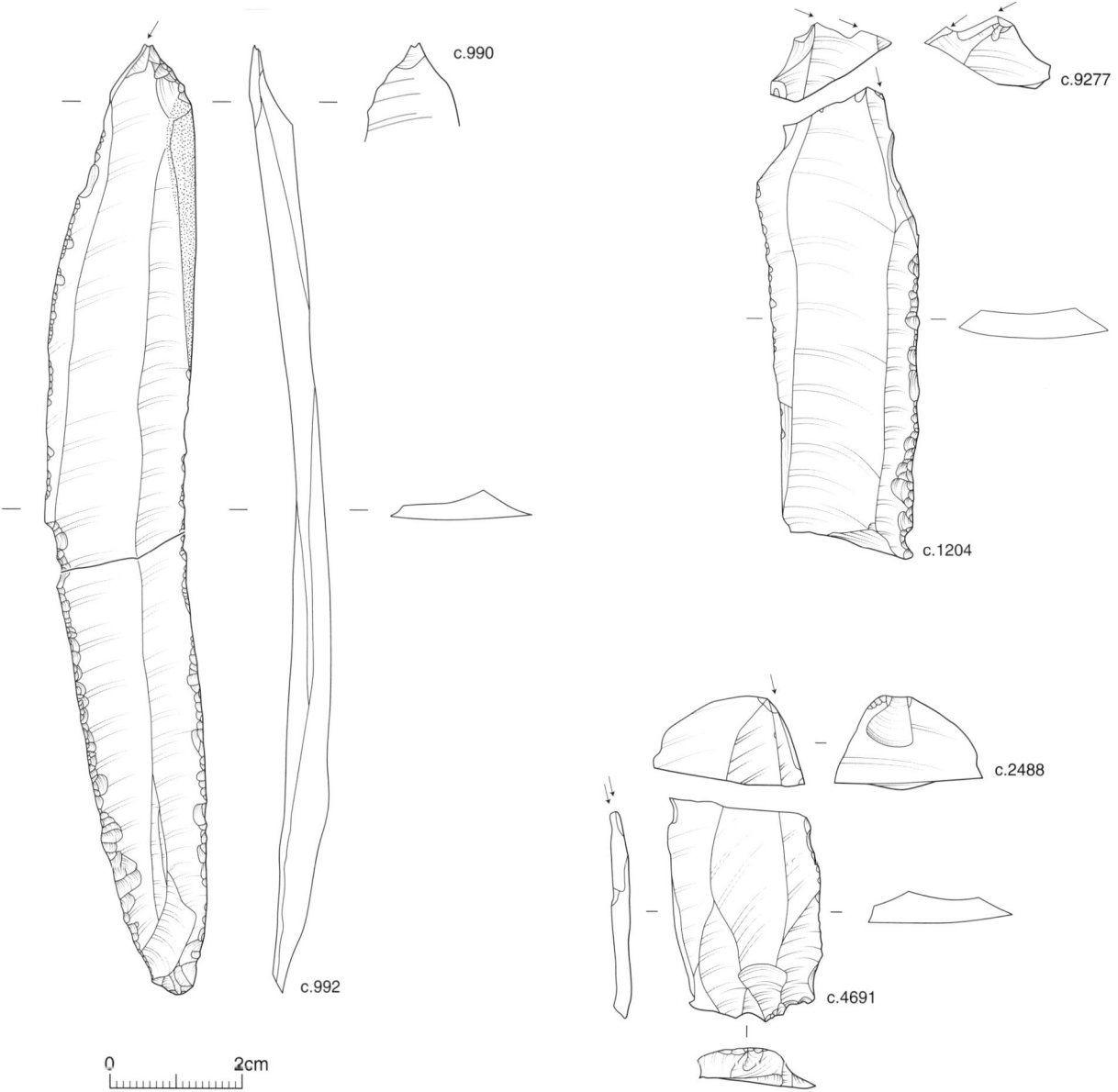

Fig. 6.15 Burins. Dihedral burin on blade with rasante retouch (c.990/c.992); refitting burin on a break and unclassified burin (c.4691/c.2488); and dihedral burin on blade with **rasante** retouch and a refitting spall (c.1204/c.9277)

eight burins in total. These include the four examples mentioned above and four others (two on truncations, c.19 and c.990; one on a break, c.362, and one on an unclassified burin, c.1370).

Of the nine burins on truncation, five have oblique truncations, two have a concave truncation and two are difficult to classify. All but one of them are made on the distal portions of blades. The truncation burins are on *plein debitage* and half occur on blades of substantial size including two with surviving lengths of 107mm (c.19) and 130mm (c.990/c.992). These two burins (Figs 6.12 and 6.15) are on the distal tips of blades with *rasante* (scalar) retouch on their lateral edges. Curiously neither burin shows signs of microwear traces. One of the truncation burins (c.699) is made up of refitting blade segments that show successive stages of reduction beginning with a retouched blade (c.7448) then a burin on a break (c.2313) and a burin on truncation (Fig. 6.18). Only the burin on truncation

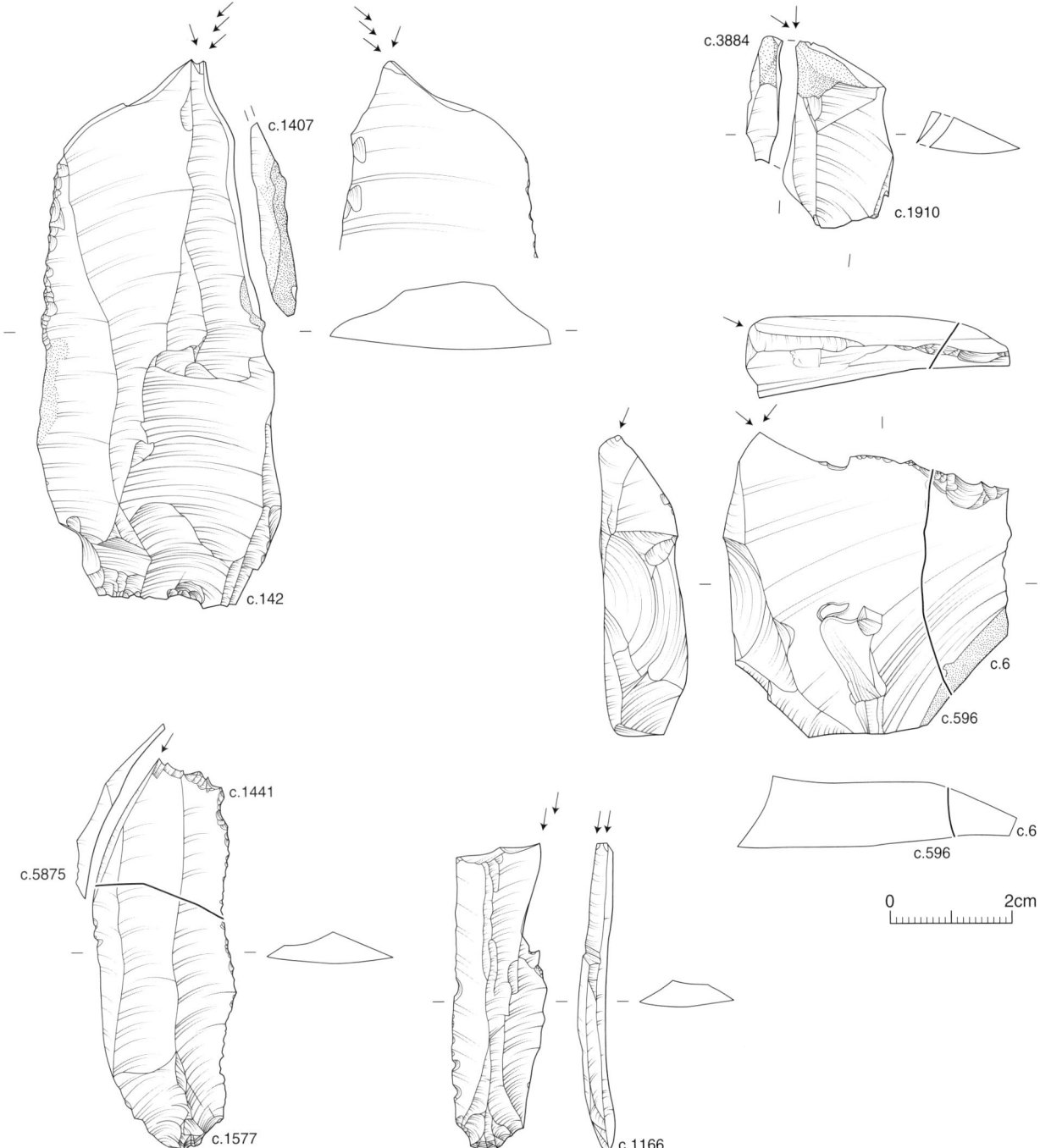

Fig. 6.16 Burins. Dihedral burins with refitting spalls (c.142/c.1407, c.1910/c.3884); dihedral burin with refitting spall and part of original flake blank (c.596/c.6); burin on break (c.1166); burin on natural surface with refitting spall and part of original blade blank (c.1441/c.5875/c.1577)

(c.699) was examined for microwear and showed possible signs of use. The only slightly unusual truncation burin was c.2207 which was made on the end of a crested blade.

The two double burins have burin removals at both ends (Fig. 6.18). The first (c.319/c.524) is on a blade with a burin on a break (proximal) and a dihedral burin (distal). There is also *rasante* retouch on its right lateral edge. A distal portion of the blade can be refitted and shows that it was deliberately removed by a transverse blow. In addition, there are two refitting burin spalls (in three pieces) from which it has been possible to reconstruct the sequence of manufacture and use (see below). The second example (c.459) is on a mesial portion of a thin blade and consists of a burin on concave truncation (proximal) and a burin on a break (distal). The distal end of this blank (c.1242) has been refitted and indicates that the original blade was probably broken into segments before being transformed into a tool.

There are two transverse burins. These are typified by burin edges perpendicular to the axis of the tool, produced by a deliberate side blow. One of the tools (c.3120) is a tiny fragment that is heavily burnt and has a large remnant of cortex.

There are six burins on breaks. It is assumed that they were all made on deliberately broken ends of blades although none exhibit the diagnostic features of intentional fracture (cf Barton *et al.* 1983). In one case (c.2313) it is clear that a burin on a break was subsequently modified into a burin on truncation

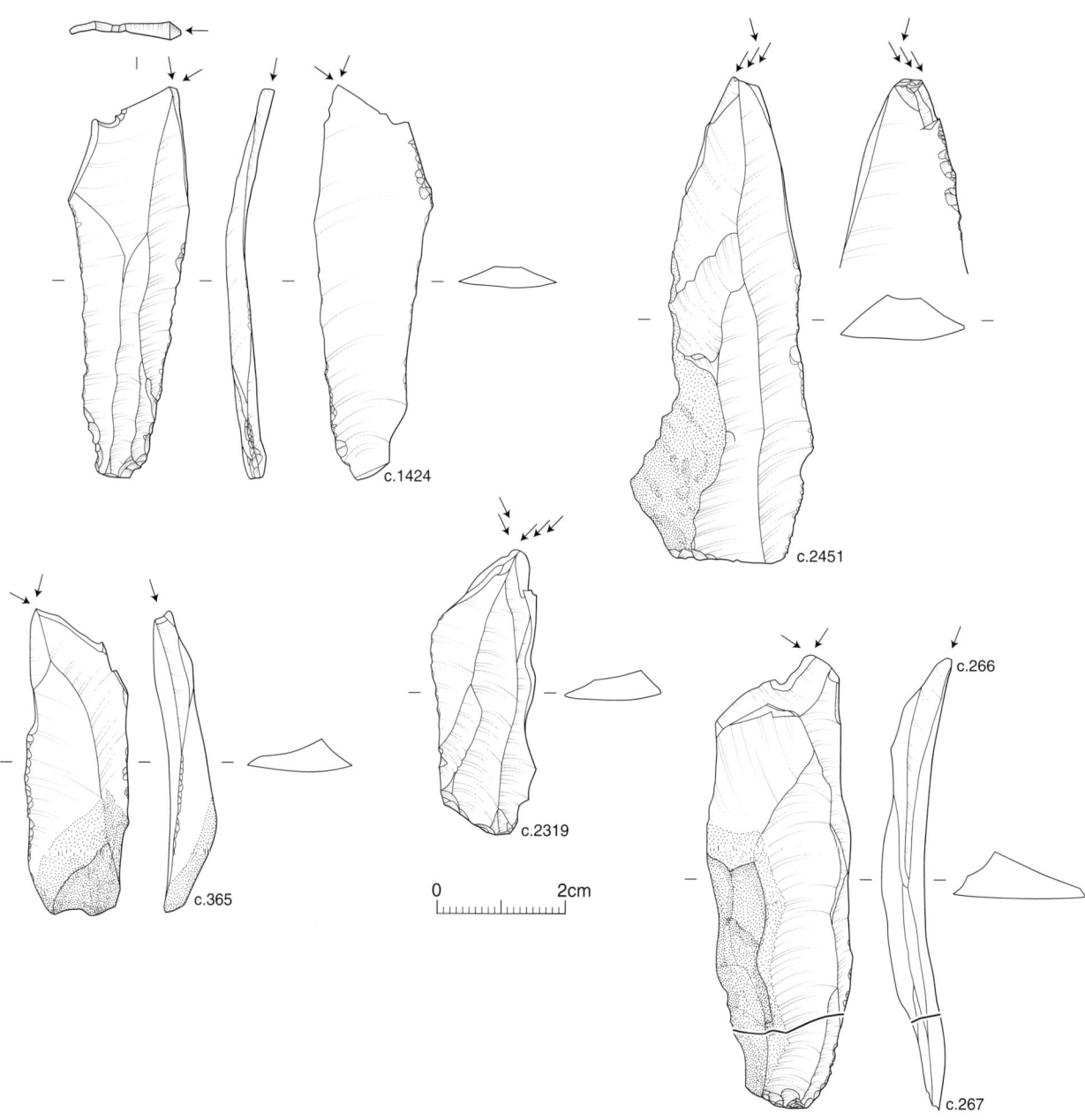

Fig. 6.17 Dihedral burins (c.1424, c.2451, c.365, c.2319, c.266/c.267)

(c.699) by removing the distal portion of the blade with a transverse blow (Fig. 6.18). Another part of the same blade (c.7448) can be refitted to this piece and shows how manufacture began with the removal of the distal end to prepare a platform for detaching the first spalls. One of the burins on a break has minor signs of *rasante* retouch along both edges (c.362) which terminate where the blank was broken in two. Unfortunately, the distal portion of the tool is missing.

There is a single example of a burin on a natural surface (c.2488) which refits to a burin on a break (c.4691; Fig. 6.15). The other burins consist of two tools prepared on a notch, one of which (c.1557) has a refitting burin spall (c.4158), removed with an oblique transverse blow. The second burin of this

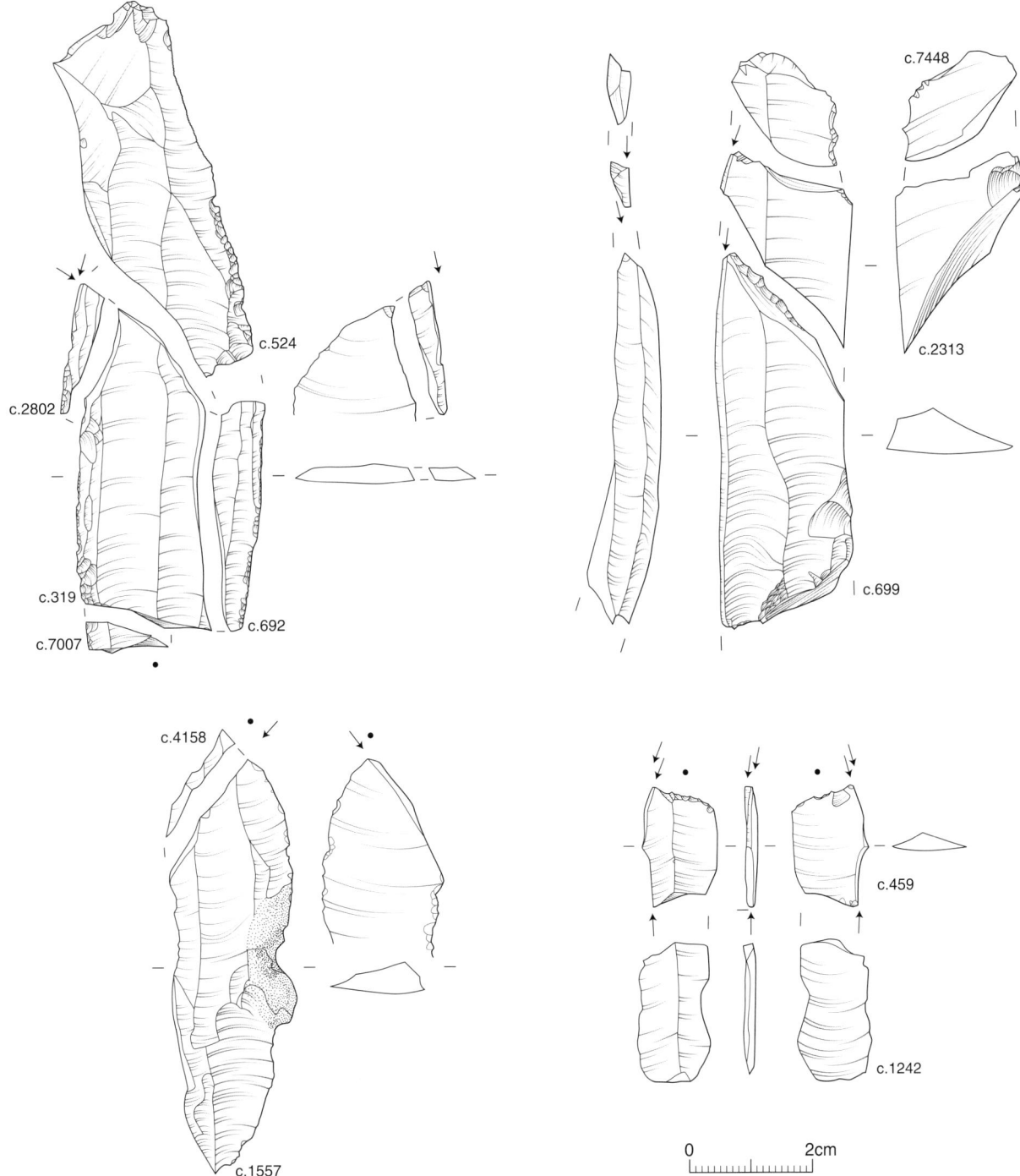

Fig. 6.18 Burins. Double burin (dihedral and on a break) with three refitting spalls and part of the original blade blank (c.319/c.524/c.692/c.2802/c.7007); two refitting burins (on a truncation and on a break) and a refitting retouched blade fragment (c.699/c.2313/c.7448); burin on a notch with a refitting spall (c.1557/c.4158); double burin (on a break and on a truncation) (c.459) with a refitting part of the blade blank (c.1242)

type (c.1647) also displays a transverse facet but at the proximal end. The fact that it runs partly on to the ventral surface suggests that it could be a *'burin de fortune'*. Finally, two of the burins cannot be identified to type. One has a refitting spall (c.1617 and spall c.690) but provides no clues as to the original preparation surface; the other (c.1370) is slightly doubtful, being characterised by a single, very narrow facet at the distal end of a well-made blade with remnants of cresting.

Seven burins form parts of refit groups: c.701 is part of RG 04, c.4064 is part of RG 43 (visible in Fig. 6.83), c.596 is part of RG 14, c.1564 is part of RG 56 (visible in Fig. 6.86), c.887 is part of RG 75 (visible in Fig. 6.89). Refitting burins c.699 and c.2313, together with retouched distal blade fragment c.7448, together form the blade blank that joins the two major sections of RG 02 — an earlier phase of core development and a later stage of blade removals and core maintenance. Several other blades seem to have been removed sequentially along with c.699/c.2313/c.7448 but could not be located within the assemblage.

The distribution of burins and burin spalls presents a complicated picture (Fig. 6.19). Two burins (c.2267 and c.1647) belong within the southern concentration, while four (c.319, c.459, c.4064 and c.701) occurred within the northern concentration. The rest are spread in a semicircle from the north-east to the south of this concentration. There appears to be no immediately obvious spatial link between the eight burins with *rasante* retouch. Apart from square G8 (covering part of the northern concentration), the densest focus of burins is in square I10 which also contains four unrelated burin spalls (Fig. 6.19).

Burin spalls

It is sometimes difficult to distinguish burin spalls from ordinary pieces of debitage, especially in relation to broken examples, but by using criteria of

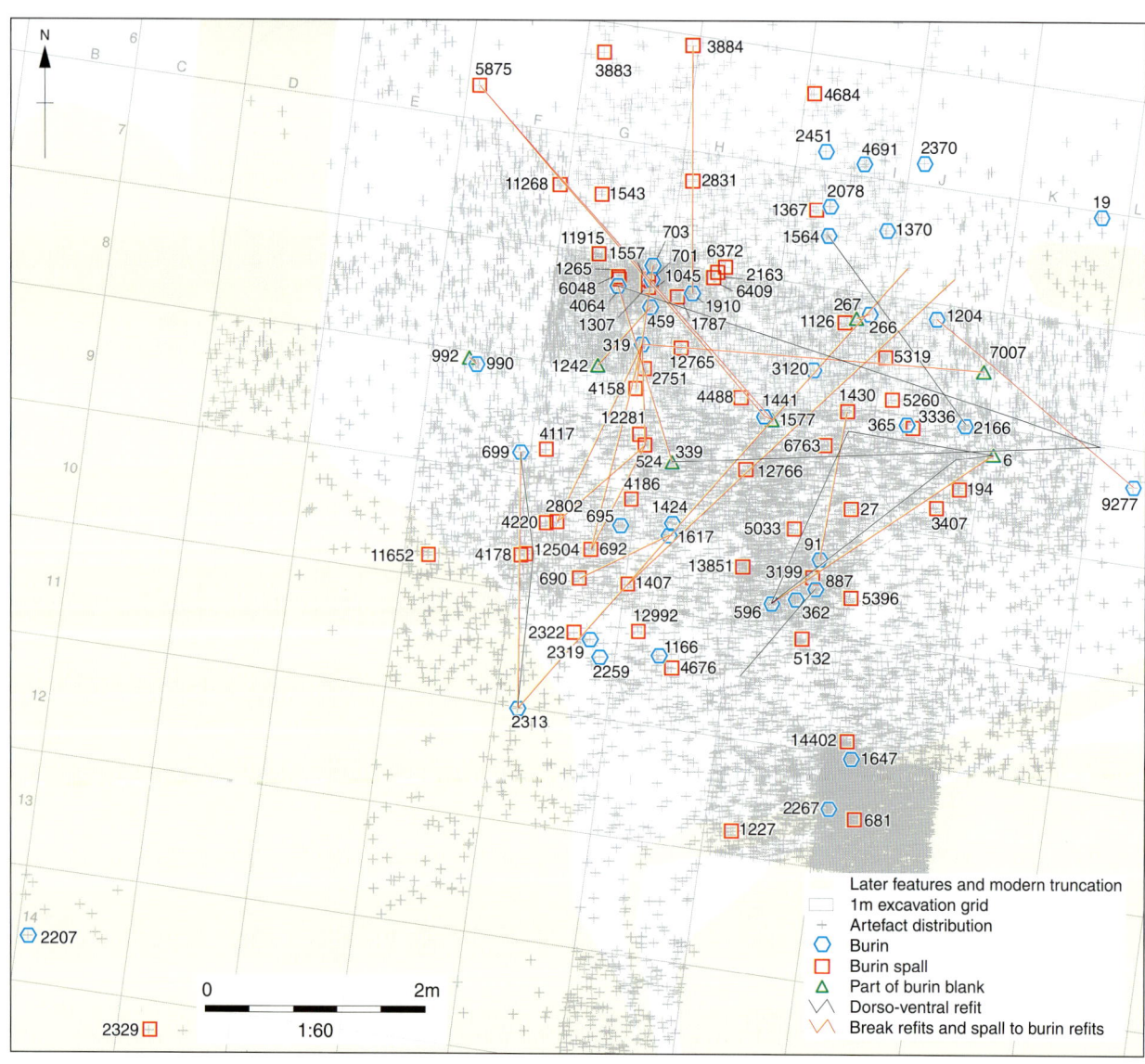

Fig. 6.19 Distribution of burins, spalls and burin fragments

Table 6.7 Burin spalls

Type of burin spall	Number
Primary spalls	19
Secondary spalls	18
Not identified	8
Burin spall total	45
Transverse spalls	10
Lateral damage or discontinuous retouch	14

thick cross-sectional shape, lateral damage or retouch traces and removal direction, it was possible to identify at least 45 burin spalls (an additional six are considered doubtful). In 12 cases it was possible to fit spalls to burins, clearly establishing them as the by-products of the burin blow technique. In one example it has been possible to refit two burin spalls to a burin (c.319; Fig. 6.18) with the position of the spalls suggesting a multi-stage use of the tool. Judging from the small size and nondescript shape of some of the refitting spalls it is likely that there are others in the collection that have been overlooked.

As can be seen from Table 6.7 there was a roughly equal number of primary and secondary spalls (the latter showing earlier removals). Ten spalls appear to have come from transverse burins although only one (c.4158) could be refitted to a burin (c.1557) in the collection (Fig. 6.18). Eight of the spalls displayed signs of damage or retouch that was incurred before the spall was detached. Only five spalls had evidence of pre-existing cortex.

The distribution of burin spalls largely mirrors that of the burins and as with the latter, the highest number of burin spalls occurs in the area between the two knapping concentrations. An interesting observation is that the spalls extended into an area in the north where virtually no burins were present, around squares F/H6/7, and conversely into squares I6/7 where there were few burin spalls but five burins. The area lacking burins may have been an activity zone where burins were used and resharpened; the neighbouring squares may have been where the burins were discarded. Several spalls can be refitted to burins (Fig. 6.19). These are discussed in more detail in the section on refitting below.

Truncations

Seven tools are classified as truncations (Fig. 6.20). Six are made on blade blanks and one on a distal bladelet fragment (c.2589). They are typified by straight (4: c.9, c.42, c.1274 and c.2612) and oblique (3: c.453, c.2589 and c.5202) truncations. All of the truncations are made by direct semi-abrupt or abrupt retouch at the distal end. One (c.2589) has a hyper-oblique truncation and may be from a very

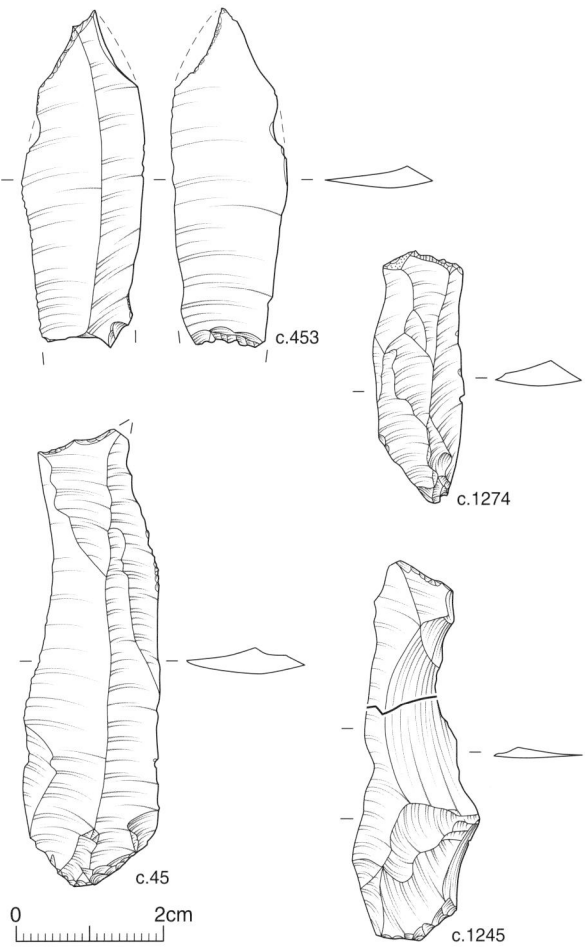

Fig. 6.20 Truncations. Oblique distal truncation (c.453); straight truncations (c.45, c.1274, c.1245/c.2612)

small tool. The assemblage also contains some examples of thin bladelets with nibbled marginal direct retouch at their distal ends that are more likely indicative of 'spontaneous' retouch (eg c.5708; cf Newcomer 1976). No truncations form parts of refitted groups. The truncations show no preferential distribution pattern (Fig. 6.13), except that most of them occur in the area between the two knapping foci.

Notches and denticulates

There are 22 notches and 4 denticulates (Fig. 6.21). The denticulates (c.7, c.697, c.915 and c.3343) are identified by a series of contiguous small notches or nicks on the lateral edges of flakes, except in one example where the denticulation appears at the distal end (c.697). Notches are far more numerous. They consist of 15 flakes with single notches (c.222, c.324, c.817, c.1056, c.1312, c.1637, c.1725, c.2432, c.3203 and c.5325), five blades with single notches (c.252, c.684, c.1069, c.2004 and c.10732), four flakes with double notches (c.592, c.679, c.1458 and c.2028) and two blades with

Fig. 6.21 Notches (c.1056, c.1069, c.1725) and denticulates (c.7, c.697/c.959)

double notches (c.1391 and c.1969). One of the notches defined by a large single cortical notch also has two separate notches on its left lateral edge (c.1056). Notches are also present in combination with fine retouch on a number of flakes. We illustrate one example (c.1725; Fig. 6.21) where a large notch is present at the distal end accompanied by fine direct retouch on the rest of the distal margin. There is also edge damage or fine retouch along the right ventral edge. Unfortunately, this piece was not examined for use-wear. Two of the notched tools are somewhat unusual in that the notches occur on opposite sides of the same blank. In c.1391 the modification gives a 'strangulated' appearance to the short blade; in the other (c.1458) the notches on either side of a flake have been truncated by a break at the distal end of the blank. None of the notches that were submitted for analysis (10) yielded any evidence for use-wear. Interestingly, seven notches have been re-incorporated into larger refit groups: c.1391 in RG 01, c.1458 in RG 09, c.1637 in RG 13, c.679 in RG 15, c.598 in RG 19, c.1069 in RG 31, and c.817 in RG 37 (visible in Fig. 6.79). No denticulates form parts of refitted groups.

The notched tools are mainly clustered close to the northern and southern concentrations (Fig. 6.22). The four denticulates are all distributed in the zone between the two knapping concentrations.

Backed blade/lets and points

There are 20 backed tools made on blades or bladelets with characteristic direct semi-abrupt or abrupt retouch to form the backing (Fig. 6.23). All of them are broken to some degree and three are burnt. The tools can be subdivided into curve-backed points, straight-backed blade/lets, oblique points and a variety of broken, backed fragments. There are also four Krukowski microburins representing the broken tips of backed tools (Table 6.8). Although, strictly speaking, the oblique points are types of truncation, they are grouped in the backed category because of characteristics in blank thick-

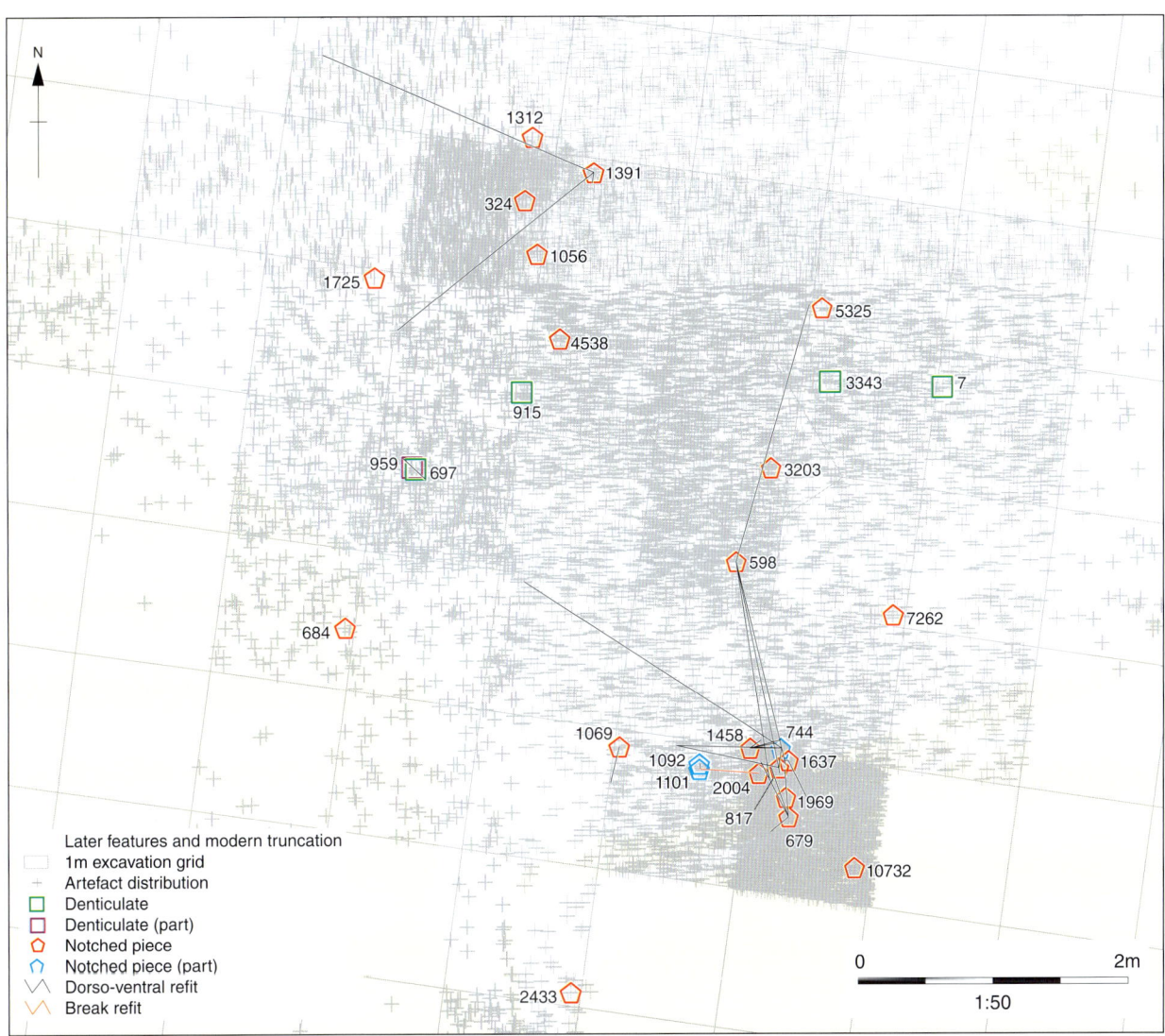

Fig. 6.22 Distribution of denticulates and notched pieces

ness and obliqueness of truncation that overlap with the other subtypes. All of the more complete backed pieces display a straight profile.

The low numbers of backed tools and their fragmentary nature makes it difficult to give precise typological descriptions or meaningful dimensions for all but a few tools. Most of them fall into the category of blades as they have widths of >9mm (Barton 1992; Tixier 1963), except two that are too fragmentary to determine the original blank type. The mean width and standard deviation of the backed pieces is 10.8 ± 1.6mm. The most complete piece (c.308) is a curve-backed blade pointed at both ends (*bi-point*; Fig. 6.24). One of its tips is missing but

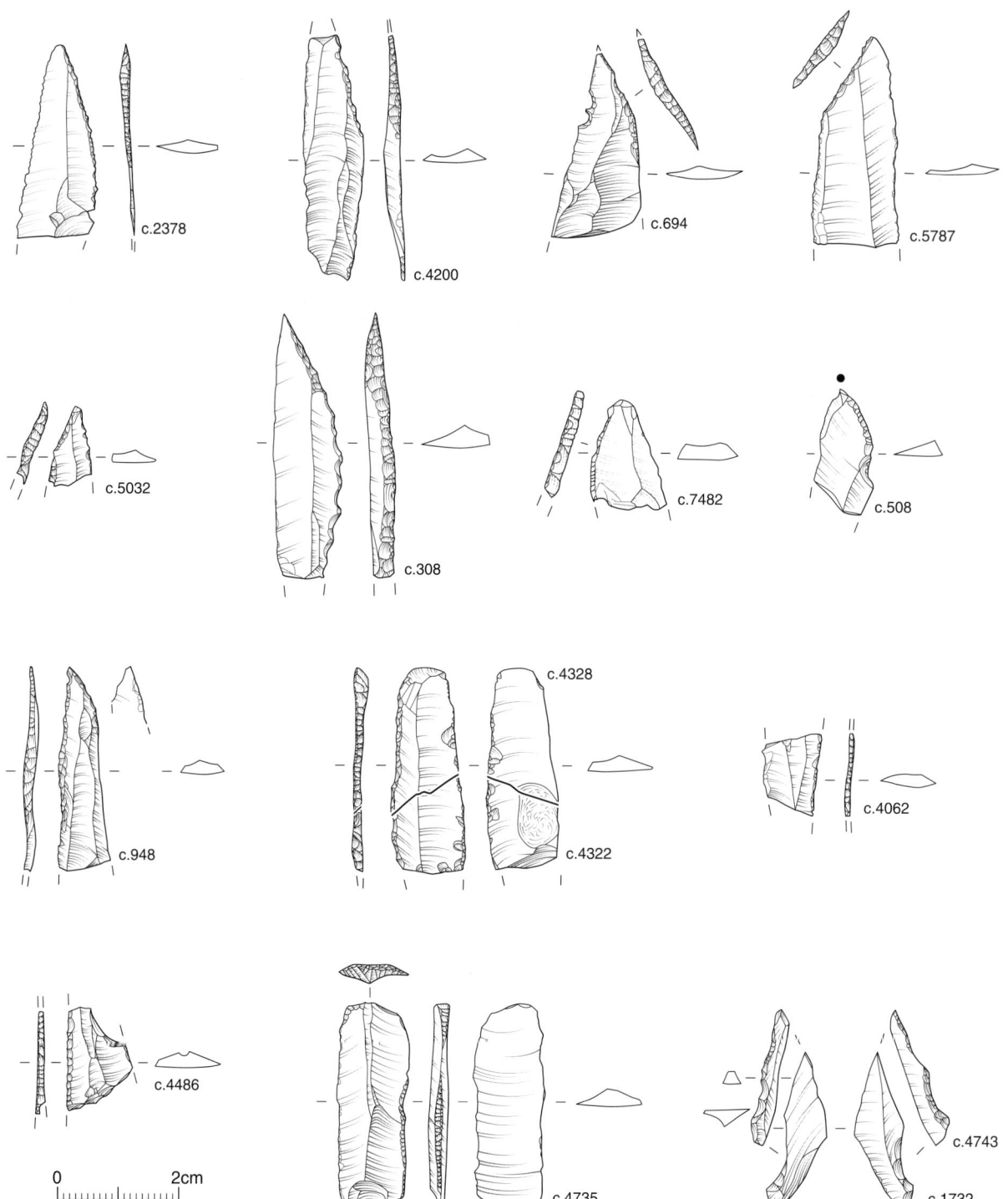

Fig. 6.23 Backed blades, bladelets and points. Oblique points (c.2378, c.4200, c.694, c.5787, c.5032); curve-backed bi-point (c.308); curve-backed point (c.7482, c.508); straight-backed bladelet with oblique truncation (c.948); backed blade fragments (c.4322/c.4328, c.4062, c.4486); partially backed and truncated blade (c.4735); two refitting Krukowski microburins (c.1732, c.4743)

Table 6.8 Backed tools and fragments

Backed tool type	Number
Curve-backed point (bi-point) (c.308)	1
Curve-backed point fragment (c.508, c.7482)	2
Straight backed bladelet with oblique truncation (c.948)	1
Oblique point (c.4200)	1
Oblique point fragment (c.694, c.2378, c.5032, c.5787)	4
Partially backed blade with proximal truncation (c.4735)	1
Backed blade fragment (c.275, c.4062, c.4322, c.4328, c.4486)	5
Backed bladelet fragment (c.5114)	1
Krukowski microburin (c.1732, 4539, 4743, 7262)	4
Total	20

it has a length of 47mm and width and thickness measurements of 11mm and 3.2mm, respectively. Other likely examples of this type are two preserved proximal portions of blades with curved backing (c.508 and c.7482). Also included in the points are five oblique points and fragments, some of which may be the incomplete parts of larger tools. All of them are obliquely pointed at the distal end.

Amongst the other identifiable types are a straight-backed blade with an oblique truncation (c.948) and a partially backed blade with a straight truncation at its proximal end (c.4735). In addition, there are four Krukowski microburins (Fig. 6.23 and see Barton 1992), the by-products of manufacturing or resharpening of backed blades. Two of them can be refitted (c.4743 and c.1732) and are interesting because they indicate successive stages of retouching a backed point and confirm that some of these tools were made on site. The maximum thicknesses (4.1mm) of these Krukowskis are greater than all but one of the other backed pieces in the assemblage. The exception is another small backed fragment (c.5114). Together they imply that new replacement backed tools were being made and taken away from the site.

Only four of the backed tools are burnt. They comprise three backed blade fragments, two of which can be conjoined (c.4322 and c.4328), and a tip of a curve-backed piece (c.7482). Although such breakages probably resulted from thermal fracture, it is interesting to note a very high incidence of breakage amongst the unburnt backed pieces as well. Use-wear studies of this collection have shown that at least four of the tools (the aforementioned burnt backed blade), the two mesial backed blade fragments (c.4486 and 4062) and the curve-backed point (c.308) all carry evidence of projectile impact damage.

The backed blade distribution indicates that they were discarded mainly in the area around the northern knapping concentration (Fig. 6.25). The

Fig. 6.24 Photograph of curve-backed bi-point (c.308)

refitting Krukowskis were found more than a metre apart in the same area but there is nothing in their condition to suggest major disturbance.

Rubbed end tools

There are only two clear examples of this type (Figs 6.26–6.27). One is a complete, patinated blade 83mm by 20mm by 9mm (c.205). It is heavily retouched at the distal end with a truncation formed by direct semi-abrupt retouch and scalariform *rasante* retouch extending on to the ventral surface and laterally near the tip. There is evidence of localised rounding at the distal extremity. The blade has a plain butt and signs of soft stone percussion. It is no different from many of the blades in the flint assemblage. The second tool is an unpatinated blade (c.2555), proximally broken, with a heavily abraded and rubbed distal end (Fig. 6.27). There are signs of edge damage along both lateral edges. Functional analysis has indicated that this piece was used as a strike-a-light (Chapter 7). A possible third example is an end-scraper c.1315 (Fig. 6.11) that has a heavily abraded arête at the distal (scraper) end.

Miscellaneous retouched blade/lets and flakes

Blades with rasante (scalar) retouch

Artefacts in this subcategory (10) are characterised by a distinctive form of flat, stepped and scaled retouch located on parts of one or both lateral

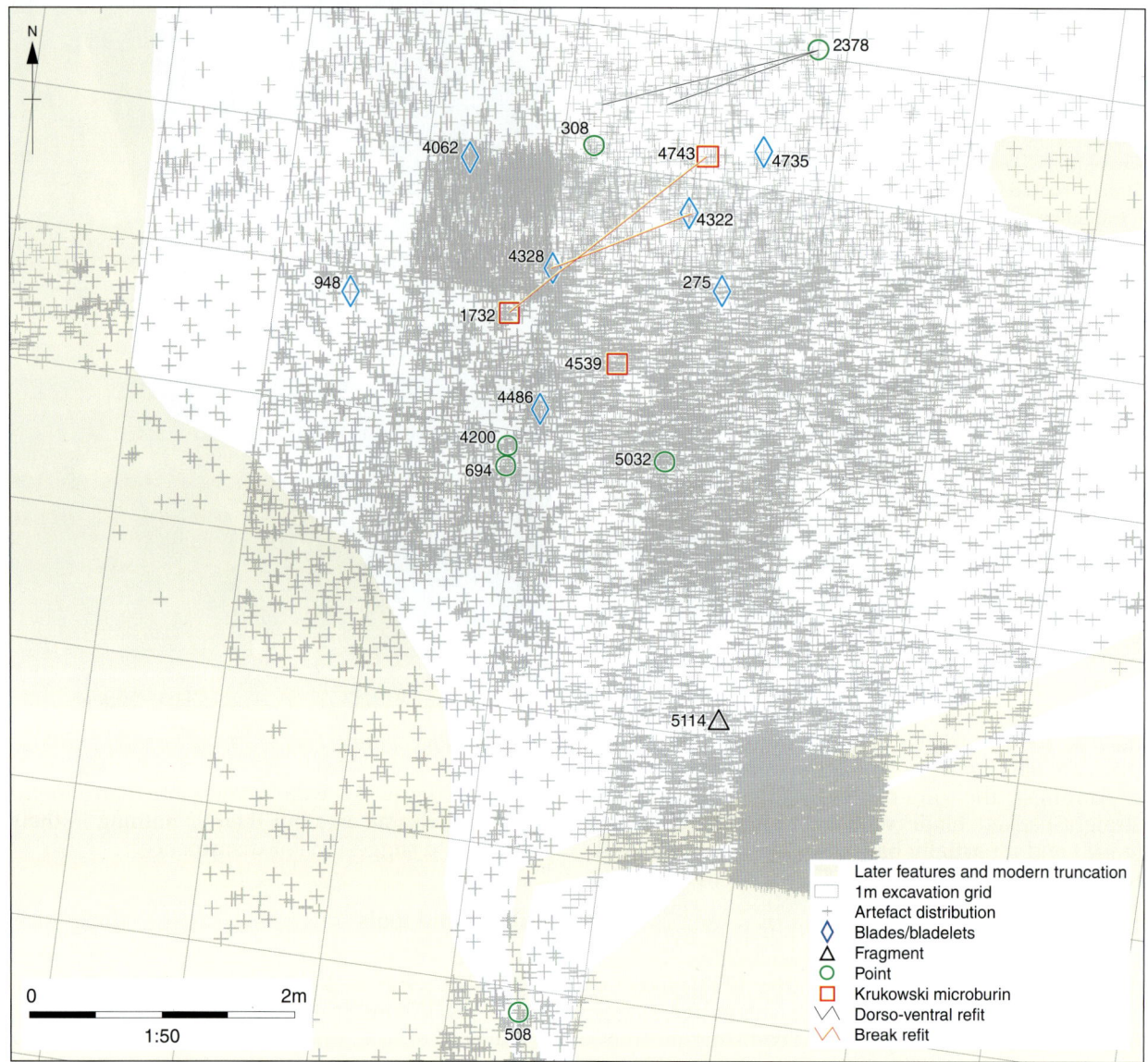

Fig. 6.25 Distribution of backed material

margins of the blank. There are nine blades and blade fragments with *rasante* retouch (c.143, c.297, c.558, c.559, c.926, c.992, c.1322, c.1744 and c.1826; Fig. 6.28). There is also a flake with this feature (c.6). Identical examples of invasive scalariform retouch have also been recorded on the edges of 12 formal tools, and some of the scalar retouched blade fragments listed above refit the tools. The formal tools with *rasante* retouch are: two end-scrapers (c.924/c.558/c.559 and c.2471; Fig. 6.12), one perforator (c.99/c.143; Fig. 6.14), eight burins (c.19, c.142/c.1407, c.319/c.524/c.692/c.2802/c.7007, c.362, c.990/c.992, c.1204/9277, c.1370 and c.2451; Figs 6.12 and 6.15–6.18) and a rubbed end tool (c.205; Fig. 6.26). All of the formal tools with *rasante* (scalar) retouch are on well-made blades from the main debitage sequence (*plein débitage*). Blades with similar retouch, described as '*une retouche rasante*' are well known in the French Azilian of the Paris Basin (Bodu and Mevel 2008), where they are considered to be the result of deliberate resharpening of the edge.

The distribution of *rasante* blades (Fig. 6.29) shows proximity with some of the burins in the northeastern area. These include burins c.1370 and c.2451 which also show evidence of *rasante* retouch on their lateral edges and may suggest some connection of activities.

Retouched blade/lets and flakes

The 46 items under this heading constitute a group of artefacts that cannot easily be integrated into any of the existing tool categories. Instead, they display signs of usually discontinuous semi-abrupt or abrupt retouch on one or more of their edges (including the distal end). The patchiness of the retouch makes it difficult to interpret. Sixteen of the retouched pieces are on blades, 5 on bladelets, 14 on flakes and 11 on unclassifiable

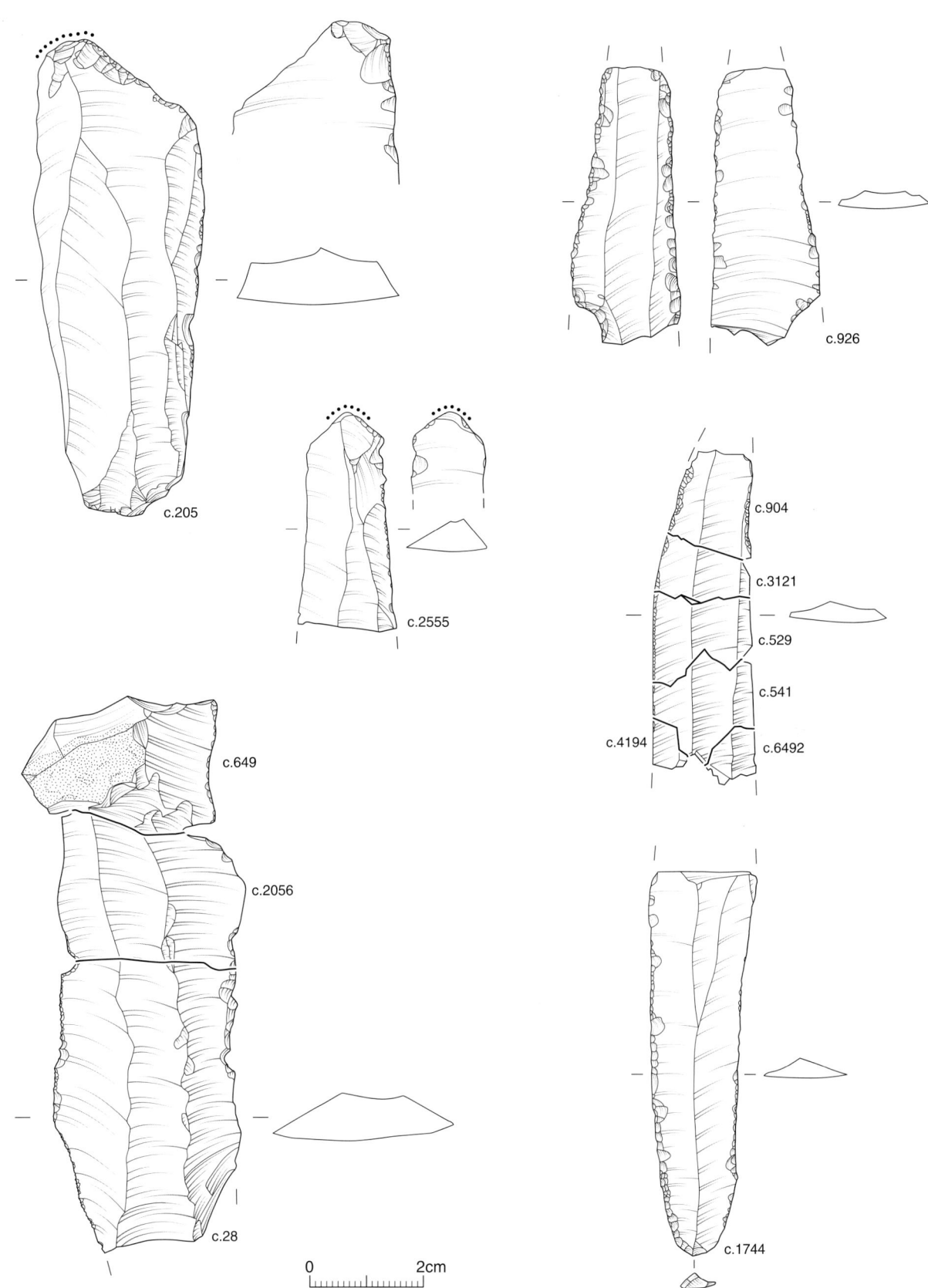

Fig. 6.26 Rubbed end tools (c.205, c.2555); blades with rasante *retouch (c.1744, c.926), blade with fine lateral retouch (c.904/c.3121/c.529/c.541/c.4194/c.6492); blade with fine and denticulated retouch (c.28/c.2056/c.649)*

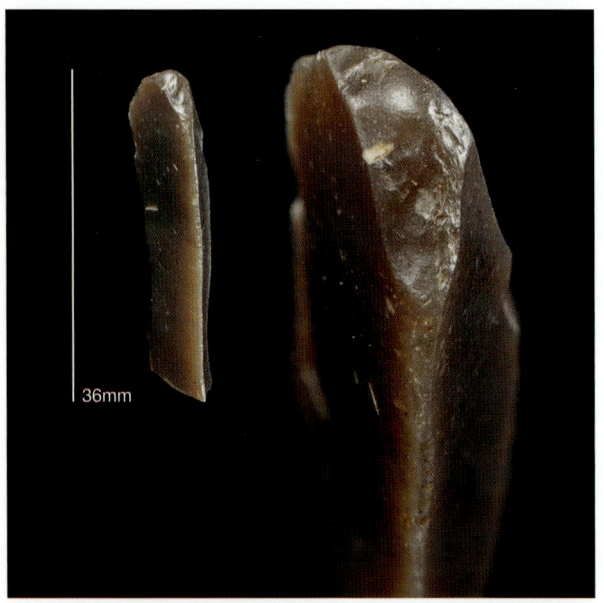

Fig. 6.27 Detail of rubbed end blade (c.2555)

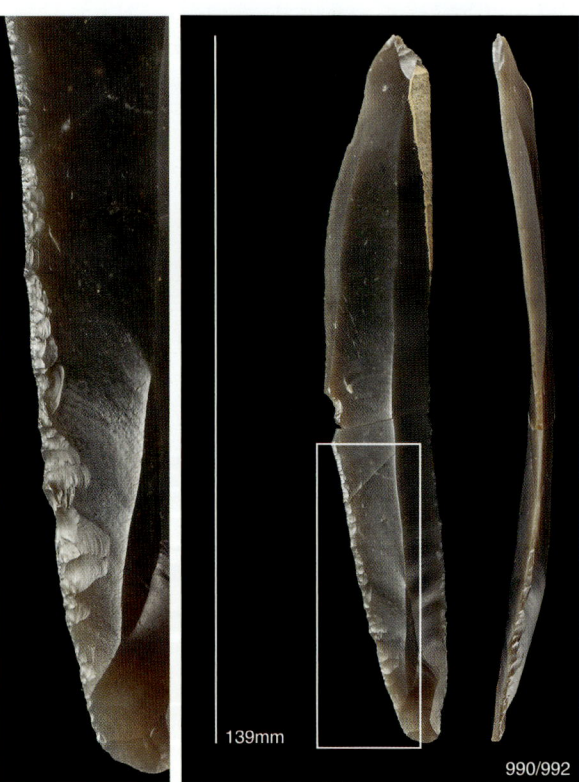
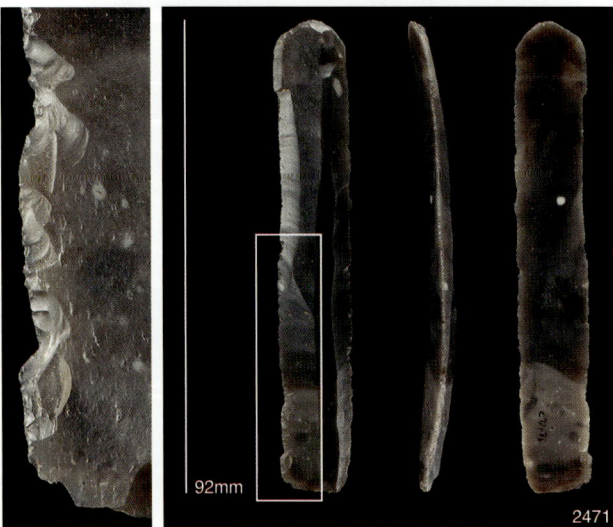

Fig. 6.28 Blade tools with rasante (scalar) retouch: dihedral burin (c.1204), end-scraper (c.2471), rasante retouched blade (c.992, the proximal part of truncation burin c.990)

fragments. Apart from an unclassifiable fragment with stepped and scaled retouch, most of the unclassifiable fragments are small and under 20mm in length. Three of these unclassifiable fragments appear to be the broken tips of tools, but it has not been possible to find the missing parts. Others may result from tool resharpening. Twenty-five of the 35 retouched blades, bladelets and flakes are fragments. One of the complete blades is on a crested blank with the retouch situated at the distal end (c.1473, which is part of Refit Group 53: Fig. 6.84) and in some ways resembles a perforator.

Five of the artefacts (one blade and four flakes) have preserved areas of cortex but only in one example does the retouch occur opposite the cortical edge. The latter (c.657) may be described as a naturally backed knife. None of the artefacts in this category is burnt. Fourteen of these artefacts form parts of ten different refit groups (RGs 01, 02, 03, 08, 10, 12, 24, 25, 41 and 53).

There is no clear pattern in the distribution of retouched blade/lets and flakes, which extend into and between the areas of the two knapping concentrations (Fig. 6.29). Further investigation of some of

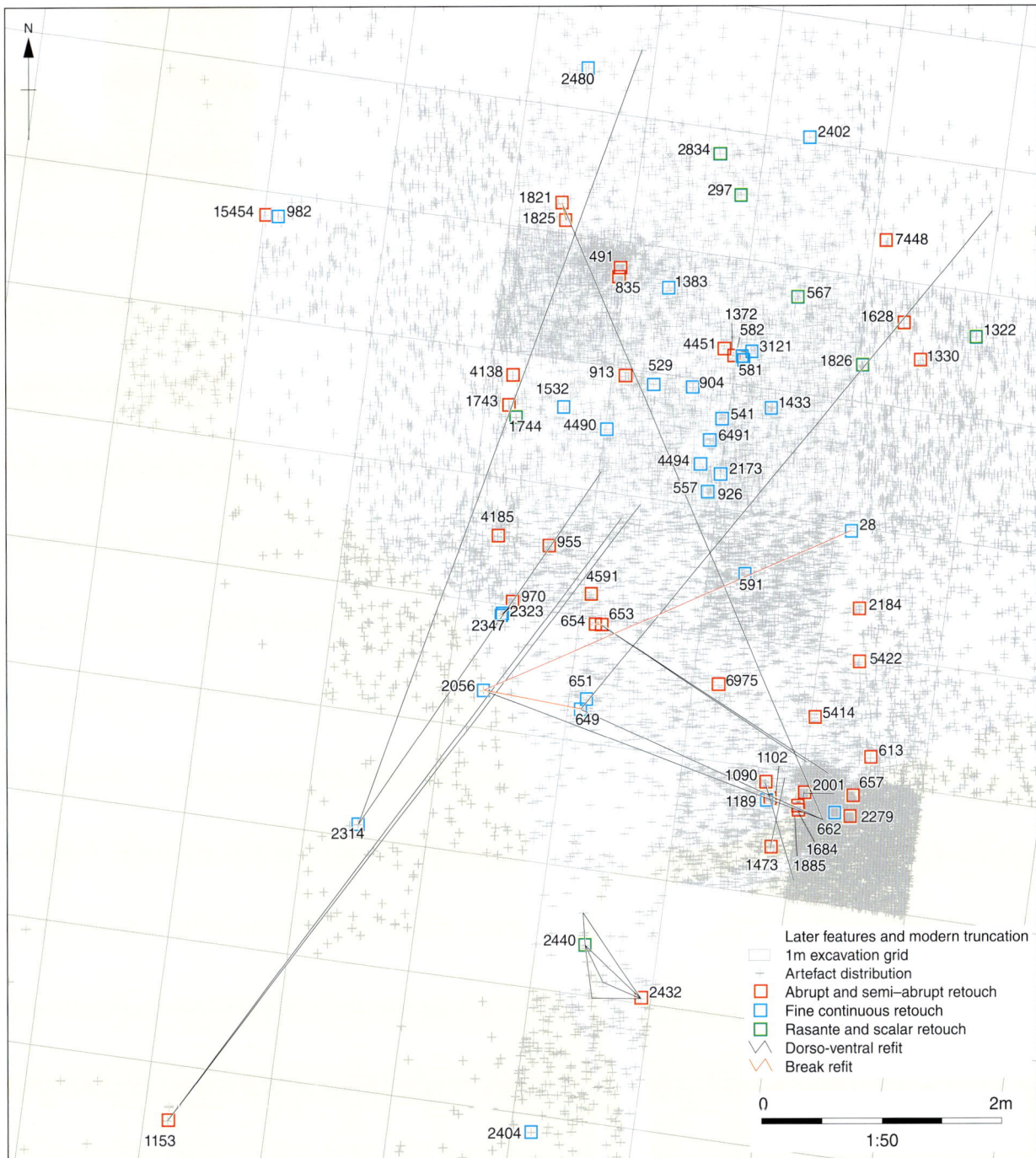

Fig. 6.29 Distribution of retouched pieces

them (eg the tips of tools) may yield some further useful information.

Blades and flakes with fine retouch

This category consists of a group of 20 blades and blade fragments and three flakes and flake fragments all of which have discontinuous, fine marginal retouch along their edges. For the flake and the two distal flake fragments it is possible that the retouch occurred spontaneously during the debitage process (cf Newcomer 1976) as all three of these artefacts have distal fine retouch. For the blades and blade fragments it is clear that the fine retouch could be associated with utilisation damage (see below). Of the 23 artefacts in this category eight are burnt and can be shown by refitting to belong to three separate blade blanks. One of them is made up of six fragments (one unretouched) that can be refitted to form a substantial portion of a large regular blade (c.904/c.529/c.541/c.3121/c.4194/c.6492; Fig. 6.26). The retouch is mainly confined to one edge. In the absence of the missing ends it is impossible to tell if it had been part of a formal tool. Two of the blade fragments are part of refit groups: c.649 in RG 10 and c.2314 in RG 38.

This category is fairly widely dispersed across the site except in the area of the northern knapping scatter (Fig. 6.29).

Edge-damaged blades and flakes

The 47 objects in this category are an indicative estimate only. They comprise 36 blades and blade fragments, 2 bladelets, 2 crested blades, 1 core platform rejuvenation flake and 6 flakes. None of these artefacts are burnt. They represent artefacts that display significant signs of edge damage on one or both edges. The damage usually occurs as a series of nicks, sometimes associated with isolated areas of retouch. It is difficult to separate these with any confidence from accidental effects, such as spontaneous retouch or trampling damage. However, similar features have been observed experimentally, and it is also possible that some of the artefacts are examples of utilised tools. Of the examples examined for microscopic use-wear traces none has so far produced any positive results. Nine of these artefacts form part of six different refit groups (RGs 01, 02, 03, 18, 39 and 67). One of the refitted artefacts is unidirectionally crested blade c.1093 that is the major part of RG 67 (Fig. 6.87). The tip of this crested blade is missing, and the distal

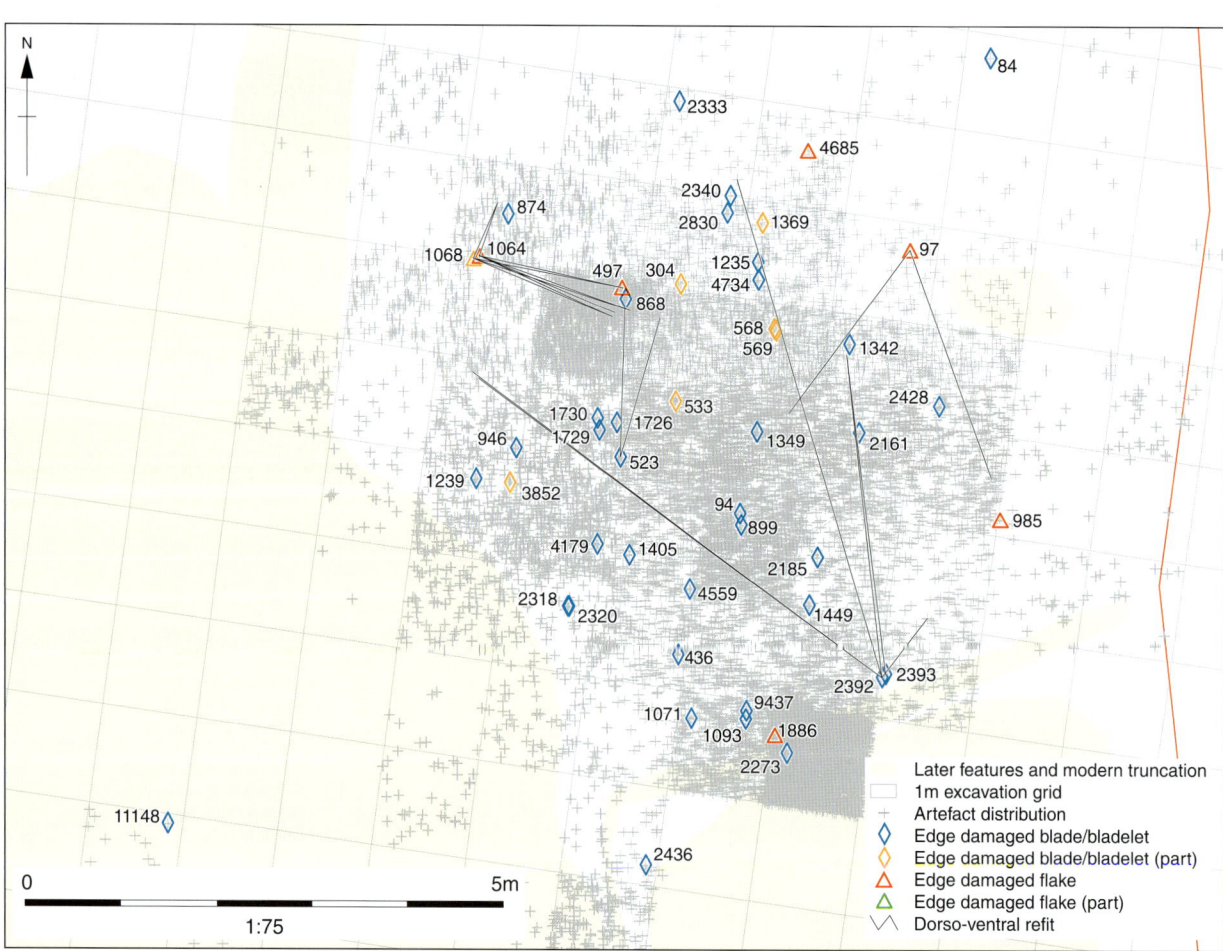

Fig. 6.30 Distribution of edge-damaged pieces

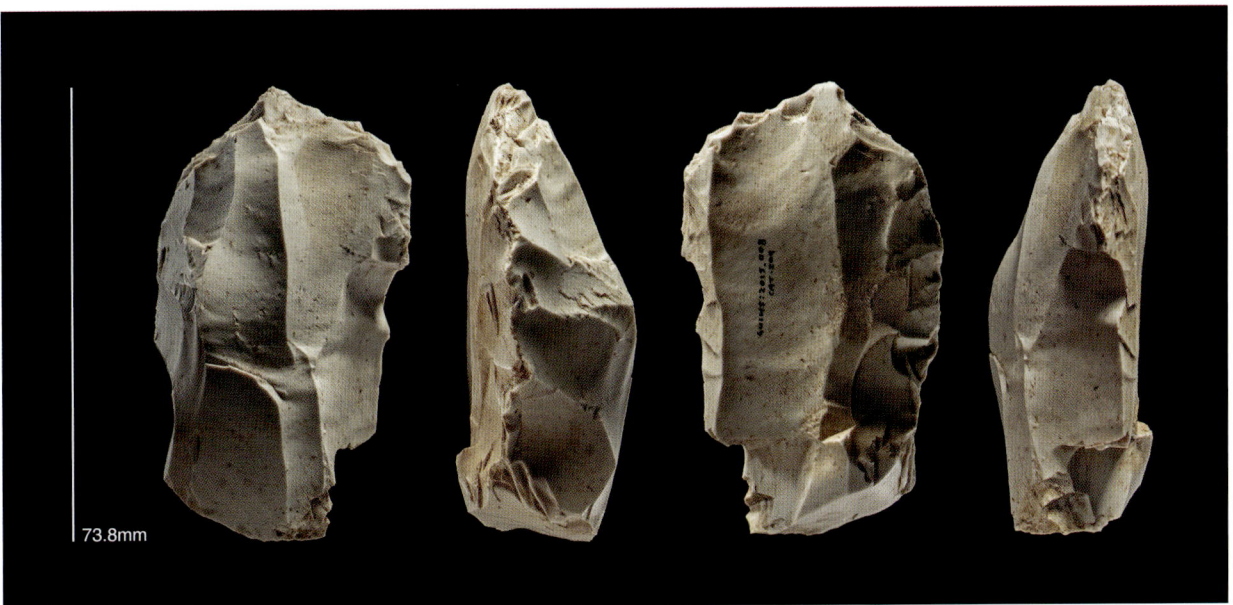

Fig. 6.31 Photograph of Mesolithic axe fragment reused as a bladelet core (c.209), surface find

end has indirect scalar edge damage on the left edge and similar direct damage on the right edge. There might also be some edge damage to the crest arête distally. It is likely that edge damage on this piece resulted from use.

The distribution of edge-damaged pieces is fairly evenly distributed across the whole site (Fig. 6.30)

POST-PALAEOLITHIC ARTEFACTS

Thirteen artefacts were identified as post-Palaeolithic types. They were mostly on patinated flints and included typical Mesolithic artefacts such as a bladelet core on an unpolished axe fragment (c.209, Fig. 6.31), a bladelet made of the same chert raw material (c.17), two microdenticulates (c.1150 and c.22), three microburins (c.1217, c.7412 and c.13376) and a possible oblique microlith fragment (c.232). There were also three retouched flakes (c.518, c.2494 and c.2528) and a retouched blade (c.323) of similar patina and a probably later prehistoric, possibly even modern multi-platform core (c.2557). All came from the surface or relatively high up in the stratigraphy and away from the main Upper Palaeolithic scatter.

REFITTING ANALYSIS

Introduction, methods and aims

A systematic refitting analysis was undertaken of the lithic artefacts (Fig. 6.32). It was conducted after the microwear study had been completed so as not to compromise any of the use-wear results by frequent handling of the flints.

A standard approach was used beginning with the area of greatest finds density in the northern part of the scatter and then proceeding methodically across its whole extent. The first stage of the work involved identifying refits within excavation squares, to make an initial assessment of the entire assemblage and the potential for more detailed refitting, and to raise research questions for further investigation. The next stage involved identifying refits between excavation squares with an emphasis on cores and core maintenance material and retouched tools and their debitage. A reversible acetone-soluble adhesive (Paraloid B72) was used to lightly glue refitting pieces together.

Refits can be divided into two basic types: break refits that describe conjoins across ancient snaps, and dorsal-to-ventral refits which reposition artefacts into their original places in the knapping sequence. Both types of refits were recorded for the Late Upper Palaeolithic assemblage.

The aims of the refitting analysis were fourfold:

1. To characterise the lithic technology and methods of manufacture. Refitting allows for a more precise analysis of the *chaîne opératoire*, enabling the related stages of the knapping process to be studied from initial shaping of a flint nodule through the various stages of core reduction to final discard. This analysis can also identify gaps in the refitting sequences where blanks were removed for use elsewhere. The latter has implications particularly for interpreting behaviours such as curation of knapping products and concerning forward planning.

2. To examine individual tool lifecycles through stages of initial manufacture to resharpening and discard.

3. To locate site activities and identify discard patterns at the site.

4. To test the integrity of the lithic scatters. Refitting can sometimes help verify if a site was occupied once or many times, and if the assemblage was

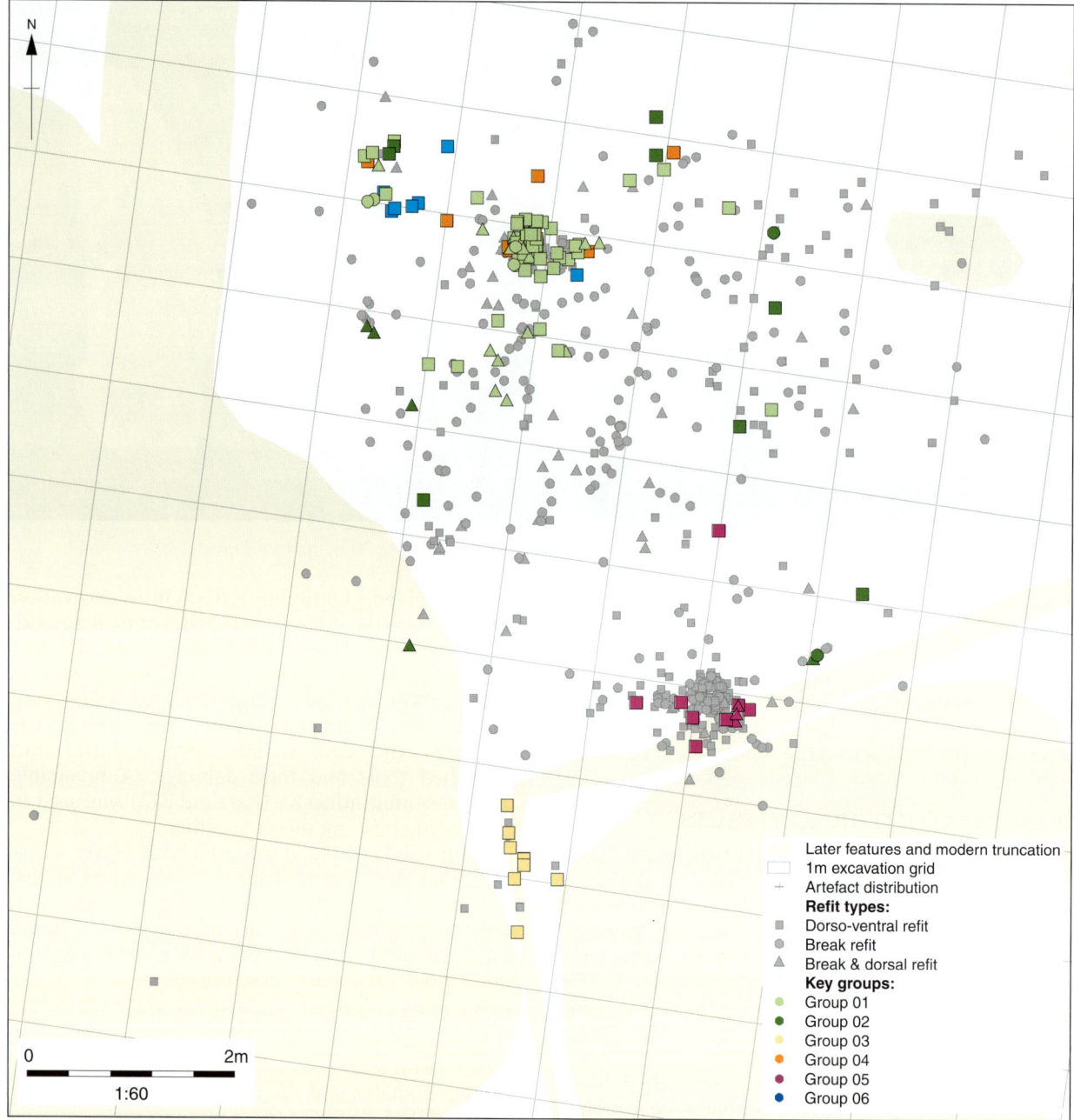

Fig. 6.32 *Overall distribution of all refitting artefacts*

affected by significant post-depositional disturbance. Such taphonomic processes can be examined via the vertical and horizontal distribution of refitted artefacts (see Chapter 5).

Break and spall refits and individual tool lifecycles

There are 174 sets of break refits involving 349 broken blades, bladelets and flakes (Fig. 6.33). The break refits include mends for broken tools but not refits of burin spalls to burins which are treated as a separate category (see below). Nearly all of the break refits represent flexional snaps that are often associated with knapping accidents (Barton *et al.* 1983). No patterning can be seen in the types of blanks with refitting breaks, which seem to reflect all stages of knapping. Eighteen are directly related to the production or maintenance of blade cores (crested pieces, core tablets and other core rejuvenators). Twenty of the break refits involve formal retouched tools and a further 37 relate to other retouched categories including edge-damaged pieces. Most of the breaks in the formal tools probably occurred during use and resharpening, as in end-scraper c.924/c.558/c.559 (Fig. 6.12). There is little evidence in the assemblage for the use of intentional breakage techniques (*fracture volontaire*, cf Barton *et al.* 1983) to create tool blanks.

The break refits represent about 17% of the total number of broken pieces in the assemblage, and it is likely that further examples could be found given more time. The mended breaks mainly occur within a metre of one another, and there are only a few examples that were found over longer distances. Interestingly, there are fewer break refits than dorso-ventral refits in the assemblage with 440 artefacts having dorso-ventral refits to at least one other artefact. This is consistent with the assemblage not having been subjected to high levels of trampling or other post-depositional disturbance.

The use of refitting is advantageous because it enables tools to be seen as part of a dynamic process which encompasses all the stages of manufacture and utilisation until discard. In addition, by mapping the spatial distribution of refits it is possible to establish a direct relationship between waste products and implements and to identify areas of concentrated activity that may otherwise have gone unrecognised. At Guildford Fire Station, it has allowed us to see how certain tools were made but also to determine the intensity of resharpening before they were discarded. Some of the results are discussed below, while the wider implications will be considered together with the microwear analysis in Chapter 8.

Amongst the retouched tool debitage it was possible to classify 45 burin spalls and nine tool retouch flakes (Table 6.5) of which some may have been from sharpening end-scrapers. The apparent scarcity of tool retouch flakes is not surprising given the difficulty in distinguishing small retouch flakes from other forms of debitage, and the fact that end-scrapers made up only a modest component (10) of the total tool assemblage. None of the tool retouch flakes could be shown to refit to any of the tools.

Before attempting to refit the burin spalls to burins, these pieces were first divided into lateral (28) and transverse types (10), the latter representing removals perpendicular to the axis of the tool and identifying themselves as by-products of transverse burins. Seven spalls or spall fragments could not be classified. The spalls were also subdivided into what might be interpreted as 'primary' and 'secondary or subsequent' removals. The primary spalls displayed the original edge of the tool, while the others showed facets from previous removals on their dorsal aspect. Of the 37 spalls which could be classified, 19 could be recognised as primary spalls and 18 as secondary spalls (Table 6.7).

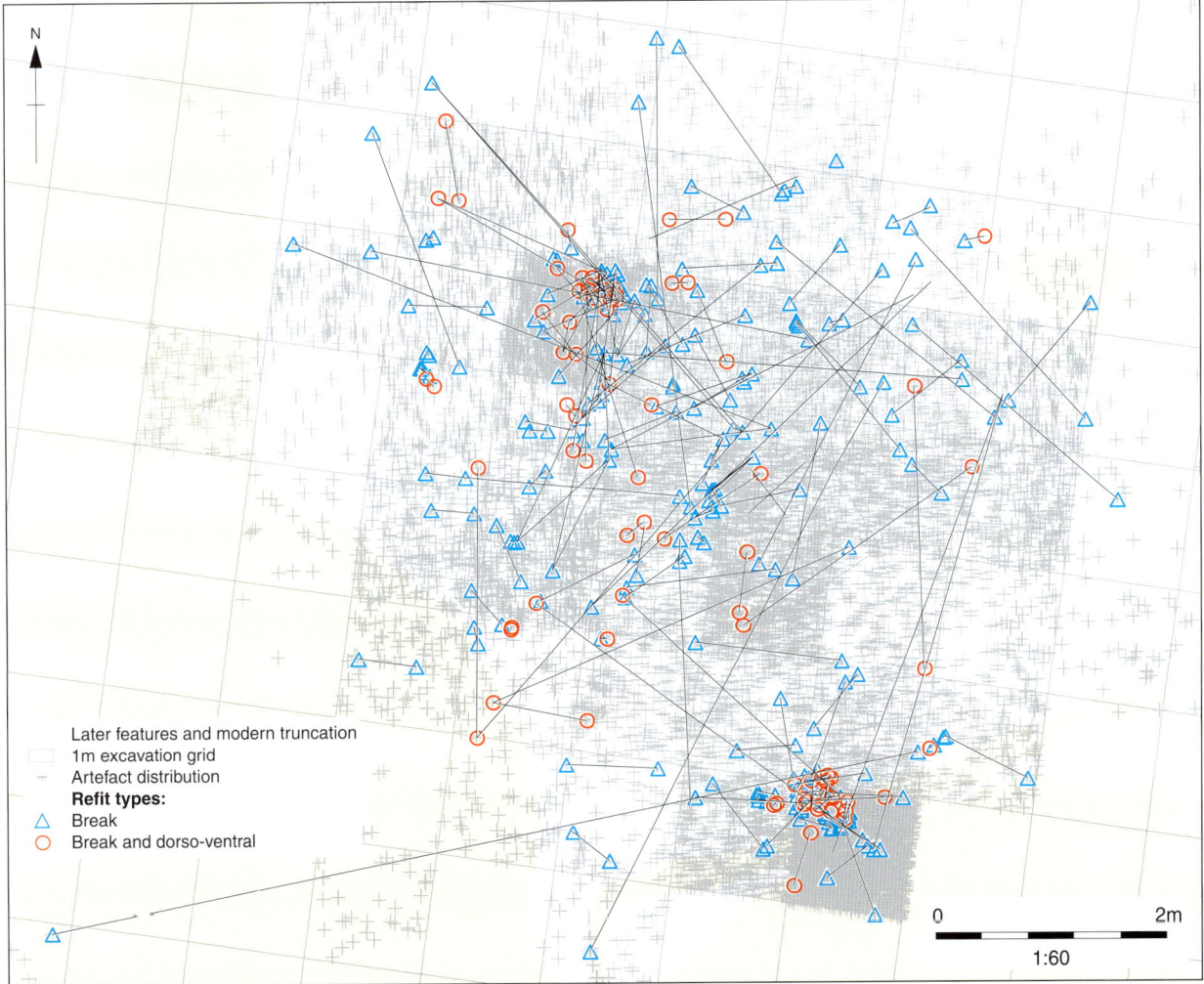

Fig. 6.33 Distribution of all break refits

Refitting was possible between eight burins and nine complete burin spalls, one made up of two refitting fragments (c.692/c.524; Fig. 6.18). In three cases primary spalls were refitted, while six secondary spalls could be conjoined, including two transverse forms. Amongst the interesting features shown by the secondary spall refits was the surprising lack of damage on one of the transverse spalls (c.4158; Fig. 6.18) as opposed to visible scarring on the burin facet itself. In another example both the refitting secondary spall and burin revealed signs of lateral edge damage, showing why resharpening had become necessary (c.2802 and c.319; Fig. 6.18). Little damage was visible for the primary spalls except on c.692/c.524 which formed part of the group fitting back on to burin c.319 (Fig. 6.18). Both of the spalls refitting this burin (c.692/c.524 and c.2802; Fig. 6.18) were found in close proximity to one another and only a short distance of no more than a metre or so from the burin.

One of the most interesting refits amongst the burins was a burin on a break (c.2313; Fig. 6.18) that could be fitted back to a burin on truncation (c.699; Fig. 6.18). The refit shows how the tool began as one typological form and was then modified into another by an oblique side blow (removing the distal end of the tool). It was then retouched and turned into a truncation burin. Without refitting it would have been impossible to identify this transformation or see the connection in the process. Both burins were found some distance apart, implying that the tool had been reused, perhaps in different activities. Another of the burins (c.1564; Fig. 6.11) can be dorso-ventrally refitted to an end-scraper (c.1315; Fig. 6.11). The two blades making up the blanks for these tools were found within a metre of one another and imply that they were both used within a fairly short space of time, perhaps in related activities.

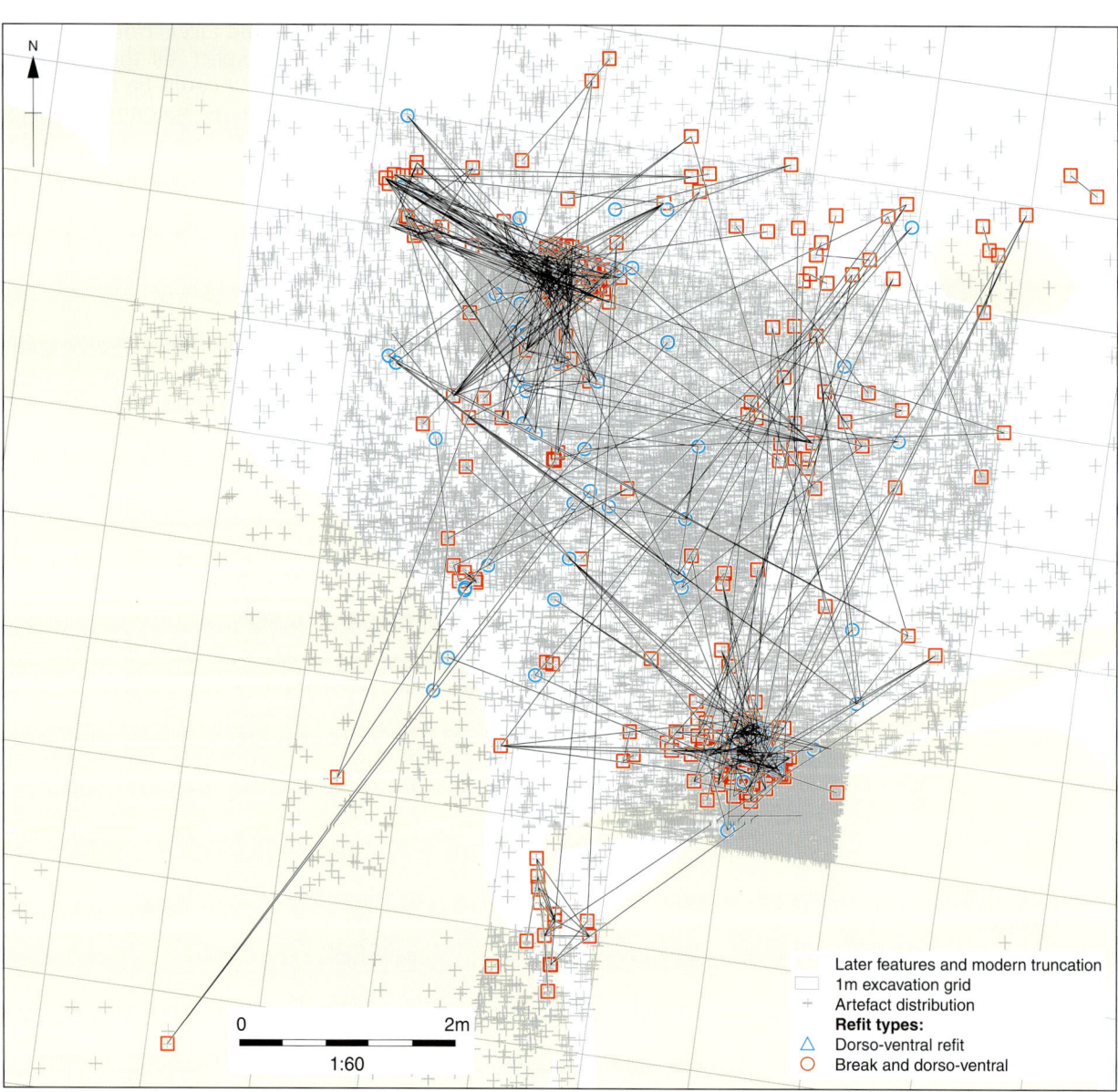

Fig. 6.34 Distribution of all dorso-ventral refits

Amongst the backed pieces were two Krukowski breaks (by-products of retouching the tip) that could be refitted (c.1732 and c.4743; Fig. 6.23). Both were in very fresh, sharp condition. These successive removals would be expected to be part of the same process of retouching the tip of a backed point and therefore should have been found close together. However, in this case the two fragments were recorded several metres apart and may suggest a more complicated life history of a backed tool that is not otherwise present on the site.

Dorso-ventral refits and refitting groups

Dorso-ventral refits are defined as conjoins which represent successive removals from a core, with the dorsal (upper) surface of one artefact fitting the ventral (lower) surface of another. At Guildford Fire Station, dorso-ventral refits were recorded for 439 artefacts, many refitting more than one other object. These types form 83 refit groups (RG) ranging in size from 73 objects (RG 01) to only 2 objects (38 groups). The distribution of all dorso-ventral refits is shown in Figure 6.34. The technological sequence of removals within each refitting group was recorded using a simplified version of the method described by Hiscock (1986).

The descriptions of the refit groups are presented below as a 'Catalogue of refit groups'. Individual distribution diagrams are presented for the twenty largest groups and for RG 25. Figure 6.93 shows the combined distribution of material from the remaining refit groups. Eleven groups contained cores or core fragments (RGs 01, 03, 04, 05, 06, 10, 13, 17, 20, 35 and 68) and provide information about how cores were used and abandoned at the site. Forty-four tools form parts of 27 different refitting groups (RGs 01, 02, 03, 04, 08, 09, 10, 12, 13, 14, 15, 18, 19, 24, 25, 31, 37, 38, 39, 41, 42, 43, 53, 56, 67, 75 and 83; see individual RG distributions and Fig. 6.92). The inclusion of so many tools within the refitting groups confirms that many of them were both knapped and used at the site. Overall, the larger refitting groups provide information about the knapping strategies used at the site, while the smaller groups provide information about the use of specific techniques. The behavioural implications of the refitting groups is discussed in a later section of this chapter. Refitting of the lithic assemblages provides strong evidence that Guildford Fire Station is an *in situ* Late Upper Palaeolithic site with little disturbance (see Chapter 5).

Catalogue of artefact refit groups (RG)

Three refit group numbers are missing from the catalogue as they were incorporated with other groups. These are former RG 44 (now part of RG 39), RG 52 (now part of RG 05), and RG 79 (now part of RG 68). Further details of the refit groups is contained in the site archive.

Refit Group 01 (n=73; Figs 6.35–6.36)

Refit Group 01, a complex group of 73 refitting elements, represents most of an entire knapping sequence. It has been photographed in three parts so that the reduction sequence can be seen properly. The first part represents initial core shaping and blade manufacture. Many of the artefacts in this part retain the outer cortex of the nodule. The second part is the exhausted core and its final removals. The third part is a small mainly cortical group of initial core shaping removals that joins the other two parts, but which are difficult to see when the whole block is refitted. Figure 6.35 shows all three parts and indicates where they join.

The group centres on single-platform core, c.504, that appears to have been abandoned when it was no longer viable for blade production (maximum length 65mm). Refitting shows that the core was originally much larger, with an opposed platform, and at one point also had a different orientation that was perpendicular to the axis of the final core. The components of the group directly related to core maintenance are a *sous-crête* blade (c.910) and refitting cresting flake (c.869), one crested flake, a *sous-crête* flake and three core rejuvenation flakes. The primary aim of knapping was blade production, and there are 21 blades in the group, five of them made of two refitting fragments each. All but one are soft stone hammer struck. One blade that directly refits the core is hard hammer struck. Most blades have plain butts, seven with platform abrasion. Two have cortical butts, one dihedral, and a single faceted example with platform abrasion. These include one tool, a double-notched blade, c.1391. There are also 34 flakes, four made up of a total of nine fragments, many of which seem to have been removed to maintain the core shape. The flakes include three tools: a retouched flake, c.1390, and two edge-damaged flakes, c.1064 and c.2200/c.4069. Most of the flakes are soft stone hammer struck, with two made by soft organic hammer, and two, refitting the core directly, by a hard stone. A variety of butt types are represented, the majority being plain. Six flakes have platform abrasion.

The majority of the artefacts in RG 01 were tightly grouped in a small area no more than 0.5m in diameter in the northern concentration. The distribution suggests that this group might also have had a clearly defined edge to the north, and it is possible that this could indicate the position of the flintknapper, sitting facing the area between the scatters. Most other elements of the refit group were located in the near vicinity with only a *sous-crête* blade (c.910) being located more than 2m away in the area between the two concentrations. A small linear group of ten artefacts was located just to the east of the main concentration. This group consists of six blades and three flakes, one blade-like. Tools c.1390 and c.1391 form part of this group. It is tempting to interpret this group as artefacts put to

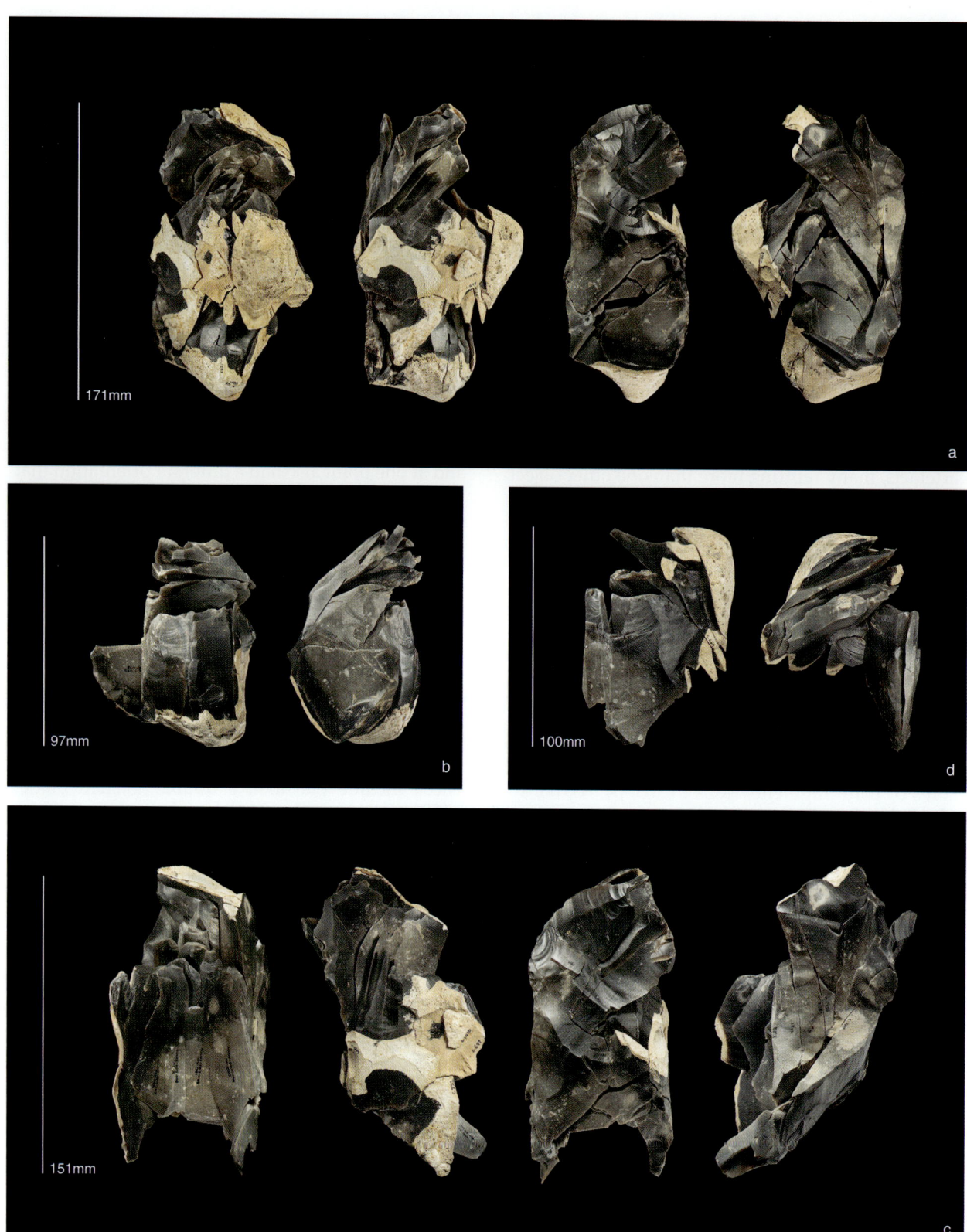

Fig. 6.35 Photograph of Refit Group 01: a) complete refit group; b) core and final removals; c) core shaping and blade manufacture; d) core shaping

one side by the knapper. Another small group of six artefacts was located in the area to the west where the 'novice' RG 06 was located. This group includes a large blade (84mm), a large *sous-crête* flake (93mm) and three other flakes. The group also contains the edge-damaged flake (c.1064/c.1068). This group perhaps represents material collected by, or passed to, the 'novice' for practice.

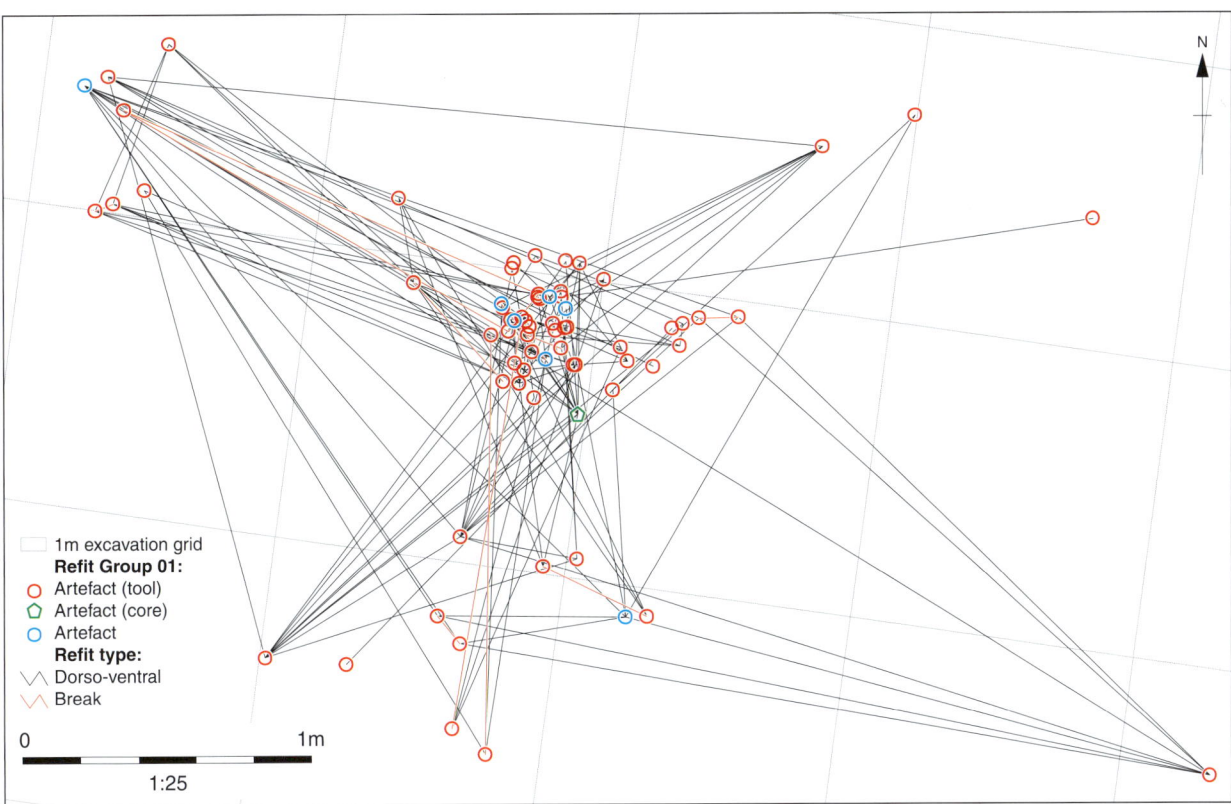

Fig. 6.36 Distribution of Refit Group 01

Refit Group 02 (n=15; Figs 6.37–6.38)

Refit Group 02 represents core shaping and the early stages of blade removal. The group does not include a core and no elements of the group retain cortex. The group consists of two parts: one representing an early stage of core shaping, and the other representing later primary blade removals from the core. The two parts are joined by a blade blank consisting of two refitting burins (on a truncation and on a break) and a refitting retouched blade fragment (c.699/c.2313/c.7448; Fig. 6.18). None of the other *plein debitage* removals from between the two groups were located in the assemblage. The group contains one other tool, a large plunging blade with ventral edge damage (c.2392/c.2393; length 113mm).

The combined group consists of seven blades and four flakes, most of large size. Three of the blades are made up of fragments (both tools and a large plunging blade) and one is a proximal fragment. The flakes include two large distal fragments lacking only the butts. All were soft stone hammer struck with plain butts and only one has platform abrasion. Elements of the group were found dispersed over the site and do not seem to be associated directly with either concentration. The burins were found about 3m apart, one just south-west of the northern concentration, and the other south-west of the southern concentration. The two refitting fragments of the edge-damaged blade (c.2392/c.2393) were found just to the east of the southern concentration. Two refitting large distal fragments of large plunging blades (c.823 and c.877, from the earlier group) were found in the area of the 'novice' RG 06 next to the northern concentration.

Refit Group 03 (n=12; Figs 6.39–6.40)

Refit Group 03 centres on a blade core fragment (c.2542) and several other large refitting fragments all relating to the early stages of shaping a core. These include two crested pieces (a blade and a flake), two core platform rejuve-

Fig. 6.37 Photograph of Refit Group 02

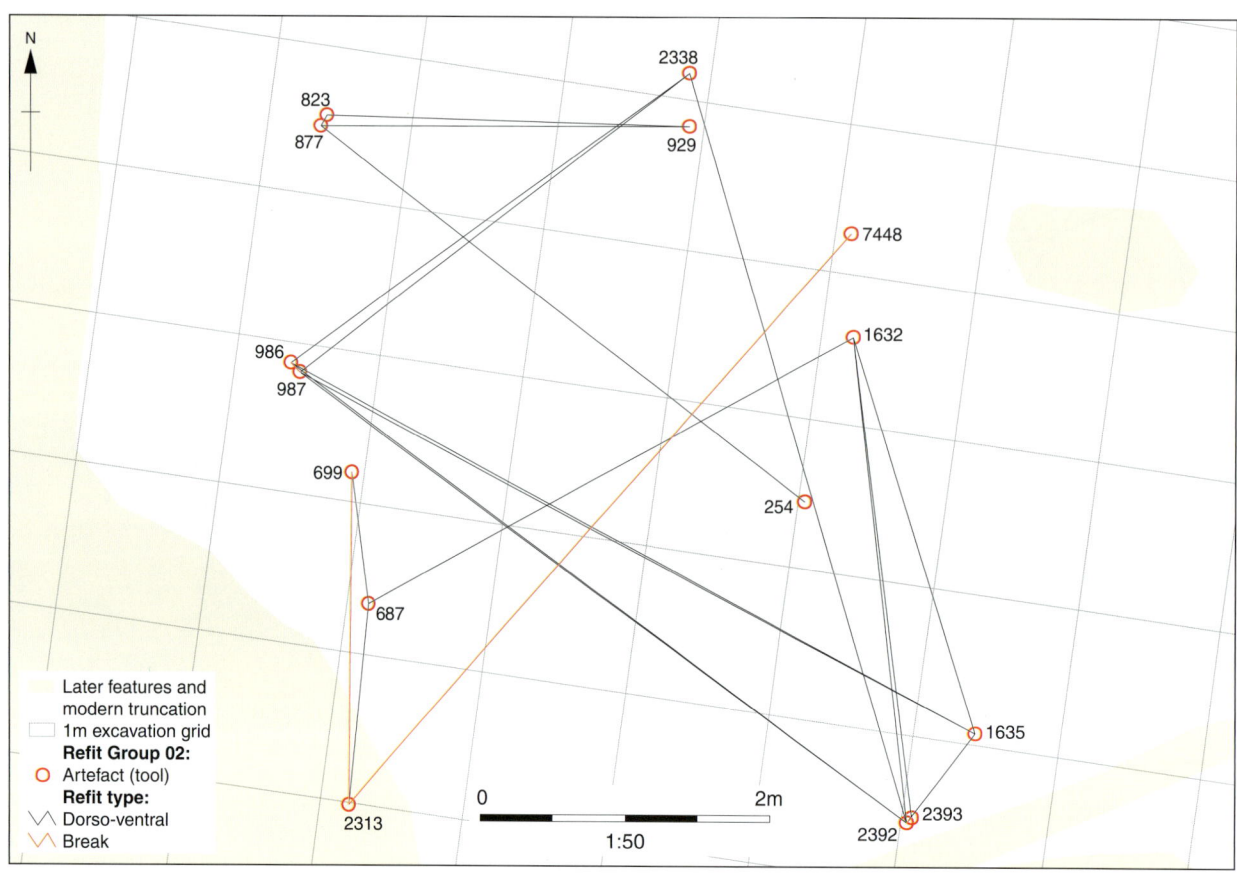

Fig. 6.38 Distribution of Refit Group 02

nators, six flakes (two of them tools), and a piece of irregular waste. Removals were by both hard and soft stone hammers and all butts were plain with no platform abrasion. The two tools are a flake, c.2432, with semi-abrupt and invasive retouch at the distal end, and edge-damaged flake distal fragment c.2440. Some of the breaks in this group seem to relate to a natural fracture in the flint associated with fossil inclusions. The refits also define a large piece of flint now missing from the site (at least 60mm by 70mm by 60mm). This flint block might have been used for other purposes, including as a smaller core, but no evidence for it could be found in the assemblage. Eight elements of the group were found on the surface but have 3D coordinates and can be located to an area 2m to the south-west of the southern scatter. One of the larger flakes was later excavated from the same area (c.520). The other pieces are unlocated. The flint has reddish tinges.

Fig. 6.39 Photograph of Refit Group 03

Chapter 6

Refit Group 04 (n=10; Figs 6.41–6.42)
Refit Group 04 consists of a small cortex-backed opposed-platform blade core and a sequence of refitting blade removals. The core was carefully maintained and appears to have been abandoned when the size became too small for effective blade production (below a length of *c* 60mm). The group centres on opposed-platform blade core c.1399 and also includes five blades and three flakes, two of which were for platform rejuvenation, and another, which is made up of two fragments. One of the blades is a tool, a transverse burin (c.701). The burin is on the thick distal end of a plunging blade. A siret break at the proximal end may have provided a potential working edge as is suggested by lateral damage on its surface. Where preserved, all the blanks have plain butts and were detached by soft stone hammer. Platform abrasion is only present on one small flake that might have been a platform rejuvenator. The group was located in the northern concentration except for one large plunging blade that was from the adjacent area where RG 06 is located (the 'novice' group). The flint has reddish tinges.

Refit Group 05 (n=11; Figs 6.43–6.44)
Refit Group 05 consists of a broken blade core with refits relating to initial core shaping. Many of the intervening elements of blade reduction are missing and presumed to have been moved into another

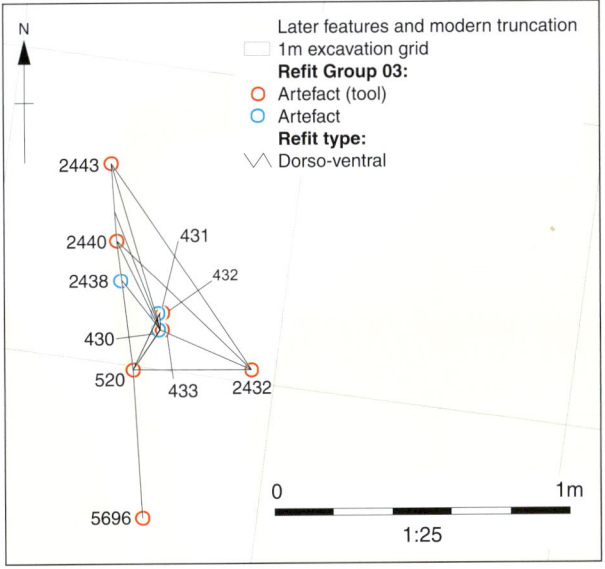

Fig. 6.40 Distribution of Refit Group 03

Fig. 6.41 Photograph of Refit Group 04

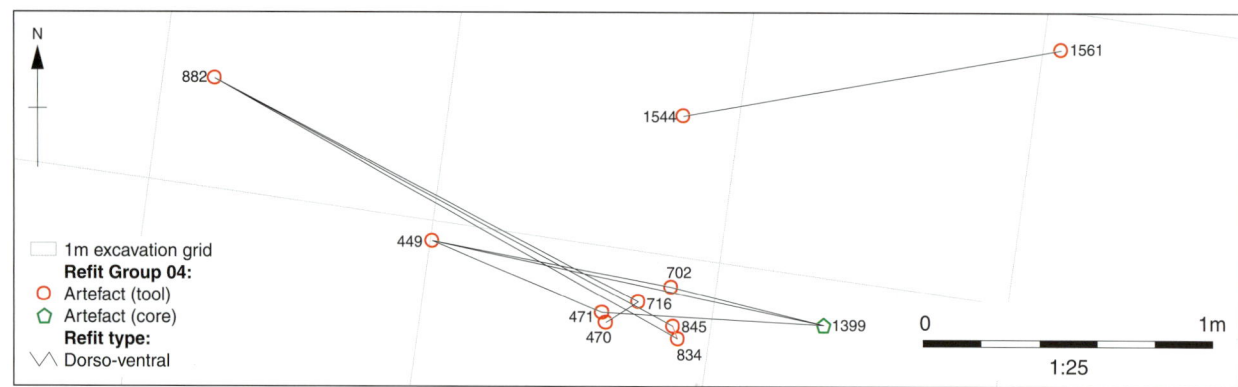

Fig. 6.42 Distribution of Refit Group 04

area or away from the site. The group centres on a single-platform blade core, c.1940, with a refitting basal core fragment (c.1181) and a large semi-cortical unidirectionally crested blade (c.1106; length 118mm). It also includes a core platform rejuvenation flake (c.1898), a blade distal fragment (c.14; length 59mm) and four flakes, one of them made up from three fragments. All removals were by soft stone and have no platform abrasion. Most have plain platforms, except for the platform rejuvenation flake which is faceted. The number of possible blade removals may have been reduced by natural fracture planes within the flint. A break along a natural fracture also detached the base of the core and led to its abandonment. The group had a tight distribution in the southern concentration except for the large blade fragment which was located about 2m to the north in the area between the concentrations.

Refit Group 06 (n=8; Figs 6.45–6.46)

Refit Group 06 is the only group that does not seem to be entirely the product of skilled flint working, and it is hypothesised to be the work of an inexpert, seemingly novice knapper (Roberts and Barton 2021). The group centres on a single-platform flake core (c.1905) which is cortically-backed and made on a river cobble. No other cores from the site are made on this material, and only a small proportion of the debitage and debris retains cortex with these features (at most 7%). The group also contains four flakes, two blades and a core platform rejuvenation flake. The flakes are laminar and soft stone hammer struck with large plain butts and no platform abrasion. One is cortical and two others retain cortex. The other flake shows damage to the platform surface by repeated blows prior to removal. One blade is near complete, lacking only the proximal end and has cortex at the distal end. The other is the first removal of the series and is a well-made blade produced by soft stone hammer and with an *en éperon*-like butt and platform abrasion (c.2403). It has a slightly curved profile. The core platform rejuvenation flake (c.1908) is part cortical and shows extensive damage and crushing of the core platform due to repeated prior blows. The four blades and the blade fragment were removed after the platform rejuvenator and were reasonably well executed although generally lacking the precise technical skill shown on debitage from other refitting groups. Dorsal scars on the core show that the final two to three removals were of a different, less controlled nature and were apparently

Fig. 6.43 Photograph of Refit Group 05

Chapter 6

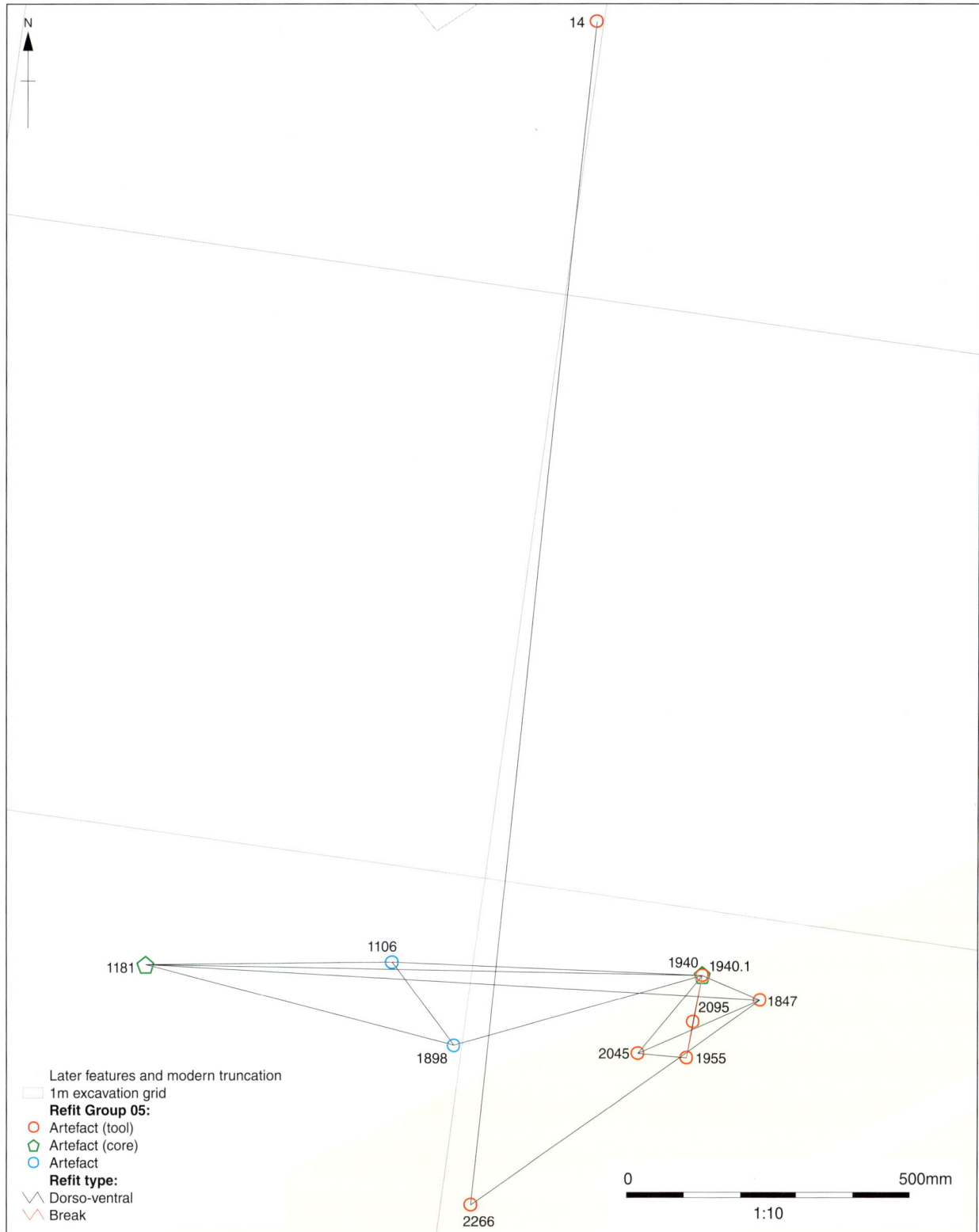

Fig. 6.44 Distribution of Refit Group 05

either hard hammer struck and/or detached with considerable force. The core was abandoned following these removals. The core, flakes and blade fragment were all found near each other about 1.0–0.5m to the west of the northern concentration. The core rejuvenation flake was found in the northern concentration and within the distribution of RG 01. The well-made blade was found about 3m away to the north-east of the main RG 06 distribution.

The core seems to have been set up on a river cobble by an expert knapper, who removed the well-made blade (c.2403). The butt of this blade

Fig. 6.45 Photograph of Refit Group 06

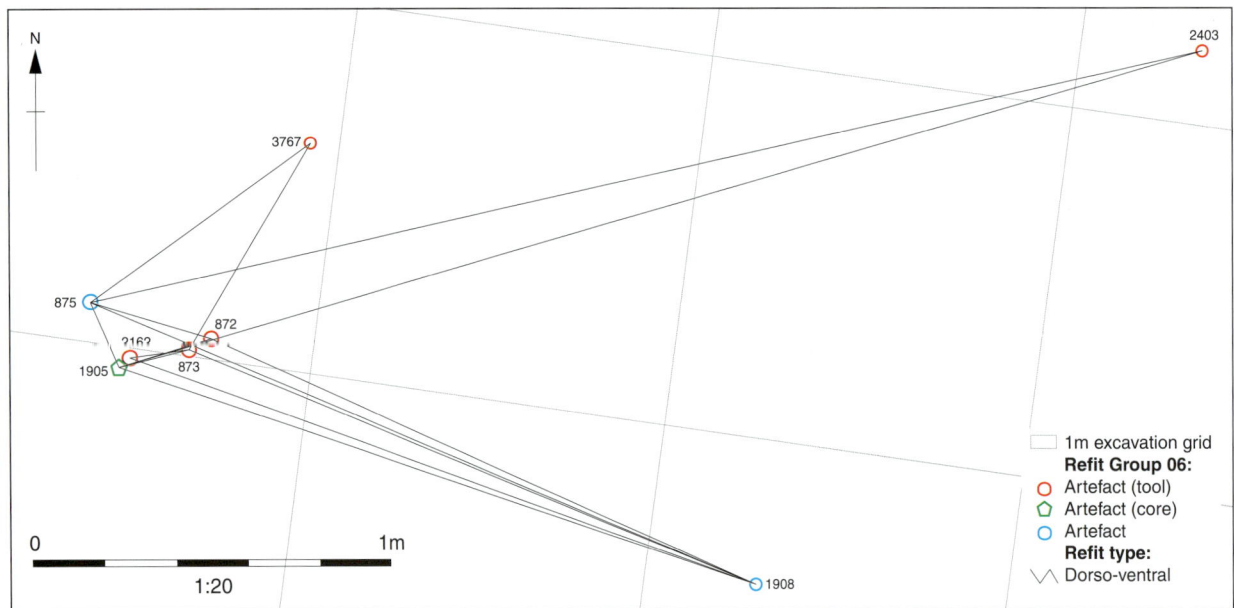

Fig. 6.46 Distribution of Refit Group 06

Chapter 6

seems to be on the same alignment as the core platform at the start of reduction. The core preparation appears to have taken place in the northernmost part of the site (in the direction of the river). Gaps in the reduction sequence show that several removals were made before the unsuccessful attempts at refreshing the core platform that damaged the core. The nature of these removals and where the knapping took place is unknown as none of these removals have been located. Dorsal scars suggest that at least some were laminar flake removals rather than blades. The successful core platform rejuvenation flake (c.1908) was removed in the northern concentration by a skilled flintknapper, and perhaps took place contemporaneously with the knapping of RG 01. The knapping activity and core abandonment represented by the majority of RG 06 then took place next to and west of the northern concentration. It is hypothesised that this refitting group represents the activity of a novice flintknapper learning the skill (per Grimm 2000), and that the removal of the platform by the northern concentration knapper to repair the core could be seen as an 'educational interaction' with the novice of the type proposed by Johansen and Stapert (2004), in this case possibly demonstrating how to refresh a core platform.

Refit Group 07 *(n=14; Figs 6.47–6.48)*

Refit Group 07 represents the initial stages of core shaping and core reduction. The sequence

Fig. 6.47 Photograph of Refit Group 07

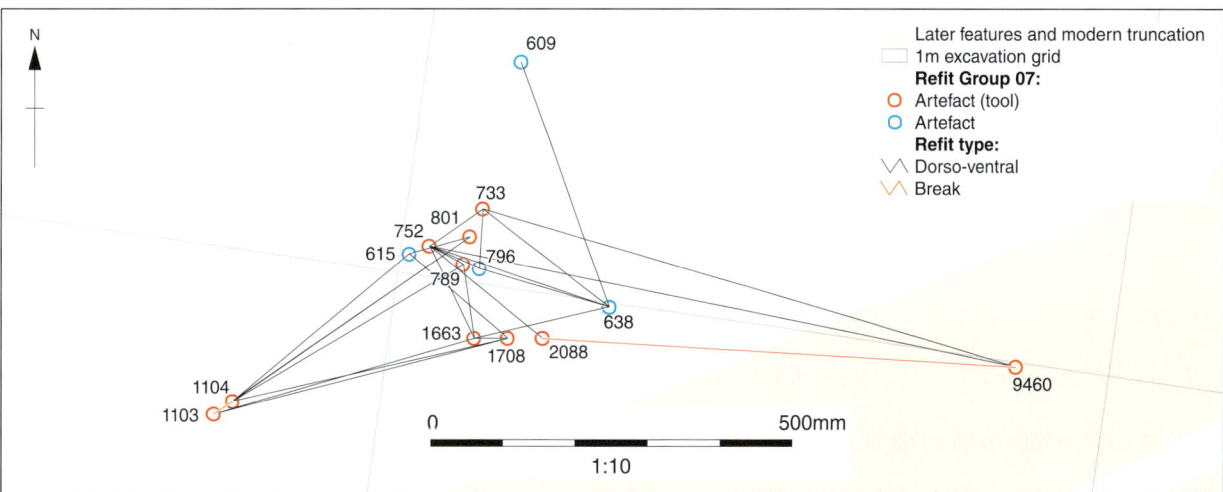

Fig. 6.48 Distribution of Refit Group 07

began with the removal of three thick cortical flakes, one made up of two fragments, and a flake mesial fragment. The thick flakes have plain cortical butts that were soft stone hammer struck. These were followed by a small piece of irregular waste and a distal flake fragment affected by a large internal fossil inclusion in the flint. A gap shows that other removals were made at this time around the inclusion. The final removals of the group are a sequence of five refitting core platform rejuvenation flakes, two of them made up of two fragments. They were all made by soft stone hammer percussion and have faceted butts with no abrasion. The group was tightly distributed in the southern concentration.

Refit Group 08 (n=16; Figs 6.49–6.50)

Refit Group 08 consists of a sequence of nine refitting core platform rejuvenation flakes, some of them typical core tablets, one distal flake fragment flake (that might originally have been from another platform rejuvenator) and three pieces of irregular waste. Three of the platform rejuvenators are made up of two mended fragments. The final platform rejuvenation flake removal has semi-abrupt retouch on the right edge distally and might once have been a scraper although the distal end is missing (c.1090). The sequence of removals shows how the core face was worked with platform angles adjusted during blade removal. The position of the bulbs of percussion on the platform rejuvenators shows that the core was rotated sequentially in an anticlockwise direction, until the final removal where the core was struck from the original direction. The core face seems to have been reduced by about 20mm during the reduction process. All of the removals were by soft stone hammer. The fragments of irregular waste all refit each other, and the largest (c.1881) appears to have been detached from the back of the core at the same time as the removal of the third from last platform rejuvenation flake and might represent an accident of knapping. Some cortex survives on two pieces of irregular waste, and several of the earlier removals show evidence of a large internal fossil inclusion. The group was tightly distributed in the southern scatter apart from two elements that were located in the area between the concentrations. The dispersed elements are a small piece of irregular waste, found just north of the southern scatter, and a platform rejuvenation flake (c.135), found about 4m distant.

Fig. 6.49 Photograph of Refit Group 08

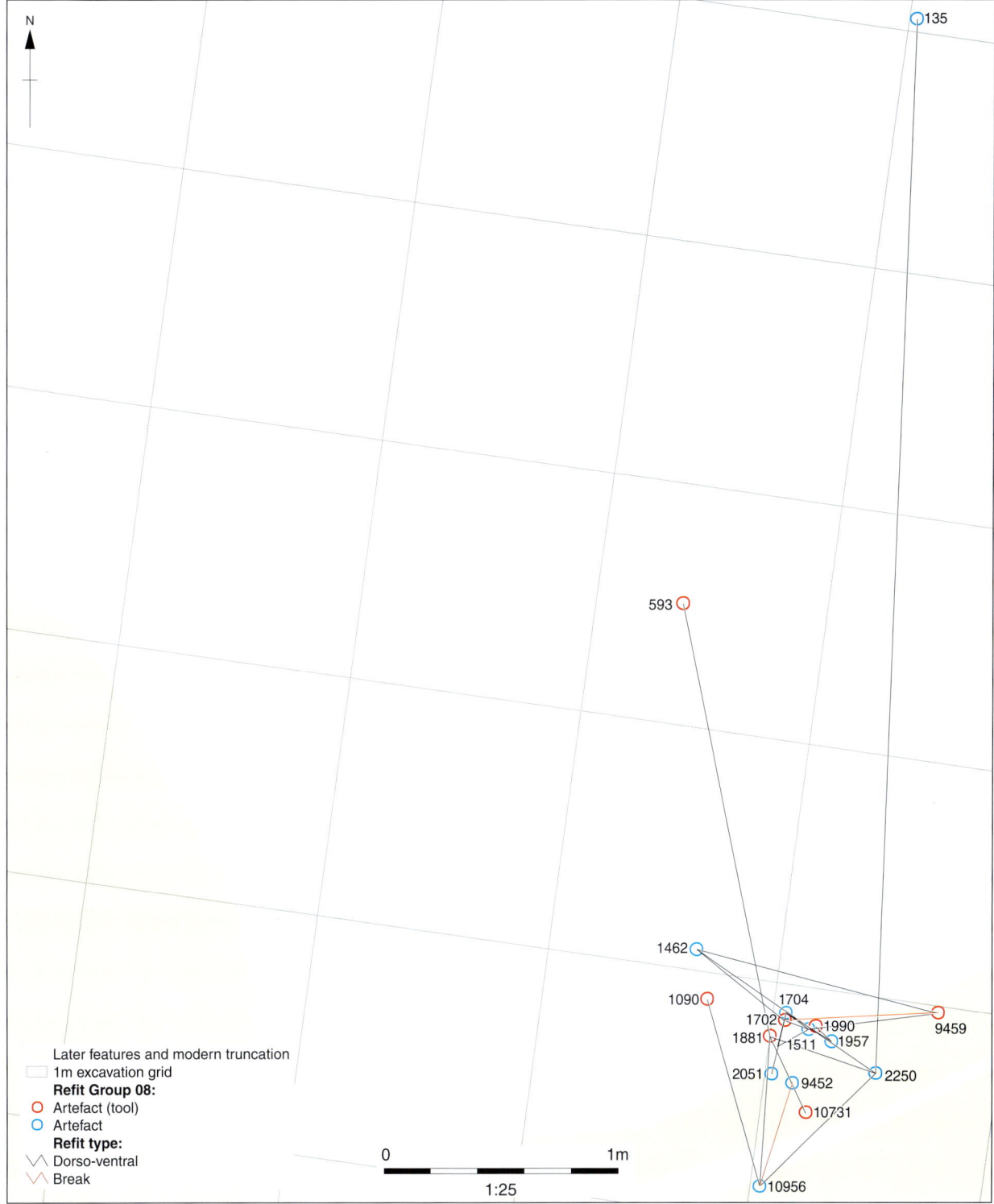

Fig. 6.50 Distribution of Refit Group 08

Refit Group 09 *(n=11; Figs 6.51–6.52)*

Refit Group 09 represents an initial stage of knapping and shaping a core, and consists of a sequence of eight removals: six flakes and two blade proximal fragments. Two of the flakes are made up of mended fragments, one of two and the other of three. All removals were struck with a soft stone hammer and most of the butts are plain apart from two flakes that have dihedral examples. There is no use of platform abrasion. Traces of cortex survive at the distal ends of the two largest flakes. The third from last removal is a double-notched flake (c.1458) with a notch on both sides below a distal break. The group was tightly distributed in one square of the southern scatter apart from a

Fig. 6.51 Photograph of Refit Group 09

proximal blade fragment (c.2298), which was found about 0.5m away.

Refit Group 10 *(n=13; Figs 6.53–6.54)*

Refit Group 10 centres around a substantial core fragment, c.675, that seems to have been the base of a heavily reduced opposed-platform blade core before it was broken into two pieces along a natural fracture plane. The final removal seems to have been an attempted platform rejuvenation flake terminated by the natural break. Before that a group of a blade, a flake and irregular waste were removed, all seemingly also affected by the same natural fracture surface. The removals and the core fragment show that the core had a cortical back. Refitting shows that in an earlier stage of reduction the core had a different orientation to the one evidenced on the fragment. A sequence of four earlier refitting blades are oriented perpendicular to the axis of the core fragment and provide evidence of the original orientation of the core. One of these blades, made of

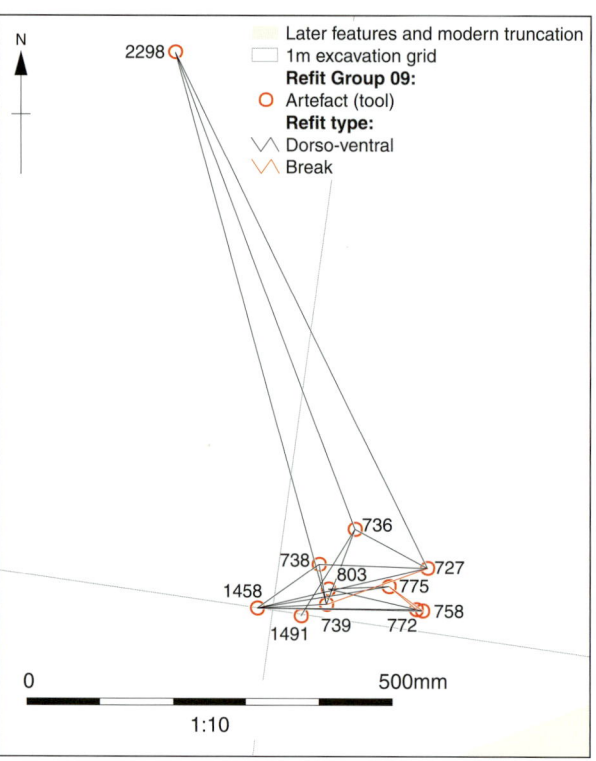

Fig. 6.52 Distribution of Refit Group 09

three fragments, has fine continuous retouch proximally on the left edge (c.28/c.2056/c.649; Fig. 6.26). Another blade, made of two fragments, has semi-abrupt and scalar retouch on the left edge (c.1821/c.1825). In general, the refitting artefact removals were by soft stone hammer and had either faceted or plain butts. The core fragment and the last removal were found in the southern concentration; the other elements of the groups were widely dispersed on the site, including one blade which

Fig. 6.53 Photograph of Refit Group 10

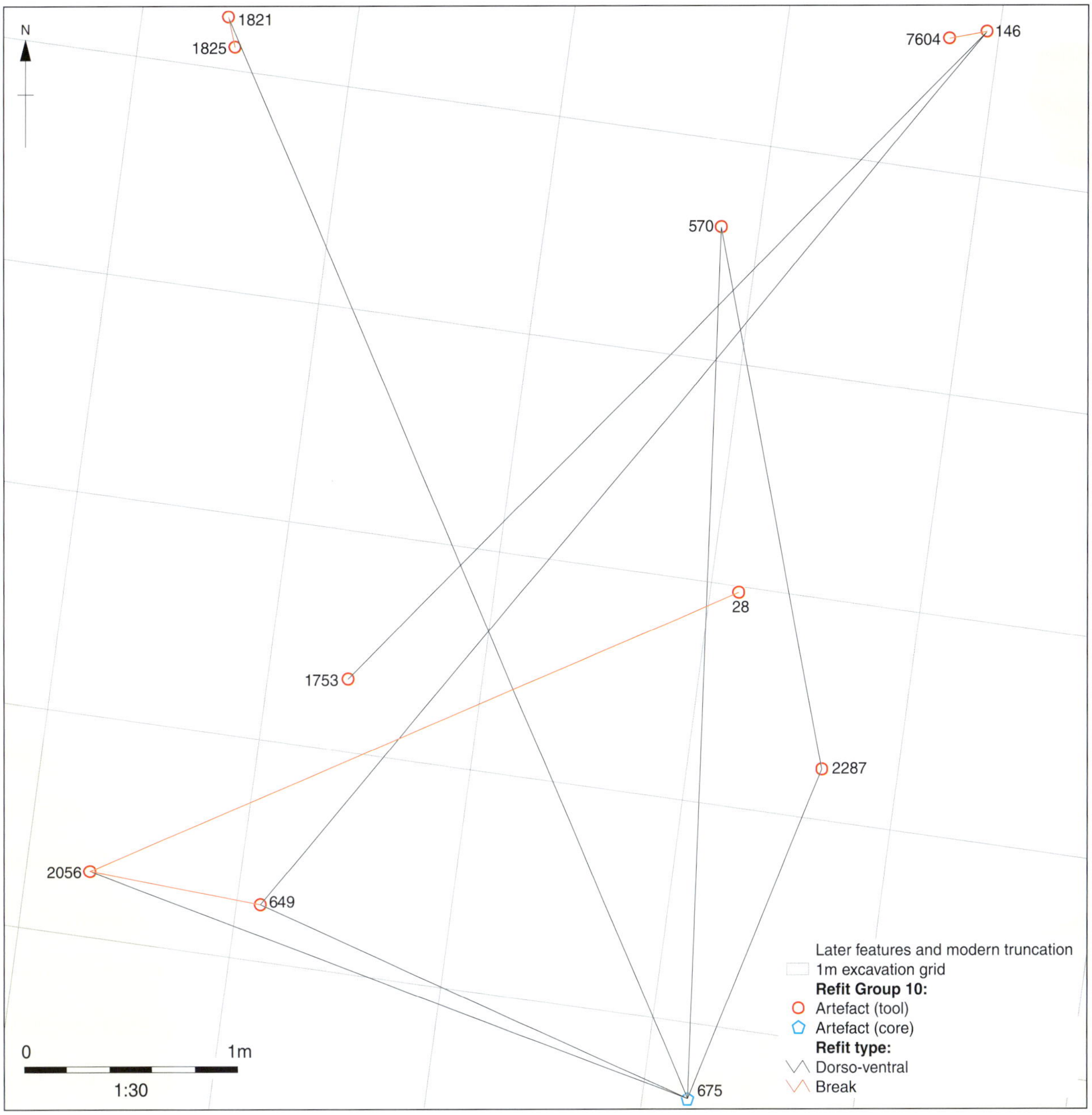

Fig. 6.54 Distribution of Refit Group 10

was found close to the northern concentration. The flint has reddish tinges.

Refit Group 11 *(n=10; Figs 6.55–6.56)*

Refit Group 11 is a sequence of four core platform rejuvenation flakes. They are all soft stone hammer struck with no platform abrasion. A small piece of irregular waste was detached at the same time as one of the rejuvenators. There are three additional flakes, one made up of three fragments. They are located either side of the platform rejuvenator sequence and relate to shaping the top of the core. Cortex is present on two of the flakes. The flakes are also soft stone hammer struck and two have plain platforms and

Fig. 6.55 Photograph of Refit Group 11

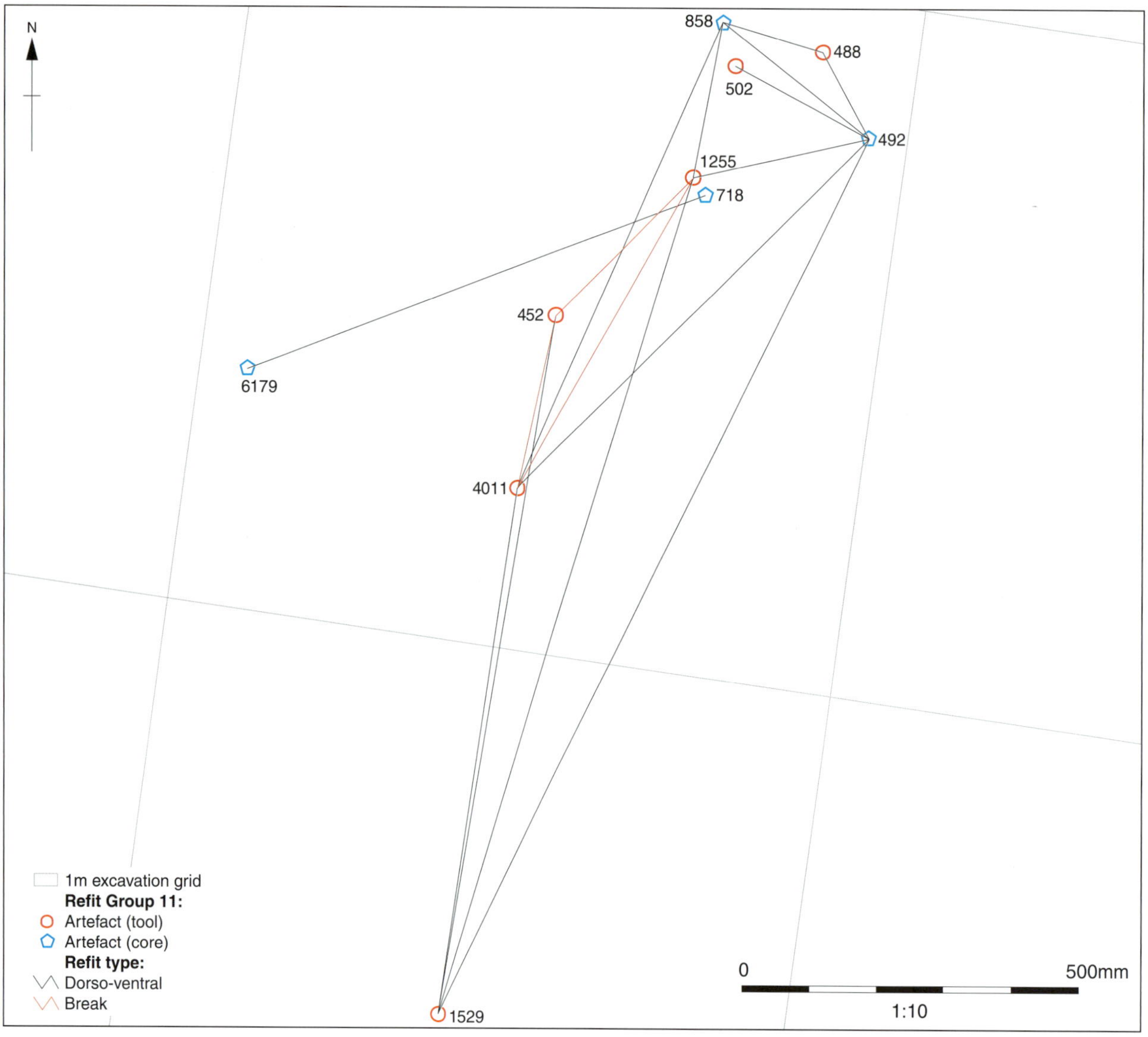

Fig. 6.56 Distribution of Refit Group 11

one is dihedral. The group was tightly distributed in one square of the northern concentration. The only outlier was the largest flake (c.1529), which was from the adjoining square about 0.5m away.

Refit Group 12 *(n=10; Figs 6.57–6.58)*

Refit Group 12 consists of blades removed alternately from an opposed-platform core. The presence of cresting and *sous crête*, and the curvature of the profiles, shows that the blades belong to an early part of the production sequence. The first refitting removal of the sequence is a *sous-crête* blade (c.653/c.654), with semi-abrupt retouch at the tip and some discontinuous retouch on the left edge. It is soft organic hammer struck with a plain platform and no abrasion. This blade was followed from the opposed end by a unidirectionally crested blade which has three refitting cresting flakes, one of which removed part of the crest edge. The crested blade is soft stone hammer struck and has a faceted platform with no abrasion. The cresting

Fig. 6.57 Photograph of Refit Group 12

Chapter 6

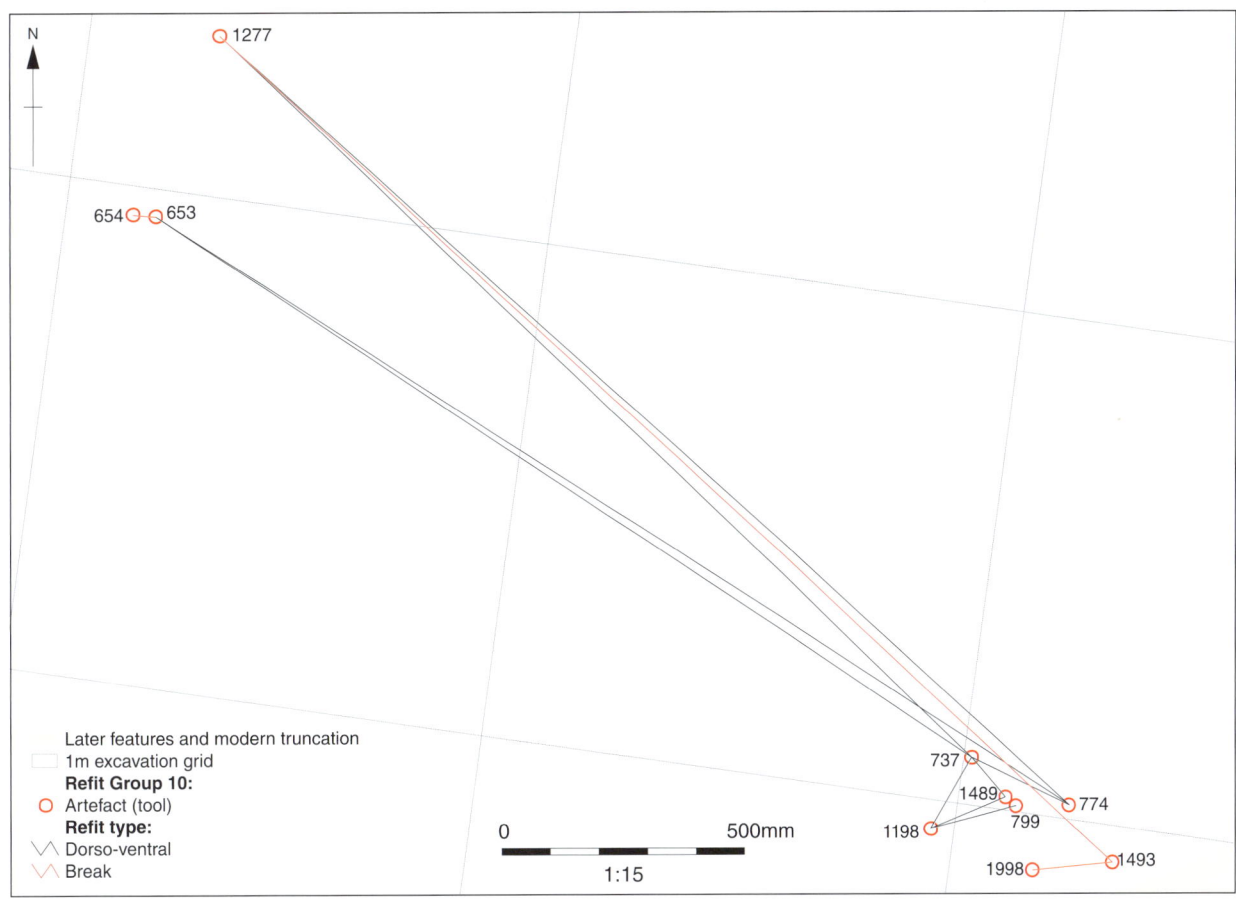

Fig. 6.58 *Distribution of Refit Group 12*

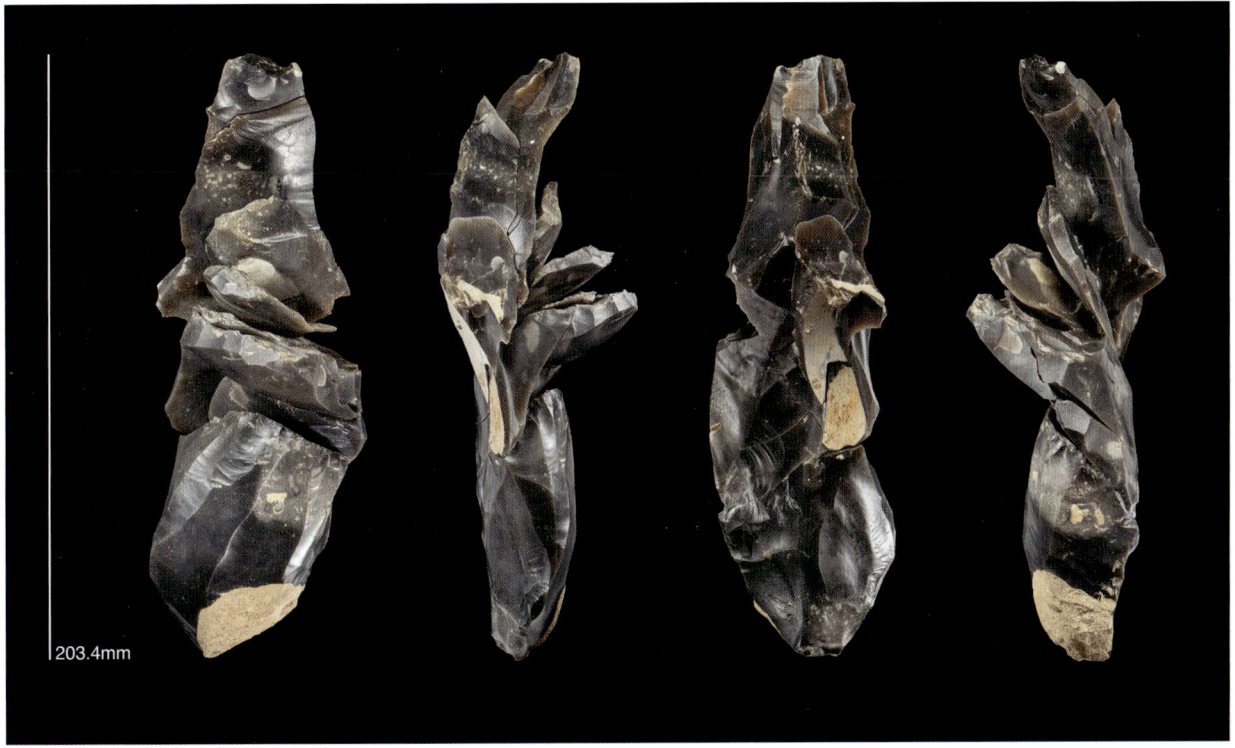

Fig. 6.59 *Photograph of Refit Group 13*

flakes are soft stone hammer struck with plain platforms. Cortex is retained on the crested blade and two of the cresting flakes. At this point the core was again turned, and a series of further blades removed from the opposite end. These are represented by two broken blades, c.1277/c.1493 and c.774. The maximum length of the refitted group is 137.4mm which provides an estimate of the size of the original opposed-platform core. The group was tightly distributed in the southern concentration apart from two outliers that were located in the area between the concentrations about 2m away; these are the retouched *sous-crête* blade (c.653/c.654) and the blade fragment that succeeded it.

Refit Group 13 (n=10; Figs 6.59–6.60)

Refit Group 13 centres on single-platform blade core c.1094, with evidence of rear cresting and a partially faceted platform. Refitting the core platform is a series of six core platform rejuvenation flakes, three of them over 50mm in length, and including some true core tablets. Gaps in the succession indicate where additional core platform rejuve-

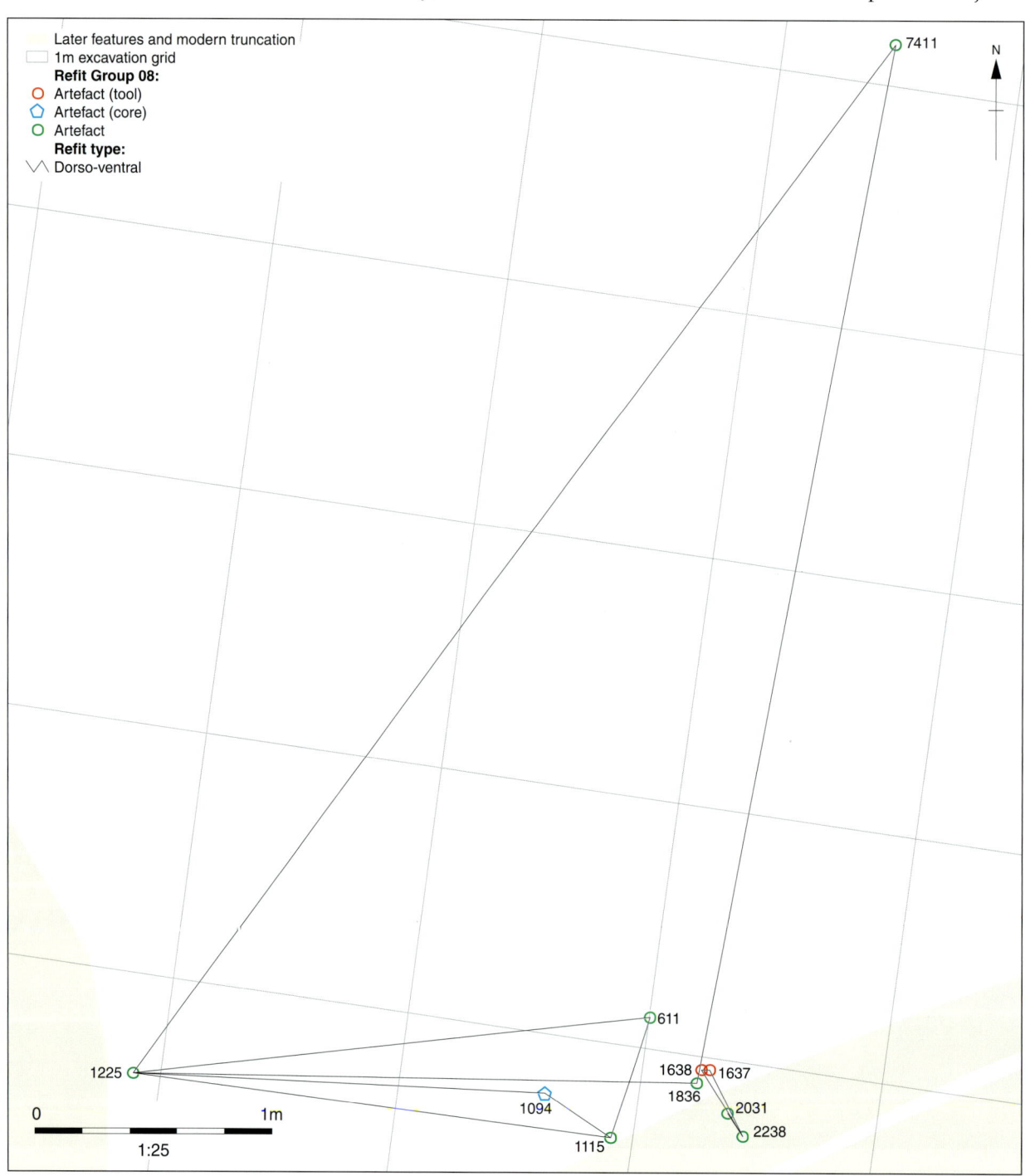

Fig. 6.60 Distribution of Refit Group 13

Fig. 6.61 Photograph of Refit Group 14

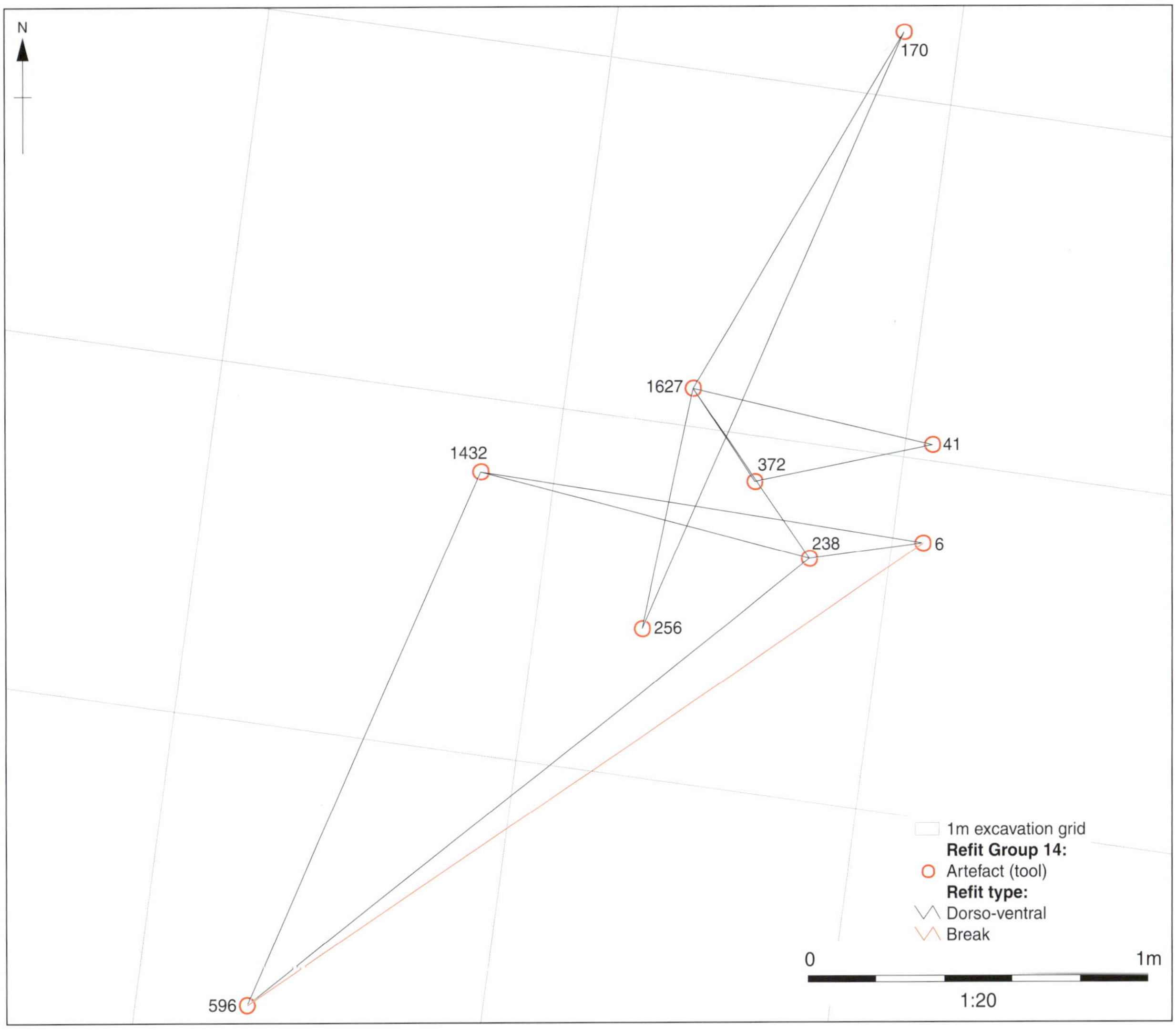

Fig. 6.62 Distribution of Refit Group 14

nation took place. The locations of the bulbs of percussion on the platform rejuvenators indicate that the platform was rotated clockwise. Preceding the core rejuvenation removals were a unidirectional crested blade distal fragment (c.2238) and two underlying flakes, one of them a tool (single-notched flake c.1637). These represent an early stage of core shaping but a phase of major *plein debitage* removal can be recognised after core tablet c.611. These removals cannot be identified in the assemblage but would have included large examples of blades up to 100–110mm in size. The maximum combined length of the group is about 200mm, providing an estimate of the size of the original core. All of the artefacts in the group were soft stone hammer struck and most had faceted butts, although two platform rejuvenators had plain ones. There is no evidence of platform abrasion. Thin cortex survives on the crested blade and the largest platform rejuvenator and is related to the back of the core. All elements of the group were located in the southern concentration apart from the largest core rejuvenator (c.1225) which was found on the surface about 2m to the west, and another platform rejuvenator found about 4m to the north.

Refit Group 14 (n=10; Figs 6.61–6.62)

Refit Group 14 comprises a succession of six flakes struck from the same end of the core and including an earlier sequence of a blade and two flakes removed in a perpendicular direction. The first of the six flakes includes a thick dihedral burin (c.596/c.6; Fig. 6.16), broken into three, with the third piece missing. Part of the burin displays *rasante* retouch that was evidently made before the tool was broken and discarded. The pieces making up the burin were found about 2m apart. All of the artefacts in this refit group have areas of either cortex and/or weathered natural dorsal surfaces, which indicate that they come from an early stage of core shaping. The artefacts were all soft stone hammer struck and have either plain or faceted butts with no platform abrasion. The refits formed a dispersed group in the central area between the knapping concentrations. The flint displays reddish tinges.

Fig. 6.63 Photograph of Refit Group 15

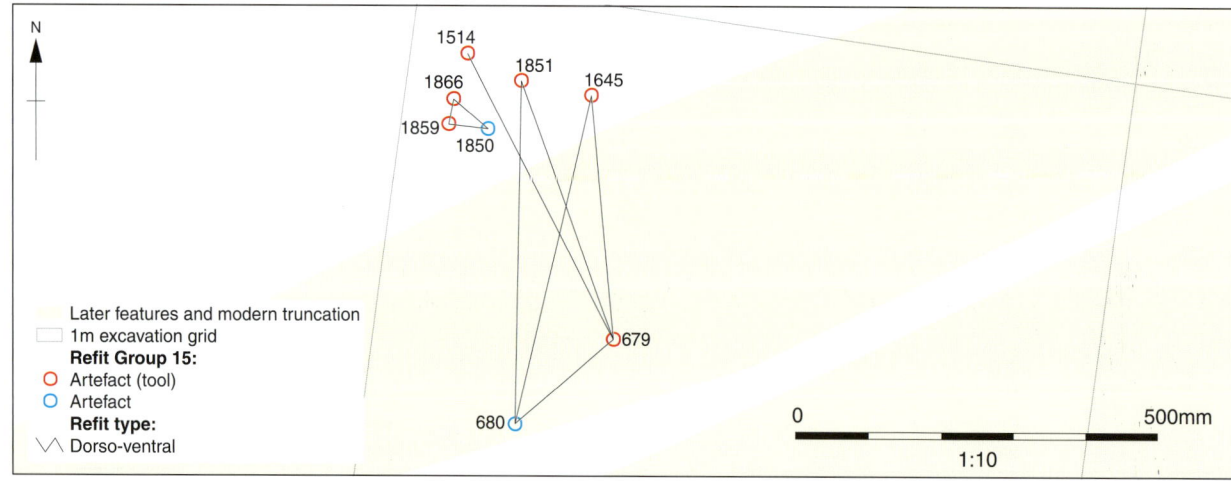

Fig. 6.64 Distribution of Refit Group 15

Refit Group 15 *(n=8; Figs 6.63–6.64)*
Refit Group 15 consists mainly of large refitting artefacts and probably relates to an early stage of core shaping. The large elements include a crested blade, c.680 (107.6mm long), a core platform rejuvenator, c.1850 (49mm by 56.3mm), a double-notched flake, c.679 (90.6mm) and an unretouched flake (82.5mm).

Fig. 6.65 Photograph of Refit Group 16

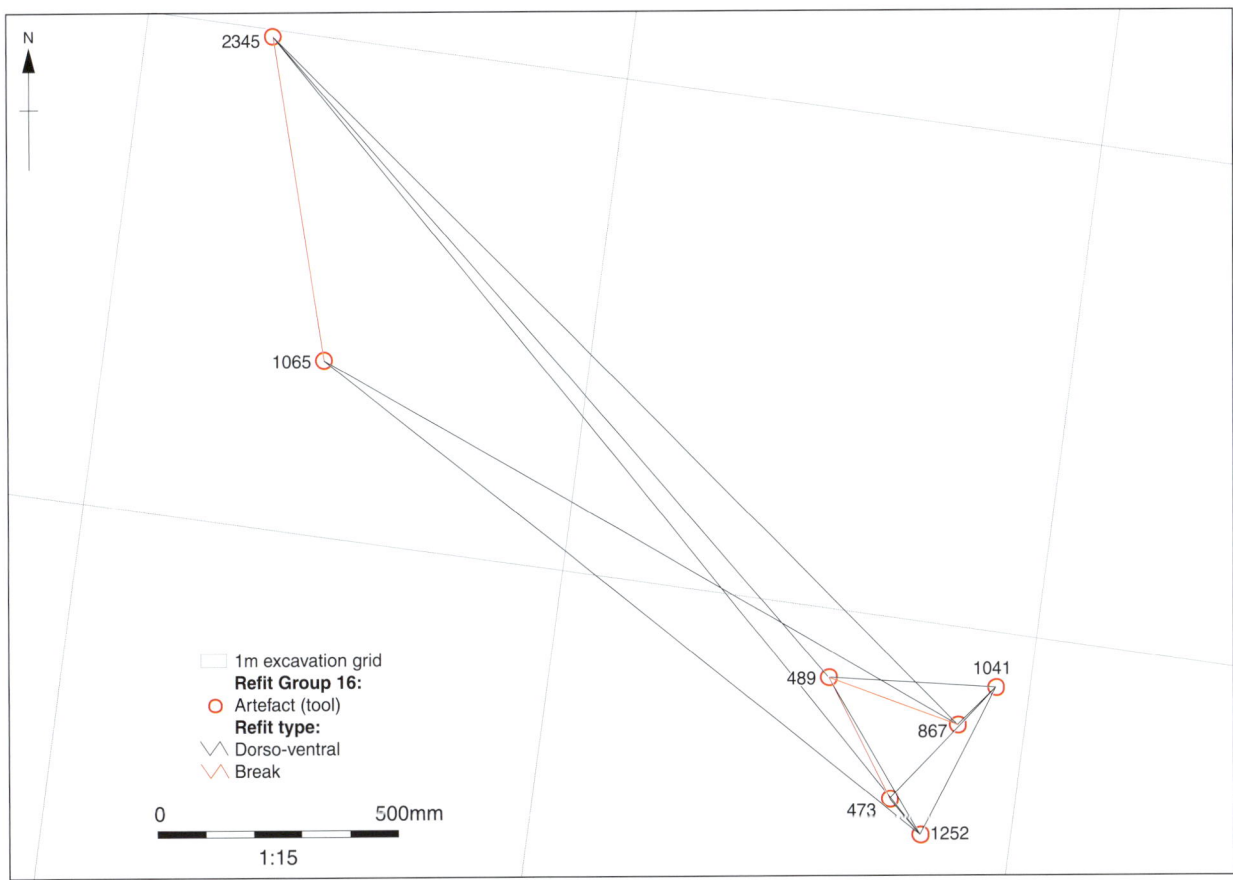

Fig. 6.66 Distribution of Refit Group 16

Fig. 6.67 Photograph of Refit Group 17

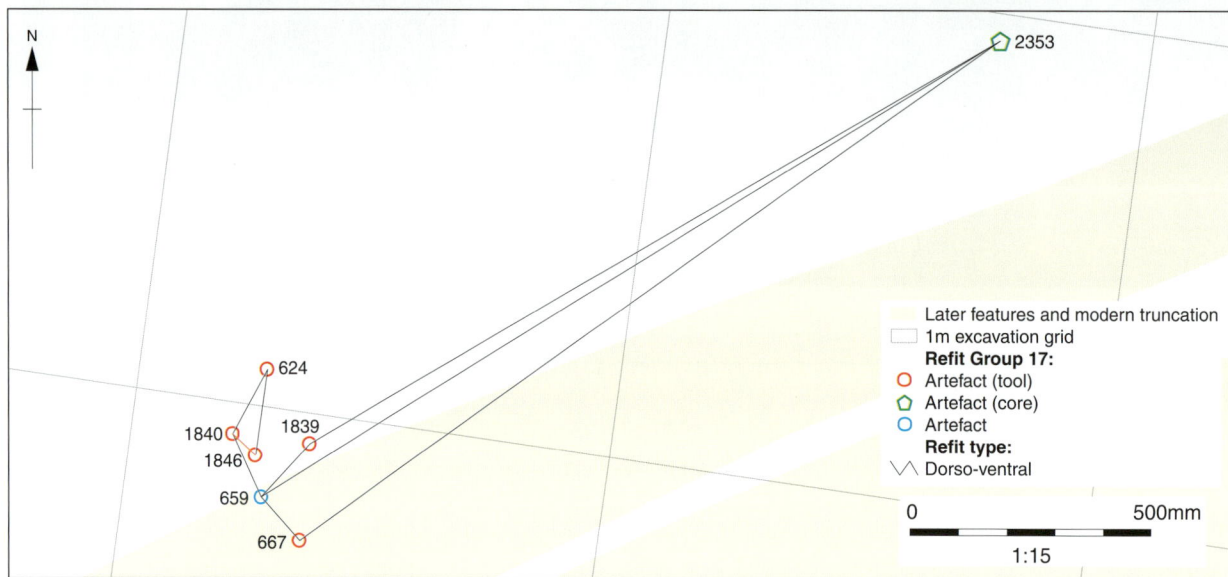

Fig. 6.68 Distribution of Refit Group 17

Fig. 6.69 Photograph of Refit Group 18

Associated with these pieces are two flakes, one of them plunging, a bladelet that might have been detached at the same time as the platform rejuvenator, and a large piece of irregular waste. A small amount of cortex survives on most of the artefacts, and the piece of irregular waste has a natural weathered surface.

The two largest artefacts were hard hammer struck and had plain butts with no platform abrasion. The others were either soft stone hammer struck or could not be classified and had either a faceted or plain butt with no abrasion. The group had a tight distribution in one square of the southern concentration.

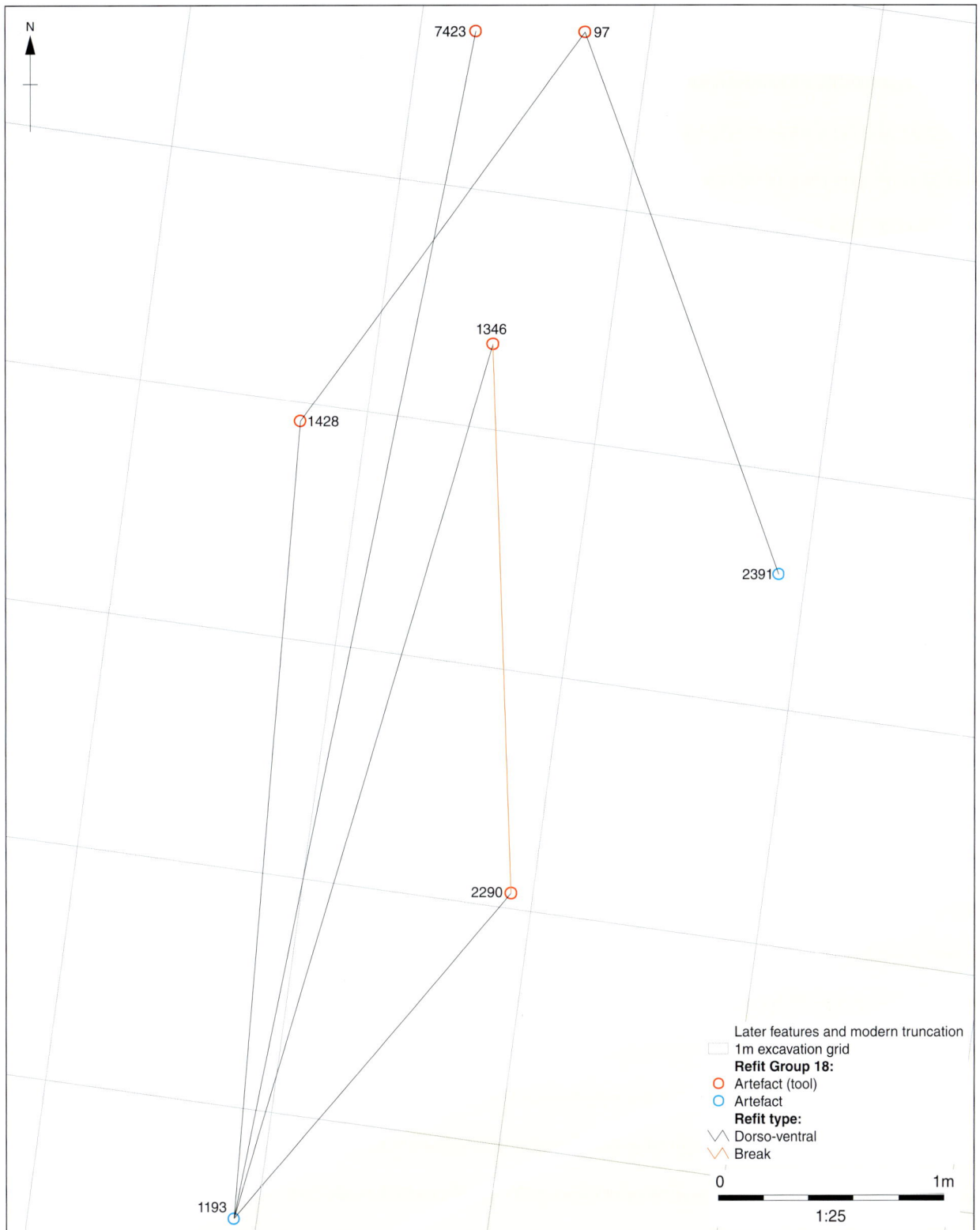

Fig. 6.70 Distribution of Refit Group 18

Refit Group 16 *(n=7; Figs 6.65–6.66)*
Refit Group 16 consists of a sequence of five partially cortical flakes, two made up of mended breaks. The butts are plain or cortical with no platform abrasion and seem to be soft stone hammer struck. The group appears to represent a stage of core shaping (or setting up a crest). All elements were from the northern concentration except for the final removal, a refitted large flake, that was from the area of the 'novice' group just to the north-west of the northern concentration.

Refit Group 17 *(n=10; Figs 6.67–6.68)*
Refit Group 17 centres on opposed-platform blade core c.2353 with its refitting final removals: blade c.797, incomplete blade c.5419 and flake c.1839. The flake terminates in a step fracture associated with an inclusion in the flint and might represent a failed attempt at clearing the core face. Refitting the main core is a platform rejuvenation flake, c.667, that shows that the core face had regressed about 17mm, indicating what must have been an impressive number of blade removals (none unfortunately located). Fitting on the right side of the core is an earlier sequence of three large thick flakes that all have cortex at the distal ends and were disrupted by a large internal inclusion in the flint. The first removal of the sequence has a lateral snap. The second removal was split by a large siret fracture. The final removal also apparently split but the refitting fragment has not been located. The final removal has evidence of cresting and *sous crête* removals, and the entire group of three flakes seems to relate to an earlier stage in cresting preparation. The back of the core (c.2353) shows the remains of cresting that might have been part of this earlier process as the cresting scars are from the same direction. Most of the removals were by soft stone hammer and all platforms were plain, except one incomplete blade and a platform rejuvenation flake which were faceted. There was no platform abrasion on the removals or on the final core platform. All of the objects were tightly grouped in the southern scatter except the core that was found just over a metre away to the north-east. The flint contains reddish tinges.

Refit Group 18 *(n=8; Figs 6.69–6.70)*
Refit Group 18 comprises a sequence of elongated platform removal and rejuvenation flakes all struck from the same direction. Four initial flakes show preparation of platforms for blade production perpendicular to the flake removal surface. Although the blades themselves are missing the negative scars are visible on the proximal ends of two of the flakes. There is then a considerable gap (presumably representing further blade removals and regression of the core face) before a further two tablets were detached to adjust the platform angle

Fig. 6.71 Photograph of Refit Group 19

probably in preparation for more blade removals. All of the flakes show some degree of cortical covering. One of the earlier rejuvenation flakes was transformed into a perforator (c.1428; Fig. 6.14). The group was widely dispersed in the area between the two knapping concentrations. Only one artefact, a thick flake (c.1193) from the earlier part of the sequence, was associated with the southern concentration.

Refit Group 19 *(n=6; Figs 6.71–6.72)*
Refit Group 19 consists of a sequence of three flakes and two blades struck from the same direction. The flakes and one of the blades are from the outer parts of a nodule and represent core shaping. The latest removal is a straight blade that seems to belong to a *plein debitage* series. Two flakes have plain butts, the other a faceted butt as does one of the blades. The exception is the inner blade which has a small punctiform butt with platform abrasion. All were struck with a soft stone hammer except the last blade that was removed with a soft organic hammer. The refit group contains a double notch tool on one of the elongated cortical flakes (c.598; 78.7mm by 34.5mm by 19.9mm), with a notch on either side of the tip. The group was from the southern concentration with two dispersed elements: the double notch flake is from the area between the concentrations, and the inner blade was from the area of the 'novice' group just north-west of the northern concentration. The flint has characteristic reddish tinges.

Refit Group 20 *(n=6; Figs 6.73–6.74)*
An opposed-platform blade core, c.1195, is the central focus of Refit Group 20, which also includes two blades and three core rejuvenation flakes. Blade c.2301 was the final removal from the core and is a well-made blade with a small plain butt and platform abrasion. It was found in the northern part of the site about 5m distant from the rest of the group, which was located in the southern concentration. The flint contains reddish tinges.

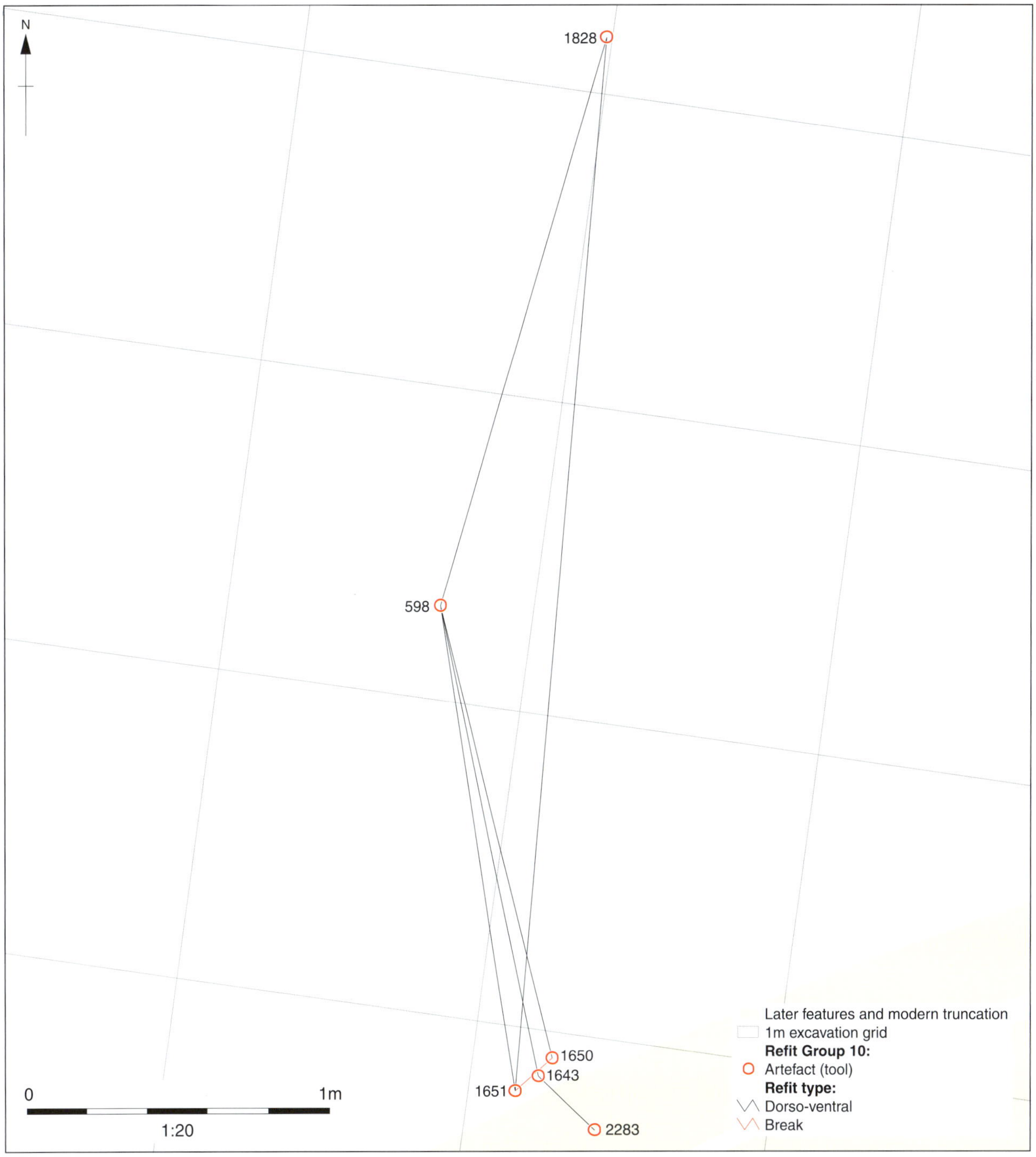

Chapter 6

Fig. 6.72 Distribution of Refit Group 19

Fig. 6.73 Photograph of Refit Group 20

Refit Group 21 (n=6)

Refit Group 21 comprises two blades and two near-complete blade proximal fragments that were struck from the same core platform. The two blades are both mends of two broken fragments. The blades have straight or slightly curved profiles and small plain butts with heavy platform abrasion. Three of the blades were struck with a soft organic hammer, and the final removal with soft stone.

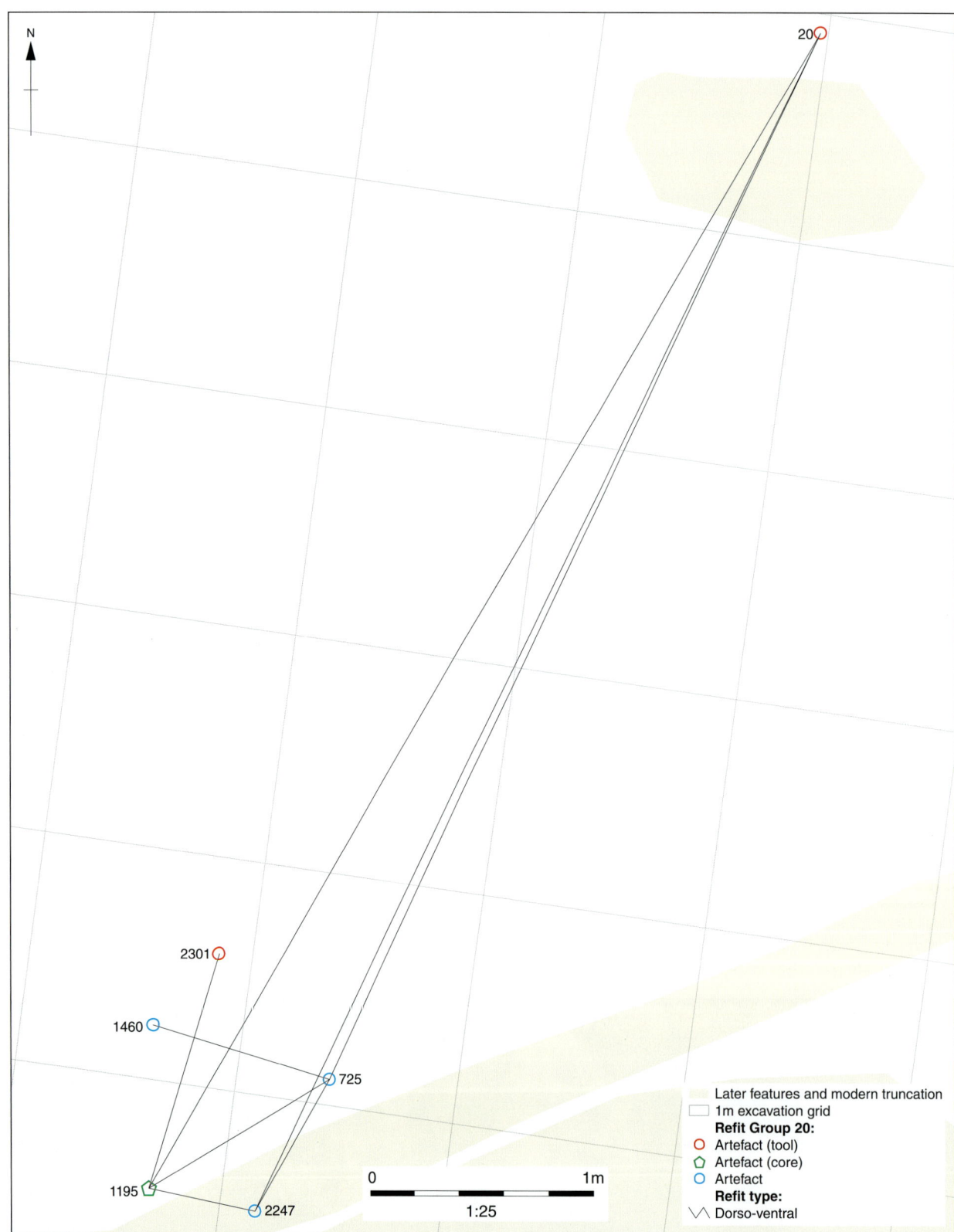

Fig. 6.74 Distribution of Refit Group 20

Incomplete blade c.1745 was the first removal of the sequence and has cortex at the broken distal. It was found just south of the northern concentration. The two succeeding removals, the mended blades, were both from the area between the concentrations. The final blade removal is unlocated.

Refit Group 22 (n=5)

Refit Group 22 consists of four part-cortical flakes, one a mend of two refitting fragments. The two middle removals are from a different platform than the other two and the group probably represents an initial stage of core shaping and platform preparation. The final removal was a large flake (c.811) with curved profile, crossed dorsal scars and a large plain platform with platform abrasion. The flakes were tightly grouped in the southern concentration.

Refit Group 23 (n=5)

Refit Group 23 consists of a sequence of three straight blades from the same platform direction. One blade is complete (c.1747), and the other two are incomplete, one a mesial fragment, and the other a proximal fragment made up of three refitting pieces. Cortex survives on the right edge of all three blades and also on the distal end of the complete blade. The platforms are plain without abrasion and have features of soft stone hammers. The complete blade was the last removal of the group, and its platform is 25mm lower than that of the first removal, suggesting that a significant adjustment of the core platform took place between the two removals. The complete blade was found just south of the northern concentration and the other pieces were found about 3m away in the southern concentration. The flint has reddish tinges.

Refit Group 24 (n=5)

Refit Group 24 consists of four flake fragments, two of them crested, and a complete flake with discontinuous semi-abrupt retouch on the left edge (c.2001). They all appear to come from the same core platform. The complete retouched flake has a plain butt with no platform abrasion and was struck with a soft stone hammer. All the pieces are cortical or part cortical and the group is presumably from an early stage of cresting preparation. They were all tightly grouped in the southern concentration.

Refit Group 25 (n=5; Figs 6.75–6.76)

Refit Group 25 comprises a sequence of three flakes and one blade from the same core platform. One of the flakes is retouched (c.2323) and consists of two refitting fragments. The three unretouched removals have large plain platforms with no platform abrasion and were hard hammer struck. The retouched flake was the last to be removed and has a dihedral butt and was removed with a soft stone hammer. The raw material shows the variation in colour within the raw material used at the site and grades in appearance from the usual black with white speckles to a patterned grey colour. All elements were located close to each other in the western part of the area between the two concentrations.

Refit Group 26 (n=5)

Refit Group 26 consists of two flakes: a large cortical flake consisting of three refitting fragments and a smaller, part cortical flake made up of two refitting fragments. They are from an initial stage of core preparation and were found tightly grouped in the northern concentration.

Refit Group 27 (n=4)

Refit Group 27 is a sequence of four non-cortical core platform rejuvenation flakes. The location of the bulbs of percussion on the flakes indicate that the core was rotated first in an anticlockwise direction and then clockwise. All of the flakes were soft stone hammer struck and all were found clustered in the southern concentration.

Fig. 6.75 Photograph of Refit Group 25

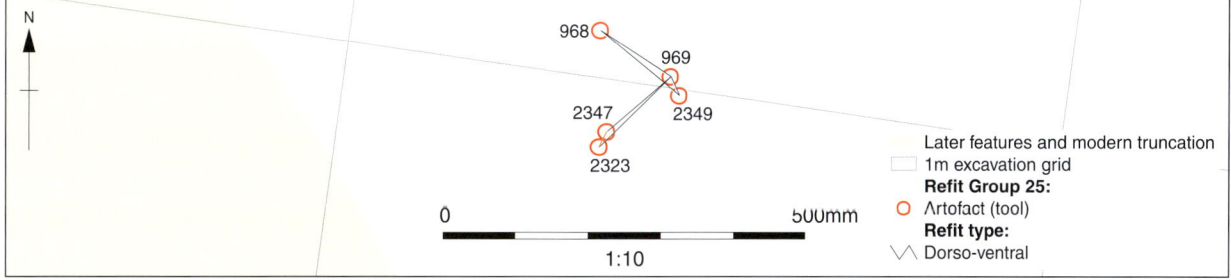

Fig. 6.76 Distribution of Refit Group 25

Fig. 6.77 Photograph of Refit Group 28

Refit Group 28 (n=4; Fig. 6.77)

Refit Group 28 is a sequence of four small straight blades of *plein debitage* from the same core platform direction. One blade, represented by a proximal fragment (c.2140) was removed first and has a steeply angled, *en éperon*-like, isolated butt and platform abrasion. The third removal (c.806) has the same features, but the butts are crushed on the other two blades. The platform of the last removal appears to be 14mm below that of the first, implying that platform maintenance took place between the removals. The blades were tightly grouped in the southern concentration.

Refit Group 29 (n=4)

Refit Group 29 is a sequence of two refitting blades, struck from the same direction and each composed of two broken blade fragments. Both blades have traces of cortex on the dorsal surface right edge. The first removal (c.2071/c.4350) is from the northern concentration. The large (73mm long) distal part of the second removal (c.680) was found on the western side of the area between the two concentrations. The proximal end of the second removal was found in the southern concentration.

Refit Group 30 (n=3)

Refit Group 30 consists of three refitting pieces of irregular waste, all with weathered cortex, possibly of a river cobble. The breaks may be natural. All three pieces were from the northern concentration.

Refit Group 31 (n=3; Fig. 6.78)

Refit Group 31 consists of a sequence of two blades and a flake from an opposed-platform blade core. The first removal was a large semi-cortical distal flake fragment struck from the non-preferential end of the core. The succeeding two non-cortical blade removals were from the main platform. One of the blade removals (c.1069) is retouched, with a single notch on the right edge. The other blade is long (98.5mm) and thick (20.5mm) with the remains of several hinge and step fractured incomplete removals on its dorsal surface. This blade appears to have been detached to clear the core face of the

Fig. 6.78 Photograph of Refit Group 31

step and hinge fractured area. The pieces were tightly grouped in the southern concentration. The flint contains reddish tinges.

Refit Group 32 (n=3)

Refit Group 32 consists of a crested flake distal fragment and two flakes with some cortex on the left edges. One flake was removed before the crested flake, and one after. Both flakes were struck perpendicular to the direction of the crested flake. The group relates to core reduction and the pieces were found tightly grouped in the southern concentration.

Refit Group 33 (n=4)

Refit Group 33 is a sequence of three blades and a small flake struck from the same core platform. One blade was plunging and one a proximal fragment. The three blade platforms are all plain, and the flake platform punctiform, and all removals were by soft stone hammer. The flint is patterned grey in colour and contains crystalline inclusions not seen on other artefacts in the assemblage. The material may have been brought to the site. However, Refit Group 25 (Fig. 6.75) shows that patterned grey areas can be found within the black speckled flint usually worked at the site. RG 33 was widely dispersed. The plunging blade and fragment were found about 2m west of the southern concentration, while the flake was found east of the northern concentration. The other blade was found in the area between the two concentrations.

Refit Group 34 (n=3)

Refit Group 34 consists of three successive flakes from the same core platform. All of the flakes have cortex on the right edge, and one has a largely cortical butt. All were tightly grouped in the southern concentration.

Refit Group 35 (n=3)

Refit Group 35 consists of two core fragments (c.305 and c.2435) and a piece of irregular waste. The group seems to relate to an initial stage of core preparation and the original nodule appears to have fractured during core flaking due to a large internal fossil inclusion. The distribution was widely dispersed.

Refit Group 36 (n=3)

Refit Group 36 comprises three partially cortical flakes, two struck from the same core platform. The third has a natural ventral surface and has an orientation crossed with respect to the others. It shows possible signs of cresting. This flake was found in the area between the concentrations; the other two in the southern concentration.

Refit Group 37 (n=3; Fig. 6.79)

Refit Group 37 consists of a large single-notched flake (c.817), made from two broken fragments, and a small refitting distal fragment of a cortical flake. The notch is on the left edge at the distal end of the flake. The flake has a large plain platform and was struck with a soft stone hammer. Both were from the southern concentration.

Refit Group 38 (n=3)

Refit Group 38 is a sequence of three blades all struck from the same core platform. The first two removals are unretouched and have curved profiles. The final blade in the sequence has a straight profile and has fine retouch along the right edge (c.2314).

Fig. 6.79 Photograph of Refit Group 37

The first removal retains cortex at the distal end, and there is a trace of cortex on the second removal. There is no cortex on the retouched blade. The platforms are plain and abraded. The group was dispersed across the site and none of the pieces are associated with either knapping concentration.

Refit Group 39 (n=7)

Refit Group 39 comprises a short sequence of six flakes and blades from the same core platform, one flake made up of two refitting fragments. All of the artefacts have thick cortex on the right edge and are soft stone hammer struck with plain platforms and no abrasion. The first removal from the sequence is an

Fig. 6.80 Photograph of Refit Group 40

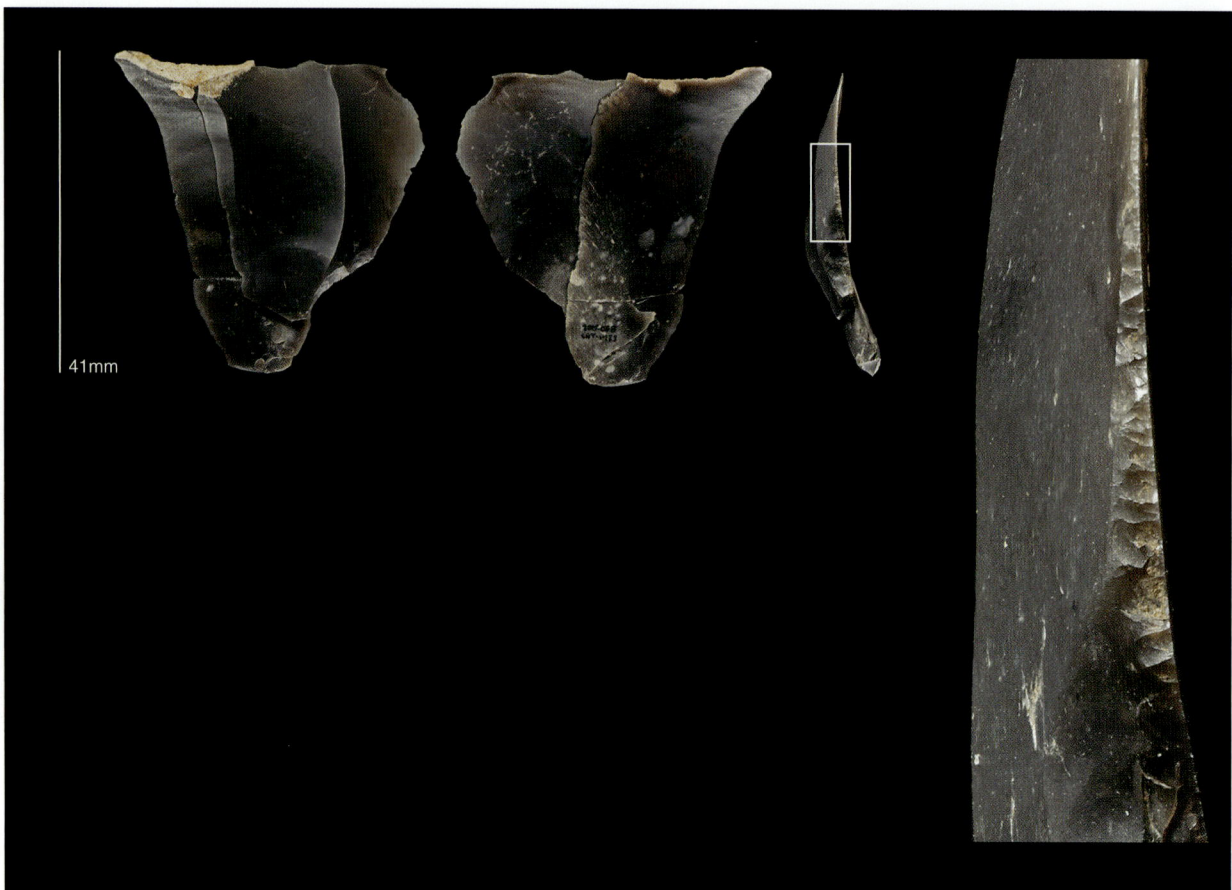

Fig. 6.81 Photograph of Refit Group 41

edge-damaged blade (c.523), with the edge damage located at the thick and wide distal end. Cortex forms a natural back on the right edge. With the exception of the edge-damaged blade, the group was located in the northern concentration. The edge-damaged blade was found about 6m away, south of the southern concentration. The flint displays reddish tinges.

Refit Group 40 (n=4; Fig. 6.80)

Refit Group 40 is a sequence of two flakes and two core platform preparation flakes representing an early stage of core preparation. The two flakes were removed first and are from the same platform. The two core preparation flakes are from a platform that is about 90° to the right and shows that the core was rotated anticlockwise. Most have thick cortex on the right edge (two flakes) or distally (one core preparation flake). One of the flakes is burnt (c.108). The distribution cannot be determined as three pieces are unlocated. The more distinct core preparation flake is from the area between the two concentrations.

Refit Group 41 (n=3; Fig. 6.81)

Refit Group 41 comprises a large distal portion of a retouched flake (c.1153) and an unretouched blade made up of two broken fragments. Both were struck from the same core platform and are curved in profile with cortex at the distal end. The flake has abrupt to semi-abrupt retouch on the right edge proximally, but the end of the tool is broken. The blade has a large plain platform with abrasion and is soft stone hammer struck. Both were found in the area between the two concentrations. There are reddish tinges in the flint.

Refit Group 42 (n=3; Fig. 6.82)

Refit Group 42 consists of a truncation burin (c.4064) and a joining proximal fragment with a later blade removal. Both blades have straight

Fig. 6.82 Photograph of Refit Group 42

profiles, small plain platforms with abrasion, and were struck with a soft organic hammer. The unmodified blade has very thin weathered cortex on the left edge. The proximal part of the burin's original blade blank was found in the northern concentration, and the burin was found in an adjacent square. The later blade removal was found about 4m to the east on the edge of the site.

Refit Group 43 (n=3; Fig. 6.83)

Refit Group 43 comprises an oblique backed point distal fragment (c.2378; Fig. 6.23) and a refitting blade consisting of two broken fragments. The blade was removed from the core first and provides an indication of the size of blank selected for making the tool (73.2mm by 18mm by 3.6mm). The blade has a slightly curved profile and linear butt with abrasion, and was struck with a soft stone hammer. The distal part of the blade has been burned. The blade was found close to the northern concentration and the point at least a metre away to the east.

Refit Group 45 (n=2)

Refit Group 45 consists of a flake and a refitting piece of irregular waste, both from the same square of the northern concentration.

Refit Group 46 (n=2)

Refit Group 46 comprises two flakes, one a distal fragment with cresting and the subsequent removal *sous crête*. The *sous-crête* flake has a dihedral butt with no abrasion and was struck with a soft stone hammer. Both flakes were recovered from the same square of the northern concentration.

Refit Group 47 (n=2)

Refit Group 47 consists of two very small refitting core platform rejuvenation flakes (11.6mm and 13.2mm long). Both flakes were from the same square of the northern concentration.

Refit Group 48 (n=2)

Refit Group 48 comprises two small refitting core platform rejuvenation flakes. Both flakes were from the same square of the northern concentration.

Refit Group 49 (n=2)

Refit Group 49 consists of two blades, one a mesial fragment. Both are lacking their proximal ends but the near-complete blade has a curved profile with cortex at the distal end. They were from the same square of the southern concentration.

Refit Group 50 (n=2)

Refit Group 50 comprises a blade and a refitting distal

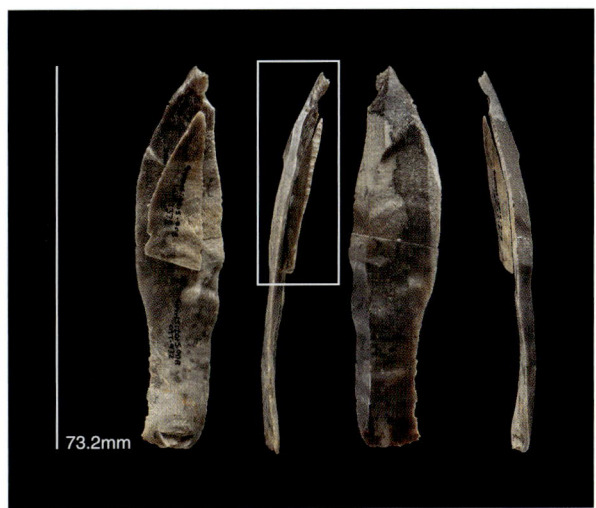

Fig. 6.83 Photograph of Refit Group 43

portion of a large blade struck from the same core platform. The underlying blade has cortex on the left lateral edge and a plain butt with no abrasion. Both were from the southern concentration.

Refit Group 51 (n=2)

Refit Group 51 consists of a semi-cortical large flake and refitting cortical natural flake from a 'potlid' natural although they were found in the same square of the southern scatter.

Refit Group 55 *(n=3; Fig. 6.85)*

Refit Group 55 comprises a unidirectional crested plunging blade (c.438) with an underlying *sous-crête* distal blade fragment. The subsequent flake removal from the opposed end of the core is also *sous crête*. The main crested blade has a small punctiform butt with platform abrasion. The underlying flake has a large plain butt with no abrasion. Both were struck with a soft stone hammer. Cortex is present on the left edge of the crested blade and the flake. The crested blade and blade fragment were found close together in the southern scatter. The flake was found about 3m away in the area between the concentrations.

Refit Group 56 *(n=2; Figs 6.11 and 6.86)*

Refit Group 56 consists of an end-scraper (c.1315) and refitting underlying dihedral burin (c.1564), both on large finely-made blades (see above for details). The tool blanks were struck from the same end of an opposed-platform blade core and are both soft stone hammer struck blades with straight profiles and plain butts. The burin blank has platform abrasion. They were found about a metre apart in the area to the east of the northern concentration. The flint displays reddish tinges.

Refit Group 57 *(n=2)*

Two refitting core rejuvenation flakes, possibly resulting from cresting, form Refit Group 57. They have dihedral/faceted butts with no abrasion and were soft stone hammer struck. They were from the area between the concentrations.

Refit Group 58 *(n=2)*

Refit Group 58 consists of two very small successive flakes from platform rejuvenation. Both were from the same square adjacent to the southern concentration.

Refit Group 59 *(n=2)*

Refit Group 59 consists of a flake and subsequent bladelet removal, both partly cortical. The flake has a plain butt without platform abrasion and is soft stone hammer struck. Both were found in the same square of the southern scatter.

Refit Group 60 *(n=2)*

Refit Group 60 comprises two successive partially cortical blades from the same platform of a blade core. Both were struck with a soft organic hammer and have small faceted platforms with abrasion. They are from just north of the northern scatter.

Fig. 6.84 Photograph of Refit Group 53

fracture. They belong to an early stage of core preparation. Both were from the same square of the southern concentration.

Refit Group 53 *(n=2; Fig. 6.84)*

Refit Group 53 consists of a retouched bidirectionally crested blade (c.1473, length 101.3mm) with a refitting cortical flake. The crested blade has semi-abrupt retouch at the distal end. It has a large plain platform with no abrasion, and was hard hammer struck. The two pieces were found close to each other in the southern concentration.

Refit Group 54 *(n=2)*

Two pieces of irregular broken waste with heavily weathered cortex, probably from a river cobble, form Refit Group 54. The pieces are probably

Fig. 6.85 Photograph of Refit Group 55

Fig. 6.86 Photograph of Refit Group 56

Refit Group 61 (n=4)

Refit Group 61 is a sequence of a flake and three blades, one a proximal fragment and another a distal fragment. All four were struck from the same platform of a core. The butts are plain with platform abrasion and have been struck with a soft stone hammer. The complete blade and the distal fragment have cortex at the distal end. The pieces were dispersed. The proximal blade fragment was found in the southern concentration and the other three in the north-east part of the site.

Refit Group 62 (n=2)

Refit Group 62 comprises two small flakes, both terminating in a natural surface. Both have thin cortex typical of a river cobble and both butts are crushed. Both were from the same square in the north-east part of the site.

Refit Group 63 (n=2)

Refit Group 63 consists of two short thick flakes terminating in hinge fractures. Each has a large plain butt with no platform abrasion and were both struck with a soft stone hammer. They probably represent failed attempts at blade removal and were found close together in the northern concentration.

Refit Group 64 (n=2)

Refit Group 64 comprises two small partly cortical flakes, possibly from cresting. Both have plain butts with no platform abrasion and were soft stone hammer struck. They were found close together in the northern concentration.

Refit Group 65 (n=2)

Two small flakes, possibly examples of *sous-crête* removals, form Refit Group 65. Both have plain butts with no platform abrasion and were soft stone hammer struck. They were found close together in the northern concentration.

Refit Group 66 (n=2)

Refit Group 66 comprises two small refitting core platform rejuvenation flakes, one a distal fragment. They were found in the same square at least a metre south of the southern concentration.

Refit Group 67 (n=2; Fig. 6.87)

Refit Group 67 comprises an edge-damaged unidirectional crested blade (c.1093) with a small refitting piece of cortical irregular waste on its dorsal surface. The crested blade has later invasive edge damage on three surfaces at the broken distal tip (right dorsal, left ventral, and the arête) and may have been used as a perforator. There is also possible edge damage on the proximal right edge on both the dorsal and ventral surfaces. The butt has been removed deliberately. Both pieces came from the southern concentration.

Refit Group 68 (n=2; Fig. 6.88)

Refit Group 68 consists of a single-platform blade core with evidence of cresting on both right and left sides (see blade cores section above). A flake distal fragment refits on the back of the core. The flake was from the northern concentration and the core was found about 1m to the south-west (Fig. 6.5). The flint has reddish tinges.

Refit Group 69 (n=2)

Two blades struck from the same core platform and joined at the distal end form Refit Group 69. A gap represents a missing blade removal between them. They are both soft stone hammer struck with plain butts; one has heavy abrasion. Each has traces of thin cortex at the distal end. Probably from an opposed-platform blade core. They were from the area just south of the northern concentration.

Refit Group 70 (n=2)

Refit Group 70 comprises successive removals of two semi-cortical flakes lacking their proximal ends. They were struck from different directions and probably relate to initial core shaping. The smaller flake fragment was found in the northern concentration and the larger flake fragment (58.8mm by 53.6mm) was recovered about a metre away to the north-west.

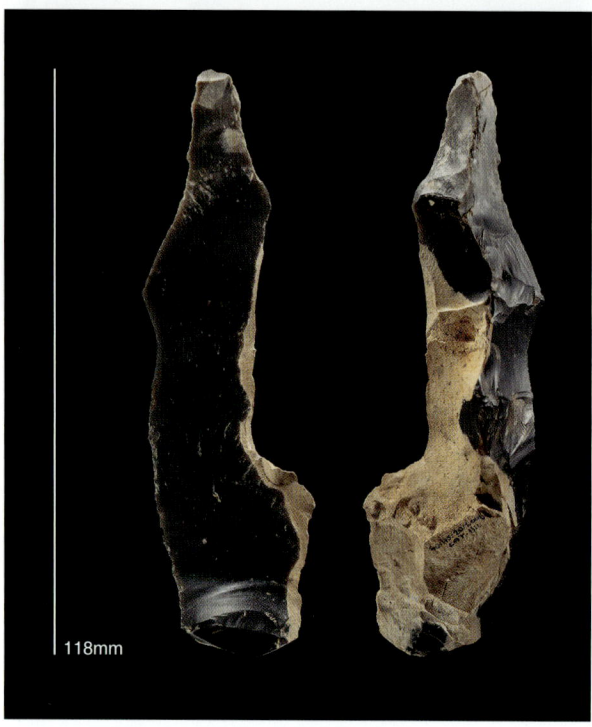

Fig. 6.87 Photograph of Refit Group 67

Refit Group 71 (n=2)

Refit Group 71 consists of a thick plunging blade and underlying blade distal fragment. The blade is soft stone hammer struck with a plain butt and no platform abrasion. Both were found close together about 2m from the southern concentration, near the bomb disturbance area. The blade was found on the surface. The flint displays reddish tinges.

Refit Group 72 (n=2)

Two refitting cortical flakes from early stages of core reduction form Refit Group 72. The underlying (larger) flake was struck from a direction about 90°

Fig. 6.88 Photograph of Refit Group 68

anticlockwise from the overlying one. Both are soft stone hammer struck and have large plain butts with no platform abrasion. They were found close together in the area between the two concentrations.

Refit Group 73 (n=2)

Refit Group 73 comprises a core platform rejuvenation flake and preceding flake removal proximal fragment. The proximal end indicates that it was soft stone hammer struck with a faceted butt and no platform abrasion. The artefacts were found close together in the northern concentration.

Refit Group 74 (n=2)

Refit Group 74 consists of two pieces of irregular waste with thin weathered cortex, probably from a river cobble. They were found close together in the north-east part of the site.

Refit Group 75 (n=2; Fig. 6.89)

Refit Group 75 comprises a dihedral burin on a distal blade fragment (c.887) and a refitting unretouched distal blade fragment. Both show evidence of unidirectional cresting. The burin was found in the area between the concentrations and no more than a metre away from the unretouched piece which was from the square just north of the southern concentration.

Refit Group 76 (n=2)

Refit Group 76 consists of two successive flakes, one with cortex on the right edge. They may have come from cresting, and were found close together in the southern concentration.

Refit Group 77 (n=2)

Refit Group 77 comprises two successive flakes without proximal ends and struck from the same platform. The overlying flake is cortical and the underlying one has cortex on both edges. Both were found in the test pit excavated in square J7.

Refit Group 78 (n=2)

Refit Group 78 comprises a sequence of two flakes joined at the distal end and with a gap representing a missing flake removal between them. Both terminate with crushing from the distal end. They are soft stone hammer struck and have large plain butts with no platform abrasion. They were recovered close together in the southern concentration.

Refit Group 80 (n=2)

Refit Group 80 consists of two very small flakes with traces of cortex on the left edge. Both were soft stone hammer struck with plain platforms and no

Fig. 6.89 Photograph of Refit Group 75

platform abrasion. They came from just north of the southern concentration.

Refit Group 81 (n=2; Fig. 6.90)

Refit Group 81 is a series of three refitting *sous-crête* blades with the uppermost one also showing traces of bidirectional cresting at the distal end. The crested blade has a large plain butt. The succeeding blade has small well-defined plain butt with platform abrasion. Both were soft stone hammer struck. The final blade is a mesial fragment. The group was dispersed. The crested blade was found about 2m north of the northern concentration. The other two *sous-crête* blades were found about 4m south in the area between the concentrations.

Refit Group 82 (n=2)

Refit Group 82 is a sequence of two refitting flakes, the uppermost a burnt proximal fragment. The unburnt flake has cortex on the left edge. The butts are large, and one is plain and the other faceted; neither displays platform abrasion. They both seem to be soft stone hammer struck. The complete flake was found just south of the northern concentration and the burnt fragment was just over a metre away to the east.

Fig. 6.90 Photograph of Refit Group 81

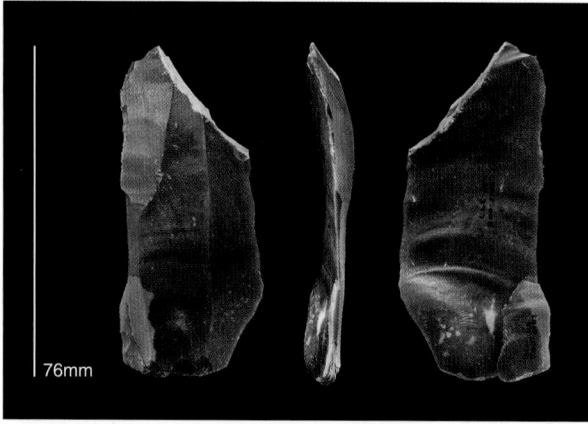

Fig. 6.91 Photograph of Refit Group 83

Refit Group 83 *(n=2; Fig. 6.91)*

Refit Group 83 comprises a partly cortical blade with *rasante* (scalar) retouch (c.297) and small flake, both struck from the same core platform. The *rasante* retouch occurs on the left edge distally and occurs on both dorsal and ventral surfaces. Cortex survives on the blade right edge distally. Both blade and flake have plain butts with abrasion and were soft stone hammer struck. The flake was found in the northern concentration and the *rasante* blade about a metre away to the north. The flint has reddish tinges.

Site activities from refits and discard patterns

Through refitting it has been possible to demonstrate that flintknapping and other site activities involving tool manufacture and tool use were focused in overlapping areas of the site: the two distinct flintknapping concentrations, the space between them, plus an area about 2m to the north and east of the northern concentration and another one about 2m to the south-west of the southern concentration. In particular, activities involving tool use and discard seem mainly to have taken place in the area between the two major knapping concentrations (Fig. 6.9), although some also seem to have occurred in the knapping concentrations themselves (represented mainly by retouched and edge-damaged pieces, and rarely formal tools). Activities involving tool resharpening and renewal seem to take place mainly outside the main knapping concentrations. While the nature of the activities needs to be considered in conjunction with microwear analysis, it can be shown that site behaviour can be broken down into a number of distinct but connected entities.

In the first place, it is clear that the production of blades formed a key activity at the site. Reconstruction of cores shows that nodules of chalk flint were transported to the Guildford Fire Station site for knapping. Where their form can be determined, these nodules appear to have been elongate in shape and generally no more than 300mm long (see in particular RG 01, Fig. 6.35, and RG 13, Fig. 6.59).

This did not preclude the occasional use of very locally derived flint, on river cobbles, although there is only one refit group in evidence (RG 06, Fig. 6.45) which we interpret as the work of a novice knapper. Overall, refitting has confirmed that most of the stages in the *chaîne opératoire* are represented in the assemblage, from initial core preparation to the production of blades and retouched tools, and the discard of broken or exhausted cores. The fact that knapping was a major activity at Guildford Fire Station is indicated by the presence of typical knapping debris, including many discarded blades and flakes with flexional breaks and *languette* fractures (Bordes 1970), and by the direct evidence of blades that can be refitted to cores. Refitting demonstrates the desired length of blades favoured by the Late Upper Palaeolithic flintknappers. Although the average length of the blades found on the site was about 45–75mm overall, the preferred blade length for tools was mainly in the size range 80–100mm with many of these blades displaying a straight or slightly curved profile. The longest blade recovered measured 137.5mm. A further estimate of desired length can be gained by considering the dimensions of negative flake scars on blade cores. A study of these reveals that the point at which blade production ceased was rarely below 50–60mm. The moderately high percentage of small blades and bladelets (width <12mm) is probably linked to the method of abrading the core edge rather than deliberate production. Similar by-products have been observed to occur accidentally during knapping experiments. There are no bladelet cores in the assemblage.

The methods of core reduction are fairly uniform. Although the natural convexity of the nodules would have enabled blades to be detached without much prior preparation, the more usual method involved the production of an anterior crest, as indicated by refits and the presence of crested blades in the assemblage. Refitting sequences and the analysis of blade scar patterns show how one platform was often dominant, with removals in the opposite direction generally used in order to correct the shape of the main flaking face. The progression of debitage was generally frontal or involved sequential removals along a core face (*semi-tournante*). Rejuvenation of core platforms, as indicated by refitting, was usually achieved by the removal of small flakes from the platform and occasionally by true core tablets removing the top of the core.

Apart from the direct evidence of blade making, it is also possible to observe important gaps in some of the refitting sequences that appear to have been left by successive series of blade removals. Significantly, these gaps sometimes correspond with blade removals larger than the average blade length found on the site. The missing blades might have been appropriate blanks for use unmodified or for transforming into tools, including tools such as end-scrapers or burins that were often made on larger blade supports. It is possible therefore that some of the missing blades were set aside or cached

Chapter 6

for future purposes. While it is possible that some transformation into tools took place on site, there are surprisingly few such examples in the refit groups. A notable exception is the blade made into two burins that links the two parts of RG 02 (c.699/ c.2313/c.7448; Figs 6.18 and 6.37). This blade was the only element identified at the site from a series of missing blade removals in RG 02.

Twenty-seven blade tools form parts of refit groups, and of these only 11 are formal tools: 1 backed point (RG 43), 1 scraper (RG 56), 1 perforator (RG 18), 6 burins (RGs 02, 04, 42, 56 and 73) and 2 notched pieces (RGs 01 and 31). The other tools are 12 retouched blades and 4 with edge damage. There are a number of reasons why the rate at which blade tools refit to the knapping sequences in the assemblage is

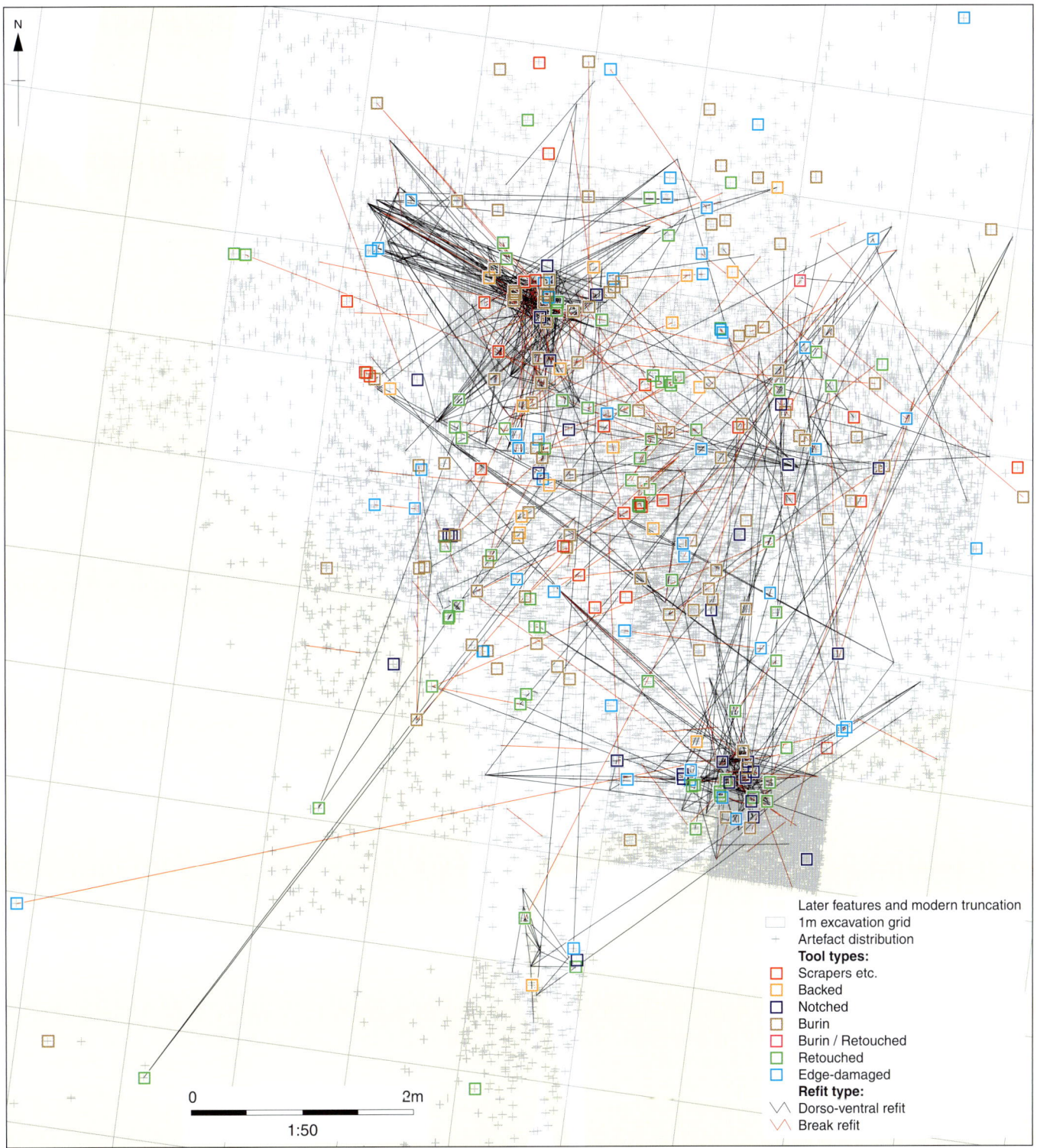

Fig. 6.92 Overall distribution of all other refit groups containing tools

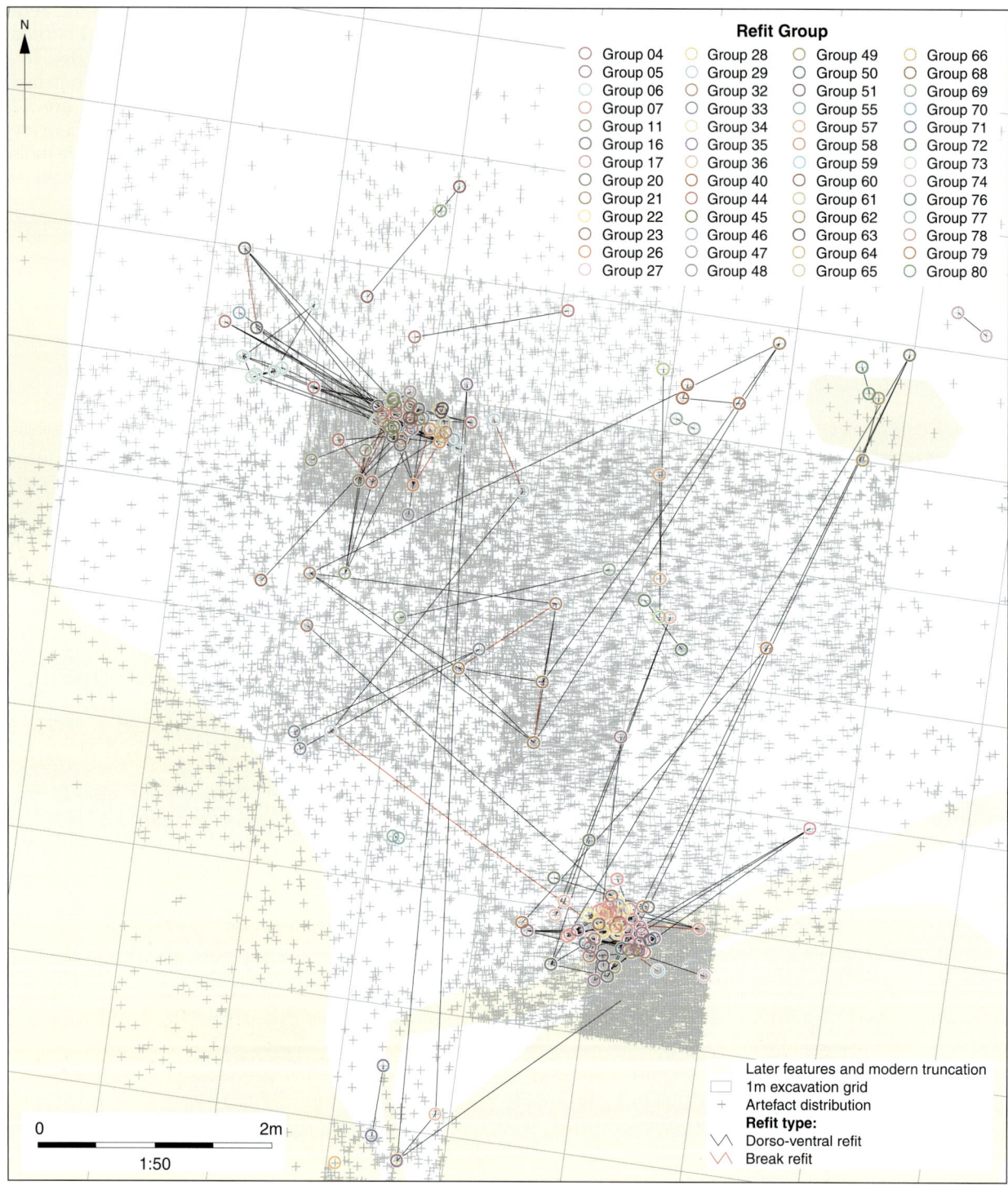

Fig. 6.93 Combined distribution of material from the remaining refit groups (not shown in other figures)

low, one being that some of the tools were brought to the site ready-made or as blanks knapped elsewhere. This might have been the case for the refitting end scraper and burin made on long blanks that make up RG 56 (Figs 6.11 and 6.86), that only refit each other, but the red-tinged flint that they are made of occurs elsewhere on the site and in several refit groups. In most cases, however, we would suggest that the retouched tools were on blanks made at the site but the difficulty of refitting them has been exacerbated by the selection of other blade blanks that were removed for use elsewhere. Further discussion of site activities can be found in Chapter 7 on microwear and in the concluding discussion (Chapter 8).

Chapter 7

Functional analysis

by Sonja Tomasso and Veerle Rots

INTRODUCTION

The aim of the study presented here was to provide insights into tool use and the range of activities at the site. In addition to direct evidence of use, attention was also devoted to hafting and prehension wear. The study combined low- and high-magnification analysis, and a small series of experiments was conducted during the work to address specific questions raised by the assemblage.

MATERIAL AND METHODS

Assemblage composition and sample selection

The lithic assemblage available for analysis at the beginning of the project (prior to more detailed analysis) consisted of ~5500 artefacts (excluding small debitage) including 139 formal tools. The whole of this assemblage was screened macroscopically in Oxford to evaluate the state of preservation of the material and to get an overview of its typological and morphological characteristics, as well as a preliminary view of edge damage on used pieces. Altogether, 600 pieces with potential use-wear were identified and were further examined with a stereomicroscope. A sample of 237 artefacts representative of the tool categories and use-wear types was subsequently selected for a more detailed microscopic analysis at TraceoLab, University of Liège.

The assemblage is dominated by blades, which are often fractured. For such pieces, it was considered relevant to determine the cause of breakage and its potential link with use, and a number of them were thus included in the final sample. Within the retouched assemblage, burins are the most frequent tool type (n=36), followed by scrapers (n=10). In contrast, here are fewer backed blade/lets and fragments (n=8) and points and fragments (n=8). For the burins and scrapers, certain variation in tool blanks was observed during the macroscopic screening. They were manufactured on blades and flakes that show considerable differences in size, thickness and elongation. This morphological variability was taken into account in sample selection to allow the evaluation of possible correlations between different morphologies and particular tool uses and/or prehensile modes. The final sample includes 100 retouched tools. In addition, 91 blades, 20 flakes, 14 burin spalls and 10 bladelets were selected from the unretouched portion of the assemblage (Table 7.1; Fig. 7.1).

Analytical methods

Artefacts were examined with a Zeiss stereomicroscope Discovery.V12 (magnifications up to 120×), a Zeiss Macro-Zoom microscope V16 (magnifications up to 160×) and a Zeiss metallurgical reflected-light microscope AxioImager (magnifications 50–500×),

Table 7.1 The sample selected for functional analysis

Tool category	Selected artefacts
Burin	27
Scraper	10
Backed blade	7
End truncation	6
Notch	2
Point	4
Awl	4
Denticulate	4
Microdenticulate	2
Piercer	3
Retouched blade	20
Retouched flake	8
Retouched misc	3
Burin spall	14
Unretouched flake	20
Unretouched blade	91
Unretouched bladelet	10
Core	1
Grinding stone	1
Others (chips, etc.)	0
Total	237

equipped with polarising filters and differential interference contrast (DIC). Artefacts were cleaned with ethanol to remove finger grease, and some were cleaned with water and sodium dodecyl sulphate (2%) in an ultrasonic bath to remove sediment. During the screening, possible residues were occasionally observed, and they were extracted with a pipette for closer examination using a Zeiss Imager A1 transmitted light microscope (magnifications 50×–1000×) equipped with rotating polarizers and DIC.

Experiments

Functional interpretations were based on comparisons with an extensive experimental reference collection available at TraceoLab. The collection consists of approximately 3000 experimental pieces and is representative of the variation in production techniques (eg Rots 2010a), tool uses, and prehensile modes (different hafting systems, hand-held use) known from Palaeolithic contexts (eg Rots 2010b). Each tool use, prehensile mode and production technique produces a typical combination of use-wear traces (eg polish, edge damage, edge rounding, striations and bright spots), which allows them to be detected in archaeological assemblages.

The experimental projectile collection (c 300 pieces) includes several projectile types used with different projecting modes (thrusting, throwing by

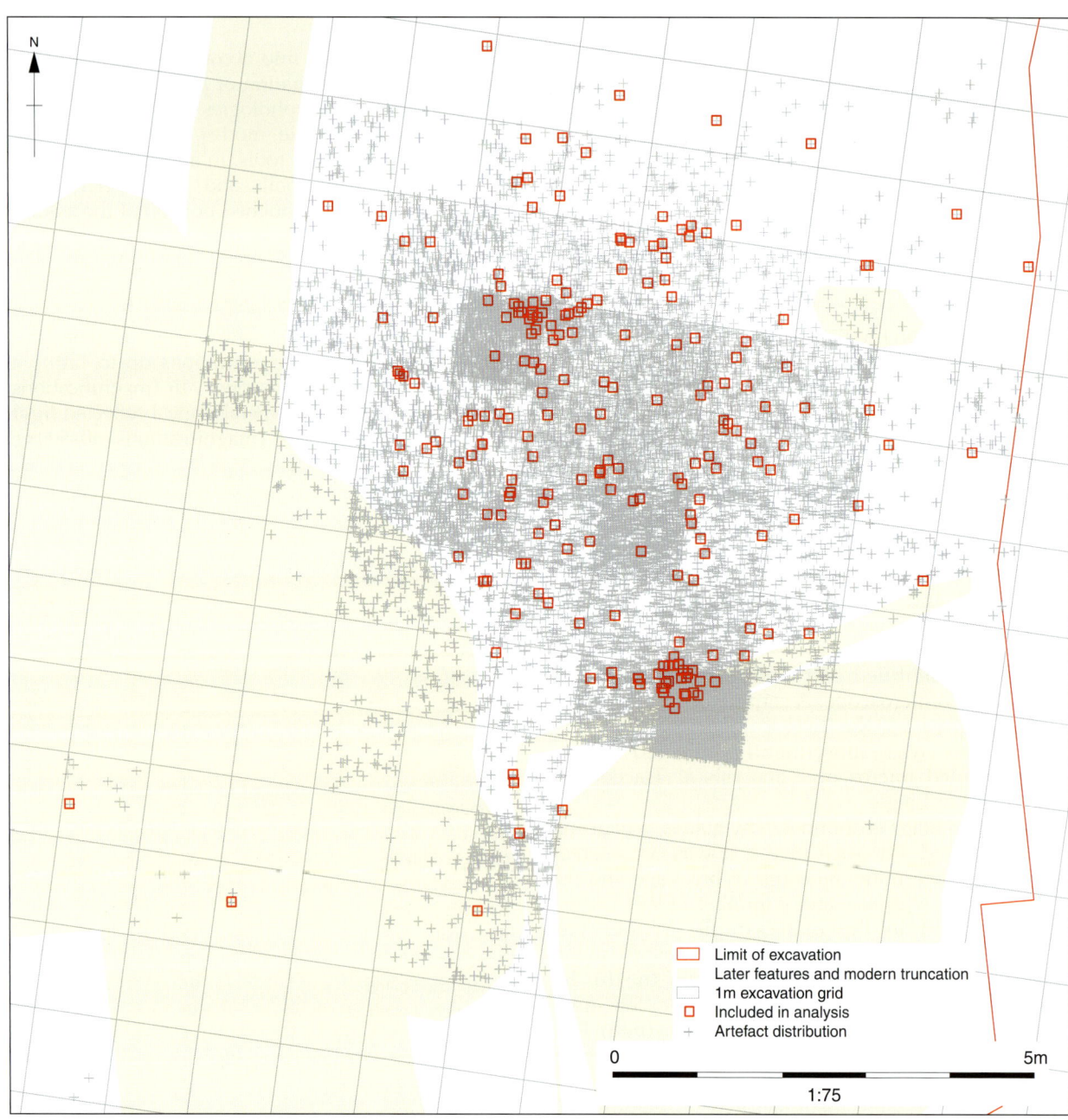

Fig. 7.1 Distribution of all objects included in the microwear analysis

hand and launching with spearthrowers and bows). The points were shot into animal carcasses and artificial targets (Coppe and Rots 2017). These experiments provided a reliable referential framework for interpreting various wear traces that result from projectile use. In addition to the physical reference collection, published studies (Barton and Bergman 1982; Fischer *et al.* 1984; Odell and Cowan 1986; Caspar and De Bie 1996; Pétillon *et al.* 2011; Chesnaux 2014; Rots and Plisson 2014) provide a useful point of comparison. Use-wear on projectiles consists of macro- and microscopic features, including fractures, edge damage, polish and striations. Of the features visible under high magnification, microscopic linear impact traces (MLITs; Moss 1983) are particularly informative. They are striations or linear polishes that are formed as the result of friction between the point and a small flint chip that detaches from it upon impact. The feature needs to start right at the termination of the impact fracture or scar to qualify as a MLIT, establishing the necessary causal link between the fracture and the secondary linear feature.

Since a number of retouched blades from Guildford Fire Station showed ambiguous wear traces, an additional small-scale experiment was designed to test some alternative hypotheses. Blades with a regular morphology similar to the archaeological ones were produced experimentally by an experienced knapper (C Lepers, TraceoLab, University of Liège). The tools were retouched and used for cutting dry raw hide and leather, and for sawing dry wood and bone. The goal was to evaluate whether similar wear traces – in particular macroscopically visible scarring and microscopic wear features such as heavily rounded edges, polish and striations – could be produced. It was impossible to exactly reproduce the archaeological wear traces, but several hypotheses could be dismissed. Further experimental work should shed more light on the use of this particular tool type.

RESULTS

Preservation of the material

The possibilities of use-wear analysis always depend on the amount and quality of post-depositional edge damage and/or surface alterations that can form on the tools during and after their burial in the soil (Grace 1990; Levi-Sala 1986). The alterations can limit the scope of high-magnification analysis to a varying degree depending on their intensity and location on the tool. Low-magnification analysis is, however, less affected by soil polish, patina and other post-depositional features, and is perfectly feasible as long as the edges show no considerable scarring from soil processes or excavation.

While the archaeological material appeared fresh when examined macroscopically, alterations with

Fig. 7.2 Examples of altered pieces: a) patination; b) heat alteration; c) post-depositional gloss; d) mechanical alteration

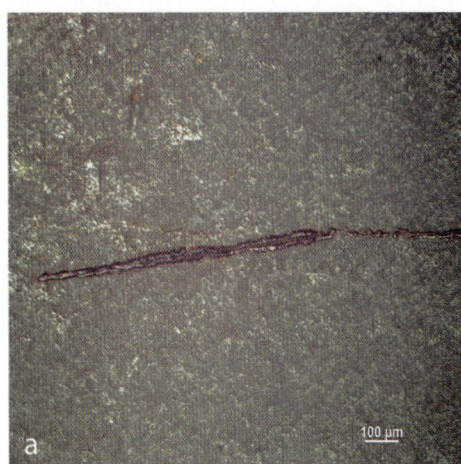 

Fig. 7.3 Residues with taphonomic origin: a) iron oxide residues on the ventral proximal face of scraper c.924 (100×); b) plant tissue (algae) preserved on the ventral face of piece c.5105, photographed under DIC (200×)

differing intensities were frequently observed during the microscopic analysis, and they limited the possibilities of the functional study. Both wear resulting from mechanical processes (abrasion, friction: Bordes 1950; Schutt 1979; Levi-Sala 1986) and chemical processes (gloss, patina: Plisson and Mauger 1988) were observed (Fig. 7.2). In the case of extensive mechanical alterations or strong patina, the analysis was restricted to examination with a stereomicroscope, which only allows the determination of the relative hardness of the worked materials and not their exact nature. The same problem was encountered with tools that displayed heat alterations. Heat damage was, however, relatively rare in the collection, with fewer than 40 pieces showing fire-induced alterations. A total of 147 pieces could not be studied under high magnification because of severe alterations that had obliterated signs of use.

Post-depositional alterations were overall frequent, but thanks to the explicit nature of the use-wear traces on some of the tools, scrapers in particular, reliable functional identifications could nevertheless be made.

Residue analysis

Residues were not the main focus of this study given that the necessary precautions during excavation and handling were not taken. (Such precautions would have included bagging the artefacts directly from the locations in which they were found without directly touching them, taking an accompanying sediment sample from below them, storing them in a refrigerator, washing them only with ultrapure water, making sure that no other analysis, marking or other handling took place prior to the residue analysis, and handling them only with clean, non-powdered gloves for the purposes of the residue analysis itself.) Nevertheless, some residues were observed during the analysis and their potential link with tool use was evaluated. The observed residues proved to be mainly taphonomic in nature, and consisted of a low number of remains of different types of plant tissue and relatively frequent iron oxide residues (Fig. 7.3), the composition of which was confirmed by elemental analysis using SEM-EDS. For only one tool, the origin of the plant tissue (Fig. 7.4) was uncertain and was possibly functional as the residue was associated with wear traces (cf below).

Use-wear analysis

Below, the analysed tools are divided into two main groups: tools used for subsistence-related activities (eg hunting, butchering) and those used for manufacturing or maintenance activities (eg woodworking, bone/antler working). Within the functional groups, results are organised by broad typological categories. The confidence level of each functional interpretation was scored on a scale of 1 (low certainty) to 4 (certain). The confidence level is determined by the degree to which the traces are explicit and diagnostic of a particular tool use, which is partly affected by the preservation state of the artefact.

Subsistence-related activities

Projectiles: backed blade/lets and unretouched blade/lets

The backed blade/lets as well as other artefacts with suitable morphologies were examined for indications of projectile use. Altogether, nine retouched and two unretouched blade/lets could be classified as potential projectiles on the basis of fracture patterns and macro- and microscopic wear features found on them (Table 7.2). It should be noted that breakage is very frequent: the sample contains only one backed blade/let that remained intact. The number of identi-

Fig. 7.4 Piercer c.99/143 with a) plant tissue and starch granules on the distal right edge of c.99. Photographed under neofluar light (1000×)

fied projectiles is too low to allow a reliable evaluation of the projecting mode used, but given the other evidence for this time period (Clark 1963; Barton and Bergman 1982; Cattelain 1997; Nuzhnyj 2000), the use of bows is a viable assumption.

Use-related damage was observed on the unretouched edges, on the tips and at the bases of the blade/lets. The tip damage consists of bending fractures with step-fissured or hinge terminations. The lateral edge damage includes concentrations of bifacial or unifacial scars with abrupt and fissured terminations, oriented parallel or slightly oblique to the cutting edge. In five cases, the macroscopic edge damage is associated with microscopic linear impact traces (MLITs), also oriented parallel or slightly oblique to the cutting edge. Judging from the orientation of the wear features, these tools were mounted either as tips at the extremity of the shaft or as barbs, positioned laterally in the shaft.

On two additional backed blade/lets and one unretouched blade/let, the wear patterns are suggestive of projectile use, but the evidence is limited and uncertain in nature, and there is no associated microscopic wear.

Table 7.2 Summary of functional interpretations for the retouched and unretouched bladelets. The confidence level (CL) of each interpretation is scored on a scale of 1 (low certainty) to 4 (certain)

ID	Type	Projectile use	Possible projectile use (undiagnostic wear)	Possibly used (extensive alterations)
4486	Backed bladelet	X (CL 4)		
4328	Backed bladelet	X (CL 3)		
4322	Backed bladelet	X (CL 3)		
4200	Backed bladelet		X (CL 2)	
4062	Retouched bladelet	X (CL 4)		
2378	Backed bladelet			X (CL 1)
1180	Unretouched bladelet		X (CL1)	
948	Backed bladelet		X (CL 1)	
308	Backed bladelet	X (CL 3)		
232	Retouched blade			X (CL 1)
32	Unretouched bladelet			X (CL 1)

On the three remaining tools, severe post-depositional alterations in combination with non-diagnostic wear did not allow a functional interpretation.

Aside from the distal edge damage, a number of tools show damage at their bases, such as bending-initiated fractures in the proximal parts of the lateral unretouched edges, and small burinations along the edges, formed by counter-pressure. This kind of damage is caused by the compression or flexion of the tool in the shaft when the projectile hits the target. Unfortunately, associated microscopic wear traces are generally poorly developed, which lowered the level of confidence of these interpretations.

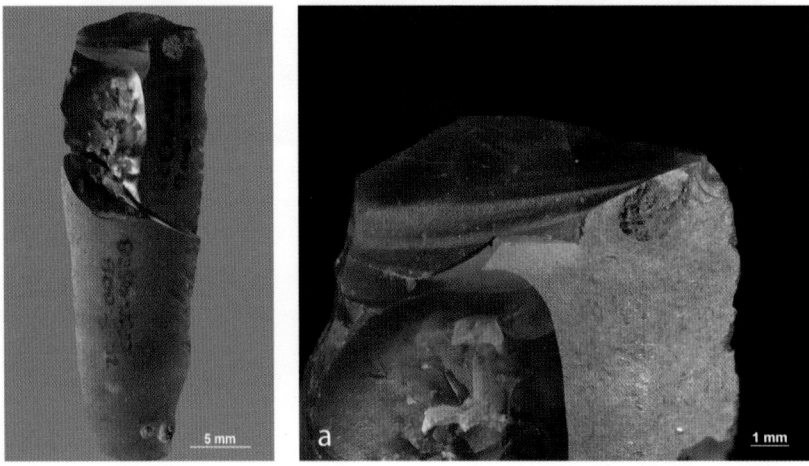

Fig. 7.5 Backed blade c.4322/4328; a) detail of the distal bending fracture with a step-fissured termination on the ventral face (16×) and later removals from heat

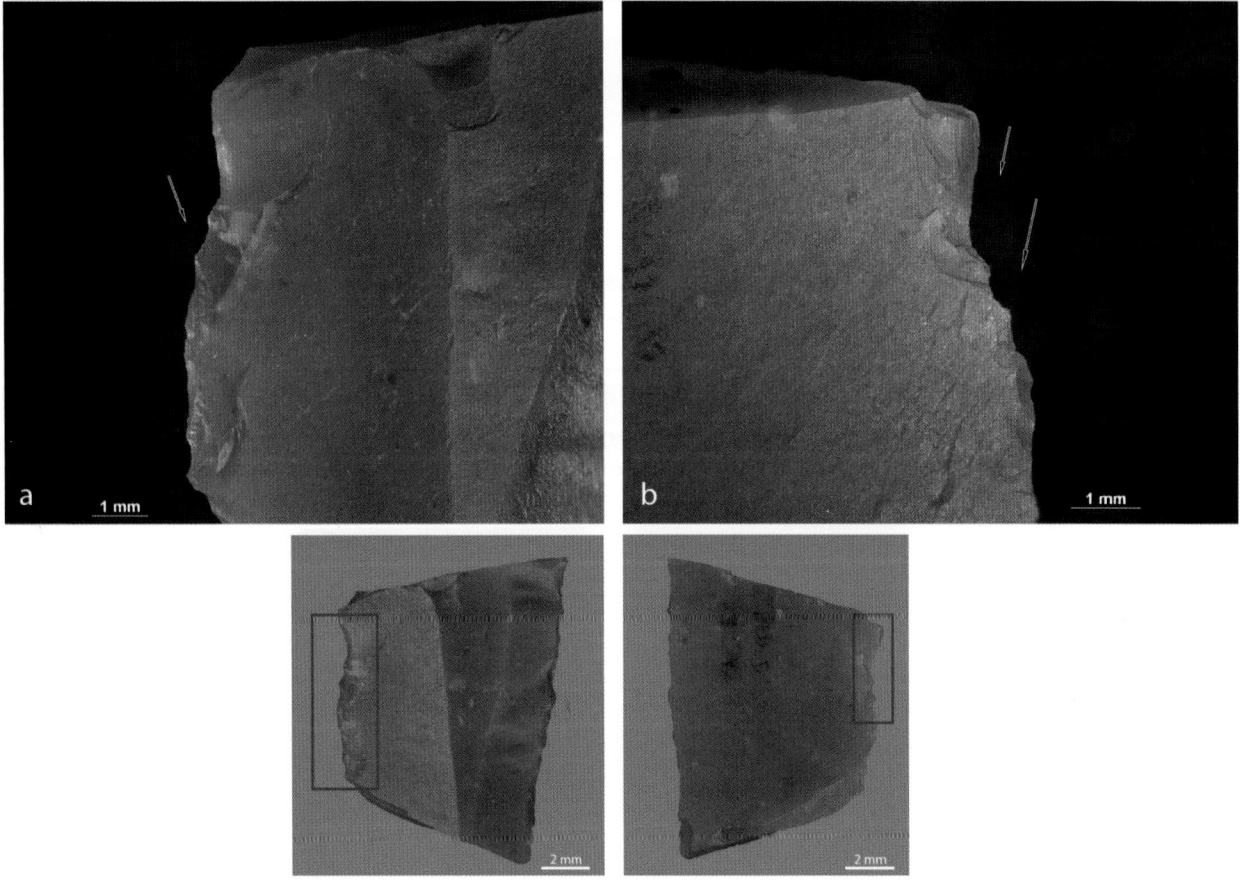

Fig. 7.6 Backed blade c.4062; a) macroscopic detail of the edge damage with step and fissured termination on the dorsal face (20×); b) ventral face of the left edge with the same edge damage (20×)

The high degree of breakage among the blade/lets from Guildford may be due to the hafting arrangement that was used. The strength of the hafting system will determine the degree of breakage, as has been demonstrated through experiments (Coppe and Rots 2017). It has been observed, for instance, that points fracture more easily when they are secured tightly in their shafts (eg when bindings and resin are combined instead of using bindings or resin only). No direct evidence of a specific hafting arrangement was found on the blade/lets, but this could be due to the use of adhesives. Experiments have systematically shown use of adhesives has a negative effect on the formation of hafting traces through the reduction of friction between the lithic point and the shaft (Rots 2002). No remains of adhesives were identified on the Guildford blade/lets, but this is probably due to the preservation conditions and does not necessarily mean adhesives were not used. It is worth noting here that several backed points and blade/lets showed heat alterations. While this may be a coincidence, it could also indicate that the tools were discarded in the fire in the process of retooling (De Bie and Caspar 2000). After all, a fire is needed when hafting with adhesives, or when de-hafting stone tools that were fixed with adhesives (eg resin, tar; Gallagher 1974; 1977; Audouze and Beyries 2007). At other Late Upper Palaeolithic and Mesolithic sites, the use of adhesives for fixing points in their shafts has been documented (eg Caspar and De Bie 1996; Clark 1954).

Wear patterns on individual pieces

Fragments c.4328 and 4322 can be refitted and were severely affected by heat. Nevertheless, relevant wear traces are still visible. The distal fragment c.4322 shows considerable use-related damage on the unretouched lateral edge: bifacial abruptly terminating scarring oriented slightly oblique to the edge, and a bending fracture on the tip with a fissure termination on the ventral face (Fig. 7.5). The mesial part of the tool (fragment c.4328) shows similar edge damage.

The left unretouched edge of the fragment c.4062 shows significant bifacial scarring with step and fissured terminations. MLITs were found linked with the distal bending fracture (Fig. 7.6). The proximal part of the tool shows a bending fracture associated with more MLITs, and a secondary elongated removal initiated on the left lateral edge.

The edge damage on piece c.4486 consists of a dorsally initiated distal break with a hinge-to-step termination, and associated fissured step-terminating removals (Fig. 7.7). The tip fracture is associated with a ventrally initiated bending fracture on the distal right edge, and with an additional fissured/step-terminating removal on the dorsal face (Fig. 7.7b). The heavy edge damage associated with MLITs is

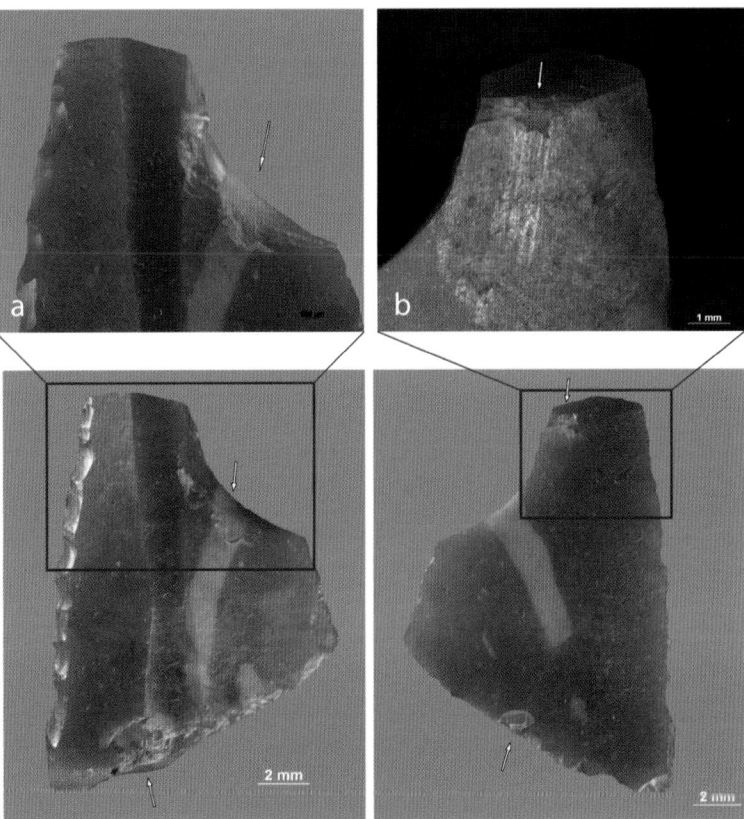

Fig. 7.7 Backed blade c.4486; a) detail of the distal edge damage: distal and lateral bending fractures (20×); b) detail of the distal edge damage associated with MLITs (25×)

oriented parallel to the lateral retouched edge. The proximal edge of the fragment is completely crushed. This crushing postdates the lateral retouch.

The combination of wear features on piece c.4200 is indicative of use as a projectile. Unfortunately the wear traces are too limited to allow a reliable determination of the position of the tool in the arrow shaft. The distal end of the piece shows a ventrally initiated bending fracture with a hinge termination. Microscopic striations were observed on the ventral face parallel to the left lateral edge and slightly oblique to the right edge. At the proximal extremity, a dorsally initiated fracture that occurred after the lateral retouch was recorded, probably caused by counter-pressure from the shaft during impact.

The single unbroken backed bladelet, c.308, only showed limited edge damage, but it nevertheless proved diagnostic of use as a projectile thanks to the distinct association between the small scars and the MLITs on the ventral aspect of the tip. In the proximal part, more intense damage was observed, including a small burination and a dorsal, abruptly terminating removal on the unretouched left edge. Like the proximal damage observed on c.4200, these features were probably caused by counter-pressure from the shaft upon impact.

Butchering activities

No obvious evidence of butchering was found. Only one scraper showed potential signs of use as a meat knife on its lateral edge, but fresh hide could not be excluded (cf below). Given the characteristics of the tool, its use in true butchering is unlikely and the traces are more likely to be due to small-scale cutting activities, probably within a manufacturing context. Meat polish forms very slowly (Unrath *et al.* 1986) and is easily affected by post-depositional surface modifications, which may partially explain its absence in the assemblage.

Manufacturing activities

Hide-working: scrapers

Previous ethnographic and experimental studies have demonstrated that hide working leads to a specific set of wear traces that is identifiable archaeologically and that allows the state of the hide and the gesture to be determined (Beyries and Rots 2008a). Hides are worked for several purposes, such as for clothing, bags and bedding. Different types of activities have been documented, including scraping, cutting and piercing (Keeley 1980; Beyries and Rots 2008b). The explicitness of the use-wear traces depends on the stage of hide processing, the positioning of the hide during work (eg on a frame, on the ground), the use of secondary items on which the hide is placed (eg a piece of wood), the use duration, the use motion and the exerted pressure (Keeley 1980). The rounding becomes more intense when the tool is used on dry hide, and the number of striations will largely depend on whether abrasives are used or not. Dry hide polish is dull and rough, while working fresh hides results in brighter and greasier polishes (Keeley 1980; Rots 2005). Given the characteristic appearance of dry hide polish and the explicit edge rounding that generally forms, this type of wear is often identifiable even if the material is affected by post-depositional alterations.

Hide-working proved to have been an important activity at Guildford Fire Station. Of the examined endscrapers, explicit use-wear was observed on eight out of ten. Certain variation was noted in the use-wear characteristics according to the tool shape, morphology and size, similar to what has been observed for the scraper assemblage from the Belgian Federmesser site of Rekem (De Bie and Caspar 2000).

The use-wear on the scrapers can be attributed to different stages of processing hides, but dry or moistened hide predominates. A single tool showed traces from working hide that could have been in an intermediate stage between fresh and dry, and possible butchering evidence on the lateral edges. The active parts of the tools were mostly the scraper-heads, with only two tools showing wear traces also on their lateral edges. Traces from working dry or moistened hide were quite symmetrically distributed over the entire scraper-heads, except for one tool on which the wear traces were clearly most pronounced in the right part of the scraper-head. The distribution of wear features has to do with the working position (position of the hide and of the artisan; De Bie and Caspar 2000; Beyries and Rots 2008a). Overall, use-wear traces are often cut by resharpening removals, attesting to prolonged use of the scrapers.

The more robust scrapers seemed to have been used mainly on dry and moistened hides by applying considerable pressure, while the scrapers manufactured on long and regular blades were probably used for a final processing stage on dry hide.

In total, three scrapers broke accidentally, two of which broke while hafted (c.924 and c.485).

For some of the scrapers, no specific gestures or other functional details could be identified. This was, depending on the case, due to partial removal of the working edges through resharpening, poor development of wear as the result of short use duration, short last use cycle, or severe surface alterations.

Wear patterns on individual pieces

In spite of the fact that c.485 showed mechanical alterations, use-related traces could be observed and interpreted as the result of scraping dry or moistened hide. The scraper shows heavy rounding on the ventral and dorsal aspects of the working edge. The rounding is associated with striations on the ventral surface, indicative of the direction of tool movement (Keeley 1980), as well as a dull polish with some friction spots within it. Judging from the intense rounding on both aspects of the edge, the tool was probably used by applying a fair amount of pressure on the hide and pushing the tool downwards. Moreover, the snap fracture, which postdates the lateral retouch, might have occurred during use, while the tool was hafted. A link between scraper breakage and hafting has been previously suggested by, for example Keeley (1978, 78): 'these broken end-scrapers were hafted and … these hafts substantially increased the amount of leverage exerted on the blank to the point that an awkward movement during use could snap them'. In addition, microscopic wear traces, such as bright spots, were observed on the ventral face close to the break, offering evidence of flint against flint friction, and therefore supporting the idea that the tool broke within its handle.

The use-related traces on scraper c.1583 were attributed to dry hide scraping. Typical dull and rough polish (Rots 2005) as well as striations were observed on the ventral surface of the scraper-head (Fig. 7.8). The working edge shows a small hinge-terminated break that postdates the retouch. It is clearly use-related, as the rounding, striations and polish extend over the entire scraper-head, showing that the work continued after this minor breakage. Another fracture finally snapped the tool in two and probably also occurred accidentally during use. The tool was curved in profile and thus susceptible to breakage under high-pressure activities.

Scraper c.2474 was positioned differently on the hide compared to the first two scrapers. This scraper was also made on a large blade, and its proximal

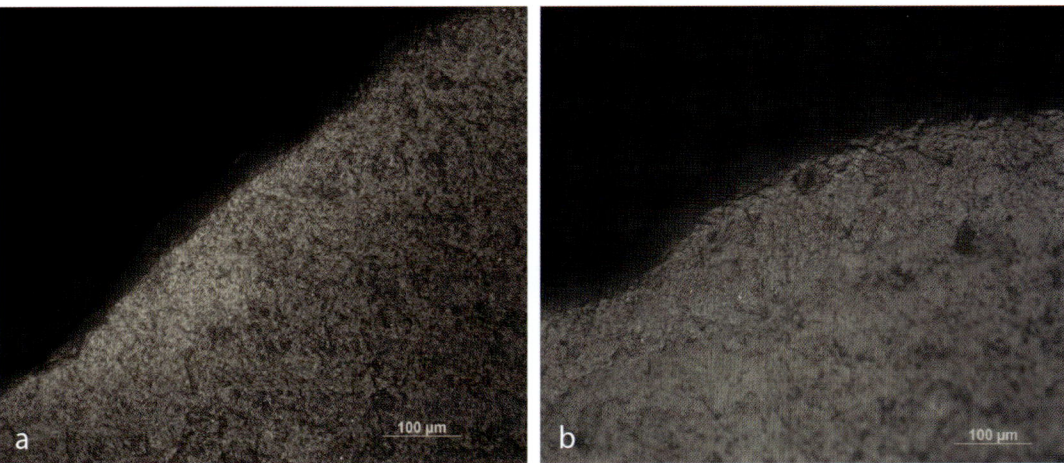

Fig. 7.8 a) microscopic detail of rounding and rough polish on an experimental scraper used on dry hide (200×); b) microscopic detail of rounding and rough polish on scraper c.1583 (200×)

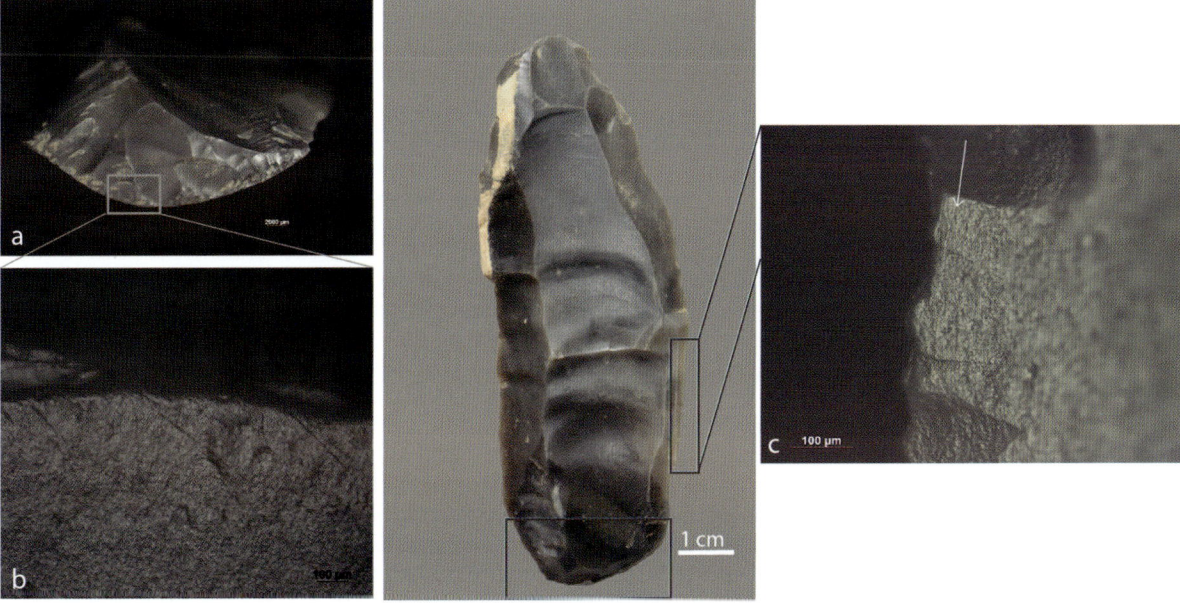

Fig. 7.9 Double end-scraper c.2474 with a) detail of the proximal used edge; b) rounding, polish and striations from scraping hide (100×); c) light rounding and striations parallel to the cutting edge, ventral face (200×)

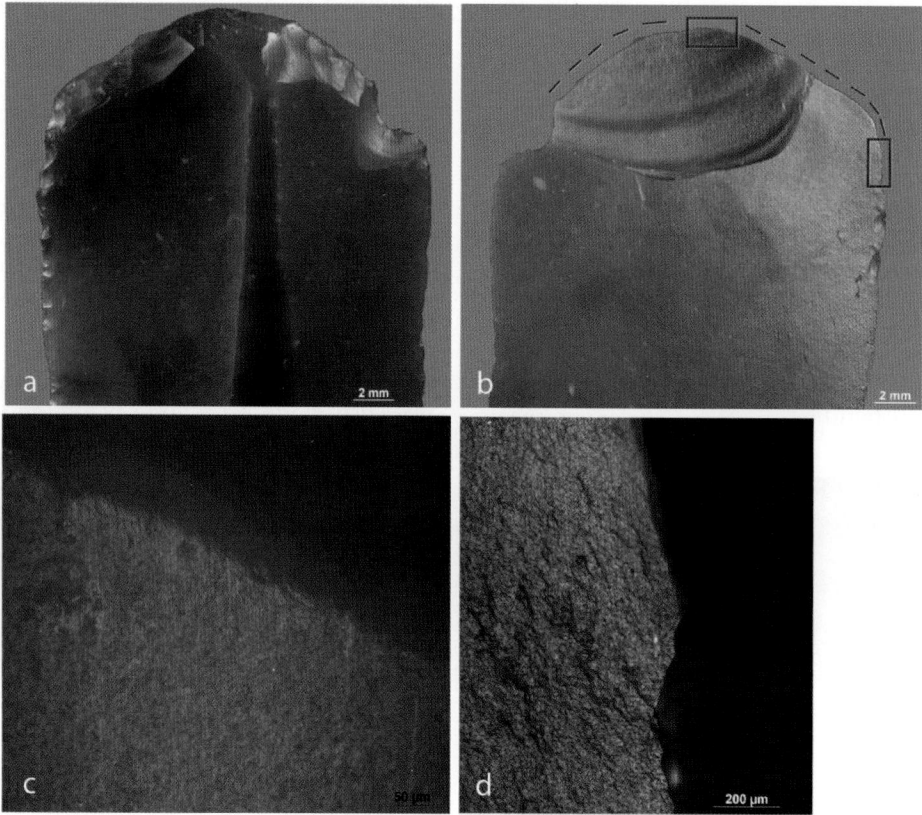

*Fig. 7.10 End-scraper on blade with **rasante** (scalar) retouch c.924 with a) macroscopic picture of the distal dorsal (10×) and b) ventral part of the tool with well-developed rounding that postdates the distal fracture (10×); c) microscopic detail of the rounded edge with polish and striations from scraping dry or moistened hide (20×); d) rounding cut by later removals from resharpening*

retouched edge was used. The rounding and polish are more pronounced on the prominent right part. This piece also has scarring (ventral bending-initiated scars) on the left lateral edge, associated with light rounding and striations which indicate that the edge was used in a parallel movement (Fig. 7.9). These wear traces may have been caused by cutting fresh hide or meat. Given the severity of the post-depositional alterations, however, the confidence level of this interpretation remains low.

Pieces c.924 and 2471 are two tools manufactured on long and regular blades. The first tool, c.924, is a distal fragment of a blade. The polish and rounding are well-developed on the ventral aspect of the distal edge. Considerable rounding was also observed on the scraper head. It post-dates the dorsally initiated step-terminating distal fracture, which in turn post-dates the retouch (Fig. 7.10). The use-wear ends abruptly in the distal part of the left lateral edge, where it is cut through by later removals. On the dorsal ridge of the tool, crushing caused by contact with an anvil during retouching can be seen. Microscopic linear bright spots were observed close to the mesial fracture. These could be due to intense friction in the haft when the tool broke. However, the evidence is too limited to be certain that the tool was hafted.

The second scraper, c.2471, was manufactured on a long regular blade (Fig. 7.11). This tool was also used intensively, but the rounding and the polish have been cut by subsequent resharpening. The lateral edges show microscopic polish, striations and heavy scarring (Fig. 7.11). On a macroscopic level, the lateral edges are damaged, showing abruptly terminating dorsal scars. The scarring is most evident on the proximal part of the tool, and it is associated with microscopic rounding on the most prominent parts, as well as spots of polish, but these wear traces are not equally distributed. Two hypotheses can be proposed: the first is that the tool had a complex life cycle, and in addition to the distal edge, the lateral edge was used for cutting or shaving hide. The second hypothesis is that these features are prehension wear, and that the association and location of these wear traces can be explained by intense contact with the palm of the hand, or with a piece of leather held between the tool and the hand during use (Rots 2002). The use of the distal end and the resulting overlapping wear patterns make it complicated to evaluate which hypothesis is the more plausible one.

Pieces c.1408 and 1272 are two very short scrapers. They were probably used and resharp-

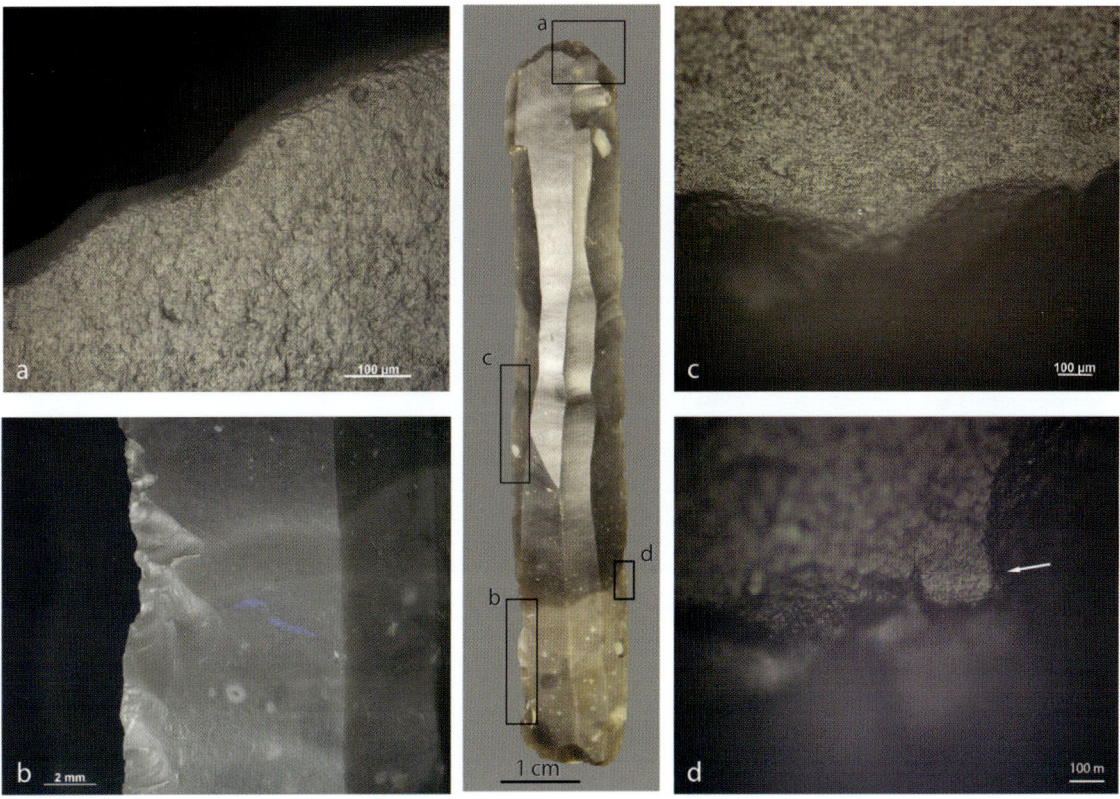

*Fig. 7.11 End-scraper on blade with **rasante** (scalar) retouch c.2471 with a) rounding from use, distal end (200×) and b) scarring, proximal left edge (12.5×); c) microscopic detail of the lateral edge with rounding and polish (200×); d) microscopic detail of the lateral edge with striations (500×)*

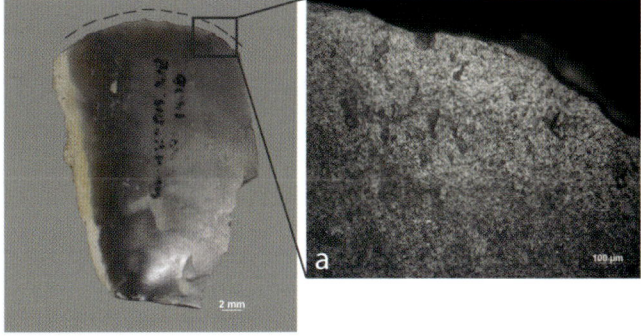

Fig. 7.12 Short end-scraper c.1408; a) microscopic detail of the polish on the scraper-head (100x)

ened up to the point of exhaustion. These tools showed some spots with very heavy rounding and polish associated with striations, but most of the use-related wear has been cut off by resharpening (Fig. 7.12).

On the remaining two tools (c.1625 and 1315), the wear was not sufficiently developed and the post-depositional alterations were too heavy to allow a functional interpretation.

Retouched blades

The blades (n=7) show irregular scarring with varying orientations and initiations (Fig. 7.13).

Similar edge damage, like that on so-called '*lames mâchurées*' (Bordes 1967), was found at the Late Upper Palaeolithic site of Nea Farm, Hampshire (Barton *et al.* 2009). On the basis of experiments made with long blades, the wear features on the Nea Farm tools were interpreted as the result of resharpening sandstone hammers or chopping hard materials such as antler (Barton 1986). Stepped retouch on Creswellian blades has also been described for the site of Three Holes Cave, Devon (Barton 1999).

The macro- and microscopic wear evidence reveals the complex life cycles of these tools. The artefacts appear to have been first used in

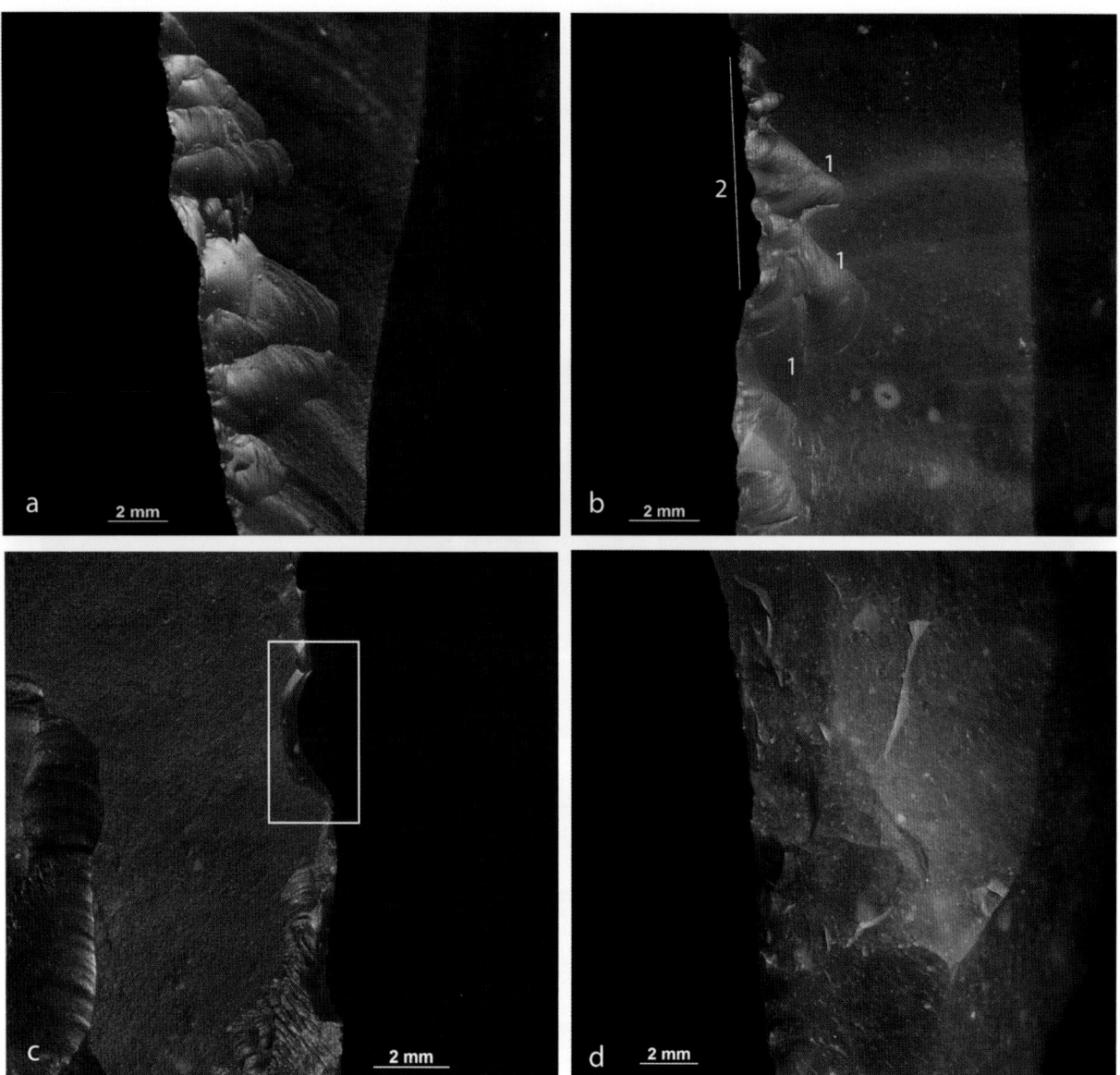

Fig. 7.13 a) Blade with **rasante** (scalar) retouch c.992 with stepped retouch, left lateral edge, dorsal face (10×); b) end-scraper on blade with **rasante** (scalar) retouch c.2471 with stepped retouch (1) cut by subsequent removals from use (2), left lateral edge, dorsal face (12.5×); c) truncation burin on blade with **rasante** (scalar) retouch c.19, dorsal face, right edge, bending-initiated scar with a hinge termination (12.5×); d) experimental tool with stepped retouch and subsequent removals from cutting and sawing bone (11.2×)

unretouched or partly retouched state, and resharpened if necessary during use. This interpretation is supported by the experiments performed during the analysis (see above). The scars with cone or bending initiations, and/or the polish and rounded edges, have been cut by later removals from resharpening or from use. The cone-initiated and bending removals suggest high-pressure use on hard material. The striations parallel to the lateral edges are consistent with cutting or sawing hard material, possibly bone or wood. On the other tools, the wear (scarring and polish in various stages of development) differs from one lateral edge to the other. Some of the pieces show additional rounding and polish oriented perpendicular to the edge, which could suggest a transverse motion, possibly shaving of dry hide or leather. It is not yet clear if these wear traces are the result of several different uses on different worked materials, or if some of the wear traces (for instance the striations parallel to the lateral edge) are the result of the tool being inserted repeatedly in a leather sheath.

Alongside the use-wear traces, hafting traces could also be observed. Hafting is also suggested by the relatively high number of broken tools (n=5). They were fractured in their mesial part, which is a typical location for hafting-related breaks (Rots 2002;

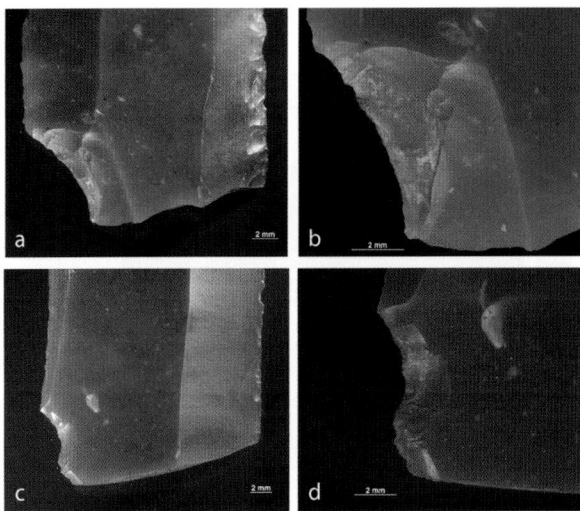

Fig. 7.14 a) Blade with rasante *(scalar) retouch c.926 (10×); b) detail of the lateral retouch/notch cut through by a later fracture (20×); c) truncation burin on blade with* rasante *(scalar) retouch 990 (8×); d) detail of the lateral retouched edge/notch cut through by a later fracture (16×)*

2010b), and the breakage proved to be posterior to the lateral notches and edge scarring (Fig. 7.14). Macroscopic edge damage is associated with microscopic bright spots or polish. These were probably formed as the result of friction between the tool and the flint particles detaching from it within the haft at the moment of breakage (Rots 2002).

It proved very difficult to identify the exact nature of the activity that was performed with these tools. The small-scale experiment was sufficient to test a number of hypotheses, but it did not provide a conclusive answer. For now, the use-wear traces remain ambiguous, similar to the well-developed but unidentified wear traces documented in Neolithic assemblages (eg 'polish 23': Van Gijn 1990). It is very likely that the traces observed on the Guildford blades, together with the Neolithic examples of enigmatic wear, are the result of specialised craft activities that are not yet entirely understood. A more comprehensive experimental programme should be designed to address these open questions in future.

Wear patterns on individual pieces

Blade fragment c.143 refits to c.99. The distal fragment (c.99) shows friction spots, polish, and rounding on its distal left edge. The wear on the tip is characteristic of working relatively hard animal material (possibly with an engraving motion). The lateral edges show light rounding and polish with striations parallel to the cutting edge. This wear suggests a cutting or sawing gesture. The worked material cannot be determined due to post-depositional alterations. The wear traces and the retouch on the left lateral edge have been cut by a bending fracture with a hinge-step termination on the ventral face. This fracture is associated with bright spots on the ventral face, which could be an indicator of hafting (Rots 2002). The proximal fragment of the tool (c.143) shows severe post-depositional gloss. On this fragment, edge damage is less intense, but microscopic striations were observed perpendicular or oblique to both edges.

Tool fragment c.926 shows a distal bending fracture with a feather termination on the ventral face. The lateral edges show rounding and polish with several friction spots, which indicate a transverse motion. When compared with the experimental tools, the observed microscopic wear features match with shaving dry hide or leather. Further, in contrast to these wear patterns, the combination of macroscopic edge damage, consisting of scars with cone or bending initiations, cut by later removals from resharpening or use, and the microscopic striations parallel to the edge, indicates a different use on a hard material.

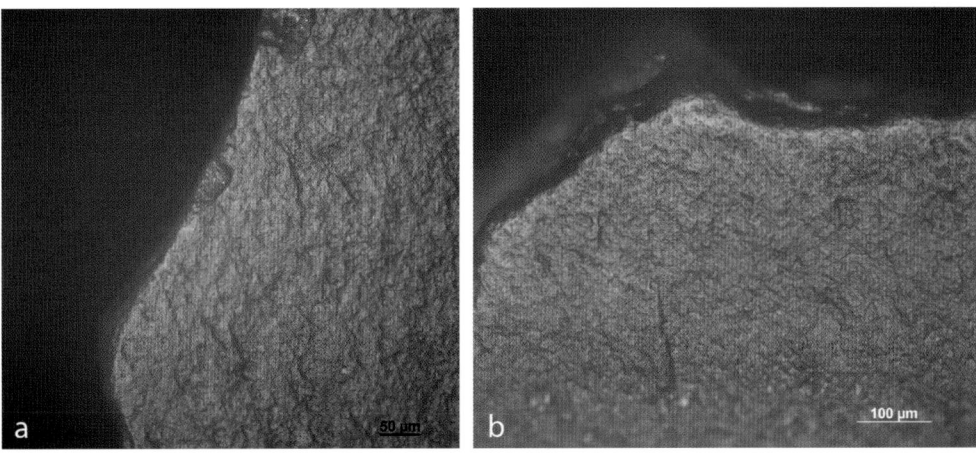

Fig. 7.15 a) microscopic detail of rounding, friction and rough polish on blade with rasante *(scalar) retouch c.992 (200×); b) detail of the same wear patterns on an experimental tool used for cutting and shaving dry hide (200×)*

Distal fragment c.990 refits with proximal fragment c.992. Both fragments were severely affected by post-depositional alterations. The observed wear traces are very similar to the wear patterns recorded on tool c.926. The lateral notch and edge scarring are cut by a later fracture. In addition, bright spots and light polish were observed under high magnification along the fracture on the ventral surface of the distal fragment (c.992; Fig. 7.15). The presence of the microscopic

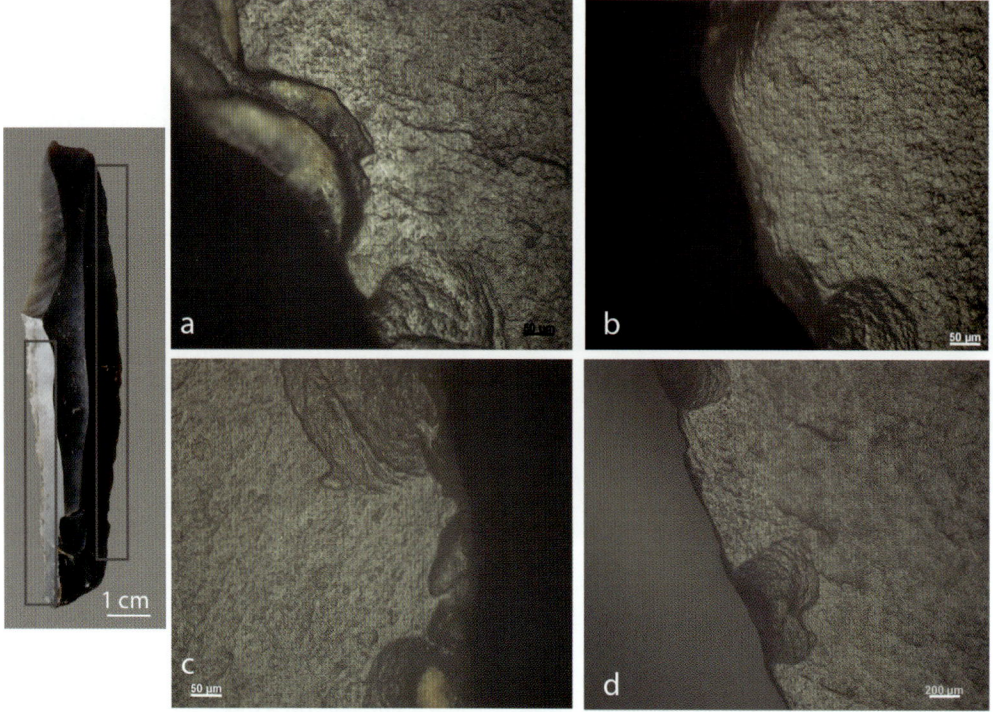

Fig. 7.16 Truncation burin on blade with **rasante** *(scalar) retouch c.19 with a) microscopic detail of the polish on the right lateral edge, mesial part of the tool (200×); b) rounding, right lateral edge (200×); c) rounding and striation on the lateral left edge of the tool (200×); d) striation and light developed polish on the lateral left edge of the tool (200×)*

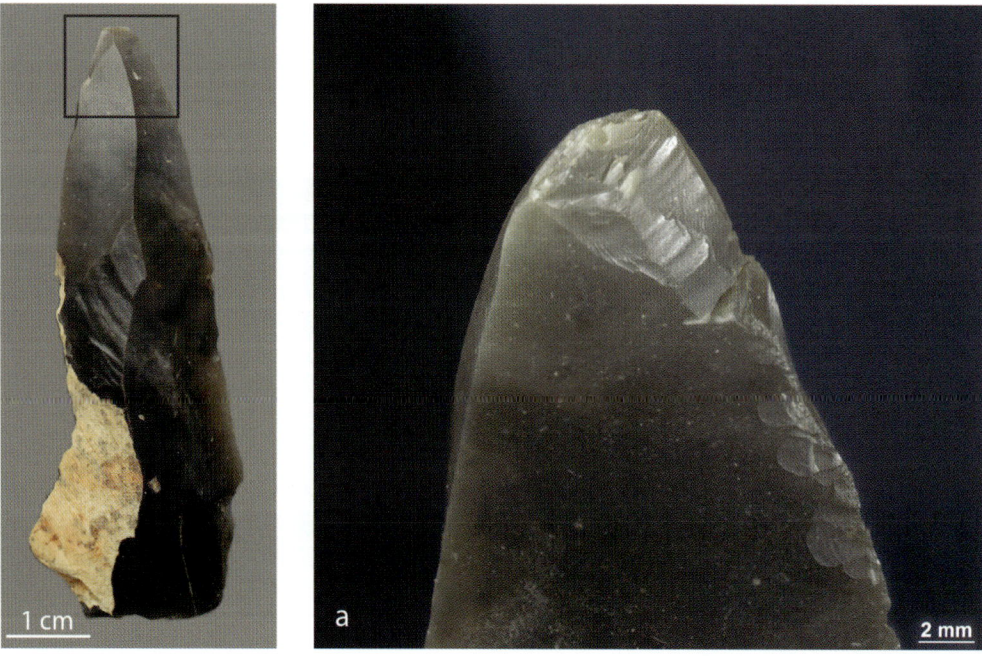

Fig. 7.17 Dihedral burin on blade with **rasante** *(scalar) retouch c.2451 with a) detail of the distal edge damage at the tip (8×)*

Table 7.3 *Summary of the functional interpretations for the analysed burins. The confidence level (CL) of each interpretation is scored on a scale of 1 (low certainty) to 4 (certain)*

ID	Used	Possible burin use	Possibly used (extensive alterations)	Unused
1280	X (CL 4)			
2451	X (CL 4)			
142	X (CL 4)			
1557	X (CL 3)			
1424	X (CL 3)			
2078		X (CL 2)		
695		X (CL 2)		
4691		X (CL 2)		
2319		X (CL 2)		
699		X (CL 2)		
2526		X (CL 1)		
459		X (CL 1)		
453		X (CL 2)		
1564		X (CL 1)		
1846			X	
4064			X	
701			X	
266			X	
2370			X	
1266			X	
953			X	
990				X
19				X
844				X
365				X
252				X
23				X

Burins

All of the burins selected for functional analysis (n=27) were examined in detail. Use-related traces were recorded on 14 tools, but with varying degrees of confidence. Burins that could be identified as used showed intense distal edge damage with crushing or abruptly terminating scarring on the tip as well as wear traces along the burin facets. The traces could be attributed to intense working of hard material by grooving and possibly by light percussion. In the case of seven tools, the examination had to be restricted to low-magnification analysis due to severe alterations (post-depositional polish), and a detailed functional interpretation could not be proposed. On six tools no use-related traces could be identified. All results are summarised in Table 7.3.

Wear patterns on individual pieces

The wear patterns on burin c.2451 indicate that the tool was used for grooving and percussion. Considerable macroscopic edge damage associated with microscopic friction traces was observed on the tip of the burin (Fig. 7.17). The distal part of the facet showed macroscopic and microscopic scarring associated with abrasion and linear polish. The combination of traces suggests that the tool was used with high pressure on hard material. Unfortunately the exact nature of the worked material could not be identified due to the presence of post-depositional alterations. Traces indicative of prehensile mode could not be identified.

The surface of burin c.1557 has been altered by post-depositional gloss and patina. Nevertheless, the examination of the tool provided sufficient evidence of use. The crushing associated with microscopic linear polish observed on the dorsal aspect of the burin facet indicates a transverse motion on hard material. No traces of hafting could be identified on the tool.

Tool c.319, a fragment of a long regular blade, had a complex life cycle. The primary use of the tool is witnessed by the remains of a striated, wood-like polish (Keeley 1980) on the left lateral edge. The tool was subsequently recycled into a burin. The first burin spall was removed from the proximal right edge of the blade, and resulted in an overshoot that removed the distal end of the blank. The proximal extremity of the blade has been snapped off by a transverse break that seems to post-date the removal of the overshot burin spall, although subsequent damage at the proximal end makes it impossible to confirm whether the initiation of the burin spall is cut off by the break. The proximal burin tip and the adjacent break edge show use polish that best matches with antler or bone (Fig. 7.18). The distal burin bit was shaped by removing a burin spall along the left edge using the

wear features associated with the fracture could indicate that they originated from the breakage of the tool in its haft (Rots 2002). The macroscopic and microscopic wear traces on the proximal part of the tool, fragment c.990, consist of intense edge damage, rounding, and polish, similar to the traces observed on tool fragment c.926.

Like the other tools or tool fragments described above, c.19 was manufactured on a long regular blade. It has numerous post-depositional features: mechanical alterations, post-depositional polishes and metal deposits. Some wear patterns were still visible on the lateral edge, but a reliable identification of the worked material could not be made. Macroscopically, scalar scars and trapezoidal scars with both cone and bending initiations were observed on the dorsal aspect of the left lateral edge. On the right edge, the removals seemed to be slightly different and are associated with light rounding (Fig. 7.16). In the tool's proximal part, the edges show more severe damage, with bending removals on the lateral and proximal edges. Microscopically, the identification of wear traces was quite difficult due to the altered surfaces of the tool. However, polish and rounding could be observed on the distal and left lateral edges. These were probably formed as the result of different uses on different materials. The rounding would suggest hide working and the polish a hard organic material.

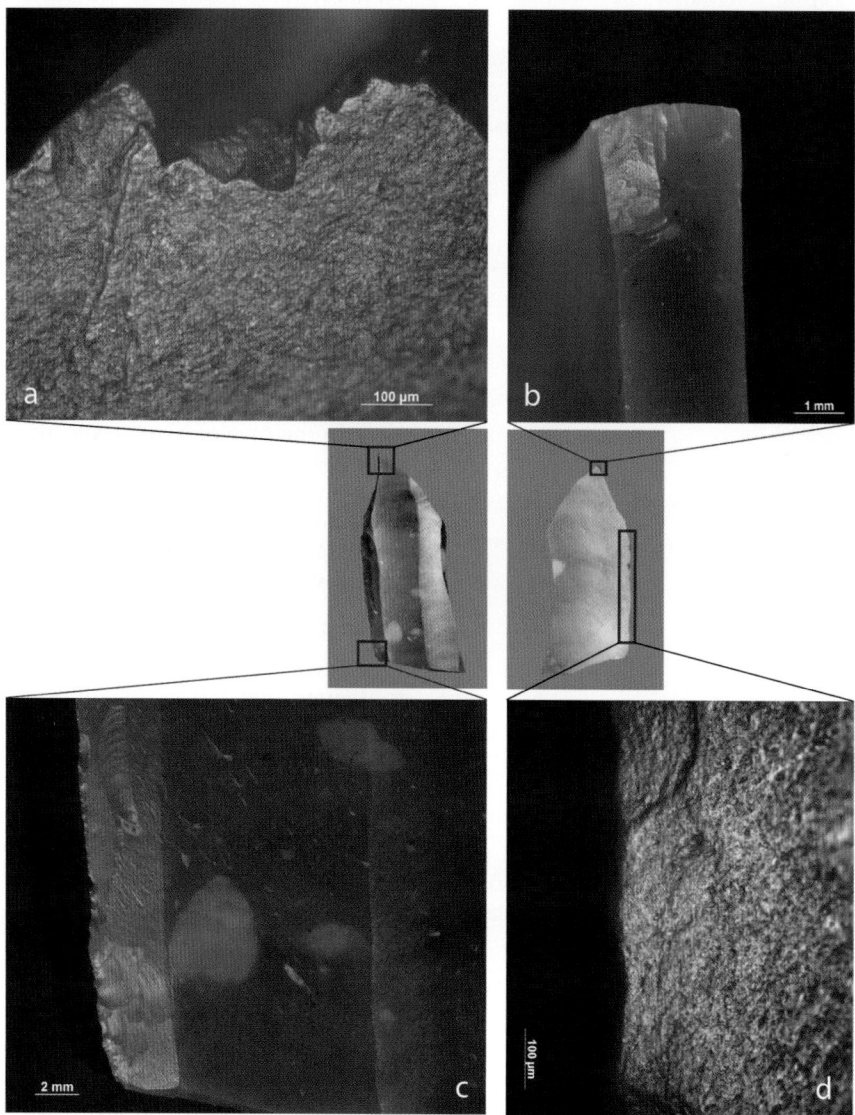

Fig. 7.18 Double burin on blade with rasante *(scalar) retouch c.319 with a) detail of the distal edge damage at the tip with polish, from use on antler or bone (200×); b) macroscopic detail of the burin tip (25.0×); c) macroscopic detail of the proximal left part of the burin with scarring related to use, cut by the transversal fracture (10.0×); d) microscopic detail of the left lateral edge with a wood-like polish (200×)*

overshot negative as the platform. The use-wear on the tip of this 'dihedral' burin is similar to that on the proximal burin tip, and occurs on both dorsal and ventral aspects of it.

Burin c.699 is manufactured on a crested blade. The dorsal ridge of the tool shows heavy crushing and intense abrasion associated with striations from cresting. The blade broke transversally either during detachment, subsequent shaping or use. Light polish on the tip of the burin suggests the tool was used, but the wear is too limited to allow a detailed interpretation.

Burin spalls

Fourteen well-preserved burin spalls were selected for microscopic analysis. All of the examined burin spalls proved to be from the primary shaping of the burins. Use-wear traces that attest a use prior to the detachment of the spall could be observed on only one piece (c.692). The wear traces consist of linear polish on the ventral surface, with additional striations parallel to the edge, cut at the proximal extremity of the burin spall by the small flakes removed during the preparation and/or removal of the spall. This wear pattern is indicative of a cutting motion on a soft material. Unfortunately, the observed traces were too minimal to infer the exact worked material. Nevertheless, the wear traces do not correspond to what was observed on the burins, which implies that various materials may have been worked with these tools.

Chapter 7

Strike-a-lights

The use of strike-a-lights is known and documented mainly from the Late Palaeolithic onwards (Stapert and Johansen 1999; De Bie and Caspar 2000), even though a rare Middle Palaeolithic example has been identified (Rots 2011). On the basis of a comparison with results from previous studies and experiments (Stapert and Johansen 1999; Rots 2011; Sorensen *et al.* 2014), it was possible to identify one tool – a rubbed end tool – from Guildford Fire Station as a strike-a-light. The

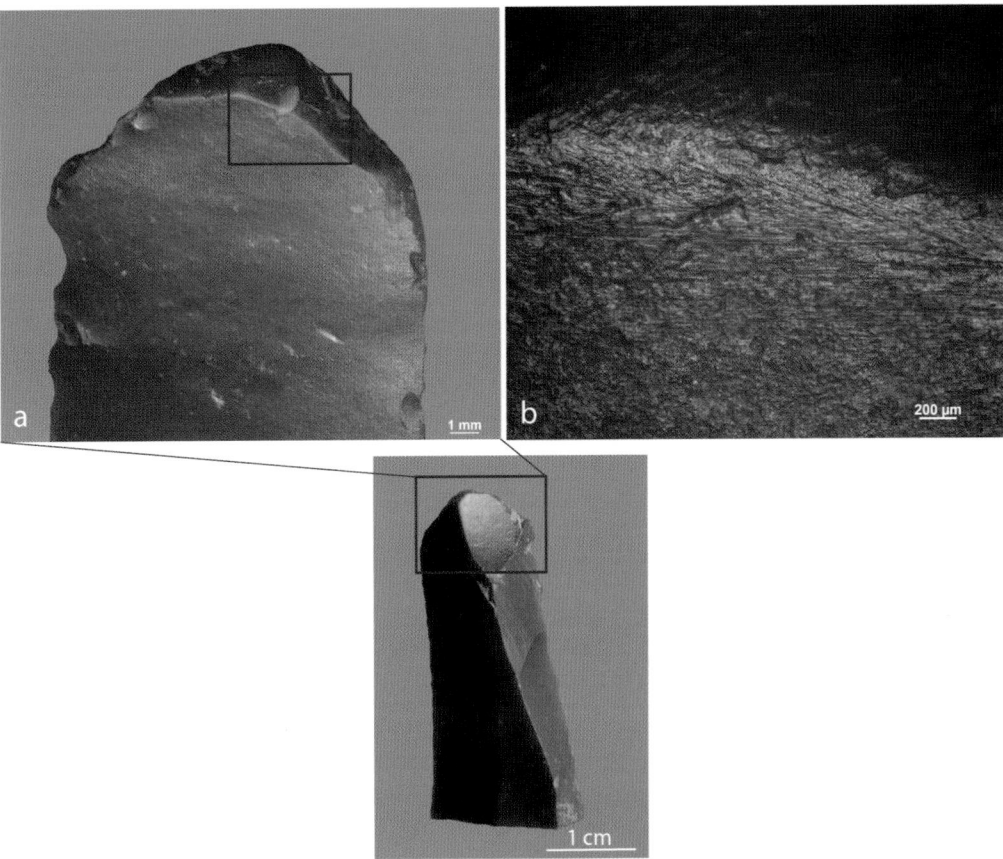

Fig. 7.19 Rubbed end blade c.2555 with a) macroscopic picture of the sturdy distal part of the blade (12.5×); b) microscopic detail of the used edge with intense rounding and striations (100×)

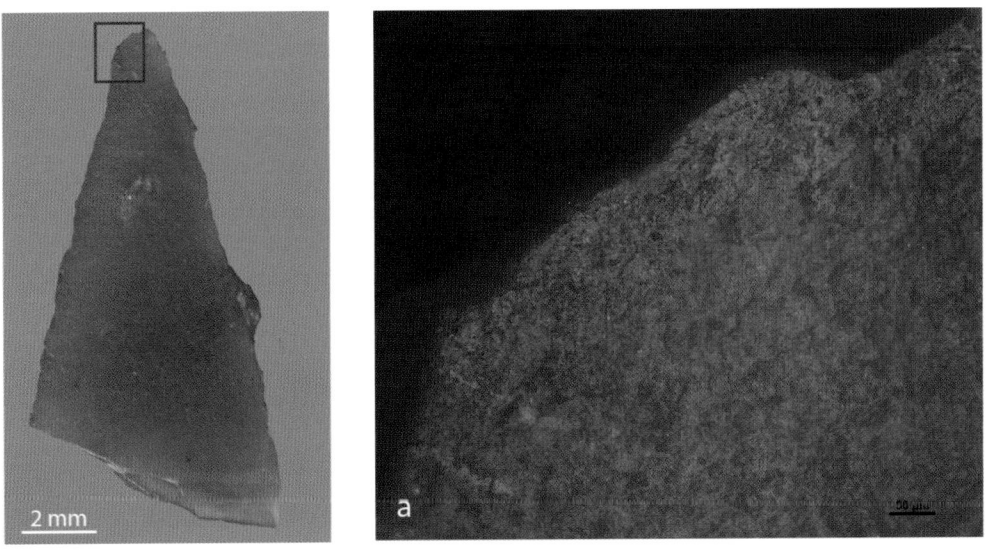

Fig. 7.20 Oblique backed point c.5032 with a) rounding on the ventral surface of the tip (200×)

Table 7.4 Summary of the functional interpretations with the worked materials and activities

	Tool category
Use related activities	
Projectile	Backed bladelets, retouched bladelets
Butchering (meat)	Scrapers manufactured on a blade
Scraping (hide: moistened or dry hide)	Scrapers
Perforating (dry hide, bone or antler)	Backed bladelets, retouched bladelets and blades
Cutting/sawing (wood, dry hide, hard material, unknown material)	Retouched/unretouched blades, burin, scraper
Shaving (dry hide, possibly leather)	Retouched blades
Grooving/graving (bone or antler, hard material)	Burins
Percussion (hard material)	Burins
(iron-rich rock)	Strike-a-lights
Subtotal	
Possibly used	
Projectile	Backed bladelets, retouched/unretouched bladelets
Scraping	Scrapers manufactured on a blade
Perforators	Retouched blades, flakes
Knives	Retouched/unretouched blades
Grooving/engraving/percussion	Burins
Subtotal	
Uncertain use	
Unused (or not interpretable, production waste, unfinished)	
Total	

piece is a robust distal fragment of a blade (c.2555) which shows macro- and microscopic wear patterns characteristic of percussion against an iron-rich rock. On its distal part, heavy edge rounding and deep striations were observed, consistent with strong friction (Fig. 7.19). It is not clear whether the tool broke during use or whether it was selected among fragmented blades. In any case, the robustness of the blade makes it ideal for use as a strike-a-light (Sorensen *et al.* 2014).

Perforators

Six artefacts were probably used as perforators. Tools with moderately altered surfaces show macroscopic edge damage and microscopic abrasion, together with polish.

The wear traces observed on a distal fragment of an oblique point (c.5032) are suggestive of use as a perforator. The tool shows heavy rounding on the ventral aspect of the tip (Fig. 7.20). This intense rounding may have been caused by perforating dry

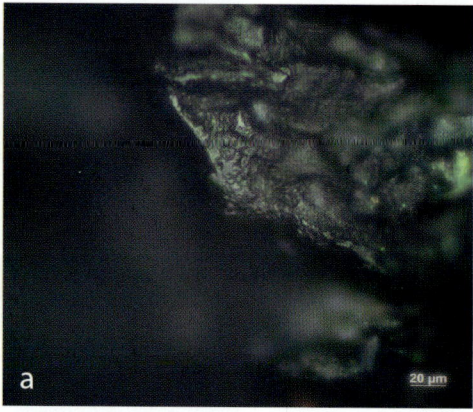

Fig. 7.21 Piercer c.5421 with a) microscopic detail of the used edge with friction polish (500×)

Total	Hand-held	Hafted	Uncertain/ unknown
5		5	
1			1
8	1 (possibly)	2	5
2		1	1
5		3	2
3		2	1
5			5
3			3
1			1
33	1	13	19
6			6
2			2
4			4
23			23
12			12
47			47
29			-
128			-
237			

hide. The proximal bending fracture and the unifacial scarring are not diagnostic of any particular use.

Tool c.5421 shows distal lateral edge damage consisting of superposing removals with step terminations on the ventral face, associated with microscopic friction polish that matches with an antler or bone working activity (Fig. 7.21). In its mesial part, the tool shows a transverse fracture associated with microscopic scarring on the lateral edges and friction polish on the ventral edge. These traces were interpreted as being possibly due to hafting (Rots 2010b).

Unretouched blades

Alongside the retouched tools, a selection of unretouched flakes (n=10) and blades (n=91) was also examined. Twenty-three pieces showed potential evidence of use as knives on soft material. Unfortunately the traces were insufficiently developed to allow a reliable interpretation. On the remaining flakes and blades, no use-wear traces were observed. Under high magnification, the artefacts proved altered by post-depositional gloss that was too intense to allow further analysis.

CONCLUSION

Post-depositional surface alterations were significant on the artefacts from Guildford Fire Station, and had affected a large number of tools. The analytical methods were therefore adjusted according to the degree of alteration on each individual piece, focusing on low-magnification analysis when the alterations were too severe to allow reliable high-magnification identifications. It was mainly the determination of exact worked materials and, in some cases, the identification of subtle traces such as prehensile wear which were hindered by post-depositional features. Relatively few tools proved to have been altered by heat or fire, with the exception of backed blade/lets, among which heat alterations were clearly more frequent. The backed blade/lets could be interpreted as projectile elements from hunting weapons. The fact that these tools were frequently altered by heat could be the result of their de-hafting. Re-tooling often takes place around a hearth to allow the softening of the glue and the replacement of damaged pieces with fresh ones (Keeley 1982; De Bie and Caspar 2000; Audouze and Beyries 2007). Alongside projectiles, hide-working tools were also identified, which offers further evidence of intense animal-processing activities. In addition, other craft activities involving plant materials as well as hard animal materials could be identified (Table 7.4). Overall, use durations appeared to be relatively short, although evidence of tool resharpening was also found. The hide scrapers in particular were regularly resharpened, some of them until exhaustion. Some retouched blades also witnessed intense use and handling. Hafting wear could be identified with varying degrees of confidence on the projectiles and on a number of scrapers and retouched blades.

To conclude, the functional analysis suggests that the site was associated with a relatively short occupation during which hunting, animal processing, and small-scale craft activities took place. The craft activities were linked with the retooling of the hunting weapons, the manufacture of hide items, and limited processing of animal and plant materials.

Chapter 8

Guildford Fire Station and the Late Upper Palaeolithic

by Nick Barton, Alison Roberts and Elizabeth Stafford

INTRODUCTION

This chapter considers the Guildford Fire Station Late Upper Palaeolithic site in its local and wider context. Beginning with the nature and age of the assemblage, the perspective is then widened to discuss the significance of the site at a national and European level. In doing so, we compare the assemblage with finds from south-east Britain and northern France (Figs 1.2 and 8.1) that share affinities with the Early Federmesser and Early Azilian industries of the Somme Valley and Paris Basin respectively. These industries are securely dated to the first half of the Late Glacial (Windermere) interstadial ~14,700 to ~12,900 years before present (Avery *et al.* 2019), the equivalent of GRIP ice core event stratigraphy phase GI-1e (Fig. 8.2). The OSL dating of the sediments that contained the Late Upper Palaeolithic assemblage at Guildford Fire Station support the idea that the British site was of similar date. Issues relating to site complexity and functional interpretation of the site are also discussed before turning to the potential for further research.

THE GEOLOGICAL CONTEXT OF THE FLINT SCATTER *by Elizabeth Stafford*

Overall, the results of the geoarchaeological investigations at Guildford Fire Station suggest that the site is underlain by cold climate fluvial sandy gravels deposited in braided stream systems prior to the onset of the Late Glacial (Windermere) Interstadial (Fig. 8.2). OSL dating of the upper part of the gravels (G1) suggests aggradation ceased at this location sometime after 22,665 ± 1605 BP, perhaps towards the end of the Last Glacial Maximum. This may be due to the migration of the main channel flow northwards away from the site and/or further incision/lowering of the floodplain during the Late Glacial period.

Gravel aggradation was superseded by the deposition of fine-grained sands, probably by seasonal floods in spring and early summer during periods of peak discharge. During drier periods, conditions probably allowed weathering and ephemeral soil formation on the surface of the sands. However, sparsely vegetated surfaces across the tops of braid bars and sand flats flanking the main channel are likely to have been subject to a degree of wind erosion and deflation. OSL dating suggests much of the sand deposition (G2a–c) occurred during the earlier part of the Late Glacial with deposition slowing or ceasing perhaps during the latter part of the Late Glacial Interstadial or the Loch Lomond Stadial. OSL dates of 10,150 ± 915 BP and 2940 ± 250 BP from the overlying sandy subsoil G2d suggest that although some deposition occurred during the early Holocene, this was not substantial, and the latter date is consistent with the horizon at which Iron Age activity was recorded across the site. A key point to note is that the OSL dating, together with the typology of the worked flint, implies that deposition of the Upper Sands G2c appears to have been contemporaneous with the period of occupation of the site, as opposed to the worked flint originating from above and having subsequently moved substantially down-profile as a result of bioturbation.

The sands were heavily affected by post-depositional processes, particularly bioturbation from worm burrowing that introduced intrusive material from above including fine comminuted charcoal and occasional charred cereal grains. Consequently, it could not confidently be said that any of the small amounts of charred material recovered from bulk samples was contemporary with the flint scatters. Tests for magnetic susceptibility did not find any evidence for heating or burning associated with the sands. The micromorphological analysis did find evidence for extensive penecontemporaneous and later fluctuating ground-water, localised leaching and iron cementation.

The topographic position and sedimentary sequence have many similarities to that of the

Fig. 8.1 Topographic relief map of south-eastern England and north-eastern France showing key sites mentioned in the text

LUP site at Wey Manor Farm, located 17.7km downstream from Guildford. There, it was concluded that human activity occurred on the surface of a low relict terrace that was subject to flooding before and during occupation, resulting in the deposition of fine to medium sand, at the same time that the Wisley (Floodplain) Gravel was aggrading at a slightly lower level on the valley floor (Green *et al.* 2013, 14). No struck flints smaller than 3mm were recovered, leading the authors to suggest that the floodwater was fast-moving and capable of entraining small items of debitage. In contrast, at Guildford Fire Station, analysis of the size class distribution of the flint shows that all size categories, including chips and small debitage, were well represented. Furthermore, artefact fabric analysis, hot spot analysis and analysis of refit orientations provides no indication that fluvial processes had affected the distribution of the flint, suggesting that the flood waters at Guildford were less frequent or not as vigorous. It may, in fact, be that mobilization of sand through wind erosion partially buried the flints which, along with the iron cementation of the sediments, afforded some protection from subsequent flooding.

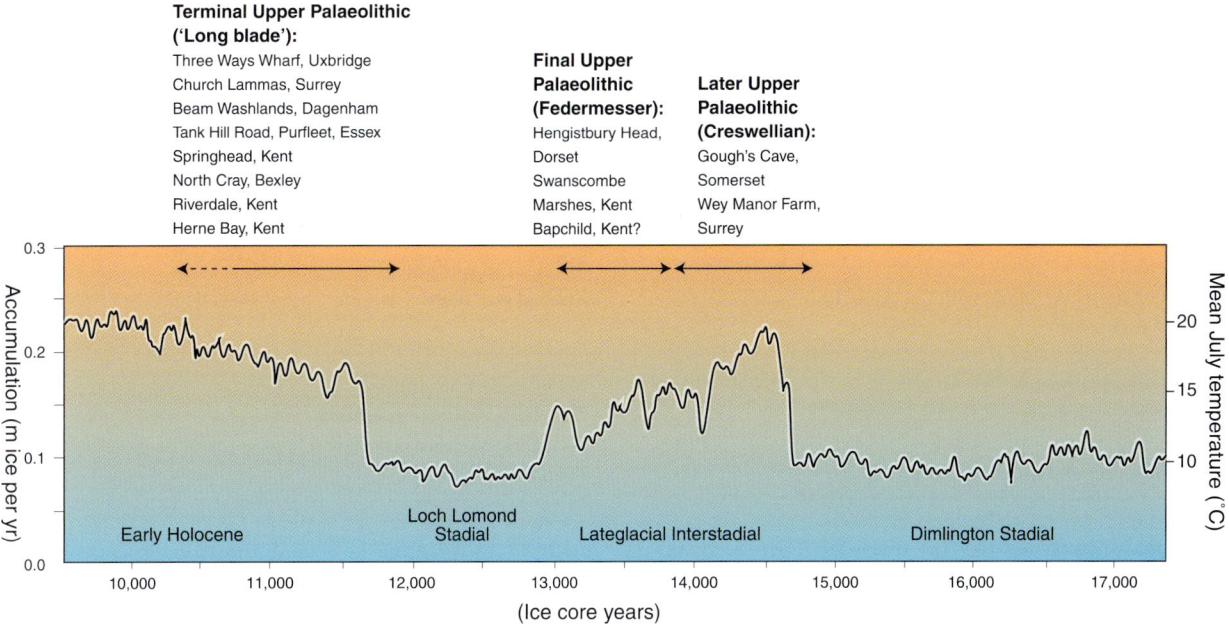

Fig. 8.2 Late Glacial climate and archaeology

THE PLACE OF GUILDFORD FIRE STATION IN THE LATE UPPER PALAEOLITHIC
by Nick Barton and Alison Roberts

Conventionally, the British Late Upper Palaeolithic of the Late Glacial interstadial is subdivided into two phases on the basis of well-established chronological and techno-typological criteria (Campbell 1977; Jacobi 1980; Barton 1986; Barton and Roberts 1996). The older of these two is usually referred to as the Creswellian, while the subsequent phase is represented by the Federmessergruppen (Federmesser) or the closely related Azilian. A third 'long blade' phase is identified in the subsequent stadial and early Holocene (Naudinot and Jacquier 2014; Barton and Roberts 2020). The Creswellian is sometimes referred to under the alternative name (Final) Magdalenian to highlight the fact that recolonisation of the British Isles in the Late Upper Palaeolithic took place as part of the dispersal of Magdalenian populations from the European mainland (Jacobi and Higham 2011a). The term Federmesser/Azilian also implies origins or parallels with industries that developed subsequently in neighbouring areas of the continent from Germany and the Low Countries to France during the Late Glacial (Schwabedissen 1954; Taute 1968, Célérier 1979). This simplified chronological scheme provides a basic framework for understanding the interstadial Late Upper Palaeolithic record, but in fact masks some subtle complexities as will be outlined below.

The techno-typological characteristics of the Creswellian have been described in detail elsewhere (Jacobi 1991; 1997; Barton *et al.* 2003). They are summarised in Table 8.1. Based on the principal attributes of blade debitage, it appears that the Guildford Fire Station assemblage has some features in common with the Creswellian. The cores are elaborately shaped, and the main objective was to produce long regular blades, straight or slightly curved in profile, and often from a single preferred flaking direction. Butts of the longer blades were carefully prepared using faceting to control the flaking angle; platform abrasion was also employed. There are, however, differences. A soft stone hammer percussion mode dominates the Guildford Fire Station assemblage which is not a characteristic of the Creswellian cave assemblages. A special method of isolating the platform prior to detaching a blade (known as the *en éperon* technique) has been reported for the Creswellian (Barton 1990) but does not appear to have precise parallels at Guildford Fire Station.

The *en éperon* technique is characterised by small-scale convergent removals that define a spur on the core edge. When placed above a dorsal ridge on the core face this serves to guide the percussive blow, especially in the manufacture of blades. Unequivocal examples of this technique have been recorded at Three Holes Cave (Barton 1990), Gough's Cave (Jacobi 2004) and Bradgate Park (Cooper 2004). However, some ambiguity has arisen over the application of this definition. Cooper initially recorded examples from Wey Manor Farm as 'approaching the *en éperon* technique', while Jacobi agreed they were an 'approximation of the technique' (Jones 2013, 23). We would concur with these observations in relation to the Guildford Fire Station assemblage, that no 'classic' examples of the *en éperon* technique are present.

Although a fairly high number of blades can be classified in the bladelet category (<12mm wide), there are no stratified examples of bladelet cores in the Guildford Fire Station assemblage and few tools are made on bladelets. It therefore seems unlikely

Table 8.1 *Main characteristics of British Creswellian and Federmesser assemblages (from Barton et al. 2009; 2003; Barton and Roberts 1996)*

Creswellian	Federmesser
Cheddar point	
Creswell points	Curve-backed point
Scraper on end of blade	Penknife point
Burin on truncation	Short end-scraper
Piercer and bec	Burin on truncation
Magdalenian blade (blade with flat retouch)	Rubbed end piece
Rubbed end piece	
Blade curved in profile	Blade straight in profile
Core with single preferred flaking direction	Core with opposed platforms
Soft organic hammer percussion	Soft stone hammer percussion
En éperon preparation of blade butt	Plain butt

that the manufacture of bladelet blanks was a priority and that many may have resulted as incidental removals (for example, when refreshing the core face). At Guildford Fire Station the final stages of core reduction, indicated by refits and negative scars on the blade cores, show instead the preferential production of short, straight blades generally made with soft stone hammer percussion.

Contrary to the debitage, few typically diagnostic backed tools of the Creswellian are present in the Guildford Fire Station assemblage. For example, there are no bi-truncated trapezoidal backed blades (Cheddar points) or single obliquely truncated backed blades (Creswell points). It is plausible that the conspicuous absence of these items may be due more to the reduced nature of the backed tool assemblage rather than its typological characteristics. However, it is also noticeable that amongst the items identified was a curve-backed blade pointed at both ends (bi-point) and several broken, backed points. Such tools (curve-backed points, but also straight-backed blades and bladelets) are more commonly reported in industries of Federmesser or Azilian types (Jacobi and Higham 2011b).

At Gough's Cave (Somerset) it has been suggested that a small number of curve-backed bi-points may have come from a stratigraphically higher position than the rest of the Creswellian assemblage with Cheddar points (Jacobi and Higham 2011). These authors have suggested that the presence of later occupation may also be inferred from an outlying age of $12,245 \pm 55$ BP on a cut-marked red deer tibia (Jacobi and Higham 2011, 233), which is significantly younger than the majority of the radiocarbon dates attributed to the Creswellian deposits. Unfortunately, it is impossible to test this interpretation more rigorously as the bulk of the finds derive from old excavations for which stratigraphic information is almost wholly lacking. Other examples of Late Upper Palaeolithic curve-backed bi-points have been recovered at Aveline's Hole, also in Somerset (Jacobi 2005), and the open-air site of Wey Manor Farm, Surrey (Jones 2013). The dating of each of these sites is based mainly on typological and technological comparisons.

This leaves largely unresolved the question of whether there was a consistent chronological separation of assemblages with angle-backed points (Creswellian) as opposed to those with curve-backed points (Federmesser/Azilian). In the case of Wey Manor Farm the situation is complicated by the presence of a curve-backed bi-point in an assemblage with angle-backed blades (shouldered points) and backed blades with a trapezoidal outline (Cheddar points; Jones 2013, fig. 2.10). As there is no reason to suspect stratigraphic mixing, could this be evidence for some degree of cultural continuity between the Creswellian and early Federmesser/Azilian or possibly offer grounds for a realignment of the Creswellian within these technologies?

Wey Manor Farm, near Addlestone in Surrey, is the closest regional parallel to the Guildford Fire Station assemblage in terms of both typological and technological composition and in site location and complexity. The site is situated only 17.7km downstream of Guildford, and occupies a similar topographic position, lying in the floodplain on the banks of the River Wey close to its confluence with the Thames (Fig. 1.2; Jones 2013, 9). Excavations there by Surrey County Archaeological Unit in 2004 recovered a small undisturbed Late Upper Palaeolithic assemblage of 371 flint artefacts including 44 retouched tools and their by-products (Jones 2013, table 2.1). Similarities with Guildford Fire Station can be observed in the prevalence of blades (30% of the debitage and retouched tool assemblage) and the methods of blade production (fairly rectilinear blanks, preferential platform use, faceting of butts, some butt abrasion and use of soft hammer percussor for longer blades). As at Guildford Fire Station, bladelets were also present (36/327 of measurable debitage) but not in sufficient quantity to suggest they were a prime objective of manufacture. The very low numbers of cores (mostly fragments) at Wey Manor Farm and the paucity of cortical debitage suggest that any initial shaping of raw material took place off-site and that the location was not used as a major manufacturing site. It may be relevant in this context that a group of blades at Wey Manor Farm may have arrived at the site ready-made (Jones 2013, 19). These blades show signs of utilisation and were on average longer than the other blades from the site (57–122mm as opposed to 35–91.5mm). Significantly, they also showed a high incidence of *en éperon*-like preparation. (In December 2019 Surrey County Archaeological Unit allowed the authors to study the Wey Manor Farm lithic assemblage for comparison with the Guildford Fire Station material. The authors agreed broadly with the original analysis (Jones 2013) and were able to add further detail for 'utilised' artefacts, and the recording of criteria not in the published report. Except where noted, statistics cited for the Wey Manor Farm assemblage in this chapter are based on the authors cataloguing for consistency with the Guildford analysis.)

Turning to the retouched tools at Wey Manor Farm, as stated above these include components of identifiably Creswellian type (one Creswell point, two shouldered points and the distal fragment of what is either another Cheddar point or a shouldered point) but also, significantly, an unmistakeable specimen of a curve-backed bi-point, typical of the early Federmesser or Azilian (Jones 2013, fig. 2.1). A near identical bi-point recovered at Guildford Fire Station (Fig. 6.23) raises the possibility that Federmesser influences were present in the Creswellian at least in these two assemblages. Figure 8.3 shows both bi-points. It should be noted, however, that the Wey Manor Farm bi-point is significantly larger and thicker than the Guildford Fire Station example. The Wey Manor Farm bi-point is 67mm long by 16.5mm wide and 4.7mm thick.

The Guildford Fire Station bi-point is missing the distal end but is only 41mm long by 11mm wide and 3.2mm thick. Indeed, most of the other backed pieces from Wey Manor Farm are larger and thicker than those from Guildford Fire Station.

Amongst other tools recorded at Wey Manor Farm are scrapers on the ends of blades, but only one displaying any form of lateral retouch. These are broadly comparable to types found at Guildford Fire Station and in other assemblages attributed to the Creswellian (Barton *et al.* 2003). Again, it is interesting to note that in amongst the Guildford Fire Station and Wey Manor Farm assemblages are a few examples of short end-scrapers more typical of the Federmesser. Five of the nine burins from Wey Manor Farm are truncation types (55%). This can be contrasted with Guildford Fire Station where slightly more examples of dihedral burins (12; 33%) than truncation types (8; 22%) have been recorded. Also present at Guildford Fire Station are micropiercers and perforators that are absent at Wey Manor Farm but that are found in some Creswellian assemblages (Jacobi 2004; L Cooper pers. comm.). If not of chronological significance, this could simply signal functional differences between the two assemblages.

One group of tools that appears common to both assemblages are blades with invasive stepped and scaled retouch (*lames à retouche rasante*). The retouch, which may extend to both edges of the blade, is present on supports of other tools such as scrapers and burins and implies a multiple or extended lifespan for such items (involving several stages of resharpening and use). In one case the scaled retouch can be found on a blade with a distinct concave truncation at one end and it may be pertinent that other examples of blades with concave truncations and *rasante* retouch have been reported at Late Upper Palaeolithic open sites at Hengistbury Head (Barton 1992, fig. 4.15) and Nea Farm (Barton *et al.* 2009, fig. 17) as well as several other isolated findspots in eastern England (Cooper pers. comm.). Blades with *rasante* retouch are regarded as an important typological *fossil directeur* at Azilian sites in mainland Europe (see below). In summary, there appear to be genuine techno-typological resemblances between the Wey Manor Farm and Guildford Fire Station assemblages. We would suggest that the similarities tend to outweigh any differences, though we do recognise a distinction in specific details such as in the relative abundance of flintknapping debris (more at Guildford Fire Station) and more generally in the nature and intensity of tool manufacture and use (again greater at Guildford Fire Station).

The Guildford Fire Station Late Upper Palaeolithic site in its regional context

The overall dating of the Guildford Fire Station Late Upper Palaeolithic assemblage is based on nine OSL measurements providing broad age estimates

Fig. 8.3 Curve-backed bi-points: Guildford Fire Station (c.308; 41mm); Wey Manor Farm (#52; 67mm)

Table 8.2 *Guildford Fire Station and Wey Manor Farm (data from Cooper in Jones 2013 and pers. obs.)*

Site	Cultural stage	Chronozone	Principal objectives of debitage	Butt preparation
GFS	Late Creswellian/ Early Federmesser	Late Bølling?	Long, regular blades Short blades	Plain and faceted 'en éperon' related Plain
Wey Manor Farm	Late Creswellian/ Early Federmesser	Late Bølling?	Long, regular blades Short blades	Plain and faceted 'en éperon' related Plain

for the sediment sequence containing the Late Upper Palaeolithic artefacts, as well as from above and below the archaeological horizon. Together they provide a highly coherent set of dates, albeit with large error brackets, that confirm the Late Glacial age of the archaeological finds (Table 4.3). The OSL samples that relate most closely to the archaeological material come from Section 1010 and show that stratigraphic unit G2c, that contains the Late Upper Palaeolithic finds, has an estimated age of 15,105 ± 1715 BP (absolute years). This would place the occupation in the first half of the Late Glacial (Windermere) interstadial (Figs 4.3 and 8.2).

Within the network of the River Wey and related valleys are several other Late Upper Palaeolithic sites and findspots that probably fall within this timeframe. They include the aforementioned site of Wey Manor Farm and Brockhill, also a substantial Late Upper Palaeolithic open air site slightly to the west of the main valley, as well as an isolated findspot at Pyrford. The latter is composed of a 'penknife point' (curve-backed point with basal truncation) made on a thick blade. Although typologically slightly different from the points from either Wey Manor Farm or Guildford Fire Station, it indicates the extent of human activity in this area during the Late Glacial interstadial.

Other open air sites in southern Britain likely to date to the Late Glacial interstadial are Hengistbury Head in Dorset (Barton 1992) and a smaller site further upstream on the River Avon at Nea Farm, Dorset (Barton *et al.* 2009). Together with Brockhill, Surrey (Cox 1976; Barton 1992, 182–3), they compare fairly closely on techno-typological grounds and offer potential differences with the Guildford Fire Station and Wey Manor Farm assemblages. Particular divergences can be recognised in the methods of core preparation and reduction of blade debitage (Table 8.2), coupled with the composition and types of tools represented (Barton *et al.* 2009). These differences seem likely to be due to chronological factors rather than site function but again the dating of all three sites is not precise enough to test such ideas further.

In terms of the overall size of the lithic assemblages, it is worth stating that Guildford Fire Station stands out both regionally and nationally, with only Hengistbury Head yielding comparative numbers of artefacts (14,377 artefacts from three phases of excavation; Barton 1992). The slightly larger size of the Guildford assemblage (15,357) undoubtedly reflects the exceptional recovery rate from the excavations with most being very small debitage and chips retrieved as a result of sieving (11,004 or 71.6% of the assemblage). This can be compared with Hengistbury where systematic fine sieving was only employed during the excavations in the 1980s (Barton 1992). Further comparison indicates that at Hengistbury Head the ratio of blade tools to unretouched blades was 1:5.7 (395 blades and bladelet tools and 2266 blades and bladelets from the 1968–9 and 1981–4 excavations; figures from Carr *et al.* 2010) in contrast to the lower ratio of 1:6.7 (173 blades and bladelet tools to 1156 unretouched blades and bladelets) at Guildford Fire Station. Even so, the volume of finds in the Guildford assemblage is still comparatively large when compared to other examples in the same region. For example, far fewer artefacts, including small debitage, were recovered from Wey Manor Farm (371: Jones 2013), Nea Farm (1600: Barton *et al.* 2009) or Brockhill (*c* 1700: Cox 1976; Barton 1992, 182–3).

European affinities with the Guildford Fire Station site

So far, it has not been possible to date with high precision any of the Late Upper Palaeolithic open-air sites in Britain, including Guildford Fire Station. It would thus appear appropriate to turn our attention to the continental European record where the chronological sequence is better developed and more fully understood. One of the closest regions of interest is the part of northern France that incorporates the Région de Picardie and the adjacent Paris Basin. An intensive programme of survey and excavation focused on the Somme, Selle and Seine valleys over the past 30 years has revealed high numbers of Late Glacial sites attributable to the Late Upper Palaeolithic Federmesser or Azilian traditions (Fagnart 1997; Bodu and Valentin 1997; Coudret and Fagnart 2006). Due to a combination of favourable preservation and meticulous fieldwork, there now exists a very detailed litho- and chronostratigraphic scheme for this region (Naudinot *et al.* 2019; Antoine *et al.* 2000; 2003; 2012; Fagnart 1997).

The terms Federmesser and Azilian are used more or less interchangeably in northern France, with Federmesser generally preferred in the Somme region and Azilian in the Paris Basin. The names

Percussive mode for blade debitage	Backed bladelets	Backed points	Other markers
Soft organic Soft stone	Absent	Polymorphic, including bi-point, curve-backed, and straight-backed	Blades with invasive 'rasante' retouch
Soft organic Soft stone	Absent	Polymorphic, including bi-points, trapezoidal-backed	Blades with invasive 'rasante' retouch

grew out of slightly different historical research traditions but essentially describe lithic industries typified by 'curve backed points' (*technocomplexe à pointes à dos courbe*) that appeared over much of Europe during the Bølling oscillation (Naudinot *et al.* 2019, 11). The process of *Azilienisation* (Valentin *et al.* 2006) is used by French prehistorians to describe a gradual transition from the preceding Late Magdalenian, a distinctive regional tradition of industries epitomised by armatures made on backed bladelets (*lamelles à dos*). Some debate still exists over whether there may have been temporal overlap between the two major technocomplexes in the Bølling (Naudinot *et al.* 2019, 6).

The technical changes that were initiated during the latest phase of the Magdalenian (early Bølling) can accurately be described at sites like Belloy-sur-Somme (Fagnart 1991; 1993). Here the principal objective of debitage continued to be the production of long regular blades but instead of backed bladelets, the majority of projectiles were made on short blades and consisted of polymorphic types including backed points (*pointes à dos*), shouldered points (*pointes à cran*) and truncated forms (*pointes à dos à troncature*). It should be noted in this context that amongst the projectile types recovered at Wey Manor Farm were shouldered forms also manufactured on small blades (Jones 2013). However, apart from this similarity, other technological attributes at Belloy-sur-Somme seem to have been different, for example, in the frequent presence of blades with *en éperon* butts, convexity in blade profiles and use of soft organic hammers for blade production (Naudinot *et al.* 2019, 11). Sites of this kind in northern France are believed to date to before 12,300 BP (uncalibrated radiocarbon years) and close to the time when reindeer disappeared as a leading game animal in the Somme region.

The oldest phase (*phase ancienne*) of the Somme Federmesser, dated to the late Bølling oscillation, reflects transitional characteristics with the Final Magdalenian (Coudret and Fagnart 1997). Assemblages of this kind are represented at the open-air sites of Hangest-sur-Somme quarry III.1 (*niveau inférieur*; Fagnart 1997; Fagnart and Coudret 2000a; 2000b) and Saleux, Sector 3 (blue/grey patinated series; Coudret and Fagnart 2015), both in the Somme Valley, Le Closeau (*niveau inférieur*) in the Paris Basin (Bodu 1998; 2000) and Grotte du Cheval at Gouy (Bordes *et al.* 1974; Valentin 1995, fig. 22).

AMS radiocarbon dates from the latter two localities place the occupations in a phase preceding the beginning of the Allerød (late Bølling). A similar age may be inferred for Hangest III.1 (*niveau inférieur*) which is stratified beneath the Allerød soil (Fagnart and Coudret 2000a, 119), while the lower layer at Saleux 3 is also dated stratigraphically to this time (Coudret and Fagnart 2015; Table 8.3).

In each of these early Federmesser assemblages the principal objective appears to have been the production of blades with relatively straight profiles, with prepared plain and faceted platforms and often manufactured using soft stone hammers. Blades with typical *talons en éperon*, known from the Magdalenian, are rare or absent. The assemblages also contain short blades and bladelets. Interestingly, at Hangest-sur-Somme III.1, backed bladelets (*lamelles à dos*) still made up a relatively high percentage of all retouched tools (37%) with macrolithic armatures (single and bi-points or *monopointes* and *bi-pointes* on small blades) also contributing a significant percentage (11%). At Le Closeau and Grotte du Cheval there is an exclusive presence of large symmetrical curved forms pointed at both ends (*bi-pointes à dos courbe*) and no backed bladelets (*lamelles à dos*). The existence of shouldered and truncated points amongst the backed tools at Hangest III.1 may be significant in the chronological development of the northern French industries (Fagnart and Coudret 2000a).

Amongst the other tools represented in this group of assemblages, burins on truncation tend to outnumber dihedral forms, and scrapers include both those on the ends of large blades as well as shorter forms (*grattoirs courts*). Distinctive Lacan burins have been recorded in the Somme Valley sites which are so far absent in the Paris Basin. In contrast, unlike the Somme Valley sites, Le Closeau includes typical examples of *lames à retouche rasante*. These tools are highly recognisable, being made on large blades with a distinctive stepped and scaled retouch, on one or both edges, resulting from a special method of resharpening (Bodu and Mevel 2008). According to these authors such tools first appear in Late Glacial technologies in the early Azilian (*l'Azilien ancien*), being largely absent in the preceding Late Magdalenian (Bodu and Mevel 2008, 510). Experimental and microwear studies suggest that they were used as knife blades (*lame couteau*) that were extensively resharpened and believed to

Table 8.3 *Development of Magdalenian to Federmesser/Azilian (after Valentin et al. 2006 with additions from Naudinot et al. 2019; Coudret and Fagnart 2015; Fagnart pers. comm. and Mevel pers. comm.)*

Cultural stage	Chronozone	Sites	Principal objectives of debitage	Butt preparation
Classic Magdalenian (Paris Basin)	Late Dryas I – Early Bølling	Pincevent Verberie	Long, regular blades	En éperon Bladelets
Transitional Cepoy-Marsangy (Paris Basin)	Early Bølling	Marsangy Cepoy	Long, regular blades Short blades	En éperon Plain?
Transitional (Somme)	Early Bølling?	Belloy	Long, regular blades Short blades	En éperon Plain
Early Federmesser (Somme)	Late Bølling	Hangest III.1 (inf) Saleux - Sector 3 Blue/grey series	Long, regular blades Short blades	Plain and faceted
Early Azilian (Paris Basin)	Late Bølling	Le Closeau (inf)	Long, regular blades Short blades	Plain, some faceting Plain
Recent Federmesser	Late Allerød	Hangest III.1 (sup)	Short blades Elongate flakes	Plain and faceted

be associated with working animal hide (*peaux*; Bodu and Mevel 2008, 541). As noted above these idiosyncratic tools are recorded at both Guildford Fire Station and Wey Manor Farm as well as at a number of other Late Upper Palaeolithic sites in southern Britain.

The later phase of the Federmesser (*phase récente*) belongs within the second half of the Late Glacial interstadial (the Allerød oscillation). Assemblages of this type are represented at a number of localities in the Somme and Selle valleys, as well as in the Paris Basin. In the Selle this phase is recorded at the Gravière du Marais at Conty (Fagnart and Coudret 2000a; Coudret and Fagnart 2012) where the lower layer is stratified at the base of a regionally defined Allerød soil. Strong typological affinities exist between the finds from this site and the upper occupation horizon in section 27 at Pincevent in the Paris Basin which has been dated to 11,870 ± 130 BP (Bodu and Orliac 1996). In contrast, the complex of sites found at Saleux (loci 109, 114, 234, 244, 244/5, 284a, 284b and 294) appear mostly to belong to the second half and end of the Allerød oscillation (Coudret and Fagnart 2015).

Although there is some regional variability, assemblages of the *phase récente* generally show an increased preponderance of simple curve-backed blades pointed at one end (*mono-pointes à dos courbe*). In the Somme valley there is an indication of a broad evolutionary change in these assemblages through time but the differences rest on slight contrasts concerning the methods of reduction and the mode of flint procurement (Coudret and Fagnart 2012; 2015). In the Paris Basin the upper level at Le Closeau, dating to the end of the Allerød, is characterised by a simplified method of debitage with a reduced emphasis on bladelet manufacture (Bodu pers. comm.). A similar feature may also be seen at one of the locations at Saleux ('La Vierge Catherine' locus 114). Here the main divergence from the early Federmesser appears to be in the preferential use of the hard hammer mode throughout the whole of the reduction sequence (Fagnart and Coudret 2000a, 120). Core preparation also seems to have been less systematic, using the natural convexity of nodules to guide the early removals and generally making infrequent use of platform abrasion. According to Fagnart and Coudret (2000a), the observed changes are accompanied by a reliance on poorer quality flint for manufacture. At Saleux (locus 114) backed mono-points make up 38% of the tool assemblage. They are on relatively thick supports, with the backed edge being much closer to the midline of the blade. Backed knives were relatively abundant (16%). In the other tool classes, burins on truncation outnumber dihedral examples by a factor of 4:1.

In assessing these variables, Guildford Fire Station and Wey Manor Farm share much greater affinities with industries of the early Federmesser/Azilian (*phase ancienne*) than with those of the recent Federmesser or Late Magdalenian of northern France. In the absence of large numbers of backed tools, it is difficult to draw any more definite conclusions. Certainly, the lack of backed bladelets and the presence of curve-backed points (*bi-pointes*) at both Wey Valley sites suggests a clear relationship with the early Federmesser or the Azilian. The occurrence of blades with *rasante* retouch suggests functional and behavioural parallels with Azilian

Percussive mode for blade debitage	Backed bladelets	Backed points	Other markers
Soft organic	Abundant	Absent or very rare	
Soft organic		Abundant and polymorphic (shouldered)	
Soft organic Soft stone	Rare	Abundant and polymorphic (including shouldered, truncated)	
Soft stone	Abundant	Abundant (bi-points) presence	Lacan burins
Soft stone	Absent	Abundant (bi-points)	Blades with invasive 'rasante' retouch
Hard and soft stone	Abundant	Abundant (mono-points)	Large backed knives

sites in the Paris Basin and elsewhere in France and may possibly be linked to a relatively short phase of activity in the equivalent of the early Bølling.

Within a European perspective, the size and complexity of sites like Guildford Fire Station and Hengistbury can be closely compared to 'smaller' Federmesser sites such as Locus 234 at 'Les Baquets', Saleux in northern France. The latter covered an area of 60m² with distinctive hearth combustion zones and about 4000–6000 artefacts (Coudret and Fagnart 2004; 2006). A slightly larger concentration with combustion zones was located about 20m distant, at Locus 244; the two loci were probably contemporary. Although of comparable size, shape and complexity to Hengistbury, the largest contemporary site in southern Britain, these two loci are considered to be relatively small by Federmesser site standards (Coudret and Fagnart 2006), and particularly in relation to locations in the Paris Basin (Bodu 2000), Belgium (De Bie and Caspar 2000) and the Rhineland (Baales and Street 1996).

SITE COMPLEXITY AND FUNCTION

The Guildford Fire Station site consists of a large sub-circular scatter of flint artefacts covering an area approximately 36m² in size (Fig. 6.1). It lies on a gradual southwards slope towards the present river but has been truncated at its southern end by the essential clearing action of a bomb disposal team prior to the excavations. Although part of the scatter around the southern flintknapping concentration is likely to have been lost during the removal of the bomb, the disturbed area is at the southern edge of the scatter leaving other areas of the site, including the central area where most of the tool use took place, unaffected.

Within the overall flint artefact scatter two dense concentrations of flint working debris can be identified. Both are slightly elongated and no more than a metre or so in diameter and separated by a gap of about 4–5m: the northern concentration (concentration 1: C1) lies in the north-west of the site, and the southern concentration (concentration 2: C2) to the south-east. The occurrence of these flintknapping concentrations was suspected during the assessment phase based on the overall distributions of artefacts. This was later confirmed by spatial analysis and the refitting programme which revealed further details of the knapping concentrations, and a more general pattern of activity and tool use in between them. The identification of the two concentrations as knapping areas was also confirmed by the distributions of cores, core rejuvenation pieces and crested pieces (Fig. 6.5) that show that these areas were foci for working and refreshing cores. In fact, the majority of all recorded cores and core fragments can be shown to come from or close to one of the two concentrations. It is also striking that these two areas also contain the largest number of pieces with a high proportion of cortex remaining on their dorsal surfaces (Fig. 6.3). This implies that not only were the cores worked in these locations, but also that the cores were prepared from original nodules in the same places.

Very similar knapping strategies were employed in both knapping locations, but they may not represent the work of the same individual flintknapper and there seem to be subtle differences in the knapping techniques used in the two locations. For example, the 'en éperon-related' technique of isolating a bulb prior to removing a blade appears to be particularly associated with the southern concentration (C2).

Refitting has also raised the possibility of the presence of a third knapper, who we have tentatively identified as an inexperienced novice (Roberts and Barton 2021). This is based on Refitting Group 06 that consists of a single-platform flake core, c.1905, on a small river cobble, a material not generally used at the site (Fig. 6.45). The core seems to have been initially set up by an expert knapper, revealed by an early removal of a well-made blade (c.2403). This occurred in the northernmost part of the site (in the direction of the river; Fig. 6.46). Gaps in the reduction sequence show how several removals were then detached before numerous unsuccessful attempts were made to refresh the platform by repeated strikes to the edge of the core. This error was corrected by a successful core platform rejuvenation flake (c.1908). The repair was done in the northern concentration (C1) by a more skilled flintknapper, who was also responsible for knapping RG 01. Continued reduction of RG 06 then took place in an area immediately to the west of the northern concentration (C1). It is hypothesised that this represented the activity of a novice flintknapper learning the skill on a small river cobble under the watchful eye of a more experienced teacher (cf Grimm 2000). Viewed in this light, the expert correction to the platform may be seen as an 'educational interaction' of the kind proposed by Johansen and Stapert (2004), in this case resolving a problem over refreshing a core platform. Although uncommon, the presence of novice flintknappers (or children) has been identified at other Late Glacial sites elsewhere in northern Europe (Johansen and Stapert 2004). It was also proposed at the nearby site of Wey Manor Farm (Jones 2013).

Refitting of artefacts has also yielded some spatial data concerning the movement of blades across the site. While most artefacts were found close to the areas where the refitting groups were located, there are also examples of artefacts found more distant from their refitting group (see Chapter 6). Most of these movements are within 2m of the original flintknapping concentration and are usually directed to the central area between the concentrations. They seem to be often related to tool use. Some movements can be over longer distances. For example, RG 02 contains two burins made from the same blade that were found about 3m apart, one just south-west of the northern concentration (C1) and the other west of the southern concentration (C2). There are also several examples of blades, especially ones of the high-quality red-tinged flint, being found at distances of several metres from the rest of their refitting parts. For example, a blade of red-tinged flint (c.2301) was found 5m distant from the rest of RG 20 in the southern concentration (C2). The same was true of a similar red-tinged flint blade that was found about 3m north of the rest of RG 21 near the northern concentration (C1). Other artefacts of red-tinged flint from RG 19 (C2) were found in the 'novice' group next to the northern concentration (C1). These examples provide evidence for the deliberate movement of blades within the site, and especially for tools and useful blanks of high-quality raw material.

No structured hearth combustion zones can be identified at the site. There are no dense accumulations of burnt or heated artefacts, the sediments containing the flints showed no signs of heating, and no examples were recovered of heated natural cobbles that could have marked the edges of a hearth. However, the possible presence of a hearth at the site may be inferred from thin traces of heated and burnt material. Figure 6.4 shows the distribution of heated and calcined artefacts at the site. Overall, the distribution is quite diffuse and in order to clarify the distribution, the plot distinguishes between larger heated artefacts and objects under 2cm in maximum dimension — the latter are assumed more likely to have been moved since incorporation in the fire (through processes such as wind action, scuffing, or cleaning disposal). The figure shows that the distribution of the larger artefacts appears to be centred just to the south and east of the northern concentration (C1), and probably suggests the original location of a hearth at the site (cf Fig. 5.19). The smaller heated artefacts also appear to be more concentrated in that area although they are spread out over a wider area, mainly in a north-westerly direction.

As discussed in Chapter 6, the fragments of backed blades and points show a higher frequency of heating than other tool types. We would attribute this to the process of repairing broken hunting equipment by removing fragments of broken projectile tips from hafts and replacing them with new ones. The activity would have required softening an adhesive (probably a plant-based mastic) by heating and presumably close to a hearth. Two refitting heated backed blade fragments c.4322 and c.4328 were found in the area identified as the probable hearth site, as was c.275 that also shows heat damage (Fig. 6.23). Most of the other broken backed material is found in the near vicinity. Other tool use also seems to have occurred around this general area and may have been associated with the same hearth that could have acted as a source of heat and light and as a centre for social activity.

From the microwear study it has been possible to infer a diversity of activities associated with hunting and processing large ungulates. Included amongst these was evidence for the use of end-scrapers in preparing animal skins with a prevalence of working dry or moistened hide. Interestingly, three of the scrapers showed hafting traces suggesting they were mounted in handles. In the few cases where little or no wear was detected it is suspected that this was due to partial removal of the working edges through resharpening and short duration use, though other explanations might be valid too (eg surface alteration of the flint). Evidence for working hard organic materials such as bone or antler was provided by different kinds of burin which displayed heavy patterns of use, especially at the tips and along burin facets. The traces could be attributed to intense working of hard material by grooving and possibly by light percussion. Further examples of edge damage and polish attributed to antler or bone working were found on one of the piercers while another example showed wear traces consistent with dry hide working. Activities that probably took place off-site can be inferred from backed blades with typical examples of linear impact traces and bending breakages. Similar effects have been recognised on experimental projectile tips and side barbs, and strongly suggest that broken projectiles were brought back to the Guildford site for repair, possibly still in their wooden or antler fore-shafts. Several burnt examples of damaged backed pieces support the idea that they were fixed in place by adhesives that needed to be reheated to allow their removal, although no remnants of resin were found on any of the artefacts. Despite the copious signs of animal processing, somewhat surprisingly, no use-wear evidence could be found for primary butchery activity. Absent too, were any signs of plant preparation or woodworking as might be expected if broken projectile equipment such as spears or arrow shafts were themselves subject to repair and replacement on site.

In terms of site structure, the Guildford Fire Station site can be considered similar to the Late Upper Palaeolithic site at Hengistbury Head. At that site the main scatter also covered an area of about 36m^2 and the presence of probable hearth combustion zones was inferred from burnt artefact distributions (Barton 1992). More locally, the Wey Manor Farm site covered an area of about 25–30m^2 (Jones 2013), slightly smaller than Guildford or Hengistbury, and the presence of fire setting at the site was suggested (Jones 2013, 41–2). In considering site size, it should be noted that other Late Upper Palaeolithic artefacts were found to the south of the Wey Manor Farm site during work elsewhere in the large quarry, and the site should not be considered in isolation (Marples 2015). Other inland Late Upper Palaeolithic sites are much smaller: Nea Farm covered about 15–20m^2 with three debitage clusters and no indication of hearth combustion zones (Barton *et al.* 2009), and La Sagesse Convent contained two closely spaced scatters of about 5m^2 and 6m^2 and no hearth or combustion zones (Conneller and Ellis 2007).

In summary, the Guildford Fire Station site seems to represent a short-term occupation on the floodplain of the River Wey by a small group of mobile hunter-gatherers. Flintknapping took place on the site, and nodules of flint were reduced to make cores and tools for use there. Other tools might have been brought in by the same people. Some elements of the knapping at the Guildford site, mainly blades, are missing and are presumed to have been removed by the occupants for use elsewhere. The proximity of the site to sources of good flint raw materials might be one factor explaining the site location. In addition to flintknapping, other activities also took place at the site. These included the repairing of hunting equipment, hide working, and other manufacturing/craft activities. There might also have been some butchery or other food preparation activity. Most of the manufacturing/craft activities took place in the central area between two knapping foci. A small hearth was probably also lit in this area. A minimum of three flintknappers has been proposed, consisting of a young novice and two more experienced practitioners. These individuals may have been part of a larger family group which moved from location to location in the extended Wey Valley catchment.

FUTURE STUDIES

Guildford Fire Station is a rare example of a well-preserved Late Upper Palaeolithic open air site in southern Britain. What gives the site its remarkable quality is the sharp and unrolled condition of the flint artefacts which lay undisturbed and largely in their original positions since the site was last occupied. This is highly unusual for a site of this kind in Britain and provides an excellent opportunity to expand knowledge about human activity in southern England during the Late Glacial period. The site can be placed chronologically in the first half of the Late Glacial Interstadial, a period that is poorly understood archaeologically due to a scarcity of recently excavated sites in Britain and a concomitant lack of scientific dating information. The investigation of the Guildford Fire Station site begins to fill this gap and provides an excellent opportunity to investigate not just the activity at the site itself, but also to start to draw comparisons with the late Bølling and early Allerød industries elsewhere in northern Europe and especially in northern France.

Two phases of work on the lithic assemblage from Guildford Fire Station are reported in this volume. The first was funded by Historic England and Surrey County Council in recognition of the national (and international) importance of the site. A second phase of refitting work was enabled by the University of Oxford through a period of research leave granted to one of the authors (AR). This phase built on and complemented the original work. Despite these studies, there are still great possibilities for further work, especially to take forward some of the existing ideas about the lithic assemblage and to further test and develop them.

One key aspect that gives the lithic assemblage great potential for future study is the undisturbed nature of the material itself and that so much of it can be refitted. As has been discussed, all stages of flintknapping took place at the site from preparing cores to the use and disposal of tools manufactured on-site. As such, refitting provides information about the complete *chaîne opératoire* for specific flint nodules and some of the tools. In turn this can yield information about the actions and activities of individuals and of groups at the site and provide clues as to possible connections with other sites in Britain and indeed in Europe. Our analysis, that covered two spells of work of a few months' duration each, cannot be considered as exhaustive and further work would certainly increase the number of refits and provide even more information about the site. In this respect it is worth remembering that refitting work at other sites of similar age in France has occurred over long periods of several years, with each phase of work complementing previous work and directed to answer specific research questions.

In relation to this, while a good start has been made, there is still much further work that could be done on aspects of the refitting. For instance, it would be crucial to know more about both on-site and off-site activities at Guildford (the latter through consideration of the missing artefacts in the refitted sequences). Equally, although the study of conjoining artefacts has already furnished important clues about the different gestures and stages involved in the manufacture and use of tools, much work in this direction is still necessary. Fortunately, the site was expertly excavated with good recovery of small debris, and this would allow more detailed refitting studies, for example to investigate the presence of further resharpening flakes and other tool debris in relation to individual implements (eg a refitting resharpening (#108) was found for an end-scraper (#250) in the Wey Manor Farm assemblage during our work). Further examples of such items might await discovery amongst the small debitage and would provide further useful details about where tools were used on site. Exercises of this type are of course enormously time intensive, especially given the size of the Guildford assemblage (including over 10,000 pieces of small debitage) and would require a detailed knowledge of flint technology.

Another aspect that would certainly repay more detailed work is use-wear studies. These could be extended to include some of the examples of tools made up of mended breaks and refitting spalls to burins which were not originally identified as tool waste. Items of particular interest would include a re-examination of tools that can now be shown to have more complex use-histories than was known during the early work, such as, for example, the refitted burins c.319/524/692/2802/7007 and c.699/2313/7448 (Fig. 6.18), or indeed all burins that can now be refitted to burin spalls. The blades and tools with *rasante* retouch provide another example. These now require systematic study which will allow a more detailed comparison with similar artefacts from sites in northern France. Equally, we would like to know more about the blades and tools that we think might have been brought into the Guildford site ready-made. Did these show signs of more intensive use than others made on site, did they have a specialist function, and were they prepared in special ways? These are some of the questions raised that might be addressed by future microwear analysis. Here it is important to mention that great care was taken in ensuring that the analysis for microwear took place before any handling of the artefacts during refitting. This was to make certain that the artefacts were in pristine condition when they were microscopically examined (some were still encased in their original sediment). In the event, one thing that the original microwear study (Chapter 7) revealed was a significant amount of unsuspected post-depositional surface alteration on the artefacts from the site, and that low magnification analysis was often the most effective strategy for the work. Such information is useful when deciding how to estimate the scale of project required for post-excavation work of this kind. It is also important to note that due to careful handling and storage the assemblage is still in a suitable condition for further investigation.

Coupled with the microwear study, one of the most successful outcomes of this project has been the spatial analysis based on refitting artefacts. This has helped characterise the nature of the two concentrations as well as defining areas of tool manufacture and discard. However, the results of this work are still at an early stage and such studies could be usefully extended. Thus, we only have a glimpse of the potential uses of the spatial analysis of refitting sequences as a tool for understanding human behaviour at a site level.

One other field of research worth considering in future is the study of raw material flint sourcing. New advances in laser ablation techniques look very promising but, as researchers undertaking studies acknowledge, the main problem are the small datasets available for different sites and the limited geological baseline. Work on the Guildford Fire Station site, which has a large well-excavated collection, could be used to address such concerns and offer a major path forward in these studies. At Guildford Fire Station, due to the extensive refitting programme, it would be possible to test the degree of variation within and between the elements of a knapped nodule, and also between different nodules worked on site. Depending on the results, this could then be used to assess whether all flints in the assemblage came from the same flint source or if some originated elsewhere (for example, the artefacts identified as probably being brought to the site). It would also be interesting to know if the flint employed at Guildford Fire Station was from the same source as that used further downstream at the Wey Manor Farm site. A final question would be to test the likelihood that the highest quality flint was specially selected from a known geological outcrop such as the chalk escarpment to the south of Guildford.

Clearly there is enormous scope for further research into sites like Guildford Fire Station within the context of their local and wider regional and international settings. At a local level, it would be instructive to know more about the relationship of this site to others in the Wey Valley and to consider the possibility that the palaeo-river served as a communications corridor in the Late Glacial landscape. From a national perspective, it is also clear that Guildford Fire Station shares close similarities with some of the French early Azilian assemblages which have included examples of mobiliary artwork and utilitarian items such as bone and antler barbed points and *sagaies* (pointed rods). These elements are so far missing from the British assemblages but given the right preservation conditions (for example, in more calcareous rich deposits to the south of Guildford) these may well survive. It is therefore important to develop appropriate strategies for identifying areas of high future potential and in employing relevant techniques of surface and below-ground prospection to locate them. It is only in this way that a coherent understanding will emerge of the human uses of landscape in Late Glacial lowland southern Britain.

Fortunately, the significance of Guildford Fire Station was recognised soon after its discovery and the archaeological contractors (Oxford Archaeology), the developer (Surrey CC) and Historic England worked in close unison to provide sufficient resources for the completion of fieldwork and for funding the post-excavation study. This is a positive example of how cooperation of this kind can and should work.

Bibliography

Adamiec, G and Aitken, M J, 1998 Dose-rate conversion factors: new data, *Ancient TL* **16**, 37–50

Agostinelli, C and Lund, U, 2023, R package 'circular': circular statistics (version 0.5–0), https://CRAN.R-project.org/package=circular

Allen, M, Blick, N, Brindle, T, Evans, T, Fulford, M, Holbrook, N, Lodwick, L, Julian D Richards, J D, Smith, A, 2018 *The rural settlement of Roman Britain: an online resource*, Archaeology Data Service, https://doi.org/10.5284/1030449

Antoine, P, Fagnart, J-P, Auguste, P, Coudret, P, Limondin-Lozouet, N, and Ponel, P, 2012 Synthèse des données: évolution des environnements de la vallée de la Selle au tardiglaciare et au début de l'Holocène et relations avec les occupations préhistoriques, in P Antoine, J-P Fagnart, P Auguste, P Coudret, N Limondin-Lozouet, P Ponel, A-V Munaut, A Defgnée, A Gauthier and C Fritz (eds), *Conty, vallée de la Selle (Somme, France): séquence tardiglaciaire de référence et occupations préhistoriques*, Quaternaire, hors-série **5**, 127–147

Antoine, P, Fagnart, J-P, Limondin-Lozouet, N, and Munaut, A-V, 2000 Le Tardiglaciaire du bassin de la Somme: éléments de synthese et nouvelles données, *Quaternaire* **11**, 85–98

Antoine, P, Limondin-Lozouet, N, Auguste, P, Lamotte, A, Bahain, J-J, Falguères, C, Laurent, M, Coudret, P, Locht, J-L, Depaepe, P, Fagnart J-P, Fontugne, M, Hatté, C, Mercier, N, Frechen, M, Moigne, A-M, Munaut, A-V, Ponel, P, and Rousseau D-D, 2003 Paléoenvironnements pléistocènes et peuplements paléolithiques dans le bassin de la Somme (nord de la France), *Bulletin de la Société Préhistorique Française* **100/1**, 5–28

Audouze, F, and Beyries, S, 2007 Chasseurs de renne d'hier et d'aujourd'hui, in S Beyries and V Vaté (eds), *Les Civilisations du renne d'hier et d'aujourd'hui: approches ethnohistoriques, archéologiques et anthropologiques. Actes des 27èmes Rencontres Internationales d'Archéologie et d'Histoire d'Antibes*, Antibes, 185–208

Avery, B W, 1990, *Soils of the British Isles*, Wallingford

Avery, R S, Kemp, A E S, Bull, J M A, Pearce, R B, Vardy, M E, Fielding, J J, Cotterill, C J, 2019 A new varve sequence from Windermere, UK, records rapid ice retreat prior to the Lateglacial Interstadial (GI-1), *Quaternary Science Reviews* **225**, 105894

Baales, M and Street, M, 1996 Hunter-gatherer behavior in a changing Late Glacial landscape: Allerød archaeology in the central Rhineland, Germany, *Journal of Anthropological Research* **52/3**, 281–316

Baddeley, A, Rubak, E, and Turner, R, 2015 *Spatial point patterns: methodology and applications with R*, Boca Raton, Florida

Ball, D F, 1964 Loss-on-ignition as an estimate of organic matter and organic carbon in non-calcareous soils, *Journal of Soil Science* **15**, 84–92

Ballantyne, C K and Harris, C, 1994 *The periglaciation of Great Britain*, Cambridge

Banerjee, D, Murray, A S, Bøtter-Jensen, L, and Lang, A, 2001 Equivalent dose estimation using a single aliquot of polymineral fine grains, *Radiation Measurements* **33**, 73–94

Barclay, A, Bello, S, Bradley, P, Harding, P, Higbee, L, Manning, A, Powell, J, Macphail, R, Roberts, A, Stewart, M, and Barton, N, 2017 A new later Upper Palaeolithic open-air site with articulated horse bone in the Colne Valley, Berkshire, *Antiquity* **91**, 1–7

Barton, R N E, 1986 Experiments with long blades from Sproughton, near Ipswich, Suffolk, in D A Roe (ed.), *Studies in the Upper Palaeolithic of Britain and Northwest Europe*, BAR Int. Ser. **296**, Oxford, 129–141

Barton, R N E, 1990 The en éperon technique in the British late Upper Palaeolithic, *Lithics* **11**, 31–33

Barton, R N E, 1992 *Hengistbury Head, Dorset, vol. 2: the late Upper Palaeolithic and early Mesolithic sites*, Oxford University Committee for Archaeology Monograph **34**, Oxford

Barton, R N E, 1999 The Lateglacial or late and final Upper Palaeolithic colonization of Britain, in J Hunter and I B M Ralston, (eds.) *Archaeology of Britain*, London, 13–34

Barton, R N E, and Bergman, C A, 1982 Hunters at Hengistbury: some evidence from experimental archaeology, *World Archaeology* **14/2**, 237–48

Barton, R N E, Bergman, C A, Collcutt, S N, and Morris, G, 1983 La fracture volontaire dans une industrie du Paléolithique supérieur tardif du sud de l'Angleterre, *L'Anthropologie* **83/3**, 323–337

Barton, R N E, Donnelly, M, Stafford, E, Thacker, G, 2016 Guildford Fire Station: post-excavation assessment and updated project design, unpubl. report, Oxford Archaeology, Oxford

Barton, R N E, Ford, S, Collcutt, S N, Crowther, J, Macphail, R, Rhodes, E, and Van Gijn, A, 2009 A final Upper Palaeolithic site at Nea Farm, Somerley, Hampshire (England) and some reflections on the occupation of Britain in the Lateglacial interstadial, *Quartär* **56**, 1–29

Barton, R N E, Jacobi, R M, Stapert, D and Street, M, 2003 The Lateglacial reoccupation of the British Isles and the Creswellian, *Journal of Quaternary Science* **18**, 631–643

Barton, R N E, and Roberts, A J, 1996 Reviewing the British late Upper Palaeolithic: new evidence for chronological patterning in the Lateglacial record, *Oxford Journal of Archaeology* **15/3**, 245–265

Barton, R N E, and Roberts A J, 2020 The transition from the Younger Dryas to the Pre-Boreal in southern Britain: some new perspectives on the spatial patterning and chronology of long blade sites, in J-P Fagnart, L Mevel, B Valentin and M-J Weber (eds), *Paléolithique supérieur ancien, Paléolithique final–Mésolithique vol. 2*, Congrès préhistoriques de France **28**, Paris, 381–389

Barton, R N E, Roberts, A J, and Roe, D A, (eds), 1991 *The Late Glacial in north-west Europe: human adaptation and environmental change at the end of the Pleistocene*, CBA Res Rep **77**, York

Benn, D, 1994 Fabric shape and the interpretation of sedimentary fabric data, *Journal of Sedimentary Research* **64**, 910–15

Bertran, P, and Lenoble, A, 2002 Fabriques des niveaux archéologiques: méthode et premier bilan des apports à l'étude taphonomique des sites paléolithiques, *Paléo* **14**, 13–28

Bertran, P, and Texier, J-P, 1995 Fabric analysis: application to Paleolithic sites, *Journal of Archaeological Science* **22**, 521–35

Bertran, P, Lenoble, A, Lacrampe, F, Brenet, M, Cretin, C, and Milor, F, 2005 Le site aurignacien de plein-air de Combemenue à Brignac-la-Plaine (Corrèze): apport de la géochéologie et de l'étude de l'industrie lithique à la compréhension des processus taphonomiques, *Paleo* **17**, 1–29

Bertran, P, Lenoble, A, Todisco, D, Desrosiers, P M, and Sørensen, M, 2012 Particle size distribution of lithic assemblages and taphonomy of Palaeolithic sites, *Journal of Archaeological Science* **39**, 3148–66

Bevan, A, 2012 Spatial methods for analysing large-scale artefact inventories, *Antiquity* **86**, 492–506

Beyries, S, and Rots, V, 2008a The contribution of ethnoarchaeological macro- and microscopic wear traces to the understanding of archaeological hide working process, in L Longo and N Skakun (eds), *'Prehistoric technology' 40 years later: functional studies and Russian legacy*, BAR Int. Ser. **1783**, Oxford, 21–28

Beyries, S, and Rots, V, 2008b Le traitement des peaux: reconstitution des outils et des procédés, *Anthropozoologica* **43**, DVD

BGS 2001 *1:50,000 geological map series, sheet 285, Guildford (S&D)*

Binford, L R, 1983 *In pursuit of the past: decoding the archaeological record*, New York

Binford, L R, 1986 An Alyawara day: making men's knives and beyond, *American Antiquity* **51**, 547–62

Binford, L, and O'Connell, J F, 1984 An Alyawara day: the stone quarry, *Journal of Anthropological Research* **40/3**, 406–32

Bird, D, 2006, *Surrey Archaeological Research Framework, 2006*, Surrey County Council, Kingston-upon-Thames, https://www.surreyarchaeology.org.uk/sites/default/files/sarf2006.pdf

Bivand, R S, Pebesma, E J, and Gómez-Rubio, V, 2013 *Applied spatial data analysis with R*, 2nd edn, Heidelberg

Bjornstad, O N, 2022, ncf: spatial covariance functions, R package, version 1.3–2

Blott, S, Croft, D J, Pye, K, Sayene, S E, and Wilson, H E, 2004 Particle size analysis by laser diffraction, *Forensic Geoscience: Principles, Techniques and Applications* **232**, 63–73

Bodu, P, 1998 Magdalenians-early Azilians in the centre of the Paris Basin: a filiation? The example of le Closeau (Rueil-Malmaison, France), in S Milliken (ed.), *The organization of lithic technology in Late Glacial and early postglacial Europe*, BAR Int. Ser. **700**, Oxford, 131–147

Bodu, P, 2000 Que sont devenus les Magdaléniens du Bassin parisien? Quelques éléments de réponse sur le gisement azilien du Closeau (Rueil-Malmaison, France), in B Valentin, P Bodu and M Christensen (eds), *L'Europe centrale et septentrionale au Tardiglaciaire: confrontation des modèles régionaux de peuplement*, Actes de la table ronde internationale de Nemours, 14–16 mai 1997, Mémoires du Musée de Préhistoire d'Ile-de-France **7**, Nemours, 315–339

Bodu, P, and Mevel, L, 2008 Enquête autour des lames tranchantes de l'Azilien ancient: le cas du niveau inférieur du Closeau (Rueil-Malmaison, Hauts-de-Seine, France), *L'Anthropologie* **112/4–5**, 509–543

Bodu, P, and Orliac, M, 1996. L'unité d'occupation de la section 27, in G Gaucher (ed.), *Fouilles de Pincevent II: le site et ses occupations récentes. L'environnement, l'Épimagdalénien et les niveaux postglaciaires*. Mémoires de la Société Préhistorique Française **23**, Paris, 69–82

Bodu, P, and Valentin, B, 1997 Groupes à Federmesser ou Aziliens dans le sud et l'ouest du Bassin parisien: propositions pour un nouveau modèle d'évolution, *Bulletin de la Société Préhistorique Française* **94/3**, 341–347

Bordes, F, 1950 Du poli particulier de certains silex taillés, *L'Anthropologie* **54**, 161–163

Bordes, F, 1967 Considérations sur la typologie et les techniques dans le Paléolithique, *Quartär* **18**, 25–55

Bordes, F, 1970 Réflexions sur l'outil au Paléolithique, *Bulletin de la Société Préhistorique Française* **67(7)**, 199–202

Bordes, F, Graindor, M-J, Martin, Y and Martin, P, 1974 L'industrie de la grotte ornée de Gouy (Seine-Maritime), *Bulletin de la Société Préhistorique Française* **71**, 115–118

Bradley, P, 1999 The worked flint, in A Barclay and C Halpin (eds) *Excavations at Barrow Hills, Radley, Oxfordshire*, Thames Valley Landscapes **11**, Oxford, 211–227

Brammer, H, 1971, Coatings in seasonal flooded soils, *Geoderma* **6**, 5–16

Bridgland, D R, 1986 *Clast lithological analysis*, Quaternary Research Association Technical Guide **3**, Cambridge

Bridgland, D R, 1994 *Quaternary of the Thames*, Geological Conservation Review Series **7**, London

Bridgland, D R, 1999 'Wealden rivers' north of the Thames: a provenance study based on gravel clast analysis, *Proceedings of the Geologists' Association* **110**, 133–148

Bullock, P, Fedoroff, N, Jongerius, A, Stoops, G, and Tursina, T, 1985 *Handbook for soil thin section description*, Wolverhampton

Bullock, P, and Mackney, D, 1970). Micromorphology of strata in the Boyn Hill Terrace deposits, Buckinghamshire, in D A Osmond and P Bullock (eds), *Micromorphological techniques and applications*, Soil Survey Technical Monograph **2**, Harpenden, 97–106

Campbell, J B, 1977 *The Upper Palaeolithic of Britain: a study of man and nature in the Ice Age*, Oxford

Carr, K W, Bergman, C A, and Haag, C M, 2010 Some comments on blade technology and Eastern Clovis lithic reduction strategies, *Lithic Technology* **35/2,** 91–125

Caspar, J P, and De Bie, M, 1996 Preparing for the hunt in the late paleolithic camp at Rekem, Belgium, *Journal of Field Archaeology* **23**, 437–60

Catt, J A, 1986 *Soils and Quaternary geology: a handbook for field scientists*, Oxford

Catt, J A E, 1990 Paleopedology manual, *Quaternary International* **6,** 1–95

Cattelain, P, 1997 Hunting during the Upper Paleolithic: bow, spearthrower, or both? in H Knecht (ed.), *Projectile technology*, New York, 213–240

Célérier, G, 1979 Inventaire morphologique de pointes aziliennes en Périgord: un projet de rationalisation, in Sonneville-Bordes, D de (ed), *La fin des temps glaciaires en Europe: chronostratigraphie et écologie des cultures du Paléolithique final*, Colloque de Talence, Paris, 461–466

Chesnaux, L, 2014. Réflexion sur le microlithisme en France au cours du Premier Mésolithique (Xe–VIIIe millénaires av. J-C): approches technologique, expérimentale et fonctionnelle, unpubl. thèse de doctorat, Univ. Paris 1

Clark, J E, 1986 Another look at small debitage and microdebitage, *Lithic Technology* **15**, 21–33

Clark, J G D, 1954 *Excavations at Star Carr: an early Mesolithic site at Seamer near Scarborough, Yorkshire*, Cambridge

Clark, J G D, 1963 Neolithic bows from Somerset, England, and the prehistory of archery in northwestern Europe, *Proceedings of the Prehistoric Society* **3**, 50–98

Conneller, C, and Ellis, C, 2007 A final Upper Palaeolithic Site at La Sagesse Convent, Romsey, Hampshire, *Proc Prehis Soc* **73**, 191–227

Cooper, L, 2012 An open-air Creswellian site at Bradgate Park, Newtown Linford, Leicestershire, *Lithics* **33**, 30–39

Coppe, J, and Rots, V, 2016 Focus on the target: the importance of a transparent fracture terminology for understanding projectile points, *Journal of Archaeological Science* **12**, 109–23

Coudret, P, and Fagnart, J-P, 1997 Les industries à Federmesser dans le bassin de la Somme: chronologie et identité des groupes culturels, *Bulletin de la Société Préhistorique Française* **94**, 349–60

Coudret, P, and Fagnart, J-P, 2004 Les fouilles du gisement paléolithique final de Saleux (Somme), *Revue Archéologique de Picardie* **1/2**, 3–17

Coudret, P, and Fagnart, J-P, 2006 Données préliminaires sur les habitats des groupes de la tradition Federmesser du bassin de la Somme, *Bulletin de la Société Préhistorique Française* **103**, 729–740

Coudret, P, and Fagnart, J-P, 2012 Les occupations préhistoriques du 'Marais de Conty' (Somme), in P Antoine, J-P Fagnart, P Auguste, P Coudret, N Limondin-Lozouet, P Ponel, A-V Munaut, A Defgnée, A Gauthier and C Fritz (eds), *Conty, vallée de la Selle (Somme, France): séquence tardiglaciaire de référence et occupations préhistoriques*, Quaternaire, hors-série **5**, 63–90

Coudret, P, and Fagnart, J-P, 2015 Recent research on the final Palaeolithic site of Saleux (France, Somme), in N Ashton and C Harris (eds), *No stone unturned: papers in honour of Roger Jacobi*, Lithic Studies Society Occasional Paper **9**, London, 135–155

Courty, M A, 2001, Microfacies analysis assisting archaeological stratigraphy, in Goldberg *et al.* 2001, 205–239

Courty, M A, Goldberg, P, and Macphail, R I, 1989, *Soils and micromorphology in archaeology*, 1st edn, Cambridge

Cox, N, 1976 Woking: Brockhill near Parley Bridge, Horsell, *Surrey Archaeological Society Bulletin* **126**, 4

Crowther, J, 2003 Potential magnetic susceptibility and fractional conversion studies of archaeological soils and sediments, *Archaeometry* **45**, 685–701

Crowther, J, and Barker, P, 1995 Magnetic susceptibility: distinguishing anthropogenic effects from the natural, *Archaeological Prospection* **2**, 207–215

Curray, J R, 1956 The analysis of two-dimensional orientation data, *The Journal of Geology* **64**, 117–31

Davies, H, 1999 Evaluation excavation at Manor Farm, Guildford, unpubl. report, Surrey Archaeological Society, Guildford

De Bie, M, and Caspar, J P, 2000 *Rekem: a Federmesser camp on the Meuse river bank*, Leuven

Dearing, J, Dann, R J H, Hay, K, Lees, J A, Loveland, P J, Maher, B A, and O'Grady, K, 1996 Frequency-dependent susceptibility measurements of environmental materials, *Geophysical Journal International* **130**, 727–736

Dick, W A, and Tabatabai, M A, 1977 An alkaline oxidation method for the determination of total phosphorus in soils, *Journal of the Soil Science Society of America* **41**, 511–14

Duchaufour, P, 1982 *Pedology*, London

Ekwall, E, 1980 *The concise Oxford English dictionary of English place names*, 4th edn, Oxford

Ellison, R A, Williamson, I T, and Humpage, A J, 2002 *Geology of the Guildford district: a brief explanation of the geological map. Sheet explanation of the British Geological Survey 1:50,000 sheet 285, Guildford (England and Wales)*, Keyworth

English, J, 2000 Evaluation excavation at Manor Farm, Guildford, unpubl. report, Surrey Archaeological Society, Guildford

Fagnart, J-P, 1991 New observations on the late Upper Palaeolithic site of Belloy-sur-Somme (Somme, France), in Barton *et al.* (eds) 1991, 213–26

Fagnart, J-P, 1993 Le Paléolithique supérieur récent et final du Nord de la France dans son cadre paléoclimatique, unpubl. thèse de doctorat, Univ. Lille

Fagnart, J-P, 1997 Paléohistoire du bassin de la Somme à la fin de temps glaciaires, in Fagnart and Thévenin, (eds) 1997, 55–77

Fagnart, J-P, and Coudret, P, 2000a Le Tardiglaciaire dans le Nord de la France, in B Valentin, P Bodu and M Christensen, (eds) *L'Europe centrale et septentrionale au Tardiglaciaire: confrontation des modèles régionaux de peuplement*, Actes de la table ronde internationale de Nemours, 14–16 mai 1997, Mémoires du Musée de Préhistoire d'Ile-de-France **7**, Nemours, 111–128

Fagnart, J-P, and Coudret, P, 2000b Données récentes sur le Tardiglaciaire du bassin de la Somme, in Pion, G (ed) *Le Paléolithique supérieur récent: nouvelles données sur le peuplement et l'environnement*, Actes de la table ronde de Chambéry, 12–13 mars 1999, Mémoires de la Société Préhistorique Française **28**, Paris, 113–126

Fagnart, J-P, and Thévenin, A, (eds), 1997 *Le Tardiglaciaire en Europe du Nord-Ouest*, Paris

Fedoroff, N, and Goldberg, P, 1982 Comparative micromorphology of two late Pleistocene palaeosols (in the Paris basin), *Catena* **9**, 227–251

Fedoroff, N, Courty, M A, and Guo, Z, 2010 Palaeosols and relict soils, in Stoops *et al.* 2010, 623–62

Fischer, A, Hansen, P V, and Rasmussen, P, 1984 Macro and micro wear traces on lithic projectile points, *Journal of Danish Archaeology* **3**, 19–46

Fisher, P F, and Bridgland, D R, 1986 Analysis of pebble morphology, in Bridgland 1986, 43–58

Fladmark, K R, 1982 Microdebitage analysis: initial considerations, *Journal of Archaeological Science* **9**, 205–220

Gallagher, J P, 1974 The preparation of hides with stone tools in south central Ethiopia, *Journal of Ethiopian studies* **12/1**, 177–182

Gallagher, J P, 1977 Contemporary stone tools in Ethiopia: implications for archaeology, *Journal of Field Archaeology* **4**, 407–14

Getis, A, and Ord, J K, 2010 The analysis of spatial association by use of distance statistics, in L Anselin, and S J Rey (eds), *Perspectives on spatial data analysis*, Heidelberg, 127–45

Gibbard, P L, 1979 Middle Pleistocene drainage in the Thames Valley, *Geological Magazine* **116**, 35–44

Gibbard, P L, 1982 Terrace stratigraphy and drainage history of the Plateau Gravels of north Surrey, south Berkshire and north Hampshire, England, *Proceedings of the Geologists' Association* **93**, 369–384

Gibbard, P, 1985 *Pleistocene history of the Middle Thames Valley*, Cambridge

Gifford-Gonzalez, D P, Damrosch, D B, Damrosch, D R, Pryor, J, and Thunen, R L, 1985 The third dimension in site structure: an experiment in trampling and vertical dispersal, *American Antiquity* **50**, 803–18

Goldberg, P, Holliday, V T and Ferring, C R, 2001 *Earth sciences and archaeology*, New York

Goldberg, P, and Macphail, R I, 2006, *Practical and theoretical geoarchaeology*, Oxford

Grace, R, 1990 The limitations and applications of use wear analysis, *Aun* **14**, 9–114

Graham, I D G, and Scollar, I, 1976 Limitations on magnetic prospection in archaeology imposed by soil properties *Archaeo-Physika*, **6**, 1–124

Green, C, Farr, L, and Branch, N, 2013 Geomorphology, site formation and landscape context, in Jones 2013, 14–16

Grimm, L, 2000 Apprentice flintknapping: relating material culture and social practice in the Upper Palaeolithic, in J S Derevenski and J Sofaer (eds), *Children and material culture*, London/New York, 53–71

Guerin, G, Mercier, N, and Adamiec, G, 2011 Doserate conversion factors, *Ancient TL* **29**, 5–8

Harding, P, Ellis, C, and Grant, M J, 2014 Late Upper Palaeolithic Farndon Fields, in N Cooke and A Mudd, *A46 Nottinghamshire: the archaeology of the Newark to Widmerpool Improvement Scheme, 2009*, Salisbury, 12–70

Hayman, G N, 1994 An archaeological site on land adjoining Barnwood School, Guildford, unpubl. report, Surrey County Council Archaeology Unit, Woking

Heiri, O, Lotter, A F, and Lemcke, G, 2001 Loss on ignition as a method for estimating organic and carbonate content in sediments: reproducibility and comparability of results, *Journal of Paleolimnology* **25**, 101–110

Hiscock, P, 1986 The conjoin sequence diagram: a method of describing conjoin sets, *Queensland Archaeological Research* **3**, 159–166

Hofman, J L, 1986 Vertical movement of artifacts in alluvial and stratified deposits, *Current Anthropology* **27**, 163–71

Inizan, M-L, Reduron-Ballinger, M, Roche, H, and Tixier, J, 1999 *Technology and terminology of knapped stone*, (trans. J Féblot-Augustins), Préhistoire de la Pierre Taillée **5**, Nanterre

Jacobi, R M, 1980 The Upper Palaeolithic of Britain with special reference to Wales, in Taylor, J A (ed.), *Culture and environment in prehistoric Wales: selected essays*, BAR Brit. Ser. **76**, Oxford, 15–99

Jacobi, R M, 1991 The Creswellian, Creswell and Cheddar, in Barton *et al.* 1991, 128–140

Jacobi, R M, 1997 The 'Creswellian' in Britain, in Fagnart and Thévein 1997, 499–505

Jacobi, R M, 2004 The Late Upper Palaeolithic lithic collection from Gough's Cave, Cheddar, Somerset and human use of the cave, *Proceedings of the Prehistoric Society* **70**, 1–92

Jacobi, R M, 2005 Some observations on the lithic artefacts from Aveline's Hole, Burrington Combe, North Somerset, *Proceedings of the University of Bristol Spelaeological Society* **23(3)**, 267–295

Jacobi, R and Higham, T, 2011a The Later Upper Palaeolithic recolonisation of Britain: new results from AMS radiocarbon dating, Developments in Quaternary Science 14, 223-247

Jacobi, R M, and Higham, T, 2011 The British earlier Upper Palaeolithic, *Developments in Quaternary Science* **14**, 181–222

Jacobs, 2012 Guildford Fire Station and adjoining land: heritage statement, unpubl. report, Jacobs, Wokingham

Jacobs, 2013a Guildford Fire Station and adjoining land; written scheme of investigation for archaeological trial trenching, unpubl. report, Jacobs, Wokingham

Jacobs, 2013b Guildford Fire Station and adjoining land: written scheme of investigation for archaeological excavation, unpubl. report, Jacobs, Wokingham

Jarvis, M G, Allen, R H, Fordham, S J, Hazleden, J, Moffat, A J, and Sturdy, R G, 1983 *Soils of England and Wales, sheet 6: south east England, 1:250,000*, Southampton

Jarvis, M G, Allen, R H, Fordham, S J, Hazleden, J, Moffat, A J, and Sturdy, R G, 1984 *Soils and their use in south-east England*, Harpenden

Johansen, L, and Stapert, D, 2004 *Oldeholtwolde: a Hamburgian family encampment around a hearth*, Lisse

Johnson, D L, and Hansen, K L, 1974 The effects of frost-heaving on objects in soils, *Plains Anthropologist* **19**, 81–98

Johnson, D L, Muhs, D R, and Barnhardt, M L, 1977 The effects of frost heaving on objects in soils, II: laboratory experiments, *Plains Anthropologist* **22**, 133–47

Jones, P, 2013 *Upper Palaeolithic sites in the lower courses of the rivers Colne and Wey: excavations at Church Lammas and Wey Manor Farm*, SpoilHeap Monograph **5**, Woking

Keeley, L H, 1980 *Experimental determination of stone tool uses: a microwear analysis*, Chicago

Keeley, L H, 1982 Hafting and retooling: effects on the archaeological record, *American Antiquity* **47/4**, 798–809

Kelsall, J E, and Diggle, P J, 1995 Kernel estimation of relative risk, *Bernoulli*, 3–16

Kühn, P, Aguilar, J, and Miedema, R, 2010 Textural pedofeatures and related horizons, in Stoops *et al.* 2010, 217–250

Kvamme, K L, 1997 Patterns and models of debitage dispersal in percussion flaking, *Lithic Technology* **22**, 122–38

Lambert, R, 2007 An archaeological evaluation at Christ College School, Larch Avenue, Guildford, unpubl. report, Surrey County Council Archaeology Unit, Woking

Lenoble, A, and Bertran, P, 2004 Fabric of Palaeolithic levels: methods and implications for site formation processes, *Journal of Archaeological Science* **31**, 457–69

Levi-Sala, I, 1986 Use wear and post-depositional surface modification: a word of caution, *Journal of Archaeological Science* **13**, 229–244

Lewis Johnson, L, 1978 A history of flint-knapping experimentation, 1838–1976, *Current Anthropology* **19**, 337–72

Lewis, J, and Rackham, K, 2011 *Three Ways Wharf, Uxbridge: a late glacial and early Holocene hunter-gatherer site in the Colne Valley*, MoLAS Monograph **51**, London

Linton, D L, 1930 Notes on the development of the western part of the Wey drainage system, *Proceedings of the Geologists' Association* **37**, 160

Lund, U, and Agostinelli, C, 2001 CircStats: circular statistics, in S R Jammalamadaka and A SenGupta (eds), *Topics in circular statistics*, River Edge, New Jersey

Macphail, R I, 2010 Bath palaeosols, Bath (SO–SGT06): soil micromorphology, unpubl. report, Museum of London Archaeology, London

Macphail, R I, and Crowther, J, 2008 Carrow Road, Norwich: soil micromorphology, particle size, chemistry and magnetic susceptibility, unpubl. report, Norfolk Archaeological Unit, Norwich

Macphail, R I, and Crowther, J, 2017, Kingsmead Quarry, Horton, Berkshire, late Upper Palaeolithic site: soil micromorphology, particle size, chemistry and magnetic susceptibility, unpubl. report, Wessex Archaeology, Salisbury

Macphail, R I, and Cruise, G M, 2001 The soil micromorphologist as team player: a multianalytical approach to the study of European microstratigraphy, in Goldberg *et al.* 2001, 241–267

Macphail, R I, and Goldberg, P, 2018, *Applied soils and micromorphology in archaeology*, Cambridge

Malden, H E (ed.), 1911 *A history of the county of Surrey*, vol. **3**, Victoria County History, London

Marples, N, 2015 The flint, in G Hayman, P Jones, N Marples and J Robertson, *Prehistoric, Roman, Saxon and medieval discoveries at Wey Manor Farm, near Weybridge 1994–2004*, SpoilHeap Publications Occasional Paper **6**, Woking, 4–106

McPherron, S J P, 2005 Artifact orientations and site formation processes from total station proveniences, *Journal of Archaeological Science* **32**, 1003–14

Moffat, A J, 1986 Quartz signatures in Plio-Pleistocene gravels in the northern part of the London Basin, in Bridgland 1986, 117–128

Moss, E H, 1983a Some comments on edge damage as a factor in functional analysis of stone artefacts, *Journal of Archaeological Science* **10**, 231–242

Murphy, C P, 1986 *Thin section preparation of soils and sediments*, Berkhamsted

Murray, A S, and Wintle, A G, 2000 Luminescence dating of quartz using an improved single-aliquot regenerative-dose protocol, *Radiation Measurements* **32**, 57–73

Naudinot, N, Fagnart, J-P, Langlais, M, Mevel, L, and Valentin, B, 2019 Les dernières sociétés du Tardiglaciaire et des tout débuts de l'Holocène en France. Bilan d'une trentaine d'années de recherche, *Gallia Préhistoire* **59**, 5–45

Naudinot, N, and Jacquier, J, 2014 Socio-economic organization of Final Paleolithic societies: new perspectives from an aggregation site in western France, *Journal of Anthropological Archaeology* **35**, 177–89

Newcomer, M H, 1976 Spontaneous retouch, in F H G Engelen (ed.), *Second International Symposium on Flint*, Staringia **3**, Maastricht, 62–64

Newcomer, M H, and Karlin, C, 1987 Flint chips from Pincevent, in G de G Sieveking and M H Newcomer (eds), *The human uses of flint and chert: proceedings of the Fourth International Flint Symposium held at Brighton Polytechnic, 10–15 April 1983*, Cambridge, 33–36

Newcomer, M H, and Sieveking, G D G, 1980 Experimental flake scatter-patterns: a new interpretative technique, *Journal of Field Archaeology* **7/3**, 345–52

Nuzhnyj, D, 2000 Development of microlithic projectile weapons in the Stone Age, in C Bellier, P Cattelain and M Otte (eds.), *La Chasse dans la préhistoire/hunting in prehistory*, Anthropologie et Préhistoire **111**, ERAUL **51**, Artefacts **8**, Brussels, 95–101

OA, 2013a Guildford Fire Station, Guildford, Surrey: archaeological evaluation report, unpubl. report, Oxford Archaeology, Oxford

OA, 2013b Guildford Fire Station, Surrey: historic building investigation and recording, unpubl. report, Oxford Archaeology, Oxford

OA, 2013c Guildford Fire Station flint scatter: addendum to a written scheme of investigation for an excavation, unpubl, report, Oxford Archaeology, Oxford

Odell, G H, and Cowan, F, 1986 Experiments with spears and arrows on animal targets, *Journal of Field Archaeology* **13**, 195–212

Ohnuma, K, and Bergman, C A, 1982 Experimental studies in the determination of flaking mode, *Bulletin of the Institute of Archaeology, University of London* **19**, 161–170

Ord, J K, and Getis, A, 1995 Local spatial autocorrelation statistics: distributional issues and an application, *Geographical Analysis* **27**, 286–306

Patterson, L W, and Sollberger, J B, 1978 Replication and classification of small size lithic debitage, *Plains Anthropologist* **23**, 103–112

Pelegrin, J, 2000 Les techniques de débitage laminaire au Tardiglaciaire: critères de diagnose et quelques reflexion, in B Valentin, P Bodu and M Christensen (eds) *L'Europe centrale et septentrionale au Tardiglaciaire: actes de la table ronde internationale (Nemours, 1997)*, Mémoires du Musée de Préhistoire d'Île-de-France **7**, Nemours, 73–86

Pétillon, J M, Bignon, O, Bodu, P, Cattelain, P, Debaut, G, Langlais, M, Laroulandie, V, Plisson, H, and Valentin, B, 2011 Hard core and cutting edge: experimental manufacture and use of Magdalenian composite projectile tips, *Journal of Archaeological Science* **38**, 1266–1283

Pettitt, P, Gamble, C, and Last, J (eds), 2008 *Research and conservation framework for the British Palaeolithic*, English Heritage and the Prehistoric Society, https://historicengland.org.uk/images-books/publications/research-and-conservation-framework-for-british-palaeolithic/palaeolithic-framework/

Pewsey, A, Neuhäuser, M, and Ruxton, G D, 2013 *Circular statistics in R*, Oxford

Plisson, H, and Mauger, M, 1988 Chemical and mechanical alteration of microwear polishes: an experimental approach, *Helinium* **28/1**, 3–16

Pope, M I, 2002 The significance of biface-rich assemblages: an examination of behavioural controls on lithic assemblage formation in the Lower Palaeolithic, unpubl. PhD thesis, Univ. Southampton

Pope, M, Wells, C, Scott, B, Maxted, A, Haycon, N, Farr, L, Branch, N, and Blinkhorn, E, 2019 *South East Research Framework resource assessment and research agenda for the Upper Palaeolithic and Mesolithic periods*, Kent County Council, https://www.kent.gov.uk/_data/assets/pdf_file/0011/98939/Upper-Palaeolithic-and-Mesolithic-Periods.pdf

Poulton, R, 2005 Excavations near Broad Street Common, Worplesdon, Guildford, in 1994, 1997 and 1998, *Surrey Archaeological Collections* **92**, 29–89

Powers, M C, 1953 A new roundness scale for sedimentary particles, *Journal of Sedimentary Petrolology* **23**, 117–119

Pryor, W A, 1971 Grain shape, in R E Carver (ed.) *Procedures in sedimentary petrology*, New York, 131–150

Richter, D, Pintaske, R, Dornich, K, and Krbetschek, M, 2012 A novel beta source design for uniform irradiation in dosimetric applications, *Ancient TL* **30**, 57–63

Richter, D, Richter, A, and Kornich, K, 2013 Lexsyg: a new system for luminescence research, *Geochronometria* **40**, 220–228

Richter, D, Richter, A, and Kornich, K, 2015 Lexsyg Smart: a luminescence detection system for dosimetry, material research and dating application, *Geochronometria* **42**, 202–209

Roberts, A, and Barton, R N E, 2021 An example of novice flintknapping in the British late Upper Palaeolithic? in S Gaudzinski-Windheuser and O Jöris (eds), *The beef behind all possible pasts: the tandem festschrift in honour of Elaine Turner and Martin Street*, Regensburg, 535–546

Rots, V, 2002 Bright spots and the question of hafting, *Anthropologica et Praehistorica* **113**, 61–71

Rots, V, 2005 Wear traces and the interpretation of stone tools, *Journal of Field Archaeology* **30/1**, 61–73

Rots, V, 2010a Un tailleur et ses traces. Traces microscopiques de production: programme expérimental et potentiel interprétatif, *Bulletin de la Société Royale Belge d'Etudes Géologiques et Archéologiques. Les Chercheurs de la Wallonie*, hors-série **2**, 51–67

Rots, V, 2010b *Prehension and hafting wear on flint tools: a methodology*, Leuven

Rots, V, 2011 Hafting and the interpretation of site function in the European Middle Palaeolithic, in N Conard (ed.), *Settlement dynamics of the Middle Palaeolithic and Middle Stone Age*, vol. **4**, Tübingen

Rots, V, and Plisson, H, 2014 Projectiles and the abuse of the use-wear method in a search for impact, *Journal of Archaeological Science* **48**, 154–165

Schick, K D, 1986 *Stone Age sites in the making: experiments in the formation and transformation of archaeological occurrences*, BAR Int. Ser **319**, Oxford

Schneiderhöhn, P, 1954 Eine vergleichende Studie uber Methoden zur quantitativen Bestimmung von Abrundung und Form an Sandkornern, *Heidelbergishce Beiträge zur Mineralogie und Petrographie* **4**, 172–191

Schutt, J A, 1979 Post-depositional edge damage on lithic artefacts, in J V Biella and R C Chapman (eds.), *Archaeological investigation in Cochitit Reservoir, New Mexico*, Albuquerque, New Mexico

Schwabedissen, H, 1954 *Die Federmesser-Gruppen des nord-westeuropäischen Flachlandes: zur Ausbreitung des Spät-Magdalénien*, Neumünster

Scollar, I, Tabbagh, A, Hesse, A, and Herzog, I, 1990 *Archaeological prospecting and remote sensing*, Cambridge

Sonneville-Bordes, D, de, 1960 *Le Paléolithique en Périgord*, Bordeaux

Sonneville-Bordes, D, de, and Perrot, J, 1953 Essai d'adaptation des methods statistiques au Paléolithique supérieur: premiers résultats, *Bulletin de la Société Préhistorique Française* **50/6**, 323–333

Sonneville-Bordes, D, de, and Perrot, J, 1954 Lexique typologique du Paléolithique supérieur, *Bulletin de la Société Préhistorique Française* **51/7**, 327–335

Sonneville-Bordes, D, de and Perrot, J, 1955 Lexique typologique du Paléolithique supérieur, Outillage lithique: III outils composites, perçoirs, *Bulletin de la Société Préhistorique Française* **52/1/2**, 76–79

Sonneville-Bordes, D, de, and Perrot, J, 1956a Lexique typologique du Paléolithique supérieur, *Bulletin de la Société Préhistorique Française* **52/7/8**, 408–412

Sonneville-Bordes, D, de, and Perrot, J, 1956b Lexique typologique du Paléolithique supérieur, *Bulletin de la Société Préhistorique Française* **53/9**, 547–559

Sorensen, A, Roebroeks, W and Van Gijn A, 2014 Fire production in the deep past? The expedient strike-a-light model, *Journal of Archaeological Science* **42**, 476–486

Spurrell, F C J, 1884 On some Palaeolithic knapping tools and modes of using them, *The Journal of the Anthropological Institute of Great Britain and Ireland* **13**, 109–18

Stapert, D, and Johansen, L, 1999 Flint and pyrite: making fire in the Stone Age, *Antiquity* **73**, 765–777

Stoops, G, 2003 *Guidelines for analysis and description of soil and regolith thin sections*, Madison, Wisconsin

Stoops, G, Marcelino, V, and Mees, F, 2010 *Interpretation of micromorphological features of soils and regoliths*, 2nd edn, Amsterdam

Taute, W, 1968 *Die Stielspitzen-Gruppen in nordlichen Mitteleuropa: ein Beitrag zur Kenntnis der späten Altsteinzeit*, Fundamenta **A5**, Cologne

Thomas, M F, 1961 River terraces and drainage development in the Reading area, *Proceedings of the Geologists' Association* **72**, 415–436

Tite, M S, 1972 The influence of geology on the magnetic susceptibility of soils on archaeological sites, *Archaeometry* **14**, 229–236

Tite, M S, and Mullins, C, 1971 Enhancement of magnetic susceptibility of soils on archaeological sites, *Archaeometry* **13**, 209–19

Tixier, J, 1963 Typologie de l'Epipaléolithique du Maghreb, unpubl. thèse de doctorat, Univ. Bordeaux

Tixier, J, Inizan, M-L, and Roche, H, 1980 *Préhistoire de la pierre taillée 1: terminologie et technologie*, Paris

Torre, I de la, Vanwezer, N, Benito-Calvo, A, Proffitt, T, and Mora, R, 2019 Spatial and orientation patterns of experimental stone tool refits, *Archaeological and Anthropological Sciences* **11**, 4569–84

Unrath, G, Owen, L R, van Gijn, A, Moss, E H, Plisson, H, and Vaughan, P, 1986 An evaluation of micro-wear studies: a multi-analyst approach, in G Unrath and L Owen (eds), *Technical aspects of micro-wear studies on stone tools*. Early Man News **9/10/11**, Archaeologica Venatoria, Tübingen

Valentin, B, 1995 Les groupes humains et leurs traditions au Tardiglaciaire dans le Bassin parisien: apports de la technologie comparée, unpublb. thèse de doctorat, Univ. Paris I

Valentin, B, Fagnart, J-P, Coudret, P, and Pelegrin, J, 2006 L'Azilianisation et ses rythmes dans le Bassin parisien: nouvelles observations sur Hangest III.1 (Somme), in B Valentin (ed.), *Habitats et peuplements tardiglaciaires dans la Bassin parisien: rapport de projet collectif de recherche, rapport d'activités pour 2006, CNRS UMR7041*, Ile-de-France, 83–92

Van Gijn, A L, 1990 The wear and tear of flint: principles of functional analysis applied to Dutch Neolithic assemblages, *Analecta Praehistorica Leidensia* **22**, Leiden

Van Noten, F, Cahen, D, and Keeley, L, 1980 A Paleolithic campsite in Belgium, *Scientific American* **242**, 48–55

Vepraskas, M J, Lindbo, D L, and Stolt, M H, 2018 Redoximorphoc features, in Stoops *et al.* 2018, 425–445

Vollmer, F W, 1995 C program for automatic contouring of spherical orientation data using a modified Kamb method, *Computers & Geosciences* **21**, 31–49

Vollmer, F W, 2015 Orient 3: a new integrated software program for orientation data analysis, kinematic analysis, spherical projections, and Schmidt plots, *Geological Society of America Abstracts with Programs* **47**, 49

Watson, G S, 1965 Equatorial distributions on a sphere, *Biometrika* **52**, 193–201

Watson, G S, 1966 The statistics of orientation data, *The Journal of Geology* **74**, 786–97

Whittaker, J C, 1994 *Flintknapping: making and understanding stone tools*, Austin, Texas

Wintle, A G, and Murray, A S, 2006 A review of quartz optically stimulated luminescence characteristics and their relevance in single-aliquot regeneration dating protocols, *Radiation Measurements* **41**, 369–391

Wood, W R, and Johnson, D L, 1978 A survey of disturbance processes in archaeological site formation, *Advances in Archaeological Method and Theory* **1**, 315–81

Woodcock, N H, 1977 Specification of fabric shapes using an eigenvalue method, *Geological Society of America Bulletin* **88**, 1231–36

Yellen, J E, 1977 *Archaeological approaches to the present: models for interpreting the past*, New York

Index

Aborigines, Australian 72
adhesive (see also mastic, resin, tar, hafting) 13, 72, 111, 169, 180
aggradation 22, 171–172
Allerød 177–178, 181
alluvium 1, 19, 22, 25, 37–38, 40, 42–43, 45
Anglian Glacial (MIS 12) 22, 32
Anglo-Saxon period 18
animal (see also hide processing, hunting) 18, 72, 153, 163, 169, 177–178, 180–181
  butchery 154, 158, 168
  processing 12, 21, 158, 169, 180–181
  red deer 174
  reindeer 177
  ungulate 180
antler 154, 161, 165–166, 168–169, 181, 183
  barbed point 183
  sagaie 183
anvil 160
arrowhead (see also projectile, point), later prehistoric 1, 6
artwork 183
Aveline's Hole, Somerset 174
axe, Mesolithic 111
Azilian 106, 171, 173–178, 183
  Azilienisation 177

Baquets, Les, Saleux, Somme, France 179
Barnfield Pit, Kent 30
Barnwood School, Guildford 6
Barvills Farm Pit, Kent 27, 30
Belloy-sur-Somme, Somme, France 177–178
Bembridge, Isle of White 27, 177
Blackwater, river 32
blade
  backed 71, 89, 103–105, 151, 156–157, 174, 178, 180–181
  bi-truncated trapezoidal 174
  bruised 161, 175, 177
  segment 97–98
bladelet
  backed 13, 71, 89, 103–106, 109, 115, 143, 149, 151, 154–158, 167–169, 174–175, 177–181
blank
  blade 1, 77, 80, 97, 99–100, 117, 143
  flake 97
  rectilinear 174
Bølling interstadial 176–179, 181

bone, working of 153–154, 162, 165–166, 168–169, 181, 183
bow 153, 155
Boxgrove, Sussex 27
Bradgate Park, Leicestershire 173
breakage, of lithic artefacts
  bending fracture 112, 148, 155–158, 160, 162–163, 169
  impact damage 55, 105, 153, 155, 158, 181
  intentional 98, 112
Broadstreet Common, Guildford 6
Brockhill, Surrey 12, 176
Bronze Age 1, 6, 111
burin
  asymmetrical 95–96
  bec 174
  on truncation 82–83, 94–95, 97–98, 108, 114, 142, 162–164, 174–175, 177–178
  dihedral 90, 95–99, 108, 132, 144, 147, 164, 166, 175
  facet 94–96, 99–100, 113–114, 165, 181
  Lacan 177, 179
  spall 13, 89, 96–101, 112–114, 151, 165–166, 182
  transverse 94–96, 98, 101, 113, 119
butchery 158, 160, 168, 181
butt, of lithic artefacts (see also core, platform)
  preparation 176, 178
  type 83, 85–86, 115
  dihedral 83, 139, 143
  faceted 86, 136, 147
  plain 86–87, 105, 115, 117, 119–120, 126, 135–136, 138–139, 143–148, 174
  punctiform 85, 136, 144

Cave Spring site, Tennessee, USA 53
chert, worked 22, 26, 29, 31–32, 43, 89, 111
child 82, 180
chip, lithic 47, 49, 61, 70, 77, 79, 81, 83, 87, 93, 151, 153, 172, 176, 182
Chobham Common, Surrey 28
Chobham Ridges, Surrey 28
Christ Church Common, Guildford 7, 16
Closeau, Le, Hauts-de-Seine, France 177–178
clothing 158
coin, Roman 6
Colne, river 45
Constantine, coin 6
Corbets Tey Gravel 30

core (see also cresting, platform)
    blade 79–84, 87, 112, 117, 119–120, 126, 130, 136, 140, 144, 146, 148, 174
    bladelet 81, 86, 111, 148, 173
    maintenance 86–87, 100, 111, 115
    preparation 77, 79, 85, 87, 123, 139, 142, 144, 148, 176, 178, 181
    rejuvenation 79, 81, 83, 85, 87, 112, 115, , 118, 121, 132, 136, 144
    tablet 49, 83, 112, 124, 130, 132, 136, 148, 179
    flake 81–82, 120, 180
    multi-platform 111
    opposed platform 79–81, 115, 119, 126, 128, 130, 136, 140, 144, 146, 174
    prismatic 80
    shaping 111, 115, 117, 119, 123, 125, 127, 132–133, 136, 139, 146, 166, 174
    single platform 79, 82, 84, 115, 120, 130, 146, 180
craft activities 163, 169, 181
cresting
    bidirectional 79, 83, 144, 147
    sous crête 83, 115, 128, 136, 143–144
    unidirectional 83, 85–87, 110, 120, 128, 132, 144–145, 147
Creswellian 6, 12, 161, 173–176
Crossways Business Park, Kent 27–28, 174–175
crushing, of lithics 120, 147, 158, 160, 165–166
curation, of lithics 13, 111

Dartford Paper Mill, Kent 27
denticulate 89, 101–103
discard, of lithics 9, 13, 64, 72–73, 101, 105, 111, 113, 132, 148, 157, 179–182
Dollis Hill Gravel 32
Dryas, late 178

Easthampstead Gravel 28
Ebbsfleet valley 28
engraving 163, 168

family 181
Federmessergruppen 6, 12, 158, 171, 173–179
flint
    burnt 11, 47, 59–60, 81, 89, 154, 180
    nodule 22, 25, 41, 77, 79, 81, 85–86, 111, 115, 136, 141, 148, 178–179, 181–182
    patinated 77, 79, 83, 105, 111, 153, 177
    raw material/sources 26, 32, 47, 49, 77, 79, 83, 111, 139, 175, 178, 180–182
    red-tinged 77, 90, 118–119, 127, 132, 136, 139–140, 142, 144, 146, 148, 150, 180
flint tool (see also specific types)
    resharpening 13, 71, 90, 93, 101, 105–106, 109, 111–114, 148, 158, 160–163, 169, 175, 177, 180, 182
    retooling 157, 169
    reuse/reworking 13, 32, 44, 72–73, 111, 114, 165
flintknapper (see also novice) 13, 25, 82, 123, 148, 179–181
food preparation 181
Frandon Fields, Nottinghamshire 45
frost shattering 25, 32

Globe Pit, Essex 30
gloss, on lithics 153–154, 163, 165, 169
Gough's Cave, Somerset 173–174
Gravière du Marais, Conty, Somme, France 178
Great Fanton Hall, Essex 27
grooving 165, 168, 181
Grotte du Cheval, Gouy, Seine-Maritime, France 177
Guildford Lido 6, 177
Gyldeford 7

hafting (see also adhesive) 71–72, 151–152, 157, 159, 162–163, 165, 169, 180
    arrow shaft 158, 181
    de-hafting 157, 169
hammer
    hard stone 83, 115
    soft organic 83, 85–87, 115, 128, 136, 138, 143–144, 174, 177, 179
    soft stone 83, 85–87, 105, 115, 117–120, 124, 126–128, 130, 132, 135–136, 138–148, 173–174, 177, 179
Hangest-sur-Somme, Somme, France 177–178
hearth 47, 60, 72–73, 169, 179–181
Hengistbury Head, Dorset 13, 53, 175–176, 179, 181
hide processing (see also leather) 72, 93, 153, 158–160, 162–163, 165, 168–169, 178, 180–181
Hog's Back, Surrey 1, 25
Hornchurch Dell, London 30
Hornchurch Railway Cutting, London 30
Hunting (see also animal) 154, 169, 180–181
Hythe Beds 32

Iron Age 5–7, 15–17, 24, 171

Kings Hill, Berkshire 28
Kingsmead Quarry, Horton, Berkshire 45
knife 72, 109, 158, 168–169, 177–179
Krukowski microburin 103–105, 115

Ladymead, Guildford 1, 6
Lambeth Group 1, 25
Late Glacial 6, 12–13, 19, 22, 24, 44–45, 171, 173, 176–178, 180–181, 183
    Late Glacial Maximum 22, 24
Lea valley 32
Leather (see also hide processing) 153, 160, 162–163, 168
    sheath 162
Linford, Essex 30
Lion Pit, Essex 30
Little Hayes, Essex 27
Loch Lomond stadial 24–25, 45, 53, 171, 173
Lodge Hill, Kent 27

Magdalenian 173–174, 177–178
Manor Farm, Guildford 7, 12, 16, 19, 172–178, 180–182
Marsangy, Yonne, France 178
mastic (see also adhesive) 180
medieval period 1, 5, 7, 15, 18
Meer, Antwerp, Belgium 53

Mesolithic 1, 5–6, 79, 111, 157
microburin (see also Krukowski microburin) 103–105, 111
microdebitage 12, 20–21, 49, 87
microdenticulate 111
microlith 111
micropiercer 95, 175
mortar, smoke round 9–10, 12, 16, 146, 179

Nea Farm, Dorset 161, 175–176, 181
Neolithic 1, 5–6, 111, 163
Netley Heath, Surrey 25
Newhaven Chalk Formation 1, 25
Northfleet Cement Works, Kent 27, 30
Northfleet West Sub-station, Kent 27
notch 94, 96, 99, 103, 125, 132, 136, 140–141, 151, 163–164
novice, flintknapper 71, 82, 116–117, 119–120, 123, 136, 148, 180–181

ochre 89
Optically stimulated luminescence dating 7, 12, 19–20, 22, 24–26, 32, 171, 175–176
Orsett Heath, Essex 30

Paris Basin 106, 171, 176–179
Park Barn, Guildford 7
perforator 89, 94–95, 106, 109, 136, 146, 149, 168, 175
piercer 83, 89, 94–95, 151, 155, 168, 174, 181
Pincevent, Seine-et-Marne, France 178
plant remains 9, 14–15, 20, 72, 154–155, 169, 180–181
　brome 14
　nutshell 14
　oat 14
　preparation of 80, 85, 136, 174, 176, 178, 181
　rye 14
　starch 155
　tissue 154–155
　wheat 14–15
platform (see also core, cresting, butt)
　en éperon 85, 94, 173–174, 176–178
　en éperon-like 84, 120, 140, 175
　faceting 79, 87, 128, 130, 144, 173–174, 177–178
　plain 79, 82, 84, 120, 127–128, 130, 139, 141–144, 147
　abrasion 83, 85–87, 115, 117–120, 125, 127, 132, 135–136, 138–140, 144–147, 173, 178
　preparation 86, 139, 142
　rejuvenation 49, 77, 79, 81, 83, 85, 87, 93, 110, 112, 115, 118–121, 123–124, 126–127, 130, 132–133, 135–136, 139, 143–145, 147–148, 179–180
point, lithic (see also antler, arrowhead, projectile)
　angle-backed 174
　backed 105, 115, 143, 149, 157, 167, 174, 177, 179
　bi-point 104–105, 174–175, 177–179
　Cheddar 174–175
　Creswell 174–175
　curve-backed 103–105, 174–178
　mono-point 177–179
　oblique 103–105, 143, 167
　Penknife 174, 176

　shouldered 174–175, 177, 179
　truncated 177
polish 88, 152–153, 158–166, 168–169, 181
polissoir 88
post-depositional processes
　argilliturbation 52–53
　bioturbation 22, 24, 47, 49, 53, 59, 70, 73, 89, 171
　burrowing 14, 18, 21–22, 24–25, 38–44, 47, 51, 70, 171
　cryoturbation 53
　deflation 25, 171
　dilation 47, 59, 61, 64–65, 67–70
　flooding 24, 38, 51–52, 57, 67, 87, 171–172
　floralturbation 53
　fluvial 19, 21–22, 25–27, 30–32, 39, 47, 49, 59, 61, 64, 67, 69, 73, 88–89, 171–172
　freeze-thaw 47, 70
　frost heave 47, 49, 51, 53, 55
　frozen ground 25, 43–45
　shrink-swell 47, 49, 53, 55, 70, 73
　solifluction 1, 25, 27, 32, 52
　sorting 51, 55–56, 60, 70
　trampling 47, 53, 55, 64, 67, 70, 73, 89, 110, 113
　wind erosion 25, 87, 171–172, 180
post-medieval period 1, 5, 7, 9, 15–18
pottery 5, 7, 15–18
　earthenware 18
　Limpsfield ware 18
　pearlware 18
　reduced ware 18
　sandy reduced ware 18
　Staffordshire white ware 18
projectile (see also arrowhead, point, spear) 13, 17, 72, 105, 152–156, 158, 168–169, 177, 180–181
　barb 155, 181
　tip 72, 180–181
prospection, below ground 183
Purfleet Esso Pit, Essex 30
Pyrford, Surrey 176

Rampart Field, Suffolk 27
Recolonisation, of Britain 173
Rekem, Limburg, Belgium 158
resin (see also adhesive) 36, 72, 157, 181
retouch
　abrupt 90, 94, 101, 103, 106, 142, 155
　denticulated 107
　invasive 90, 106, 118, 145, 175, 177, 179
　rasante (scalar) 13, 85, 89–90, 93–100, 105–110, 126, 132, 148, 160–166, 175, 177–179, 182
　semi-abrupt 90, 101, 103, 105–106, 118, 124, 126, 128, 139, 142, 144
　spontaneous 101, 110
Rhineland 179
rods 183
Roman period 5–7, 15–18
rubbed end tools 89, 105–108, 167, 174

Saleux, la Vierge Catherine, Somme, France 178
saw 6, 153, 162–163, 168
scraper
　end 89–93, 105–106, 108, 112–114, 144, 148, 150,

158–162, 174–175, 180, 182
   short 89, 91, 160–161, 174–175, 177
  robust 94, 158, 168
  scraping 158–160, 168
Seaford Chalk 1, 25, 79
Seine valley 176
Selle valley 176, 178
shaft 155–158, 181
  shaft-smoother 88
Shakespeare Pit, Kent 27
shatter, lithic 79, 87
Skinners Wick, Kent 27
Somme valley 171, 176–178
Southfleet Ringmain, Kent 27–28
Southfleet Road, Kent 27–28
Southwold, Suffolk 27
spear 181
spearthrower 153
Springhead, Kent 27–28
St John the Evangelist church, Guildford 7
St Mary's Marshes 27
Stochæ 7
Stoke Hill, Guildford 7
Stoke next Guildford 7
strike-a-light 105, 167–168
Sunninghill, Berkshire 28

Swanscombe, Kent 27–28, 32

tar 157
termination
  feathered 85–87, 163
  hinged 85–87, 140, 145, 155, 157–159, 162–163
  stepped 13, 83, 85–87, 90, 105, 109, 136, 140, 155–157, 160–162, 169, 175, 177
Thames, river 1, 19, 22, 26–28, 30, 32, 174
Three Holes Cave, Devon 161, 173
Three Ways Wharf, Uxbridge, Middlesex 53
Tilbury Marshes, Essex 30
tile 5, 15, 18
truncation 101, 103
  oblique 96, 101, 104–105

Verberie, Oise, France 178
villa, Roman 6–7

Wey and Godalming Navigations Canal 7
Wey Manor Farm, Surrey 12, 19, 172–178, 180–182
Wey, river 1, 19, 22, 38–39, 44, 77, 79, 174, 176, 181
Windermere interstadial 19, 22, 24, 44, 171, 173, 176, 178, 181
wood 154, 165–166, 181
Woolwich and Reading Beds 25